An Uncertain Age

NEW AFRICAN HISTORIES

SERIES EDITORS: JEAN ALLMAN, ALLEN ISAACMAN, AND DEREK R. PETERSON

*Books in this series are published with support
from the Ohio University Center for International Studies.*

David William Cohen and E. S. Atieno Odhiambo, *The Risks of Knowledge*

Belinda Bozzoli, *Theatres of Struggle and the End of Apartheid*

Gary Kynoch, *We Are Fighting the World*

Stephanie Newell, *The Forger's Tale*

Jacob A. Tropp, *Natures of Colonial Change*

Jan Bender Shetler, *Imagining Serengeti*

Cheikh Anta Babou, *Fighting the Greater Jihad*

Marc Epprecht, *Heterosexual Africa?*

Marissa J. Moorman, *Intonations*

Karen E. Flint, *Healing Traditions*

Derek R. Peterson and Giacomo Macola, editors, *Recasting the Past*

Moses E. Ochonu, *Colonial Meltdown*

Emily S. Burrill, Richard L. Roberts, and Elizabeth Thornberry, editors, *Domestic Violence and the Law in Colonial and Postcolonial Africa*

Daniel R. Magaziner, *The Law and the Prophets*

Emily Lynn Osborn, *Our New Husbands Are Here*

Robert Trent Vinson, *The Americans Are Coming!*

James R. Brennan, *Taifa*

Benjamin N. Lawrance and Richard L. Roberts, editors, *Trafficking in Slavery's Wake*

David M. Gordon, *Invisible Agents*

Allen F. Isaacman and Barbara S. Isaacman, *Dams, Displacement, and the Delusion of Development*

Stephanie Newell, *The Power to Name*

Gibril R. Cole, *The Krio of West Africa*

Matthew M. Heaton, *Black Skin, White Coats*

Meredith Terretta, *Nation of Outlaws, State of Violence*

Paolo Israel, *In Step with the Times*

Michelle R. Moyd, *Violent Intermediaries*

Abosede A. George, *Making Modern Girls*

Alicia C. Decker, *In Idi Amin's Shadow*

Rachel Jean-Baptiste, *Conjugal Rights*

Shobana Shankar, *Who Shall Enter Paradise?*

Emily S. Burrill, *States of Marriage*

Todd Cleveland, *Diamonds in the Rough*

Carina E. Ray, *Crossing the Color Line*

Sarah Van Beurden, *Authentically African*

Giacomo Macola, *The Gun in Central Africa*

Lynn Schler, *Nation on Board*

Julie MacArthur, *Cartography and the Political Imagination*

Abou B. Bamba, *African Miracle, African Mirage*

Daniel Magaziner, *The Art of Life in South Africa*

Paul Ocobock, *An Uncertain Age*

An Uncertain Age

The Politics of Manhood in Kenya

⌐

Paul Ocobock

OHIO UNIVERSITY PRESS ⌐ ATHENS

Ohio University Press, Athens, Ohio 45701
ohioswallow.com
© 2017 by Ohio University Press
All rights reserved

Printed in the United States of America
Ohio University Press books are printed on acid-free paper. ∞ ™

27 26 25 24 23 22 21 20 19 18 17   5 4 3 2 1

Library of Congress Cataloging-in-Publication Data

Names: Ocobock, Paul, 1980– author.
Title: An uncertain age : the politics of manhood in Kenya / Paul Ocobock.
Other titles: New African histories series.
Description: Athens : Ohio University Press, 2017. | Series: New African
  histories | Includes bibliographical references and index.
Identifiers: LCCN 2017001261| ISBN 9780821422632 (hc : alk. paper) | ISBN
  9780821422649 (pb : alk. paper) | ISBN 9780821445983 (pdf)
Subjects: LCSH: Coming of age—Kenya—History—20th century. |
  Masculinity—Political aspects—Kenya—History—20th century. | Young
  men—Kenya—Social conditions—20th century. | Conflict of
  generations—Kenya—History—20th century. | Kenya—Social
  conditions—20th century. | Kenya—Colonial influence. | Kenya—Politics
  and government—To 1963.
Classification: LCC DT433.575 .O26 2017 | DDC 967.6203—dc23
LC record available at https://lccn.loc.gov/2017001261

Contents

Illustrations

Acknowledgments

As I wrote about how young Kenyan men and the colonial state came of age, I could not help but think about the life of this book and the folks who helped me write it along the way. The idea for this book was born at St. Antony's College, Oxford, as I worked through my MPhil degree in history. Oxford still feels like my second home. I met the love of my life, learned a lot about being a historian of Africa, and made many friends, including Dave Anderson, Daniel Branch, Kevin Dumouchelle, and Richard Waller, who shaped this project from the very start.

After Oxford, my book idea and I traveled to Princeton, where we grew up spoiled by the supervision of Bob Tignor and Emmanuel Kreike, as well as the financial support of the Department of History. They gave me just enough freedom to feel rebellious. During my three-hour dissertation defense, I could not help but wonder aloud if anyone else felt like this was a kind of intellectual initiation ceremony. Long since graduation, Bob and Emmanuel have continued to read my work and offer me sound advice.

None of the research I did while at Princeton would have been possible, though, without the eighty or so men who agreed to sit with me for hours thinking about their pasts. And I would never have met those men without the help of John Gitau Kariuki and Henry Kissinger Adera. I thank them for their patience and their willingness to endure endless *matatu* journeys, translate terrible sometimes totally inappropriate questions, and tolerate my taste for White Cap *baridi*. I owe a similar debt to the staff of the Kenya National Archives. Peterson Kithuka, Evanson Kiiru, and Richard Ambani have fostered generations of historians of Kenya—our work is so much better for the time you have invested in us. My trips to Kenya would not have been half as much fun without the companionship of some incredible people: Robert Blunt, Leigh Gardner, Will Jackson, Michelle Osborn, Robert Pringle—and many others.

For the past six years, my book and I have been nurtured in the comfort of the University of Notre Dame, first as a visiting fellow of the Kellogg Institute for International Studies and then as an assistant professor in the Department of History. Surrounded by generous colleagues, I have had ample opportunity to focus on finishing this book. They have spent considerable time reading drafts and encouraging my ideas. I cannot thank them enough, especially Ted Beatty, Catherine Cangany, John Deak, Karen Graubart, Patrick Griffin, Thomas Kselman, Rebecca McKenna, and Sebastian Rosato. I also want to thank my fellow Notre Dame Africanists, whose energy and friendship inspire me every day: Jaimie Bleck, Catherine Bolten, Mariana Candido, Yacine Daddi Addoun, and Paul Kollman, as well as Erin McDonnell and Terry McDonnell.

Geraldine Mukumbi, Damek Mitchell, and Kate Squiers, three of my students at Notre Dame, did a lot of research for me, compiling and coding data and sifting through newspapers. Only occasionally did they complain about the monotony of the work. I would also like to express my gratitude to Alex Coccia, Py Killen, and Bright Gyamfi for their support and friendship as I found my footing as a teacher, mentor, and historian. As they continue their studies at Oxford, Yale, and Northwestern, I can only hope I have encouraged them in much the same way the many people mentioned here have encouraged me.

I have amassed many debts raising this book, but none of them have been financial. This is in no small part because of the rich financial resources of Notre Dame. I would like to thank the Kellogg Institute for International Studies for supporting a semester of leave, as well as the Institute for Scholarship in the Liberal Arts for funding my manuscript workshop, image reproduction costs, and indexing. Matthew Sisk and the Center for Digital Scholarship at the Hesburgh Library assisted with mapmaking. I would also like to thank William Roger Louis, who invited me to participate in the Decolonization Seminar at the National History Center in Washington, DC. That summer was truly inspiring. I learned an incredible amount from my fellow "seminarians," as well as Dane Kennedy, Philippa Levine, Jason Parker, and Marilyn Young.

There are a few people, though, whose friendship and influence on my work require a little more than passing notice. Jim Brennan, Matt Carotenuto, John Lonsdale, Kate Luongo, Julie MacArthur, Sloan Mahone,

George-Paul Meiu, Kenda Mutongi, Tim Parsons, China Scherz, and Luise White have all shared drinks and ideas with me. Without the help of Sara Bellows-Blakely, chapter 5 of this book would not exist. I spent a few wonderful years living in Chicago, writing up the dissertation and getting to know Emily Lynn Osborn. Emily became a fast friend, tireless advocate, and coconspirator. She has read this manuscript more than most and kept me on the straight-and-narrow tenure track. Special thanks go to Brett Shadle and Meredith McKittrick, who read a very juvenile draft of this book and offered me constructive feedback. But this book has matured fastest under the scrutiny of the editors, dare I say the elders, at Ohio University Press. Gill Berchowitz, Jean Allman, Allen Isaacman, and Derek Peterson have patiently pushed me further than anyone, and I am immensely grateful. And to all the wonderful people I have worked with at Ohio University Press—Omar Aziz, Nancy Basmajian, Beth Pratt, Samara Rafert, Charles Sutherland, Sally Welch, Heather Roberts Stanfiel, and especially Deborah Wiseman—my thanks for making this book a reality.

But none of these folks had to put up with me like my wife, Abi. She endured the long absences for research, writing mood swings, and endless drafts handed to her to edit, as well as the anxieties of the job market, teaching, and finishing a first book. My work would not be what it is without her constant critique. I owe no greater debt than to Abi, who has graced my life and my work with her brilliance, good humor, and love.

I would like to dedicate this book, written by a young man about young men, to five generations of women who have had an immeasurable influence on me. This book is for my grandmothers, Jean and Florence; my mothers, Patricia and Vanessa; my wife, Abi; my sister, Cara; and my daughter, Ruby.

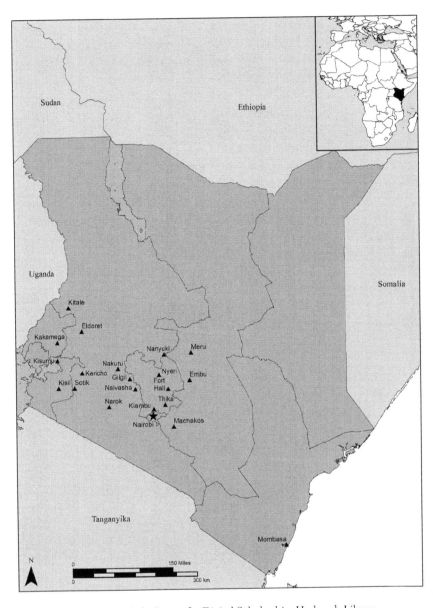

Kenya. Courtesy of Mat Sisk, Center for Digital Scholarship, Hesburgh Library, University of Notre Dame.

Introduction

ALONG THE COAST OF the British East Africa Protectorate, district commissioners left their posts in the heat and humidity of April 1914 to meet with local elders on an urgent matter.[1] Their task: to investigate when, or if ever, African boys and girls came of age. Their reason: to determine whether Christian missions had the right to keep underage Africans in their custody without parental consent. The issue had vexed British officials since the waning years of the nineteenth century. Christian missions had opened new, alternative spaces for the young. At first, a few sons and daughters converted, attended services, received an education, and worked on mission farms. Others arrived as recently freed slaves, picked up and dropped off by the British abolitionist impulse. And still others came out of desperation, made destitute by disease, drought, and famine. When parents demanded that their sons and daughters be returned home, difficult questions arose over the tangled authorities of families, missionaries, and the colonial state.

As the long rainy season began, district commissioners and African elders exchanged information about being young and growing old. They then submitted their reports to provincial commissioner Charles Hobley. Some commissioners argued that young East Africans were never free from the power of the old. To carve out a moment of independence, the colonial state would have to draw an arbitrary, entirely novel line, one with untold repercussions. Others claimed that for boys, parental control ceased when fathers helped them marry and settle down. Girls merely passed from the control of fathers to the control of husbands. A few officials felt no need to ask their African intermediaries at all. Imperial laws like the Indian Penal Code already established an age at which nonwhites became adults: fourteen for boys and sixteen for girls. The British need only exert their rule of law.[2] After reading these reports, provincial commissioner Hobley concluded that "no hard and fast ruling should be made."[3] The administration must leverage its influence carefully. Hobley warned his commissioners against disrupting elder, male authority. They must uphold the power of fathers whenever demarcating the boundaries between obedient childhood and independent adulthood. And they must be ever mindful of the encroaching influences of missionaries and one another into the realm of elders.

The inquiry failed to unknot the issue of African coming-of-age. While the British determined that boys, unlike their sisters, eventually experienced some degree of independence, they remained unsure of how much. They knew that age was a powerful part of the everyday lives of East Africans, and they presumed patriarchs had strict authority over juniors. Yet the stability of age-relations and the influence of elders seemed worryingly tenuous. For the remainder of colonial rule, and long after, the state in Kenya exerted considerable energy to understand, and then access, the power it believed inherent in age-relations.

A century later, struggles over age and state authority continue in Kenya. In the first few months of 2008, waves of postelection violence rocked the country, leaving thousands dead and an estimated six hundred thousand internally displaced. The horror called to mind similar episodes in 1992 and 1997. Even after rival presidential candidates Mwai Kibaki and Raila Odinga shook hands over a power-sharing agreement beside a smiling Kofi Annan, unrest continued in the countryside. Smoldering evidence lay everywhere of the violence perpetrated by young men and orchestrated by political elites. Senior politicians activated age-relations and the lexicon of age to instigate ethnic conflict.

In the wake of this bloodshed, I conducted much of the research for this book. In nearly all of my more than eighty interviews with Gikuyu, Kipsigis, and Luo men, talk turned to politics and postelection mayhem: an interviewee pointing out the ashy remains of kiosks and schools near his home in Saunet, another giving refuge to a displaced family in Gilgil, and still another comforting his son, who had suffered a stroke after being beaten in Bondo. These discussions gave the men I met an opportunity to vent frustrations and share anxieties. They also made connections across time. Memories of coming of age in colonial Kenya became a way for these men to talk about how generations behave today. These senior men lamented the disrespect the young showed for them but admitted their failure to dictate respectable norms. It had never been so, they claimed, in the "good old days."

After these interviews, I returned to the archive, and through the British colonial record I inhabited those "good old days": letters from fathers to district commissioners worrying about runaway sons, and warnings from chiefs about young people drinking, dancing, and singing lewd songs. The "good old" colonial days seemed a lot like the present. Decades separate the stories drawn from the archive and men's memories, yet age remains a prism through which Kenyans look to the not-so-distant colonial past to pass judgment on the present and fret about the future.

An Uncertain Age tells many coming-of-age stories of men who grew up in Kenya from the beginning of British colonial rule in the 1890s until the end of Jomo Kenyatta's presidency in the late 1970s. This is a book about boys and young men using the colonial encounter to enjoy their youthfulness, make themselves masculine, and eventually earn a sense of maturity. Age and gender drove their pursuit of new possibilities in areas such as migrant wage labor, town life, crime, anticolonial violence, and nation building. They relished being young and used these new paths to reimagine and assert their age and masculinity with one another and other generations.

Colonialism could also unmake men. British conquest had relied on the violence of British troops, the East African Rifles, and local auxiliaries like the Maasai, who saw profit in the livestock confiscated from fallen neighbors.[4] Young men who joined the conquest as soldiers or porters imagined their work as part of their coming-of-age.[5] Yet their violence crushed the manly aspirations of the countless young warriors they defeated. Among those communities that resisted, like the Gikuyu, Kipsigis, Nandi, and Gusii, conquest marked the decline of the young warrior. Although the consolidation of colonial rule and development of a settler economy offered future generations of young men new ways to earn an age, they were not always successful. The racial and economic inequalities of a settler society frustrated young men's ambitions, especially during and after the depression. As they struggled with stagnating wages and rising costs of living, as well as dwindling jobs and places at school, they endured rather than enjoyed an increasingly prolonged liminal age between childhood and adulthood. Feeling trapped, men saw colonialism as an obstacle that must be removed if they were to ever achieve adulthood.

Across Kenya, households crackled with tension over these promising new paths and disappointing dead ends. Young men argued with one another, with their parents, and with the young women and age-mates they wished to impress. Did a wage—and the flashy clothing, bicycles, and alcohol it purchased—make a migrant laborer worthy of a potential lover's attention or an age-mate's envy? Did a grasp of English and the ability to read the newspaper grant a schoolboy the right to demand from his father initiation into manhood? Were the gangs of boys forged on the mean streets of Nairobi as legitimate as the generations formed along the edge of a circumciser's blade? Could a married man who fathered children still claim the rights and respect of an adult even if he was poor, landless, unemployed, or, worst of all, uncircumcised?

The outcomes of these arguments were as complex as the conflicting views that ignited them. Debate could lead to irreconcilable conflict between young men proud of their new ways to perform masculinity and elders disgusted with such displays of disrespect and delinquency. Attitudes could be swayed, though; fathers could forcefully encourage their sons to set aside wages to buy livestock; and sons could convince their fathers to pay for another semester of school fees—each with the understanding that these new avenues would benefit the household. Such arguments never cooled; they roiled on long after colonial rule ended.

As the din rose up and out of African households, newcomers to East Africa leaned in, listening intently. Colonial rule introduced new actors into the conversation such as employers, missionaries, schoolmasters, police officers, and magistrates. Age and masculinity mattered a great deal to them, too, and they brought their own notions to Kenya. Africans included them in their arguments, borrowing, rejecting, and reappropriating these globally circulating, though sometimes very familiar, ideas. These new actors also sought to control the behavior of young men, to make them hardworking employees, God-fearing parishioners, and law-abiding subjects. Along with African parents and elder kin, they formed an ever-expanding network of competing yet complementary adult authority figures. As freeing as so many young men might have found migrant labor or town life, they found themselves under more adult surveillance than ever before. And the most important and intrusive of all these newcomers was the colonial state.

This is also a book about the British colonial state's own coming-of-age story—its search for legitimacy and authority. In Kenya, statecraft necessitated posing as an elder—producing what I call the elder state. Early in the colonial encounter, British officials came to view relationships among male generations as a potent source of power. To craft and exert their authority, the British became very willing, very active participants in age-relations. In doing so, the elder state institutionalized age and masculinity as inseparable components of statecraft. Making and unmaking mature men became a means for the British to reconcile the incongruities of nurturing a settler economy while fulfilling the lofty goals of the civilizing mission. For instance, with the help of chiefs and local elders, the British tampered with male initiation practices, pushing boys into premature manhood and the migrant labor market. The elder state wielded male initiation to discipline young delinquents, circumcising prison inmates who exhibited mature, obedient behavior.

Like the relationships between fathers and sons, state making could be a messy affair. Colonial officials' decisions and actions were nearly always contingent on the demands and desires of Africans, both young and old, and other actors such as missionaries, settlers, Colonial Office officials in London, and international welfare organizations. Entangled with so many eager participants, each with their own perspectives, the elder state became a conduit for the exchange of local African and global Western ideas about age and manhood. Stretched in different directions, the elder state pursued contradictory strategies, ones that changed over time.

As the colonial project matured, so, too, did the role of the elder state. By the 1950s, British authority was at its most uncertain. Challenged by the violence of young men frustrated with their generational station, the elder state constructed a network of institutions to instill a subordinate, subservient masculinity and maturity in captured young rebels. As they prepared to leave an independent Kenya, the British lamented the failure of the elder state, only to see its pieces salvaged by the first generation of Kenyan leaders. The elder state did not merely survive decolonization; postcolonial politicians retooled it for nation building. It ensured that postcolonial politics spun on the axis of age and gender—a gerontocratic form of politics entrenching the power of a single elder generation of male politicians over their young constituents for the next half century.

Exploring the coming-of-age stories of African men and the colonial state offers several contributions to the historiographies of Kenya, Africa, and the British Empire. First, *An Uncertain Age* positions age at the heart of everyday life in twentieth-century Kenya.[6] With a few exceptions, historians have fixed their gaze elsewhere, on other relationships and cleavages like ethnicity, class, and kinship. Unlike ethnicity and kinship, which the British categorized as traditionally African; or class, which they could claim as a modern aftershock of capitalism, age and age-relations were preoccupations shared by both Africans and the British. The colonial encounter involved intense, intimate arguments over age from which Africans and colonial officials crafted powerful practices and institutions that made age a mutually communicable form of authority.

Second, this book joins a growing number of histories of masculinity in Africa. Rallying around Luise White's call for more nuanced studies of men and masculinities, historians of Africa have begun to break down monolithic male identities like farmer, father, soldier, or student and then examine the rival masculinities with which men wrestled.[7] Yet scholars of Kenya have largely ignored White's challenge. I show that age and gender are inseparable units of historical analysis. To study a young man's coming-of-age, historians must also examine the different ways he imagined and expressed his masculinity, and then battled one another, elders, and the state over acceptable, respectable expressions of manhood.

Third, the concept of the elder state offers historians a fresh perspective on statecraft in Africa, one that straddles the blurry line between the colonial and the postcolonial periods. Historians have long examined the ways class, race, ethnicity, religion, and education influenced state power. I join a growing number of scholars who argue that both age and gender also produced the state. The elder state reveals that even the youngest imperial subjects, mere boys and girls, could compel the state to consider and control them. As they did, the British found age and masculinity powerful cultural tools with which they communicated their power.

Fourth, this is a book about not just age, but also the making of an age: youth. Since the 1990s, scholars of postcolonial Africa have been fascinated by the creative and destructive power of the young. Whether vanguard or vandals, makers or breakers, the concept of youth has become an influential, very male, actor in Africa's successes and failures. While several historians have studied the politicization of youths by political parties and Big Men, few have excavated deeper to uncover the cultural, political, and economic processes that begot the so-called youth crises that postcolonial leaders tried to resolve or perpetuate. I trace the emergence of this uncertain age through the twentieth century, exploring how youth arose from the racial and economic inequalities of settler colonialism, the fusion of emergent Western ideas about age with those in East Africa, and the desperate designs of a state struggling for authority.

Finally, the work of historians of Kenya remains ensnared by studies of single ethnic groups and their distinct, disconnected histories. Gikuyu squatters, Gusii litigants, Kalenjin politicians, Kamba soldiers, Maasai moran, or Maragoli widows—this research has produced a history of Kenya as a sum of its ethnic parts, rather than a history of the whole.[8] *An Uncertain Age* pushes scholars to reconsider their ethnicization of Kenya's past. Kenyans experienced colonial rule not in ethnic isolation but in constant contact with one another. Every young man felt the tremors of colonial power and discussed it with his peers and elders. Age and gender offer historians an opportunity to think about a shared history of Kenya.

The chapters that follow explore the roles age and masculinity played in some of the field's largest, longest-standing historiographies: migrant labor and town life, crime and punishment, Mau Mau and British counter-insurgency, as well as decolonization and nationalism. Their importance to each of these historiographies is well worth books in their own right. By bringing them together, I hope *An Uncertain Age* shows historians how mindful African men and the state were of one another's coming-of-age stories and how this mindfulness influenced so many of the decisions and actions that made up the colonial encounter in Kenya.

ARGUING ABOUT AGE

Prior to colonial rule, age was a powerful force in the lives of Kenyan communities—perhaps more so than ethnicity.[9] Early ethnographies do not reveal how far back into the past age-relations and their institutions endured.[10] Yet they confirm for historians that on the eve of conquest, how men and women lived their lives, explained their place in society, and sought mobility through it were influenced by their sense of belonging to a given generation and their relationships with their age-mates, juniors, and seniors.[11] Age also stratified these communities. Much of the early anthropological and historical literature on age emphasizes the conflict among men over access to wealth.[12] In these studies, elder men competed with one another to control the reproductive power of wives and mothers as well as the productive power of young male warriors and clients. To regulate this competition, communities organized themselves by age, ascribing rights and obligations to different age-groups and creating ritual moments when those age-groups formed and gradually moved up into positions of authority. Boys spent their childhoods herding their fathers' livestock, playing games with age-mates, and learning to navigate the social world around them. Eventually they would be made men, typically through a series of initiation ceremonies. They enjoyed their days honing their warrior skills, raiding neighboring communities' livestock, dancing, and courting sweethearts. In time, warriors would settle down, marry, start families, and become elders in their own right.

Elder men laid claim to this process of making generations as well as norms expected of different ages. They imbued themselves with ritual knowledge, demanded respect from acquiescent juniors, and relished the joys of elderhood. They created an awareness of time, a sense of order, and perceptions of masculinity and maturity within the community.[13] Yet the power of elders was never absolute. Male age-relations in East Africa revolved around reciprocal obligations.[14] An age, and the rights that came with it, had to be earned. Young men expected fathers to work hard for them, to accumulate the wealth needed for initiation and the bridewealth needed for marriage. Meanwhile, juniors had to prove themselves as well, showing respect for their elders and following the codes of conduct laid out to them during their initiations.

But not everyone agreed on what it meant to be a good father or son. Historians of age, following the lead of gender historians, have begun to challenge the earlier scholarship that proposed a linear process of aging that privileged patriarchs. Seniority was not granted to anyone simply for growing old or playing by the rules.[15] Arguing was an essential part of age-relations—part of the pursuit and performance of masculinity and maturity.[16] Generations constantly debated one another about their biological, social, and economic positions within the community.[17] If a boy showed no signs of maturity, then his father could postpone his initiation. Likewise, if fathers failed to initiate their sons, or if elders clung to the privileges of old age for too long, then younger generations could force the elders to meet their obligations.[18] Arguments could be violent and short-lived, but they could also take time and operate within the acceptable, creative moral codes of the day. For instance, at the turn of the twentieth century, as thousands of Gikuyu died of famine and disease, a generation of well-to-do men pooled their resources to push ineffectual elders out of political authority, a ritualized process known as *ituĩka*, or the "breaking." As Derek Peterson shows us, this generation retired ruling elders by buying them off with livestock. In doing so, they restored peace, stability, and hope to the Gikuyu community.[19]

Age-relations as well as their norms and institutions were flexible and creative, designed to weather demographic and climactic changes as well as to exploit new cultural and economic frontiers. Age could shift depending on the ideas and eloquence with which a generation argued, with whom a generation argued, and the wider socioeconomic and political settings in which the argument occurred.[20] As a result, as Nicolas Argenti argues, "seniority was not calculated simply on the basis of age but by means of a complex, multilayered assessment" of a range of criteria, including wealth in material goods, kinship, or knowledge.[21]

Colonialism intensified these arguments. It brought new forms of knowledge and wealth as well as alternative, obstacle-ridden routes along which the young and the old explored their age and masculinity both within and outside household, kinship, and generation. It also introduced new players. Missionaries, employers, and British officials introduced their own ideas about age and claimed the role of adults. Recently, historians have shown how ideas about age were reconfigured as young people inhabited these new spaces and argued with these new actors. Some sons and daughters left home, joined Christian missions, and adhered to the authority of a heavenly father over a corporeal one.[22] Their newfound faith and access to Western education set them apart from, and often against, their elders. Others left home in search of work and wages as soldiers, farmers, miners, or artisans. The camaraderie of the barracks, the organization of trade unions, and the struggles of town life all allowed the young to forge relationships outside their age-groups and kin groups.[23] They spent their wages on what they wanted, striking out on the path to maturity in their own unique ways—buying flashy clothes to attract sexual partners, attending beer halls and dances, or saving up to get married without their fathers' consent. Still others sought out social and economic worlds deemed distasteful by their families and colonial states. Boys joined criminal gangs, making up their own age-groups using black marketeering, violence, and street culture to express their manliness.[24] Girls joined the criminalized underworld, too, using street hawking and sex work to build successful households and families. They also refused to get married, continued their schooling, and demanded or rejected female circumcision.[25]

These experiences brought the young not only new sources of wealth and authority but also inevitable conflict with their elders and age-mates.[26] As Gary Burgess argues, colonial rule gave the young "analytical distance to question the validity and universality of gerontocratic discourse."[27] As they did, conflict often ensued. In turn-of-the-century Natal, young Zulu men embraced wage labor at a time of crippling war and epidemic disease. In time, as Benedict Carton argues, fathers and families back home became dependent on young men's wealth. Burdened by demanding fathers and colonial taxation, young men rose up against chiefs and fathers in the 1906 War of the Heads.[28] Meredith McKittrick shows how ecological and economic uncertainties in Ovamboland at around the same time also compelled the young to seek "refuge not within the familiar but within the exotic," in this case Christianity and migrant wage labor.[29] Meanwhile, elders fumed over their sons' and daughters' cultural delinquency.

Yet many of those children poured their efforts into familial goals in familiar ways. Colonialism did not always trigger irresolvable conflict among seniors and juniors or weaken age-based institutions. Having experienced the "exotic" worlds of migrant wage labor and Christianity, the "new men" of Ovamboland became more independent from their fathers and local kings than in decades past. But they still returned home, paid tribute, asked for advice, and courted kingly favor.[30] Interference from missionaries, chiefs, and British officials also inspired generations to work together to preserve ritual life. As Lynn Thomas has shown, when missions, the state, and Christian neighbors tried to block Meru girls' paths to womanhood, they circumcised one another.[31] As the price of bridewealth rose in Western Kenya, Brett Shadle argues, Gusii sons and fathers worked together to control rising bridewealth costs and prevent conflict over delayed marriage.[32] Parents across Kenya found merit in their sons' and daughters' taking advantage of new possibilities or defending old practices. Wage-earning sons returned home ready to invest in livestock and educated daughters fetched better dowries, each serving their parents' interests.[33] By the late colonial period, mothers and fathers who had been among the first or second generation to join a mission, attend a school, or tend a settler's herd understood the choices their sons and daughters made.

In *An Uncertain Age*, I argue that dissent and cooperation do not neatly characterize the strategies and outcomes of Kenyan men's arguments about age and masculinity. Throughout this book, many boys and young men pointedly interrogated and then flatly rejected the expectations of their elders and peers. There were worlds beyond kinship and generation that they wanted to explore and exploit—and it did not matter what their mothers or fathers might say to stop them. Yet even when they did contemplate the legitimacy of "gerontocratic discourse" by taking unusual or unsavory paths, the destinations young men mapped out in their minds could also be recognizable to those around them. They still wanted to enjoy their youthful years, prove their manly mettle, and earn the right to be initiated or married, as well as feel and be viewed by those around them as mature.

As colonial rule ground on, arguments about age intensified. From the 1930s onward, those once new possibilities through which earlier generations of young men had come of age began to lose their luster. The harder it became to find work, pay for school fees, and save wages, the more distant the prospects for enjoying oneself or settling down. On settler estates, African squatters endured draconian restrictions on the herds they kept and the work hours they logged. The reserves, especially in Central Kenya, simmered with frustration over chiefly misconduct, lack of education and employment, overcrowding, and soil erosion. Town life offered little respite as the costs of living soared while squalor spread.[34] For some young men, it was their fathers' poverty that let them down. They lost confidence in their fathers' ability to usher them into manhood through initiation, or into adulthood through marriage. For others, a father's prosperity bitterly reminded them that they had yet to succeed in their own right.

Coming-of-age stalled by the 1950s. Changes that might have once been imperceptible to young men were now painfully clear: many felt trapped in a prolonged age between childhood and adulthood. None of their strategies—going to school, picking tea, or fighting in a world war—provided them material wealth or moral standing. To escape, young men sought out alternative paths. They moved to towns in greater numbers to eke out a living as casual laborers and black marketeers. They joined the militant wings of political associations like the Kenya African Union and the Kikuyu Central Association. They also committed acts of organized violence, like Dini ya Msambwa and Mau Mau, against well-to-do neighbors, chiefs, and the state.[35]

The Mau Mau war in particular arose out of a crisis of age and masculinity among the Gikuyu. Following Luise White and John Lonsdale, I show that for all its complexities, the organized violence of the early 1950s was young Gikuyu men's response to a crisis of maturity in the late colonial period.[36] They argued with one another and with elders over how to best resolve their ambiguous age. During the war, they used the symbols and vocabulary of initiation, seclusion, warriorhood, and age grading to oath new members, steel fearful comrades, and establish chains of command. As they prepared for battle in the forests of Central Kenya, they reimagined what their masculinity might look like in the future, just as they looked back to history to think about how young warriors should behave. Despite their military defeat and grueling detention, these young men spent the remainder of colonial rule joining the youth wings of political parties and campaigning for their candidates. As young men did in Ghana, Guinea, and Tanzania, Kenyans rallied around age-relations as a way to make claims on the largesse of political elites. They also agitated for often-conservative gendered nationalisms—usually at the expense of young women—to make places for themselves at the table of nation building.[37]

To scholars of contemporary Africa, this uncertain age with which Mau Mau fighters or political activists struggled or appropriated might seem all too familiar; they would call it youth. A growing number of scholars have argued that youth, typically gendered male, is a liminal period of junior dependence, one marked by "waithood" or "involuntary delay" in becoming an adult.[38] Youth is described as a by-product of modernity's vicious contradictions: expanded access to and expectations of global ideas contrasted starkly by local economic constraints and political repression.[39] In their waiting, some youth have become a destructive force of change, finding their masculinity as child soldiers or gangsters.[40] Others are a force of creativity and activism, finding ways around state surveillance through social media or empowering one another through fashion and music.[41]

Much of the literature assumes that youth is the result of "a long historical process, shaped by authoritarian colonialism, postcolonial state failure, and a generally problematic engagement with material modernity."[42] But far too little research has been done to excavate if and how youth emerged over the course of the twentieth century. Deborah Durham offers historians a road map, arguing that studies of youth must go beyond the relationships and negotiations of youth and include the deeper structures that produce these encounters.[43] This book does not offer scholars yet another definition of youth. Rather, it looks back on how this prolonged, liminal age came to be in Kenya, and how past practices of age and generational relations became moral representations to hold up against the present and imagine the future.[44]

MAKING MEN

Manliness mattered as much as age in Kenya. At night, boys listened to the stories of their fathers and grandfathers, learning what it meant to be a man, debating those ideas the next morning out on the grazing fields. A boy, eager for initiation, had to prove to his father that he had the fortitude to face the circumcision knife. A young man practiced his dance moves and refined his oratory skills to catch his peers' eyes and ears. Age and gender were inseparable to these young men, and historians must treat them as tightly knotted units of historical analysis.[45] To study the entwined coming-of-age stories of young men and the state, historians must also consider how growing up and making states were both gendered processes.

Until the 1970s, histories of Africa were histories of men. Afterward, a generation of historians brought the lives of African women to the forefront of the field. Scholars of Kenya are especially lucky to have a remarkable set of studies on the lives of schoolgirls, street hawkers, sex workers, widows, divorcées, wives, and mothers. This early work pushed historians to consider the decisions and actions of women, especially their labor, to be as important as class, race, and ethnicity.[46] In the years that followed, focus shifted to the changing practices and meanings of gender and the relationships of power among women and men.[47] Histories followed of women navigating the new possibilities of colonialism, like labor outside the household, education, urban migration, Christianity, and colonial courts, to carve out spaces of autonomy for themselves and their families.[48]

Many of these same studies also reveal that African women struggled under an expanding "patchwork quilt of patriarchies"—fathers and husbands, chiefs, clerics and clergy, employers, and the state.[49] Over the course of the twentieth century, these patriarchs leaned on one another to control and marginalize women. They tried to drag women out of the public sphere of politics and streets of commerce and into the private sphere of households ruled by male breadwinners. There they were to labor as dutiful daughters, wives, mothers, and Christians, keeping their husbands and children content and out of trouble.[50] Dictating gendered roles to women and then punishing them when they broke gendered rules lay at the heart of colonial law and order.

Women were not the only ones who provoked moral panics and stampedes to correct their behavior—so, too, did young men. For a discipline originally built on the study of African men, we still know surprisingly little about how they understood their gender and sexuality, and how those ideas changed over time. In 1990, Luise White encouraged her colleagues to take the study of masculinity more seriously—and several scholars have answered her call.[51] Lisa Lindsay and Stephan Miescher define *masculinity* as "a cluster of norms, values, and behavioral patterns expressing explicitly and implicitly expectations of how men should act and represent themselves to others."[52] Like age, masculinities are relational, and because gender interacts with so many other social structures like race, class, and ethnicity, multiple masculinities can exist within a community.[53] Not all masculinities are equal. Masculinities are all pulled, as R. W. Connell argues, into the orbit of a hegemonic masculinity. Dominant as its ideas and practices may be, this hegemonic masculinity wars with rivals through coercion and consensus, destroying some and co-opting others.[54] Even men whose masculinities encircle the outermost margins enjoy what Connell calls the "patriarchal dividend," the privileged position all men share and uphold over women.[55] Gender scholars question whether Connell's hegemonic masculinity existed in colonial Africa. "It is *not* always obvious," Lindsay and Miescher write, "which notions of masculinity were dominant, or hegemonic."[56] African men experienced a succession of competing and coexisting masculinities as they crisscrossed the "patchwork of patriarchies" sewn together by fathers, chiefs, missionaries, employers, and colonial officials.[57] They also had to adjust to the changing preferences of women and their demands on the kinds of men with whom they wanted to meet, make love, or start families.

For all their work on masculinities, historians of Africa have been less interested in the relationships between local and imperial masculinities than have their colleagues studying other colonial worlds like British India.[58]

Africanists focus instead on local, African arguments about masculinity and the fractures and continuities those debates produced during colonial rule.[59] African masculinities defied definition by the colonizer, shifting rather than breaking under the weight of colonial racism and violence. Young men left home to work for wages or join mission stations; yet, as they did in Ovamboland, they still looked up to their fathers and kin as models of manliness.[60] Within young men's own households, steady paychecks from working on the Nigerian railways or in coal mines allowed them to claim breadwinner status, command the household, and demand family allowances from their employers.[61] Even under the surveillance of the state and workplace, South African masculinities were quite literally driven underground, but they still challenged the apartheid regime.[62]

In similar ways, this book explores the masculinities boys and young men felt, debated, and performed as they grew up in colonial Kenya. I explore the masculine norms boys were expected to adhere to in preparation for initiation as well as those taught to them by elders as they healed in seclusion. As initiation practices changed during colonial rule, I show how young men looked for new ways to prove their manly mettle and how their feelings and expressions of masculinity changed as a result. The travels and travails of migrant wage labor and town life offered young men new spaces, often outside family life, to reconsider the masculinities they observed in their fathers' households. As they reformulated what it meant to be male, they struggled to convince their elders back home that new styles of clothes and shoes and gang life were acceptable forms of manhood.[63] I also show how African men and women mulled over ideas about manhood in constant contact with non-Africans who weighed in, sometimes quite forcefully, with their own expectations and designs.[64] If, as Africanist gender scholars claim, colonial Africa was home to a constellation of dominant masculinities, then it is not enough to study African masculinities in relation to one another.[65] Relationships between African and colonial or imperial masculinities must matter just as much. Colonial actors might have had only the faintest influence, and their global ideologies might not have seemed so alien to Africans; yet, even in moments of recognition, of soft power, potent masculinities were made. One of the most forceful actors to intervene in African men's debates about gender was the colonial state.

Gender historians have long paid particular attention to how colonial states influenced gender relations and how gender altered the trajectories of statecraft.[66] States are gendered institutions, and the colonial state was a very masculine one. Its sundry bureaucrats, protocols, cultures, and laws were all products of their own competing masculinities that changed over time.[67]

These masculinities were made up of the prevailing metropolitan norms back home, the racial paternalism of the civilizing mission, and the lessons learned, or not, from colonial subjects. And these came to bear on African communities when they found themselves face-to-face with or working as agents of the state. Emily Osborn's study of household building in Guinea shows how the French ignored local connections between marriage and political authority and refused to marry Baté women and build households of their own. Instead, they hid their private lives from public view, denying themselves a powerful cultural component of statecraft.[68] Unlike their counterparts in Guinea, British officials in Kenya recognized the power of gender, making men and women to make the state.

Despite very rich, very separate scholarships on gender and statecraft, historians of Kenya have only occasionally connected the two. A few studies, most notably Lynn Thomas's *Politics of the Womb*, have shown how chiefs and British officials tried to use women's bodies and African gender ideologies to underwrite their authority.[69] In *An Uncertain Age*, I explore how British officials' own masculinities and the kinds of masculinity they wanted their young African subjects to inhabit guided their interventions. Moreover, inside government institutions such as approved schools, youth camps, and youth clubs, very intimate conversations took place between the state and young men about acceptable forms of manliness, sexuality, and maturity as well as the outlets through which to express those feelings: sports, hard work, education, and marriage. Colonial rule in Kenya is the story of how the British leveraged the success of their colonial enterprise on their appeal to and control over the masculinities of young Africans.

THE ELDER STATE

Scholars of Africa have long been interested in how colonial regimes exercised their power. Some cast the colonial state as powerful and authoritarian, transforming the everyday lives of traumatized Africans. The state is a crusher of rocks, a *bula matari*, as Crawford Young argues, relying on violence, private enterprise, and invested African intermediaries to extract raw materials. No less intrusive is Mahmood Mamdani's "Janus-faced, bifurcated" state, exerting two forms of power: civil laws governing urban citizens and customary laws controlling rural subjects. This decentralized despot locked some Africans away in ethnic reserves, controlled by intermediaries using customary law, and then placed them in tension with Africans living in urban spaces under a different legal logic.[70] Others, including Ann Stoler, Frederick Cooper, and Jeffrey Herbst, argue that colonial statecraft was a more contingent process. "More arterial than capillary," Cooper writes, state power did not circulate evenly to every corner of colonial society, and periodically it required a little defibrillation to keep it going. African communities living closest to the heart of state authority felt the steady, rapid pulse of rule. Further away, its effects could be but a murmur.[71] This unevenness opened a range of possibilities for Africans and many others, such as Christian missionaries and European settlers, to affect the nature of colonialism. As a result, the state was "neither monolithic nor omnipotent." It was tangled up in "competing agendas for using power, competing strategies for maintaining control, and doubts about the legitimacy of the venture"—debates that government officials had not simply with one another but with those over whom they meant to rule.[72]

In Kenya, the colonial state wrestled with these issues in its own peculiar ways. Kenya was a settler colony teeming with a diverse, vociferous cast of characters who made claims on and against the state. British officials found themselves constantly reacting to the activism of ordinary Africans, chiefs, and educated elites, as well as European settlers, Christian missionaries, international welfare organizations, and metropolitan superiors in London. Each of these voices spoke of competing, contradictory visions of what life in a settler colony should be like. Under such intense scrutiny both within and outside the colony, the state internalized these contradictions. As Bruce Berman and John Lonsdale argue, to ensure the financial viability of the colony, the state nurtured the economic fortunes of settler families it had encouraged to emigrate. The state alienated vast tracks of the choicest land from African communities like the Maasai, Kipsigis, and Gikuyu, and then coerced them to leave their homes and work for wages. British officials also had to keep the promise, or at least the pretense, of the civilizing mission. Ever fearful of being seen as an accessory to settler exploitation and virulent racism, the state also adopted "the role of even-handed arbiter, of defender of the weaker, African, interest."[73] With one hand, the state tried to extract African labor, violently if need be. With the other, it sought to shield them from the destabilizing effects of capitalism and Western culture.

For Berman and Lonsdale, considering the welfare of Africans merely made tolerable the dirty work of building an apparatus to coerce them out to work. Cooper has pointed out that their analysis of statecraft in Kenya focused more on securing "profits and peace" than "on the cultural work that colonial states do."[74] Since first conceptualizing colonial rule as a state of struggle, historians of Kenya and elsewhere in Africa have turned to locating the much deeper cultural work that went on to cope with the state's contending logics. One of the places historians looked for the state's cultural work was within the African institutions on which the British leaned most heavily to strengthen their authority. The British relied on the practice of indirect rule. Their men on the spot, known in Kenya as the provincial administration, worked with a cadre of chiefs and elders to collect taxes, enforce laws, discipline unruly behavior, and arbitrate local disputes. If African communities had no preexisting tradition of chieftaincy, as was the case in Kenya, then British officials appointed men they felt up to the task.[75] These intermediaries offered the British a way to overcome their financial limitations and exert influence beyond the barrel of a gun.[76] Together, provincial administrators and their African intermediaries created and oversaw local courts, and codified customary laws, such as marriage or land tenure rights, as well as hardened ethnic affiliations. These kinds of cultural work, Lynn Thomas argues, offered the colonial state ways to resolve the tensions between the crude necessities of coercive exploitation and ideological commitments to the civilizing mission.[77]

Rather than instruments of colonial domination, these flexible African institutions became sites of intense argument.[78] Africans often reappropriated them in ways the British had not intended. Chiefs used newly created courts to reimagine marriage rights and household relationships, yet women and young men used them to challenge the authority of their husbands or elders, respectively.[79] Ethnic affiliations solidified after the state carved out African reserves to establish racial boundaries and demarcate chiefly jurisdiction. Yet Africans trying to inspire political unity and agitation hardened ethnicity to challenge state authority.[80]

Age and gender also served the colonial state well. Almost immediately, the British set out to learn as much about African social and political life as possible. Through what Katherine Luongo has termed the "anthro-administrative complex," officials and anthropologists, in dialogue with African intermediaries, created a corpus of often functionalist, incomplete knowledge of the ways age and gender guided everyday East African life.[81] With this knowledge, the British tried to assert their authority by using and manipulating local practices of age and masculinity—a process that produced what I call the elder state.

The elder state was no "crusher of rocks," no colossus. But British efforts to harness age became a formidable instrument of statecraft—more than the distant drumbeat of "arterial" power. First, the elder state strung the sinews of the colonial apparatus together, forcing officials with different outlooks on and mandates for rule to argue and work with one another. The elder state emerged from the "constant rows" between the provincial administration, who oversaw day-to-day life in the African reserves; the departments, who managed law and order, economic planning, and welfare projects; as well as the judiciary and treasury, who enforced and funded the entire enterprise.[82] In the interwar years, labor officers, who found evidence of child labor on settler estates, argued with district commissioners, who had lowered the age of male initiation, over the appropriate age at which boys could leave home to work. Meanwhile, municipal officials in Nairobi found themselves working with magistrates and the treasury to enforce vagrancy laws and fund repatriation orders for rounded-up street boys.

The elder state manifested itself in nearly every nook and cranny of the regime. Most histories of Kenya focus on a single part, or interaction between only a few parts, of the state. The provincial administration has come under frequent scrutiny because of how closely it worked with African communities. These studies locate the real work of making law and maintaining order in the arguments between local communities, chiefs, and, sometimes, British officials.[83] Disputes over land and customary practices like marriage and female circumcision were resolved in local African council meetings attended by chiefs or court battles adjudicated by elders. British officials occasionally arrived on the scene to huddle with chiefs or fume over failed policies. In these histories, if not for their monopoly on violence, the British seem almost incidental to indirect rule.

Second, as the elder state reverberated with tension, the administrative rank and file grew attuned to the voices of those outside the bureaucracy clamoring to be heard. Kenya was a crowded, cacophonous place. As officials moved in and out of colonial society, they encountered all manner of competing ideas about ruling Africa. In conversations with Maasai elders, a district officer might learn the details of how and when they decided to transition a new generation of boys into manhood. Around a settler's dining room table, they might hear that the nimble fingers of African children were perfect for picking tea. Reading the newspaper, they might read a story about the importance of the Boy Scouts in the training of young British citizens.

Sometimes, these encounters inspired experimentally minded officials to test new technologies of rule, and they were often allowed to do so with a free hand.[84] They resourcefully borrowed and experimented with ideas and institutions practiced by the communities they sought to govern, by missionaries working just down the road, by British officials back home, and by other governments around the globe. In the 1930s, the governor sent S. H. La Fontaine, who had served in the provincial administration, to Britain to investigate the methods of juvenile incarceration and reform that could be reproduced in the colony. Twenty years later, to rehabilitate young detainees during the Mau Mau war, community development officers used a blend of Christian baptism, cleansing ceremonies adapted from revivalists, and vocational training provided by former staff of the Church of Scotland Mission at Tumutumu.

More often than not, though, unresponsive officials were compelled to act. When it appeared the state had sacrificed the well-being of Africans to the benefit of settlers, a chorus of criticism pressed the state to respond with denials, committee investigations, reforms, and even development projects.[85] Such pressures were especially acute when young Africans were involved. When Archdeacon Owen found children digging roads near Kisumu in the 1920s, he brought his outrage to the British public and to bear on the colonial state.[86] And in the 1930s, and again in the 1950s, when Protestant missionaries decided to ban female circumcision and abortion, they pushed district officials and chiefs to support them.[87]

Third, the elder state was doubly cognizant of age and masculinity—pressured by local arguments with Africans and globally circulating ideas back in Britain. The migration, labor, punishment, illiteracy, and health of young people were controversial in Kenya because they were also so contentious in Britain and much of the Western world. The Colonial Office and British parliamentarians, as well as religious and welfare organizations, were animated by the treatment of Her Majesty's youngest subjects, just as they were by the treatment of young Britons. How young Africans fared under colonial rule became a barometer for the success or failure of the civilizing mission and the superiority of metropolitan ideas and institutions.

By the end of the nineteenth century, European notions about age had undergone dramatic renovation. Social reformers, social scientists, and government officials began to carve out a new stage of the life cycle between childhood and adulthood, first among the well-to-do and later the working class.[88] Those boys and girls newly labeled as "youths" or "adolescents" became more dependent, losing their access to the economic and social worlds outside their households and coming under greater surveillance by parents, educators, and the state.[89] Once created, this new age came under close scholarly and political study. It also quickly became a repository for all manner of adult nightmares. Fears emerged that the young, especially boys, left to play in the streets of London, work in satanic mills, or languish in poorhouses suffered from moral and physical degeneration.[90] Worse still, the burgeoning field of child psychology promoted ideas that adolescence was a fragile time in the development of the human mind. The young were unstable, irrational, and malleable. When combined with destabilizing influences like town life, poverty, and loose morals, the results for society could be disastrous.[91] Governments and charitable institutions urgently defined, legislated, disciplined, and protected the young.[92]

Yet the same characteristics that made the young so dangerous also gave them great potential—if only their energies could be controlled. In times of intense insecurity, the young could be called upon to defend the nation and empire. Britain's near defeat in the Boer War inspired Robert Baden-Powell to create the Boy Scouts, which he viewed as a way to harden and discipline the next generation, prevent another catastrophic military campaign, and preserve the empire.[93] During World War I, an entire generation of young men flocked to the trenches and their deaths to fulfill a romantic, masculine fervor.[94] Over the course of the early twentieth century, states across Europe organized youth movements with militarized, propagandist flare. A creeping conformity replaced the rebellious spirit that had once defined young Europeans. Adults had reimagined them as modern warriors defending the nation and its empire as opposed to rebels erecting mid-nineteenth-century barricades.[95] After World War II, the role of the state in the lives of young men and women deepened out of the desire to rejuvenate citizenship and nationhood in the wake of the war's devastation, the emergence of welfare states, and the threat of nuclear armageddon.[96]

As elder states developed in Europe, they also formed along the colonial frontier. Metropolitan and colonial governments had worried over the welfare of European children and young people who had been spirited away to or born in settler colonies. In the seventeenth and eighteenth centuries, young English and Portuguese orphans and vagrants were seen as the very foundation of successful empires.[97] In turn, colonies became "not only a spleen, to drain the ill humours of the body, but a liver to breed good blood."[98] Colonies cured the nation of its moral decay and created sturdy subjects. By the nineteenth and twentieth centuries, the well-being and proper socialization of young British immigrants to Australia and South Africa, as well as Northern and Southern Rhodesia, became essential to strengthening the cultural ties that bound the British world system together.[99] Yet historians still know far too little about the lives of children and young people in colonized societies and their encounters with the state. In colonial Spanish America, the state defined and legislated childhood and familial relationships; and in doing so, positioned itself as a paternalistic "father king" to augur its racial domination over non-European subjects.[100] Centuries later, the British used prisons and schools in India and Nigeria to experiment with new disciplinary tools that tried to shape Indian and African children into twisted versions of a Western ideal.[101] In the mid-twentieth century, the language of development, citizenship, and youth spoken in Europe infused new institutions and new kinds of racialized, social controls in the colonies.[102]

Last, the elder state in Kenya did not materialize fully formed, but emerged gradually over the course of colonial rule. Early on, from the turn of the century until the late 1940s, the British found that the authority they gained from participating in age-relations was a very messy affair. Ruled by the financial and logistical constraints of empire-on-the-cheap, they had to work with chiefs, elders, and young men to effect change. The elder state became a process of negotiation not just among officials in different posts within the administration but also with the competing, yet not always incompatible, desires and designs of African men.[103]

At the turn of the century, officials working in the East Africa Protectorate brought with them a "self-confident Victorian mystique of progress."[104] Many of these men were holdovers from the Imperial British East Africa Company, a short-lived, financially disastrous experiment. Adventurers and entrepreneurs fashioned into administrators, they believed that "competitive individualism represented the driving force of progress and the highest stage of social development." And that spirit led, as Bruce Berman argues, to a period of "intrusive and innovative interventions."[105] These earliest fragments of the elder state began to use age and gender to free young men and women from their familial relationships as well as shield them from abuse. Using the language of racial paternalism, the state fretted over the right of Christian converts to leave home, the safety of kidnapped pawns, and the freedom of girls forced into slavery.[106] Officials developed welfare-oriented policies and institutions specifically for young people that aimed to treat them differently than adults. In 1902, young men who loitered about the railway station at Nairobi were arrested and taken to mission stations for education. Five years later, the governor ordered the construction of a reformatory where the protectorate's worst offenders would receive tough discipline and an education—in much the same way as their counterparts in Britain's famous Feltham Prison. Throughout the same period, the high court outlined regulations for a less severe form of corporal punishment for young male Africans brought before magistrates.

These "innovative interventions" supposedly ended in the 1920s as a conservative pall settled over the state. A new generation of British officials arrived who valued stability, orderliness, and traditionalism.[107] Everywhere they saw the crippling effects of what they called detribalization: unruly young warriors raiding for cattle, young men and women dancing and drinking together, women demanding the right to divorce their abusive husbands, children swarming towns and train stations to pick pockets and pilfer.

They sought ways to prevent what they believed to be the breakdown of "traditional" African life. They tried to strengthen the precarious authority of chiefs and establish local tribunals so local elder men could resolve conflicts over land, marriage, and law and order. In spite of this more conservative outlook, the innovative spirit of the early years of colonial rule did not vanish.[108] Protestant churches continued to press provincial administrators to outlaw certain cultural practices they deemed barbaric, such as female circumcision and abortion. Throughout the 1920s and 1930s—at the very height of this supposed conservatism—provincial administrators worked with chiefs to speed up the timing and shorten the duration of male initiation to free young men to seek employment. They also circumvented the authority of fathers who resisted sending their sons out to work by facilitating the sons' efforts to find recruiters. At the same time, prodded by the International Labor Organization and the Colonial Office, technocrats in the departments unveiled new age-specific legislation, including the Juveniles Ordinance and the Employment of Women, Young Persons, and Children Ordinance, to—in theory—protect young people from broken, abusive homes and workplace exploitation.

Concern for the well-being and development of the young—drawn from a sense of paternalism and driven by missionaries, metropolitan officials, and Africans—fueled the elder state's innovative work throughout the interwar years. Elsewhere in Africa, significant steps to build state power around age occurred decades later, well after the 1940s, when a developmentalist ethos emerged within the British Empire.[109] In Kenya, these efforts began long before; and when officials of the elder state felt the sudden rush of development funds after World War II, they relied on past networks of expertise, practices, and institutions.[110] Yet the postwar period did have a dramatic effect on the ambitions of the elder state—it morally and financially invigorated officials.[111] In both the departments and the provincial administration, officials busied themselves addressing the social and economic ills they believed had hampered their work for years.

In the late 1940s and 1950s, the elder state's influence was amplified by this renewed faith in the transformative power of colonial welfare and development. When the elder state came face-to-face with Mau Mau, it seized on the violence to deepen its role in the lives of young men. For officials in the department of community development as well as several provincial administrators, Mau Mau had revealed in the starkest of terms that fathers, elders, and chiefs had failed to exert sufficient control over young men.[112] One solution to Mau Mau was for the elder state to boldly step further into Gikuyu age-relations and offer itself up as an alternative elder with a new, more orderly path to manhood. The involvement of the elder state ensured that the detention and rehabilitation of young Gikuyu differed dramatically from the violence of adult detention.[113] In the waning days of empire, the British built a massive network of institutions for young men in the hopes of resolving the issues that had brought Mau Mau to life. And when independence came in 1963, many ancillaries of the elder state believed they had failed. Rather, they had strengthened the institutions of age by making them a source of state power. The elder state elevated arguments that had once occurred in households and among generations to the broader field of politics. And the first generation of African politicians eagerly took up the elder state's mantle. Political elites like Jomo Kenyatta found the language and relationships of age and the late colonial institutions for young people useful tools to craft a national culture and legitimize their authority.

SOURCES AND METHODS

This book draws on a mixed methods approach, blending archival material, life histories, and quantitative analysis. Most of the documentary evidence in this book comes from the Kenya National Archive. In the archive, I cast a wide net, examining files from nearly every corner of the colonial state, from the provincial administration, to the attorney general's office, to the departments of community development, education, labor, and prisons—among many others. This archival breadth broadens the scope of the book beyond being simply a study of the actions of local African councils and district commissioners or anxieties of municipal authorities and welfare officials. It allows me to explore the many ways a diverse group of young African men encountered an equally diverse group of colonial officials. Juggling archival evidence from these disparate corners of the state shows just how pervasive age and gender were in the cacophonous process of state making in Kenya.

I also made use of the British National Archives as well as archives at the School of Oriental and African Studies, the Rhodes House Library at Oxford University, and the London School of Hygiene and Tropical Medicine—to name just a few. Late in my research, I consulted the newly released Foreign and Commonwealth Office (FCO) files deposited in the British National Archives. While the FCO material promises new revelations on the brutalities of the 1950s, they do not dramatically alter what we already know about the period. The new FCO files tell us far more about the lengths the British went to burn or bury the paper trail—an effort to shape a particular kind of history.[114] For this book, the FCO files deepened what I had already found in the Kenya National Archives and from speaking with former detainees.

Together, this documentary evidence forms the backbone of the stories that follow.

Working with documents that detail the interactions between young Africans and colonial officials comes with a particular set of challenges. The ideas and institutions of the elder state were often propaganda pieces, very public performances of British benevolence. Labor inspections of sisal factories, camps for young Mau Mau detainees, or youth clubs for poor, illiterate country boys all tried to temper criticisms by missionaries and social reformers. If the work of the myriad people and institutions that made up the elder state was mere performance, then to tell this story risks perpetuating the very self-serving, face-saving publicity the British hoped to project all those years ago and perpetuate through a tampered archive. Much of my work, then, has been to get backstage, away from the pageantry. And there, the sources reveal much more. I found that the elder state was often at odds with itself, unsure how to best handle young African men. Sometimes, I met true believers: British officials who genuinely took interest in the well-being of young Africans and the civilizing mission.[115] Their work, often in collaboration with Africans themselves, resulted in policies and programs generated locally, from within the state, rather than as the result of unwelcome, external pressure. But the best way to tease out such troublesome sources was to corroborate them with the memories of Kenyan men who had encountered the elder state in their youth. Regardless of the propaganda inherent in so much of the elder state's work, it had real, lasting consequences for the young men it circumcised, caned, incarcerated, educated, or wounded in battle. Listening to their voices, rarely heard during the performance, as well as the murmurs of dissenting officials arguing backstage, allows us to see past the theatricality of the elder state and its archive.

I conducted eighty interviews, nearly all of them in 2008, with men who came of age during colonial rule. Several Kenyan researchers helped me recruit these men and then facilitated and translated our conversations. John Gitau Kariuki, an experienced researcher who has worked with Robert Blunt and Daniel Branch, among many others, assisted me with my work in Central and Rift Valley Provinces. In Nyanza Province, I worked with the indomitable Henry Kissinger Adera, who had previously worked with Matthew Carotenuto and Derek Peterson. He recruited Luo and Kipsigis participants. Before each interview, we asked all our participants to use the language with which they felt most comfortable, and while most chose to speak in their first language, a few opted to speak Kiswahili or English.

We began our interviews only after I had completed most of my archival work. I had waited because I wanted to recruit men with firsthand experiences of the issues and institutions I found most compelling in the documentary evidence. Once I realized how important spaces like the Kabete Approved School and the Wamumu Youth Camp had been to British efforts to shape African age and masculinity, I sought out men who had been incarcerated there. When I learned of the colonial state's preoccupation with the recruitment of young people in and migration out of Western Kenya, I conducted interviews with Luo and Kipsigis men who had left home in search of wages and a little adventure. Waiting in this way afforded me opportunities to speak with men such as Simon Kariuki, Alan Kanyingi, Thomas Tamutwa, and many others who could speak with authority about the thrill of buying clothes with their first paycheck or the agony of being caned by a prison official. In a few instances, I was able to interview men whom I had first encountered in the archival material. Take, for example, Simon Kariuki: I had read of him several times in letters among officials in the department of community development as well as a memoir of a former official, Geoffrey Griffin. Sitting with Simon in his small apartment in the three-story building he owns in Ongata-Rongai, we teased out the tensions between his memories today and colonial records filed away over sixty years earlier. Opportunities such as these revealed to me just how closely life histories and the documentary evidence aligned with one another. When I shared with men what the archive had to say about them, it gave them a chance to challenge and correct their recorded pasts.

Yet challenges shaped my research as much as these opportunities. The fading memories of the very old limited my work just as the vivid accounts of men like Simon Kariuki enriched it. I struggled to recruit men of advanced age who might tell me something of their lives in the 1920s and 1930s. When I did, I often found them too old or infirm to participate in an interview. First person life histories of men and women who lived through the early years of colonial rule are increasingly closed off to my generation of scholars. Nearly all of my interviews were with men who came of age in the 1940s and 1950s. The stories that follow are those of only a few generations; and within these generations, of a privileged few who thrived and survived. From these life histories alone, I cannot adequately track how ideas and practices surrounding age and masculinity changed over the course of the colonial period. Although I routinely asked the participants to tell me about how their forefathers came of age, I often found them using their fathers' and grandfathers' lives as a way of legitimizing their own struggles for manhood and maturity. In the end, I have relied on the archival record to show how different generations of men thought about age and masculinity over the course of the twentieth century.

I conducted these life histories in the immediate aftermath of the brutal postelection violence of 2007–2008 that left hundreds dead and hundreds of thousands displaced. The violence cast a long shadow over my conversations. I did not interview anyone who had been displaced by the violence. For some men, speaking about their pasts was a welcome distraction from the crisis. For others, age became a way of contextualizing and making sense of the violence. Numerous interviewees spoke of Kenya's most pressing problems in terms of generation, not ethnicity. Our discussions ended in refrains about the disrespect generations now had for one another, of rudderless young men run amok, and of corrupt elder politicians desperate to hold on to power.

Perhaps the most difficult challenge I faced was being mindful of the age-relations and generational politics at play during my interviews. I quickly realized that elder men felt deeply uncomfortable speaking with me until they had a better sense of my own maturity. Often after spotting my wedding ring, they nodded approvingly and explained that I could clearly understand such things. Likewise, elder men did not want to discuss the intimate details of their initiations in front of young interpreters. Take for instance a very awkward group interview I conducted in Saunet. I had agreed to work with a young Kipsigis student from the area named Sammie Kiprop Cheruiyot. During our first interview with a local elder and his age-mates, they made it clear that they could not be entirely forthcoming. He was too young, they argued, to learn such things. Sammie was also hesitant to ask his seniors probing, personal questions.

From then on, I recruited and interviewed Kipsigis men with Henry Adera, a Luo who lived nearby in Awendo. Elder Kipsigis men found it much easier to discuss their experiences with two seemingly mature outsiders than with young members of their own community. A few times, Kipsigis men would gently rib Henry that they could share their initiation stories with him because Luos did not circumcise their sons. In my conversations with Gikuyu men in Central Kenya and the Rift Valley, I had the good fortune of being joined by John Gitau Kariuki, whose own maturity facilitated my conversations with elder men. In fact, Gitau eagerly established his own generational bona fides before each interview, a strategy that put elder men at ease with talking about sometimes very difficult, intimate subjects. Such generational tensions underscore the centrality of age in Kenya and the importance of this book. They also give me pause, as they should other researchers, when relying on young, educated men and women to help us conduct research with their elders. Moreover, these still-visible frictions should call on historians to reevaluate and think more critically about earlier ethnographies by anthropologists, who often used underage interpreters to probe elders about things they had no right knowing. It begs the question of whether what we know from these early studies requires a more critical analysis of the age-relations embedded in their results.

The final method I employed in writing this book was analysis of three databases that I compiled using materials from the Kenya and British national archives. The first database consists of 10,410 cases of court-ordered corporal punishment of young men from 1928 to 1955. The second contains 7,423 cases of young offenders from 1938 to 1950 who were punished in a variety of ways, not just by corporal punishment. All these cases had been recorded into annual registers by officials in Nairobi and then sent to the Colonial Office for review. Unfortunately, the registers are incomplete. I could not locate those for the years during World War II, though it is possible that officials in Kenya did not submit them. Although incomplete, the cases provide historians with a great deal of information: among other things, an offender's age and ethnic background, the crime for which he was charged, and the location of the court where he stood trial, as well as the kind of punishment he received and its severity. I have used this wealth of information to provide rough sketches of those young men the colonial state found most threatening. The data provide historians with as much information about who these young men were as about why the British felt compelled to discipline them.

The third database is made up of 381 case files of inquiries made by the probation service into the lives of young male offenders committed to approved schools between 1947 and 1954. These reports are incredibly rich. I used these investigations by probation officers, who were often Africans, to glimpse the everyday lives and histories of Kenya's most serious young male offenders. Probation officers interviewed offenders, visited family homesteads, spoke with parents, and debated forms of punishment with one another and magistrates. The details are sometimes extraordinary—parents asking the state to incarcerate sons; offenders describing their first job, favorite subject in school, or life on the streets; and, most intriguing of all, probation officers' own biases and the characteristics they sought to aid in their decisions of whether boys should be institutionalized by the state. Together, my reading of the documentary evidence, conversations with Kenyan men, and analysis of these three data sets offer a rich, complex, and compelling history of young men's coming-of-age and their encounter with the state.

An Uncertain Age begins when a boy's manhood begins: his initiation. In chapter 1, I explore the ways British provincial administrators and chiefs altered male initiation practices and the effects of these changes on young men's coming-of-age. During the interwar years, though likely in the years before, district officials and elders lowered the age of initiates, eliminated important ritual practices, and curbed or ended young men's time as warriors. The elder state became an active participant in the most intimate moments among male generations, trying to push newly made men into the wage labor market and discipline their behavior. The crucible of manhood shifted away from a constellation of ritual practices to circumcision, which became the primary indicator that a boy had become a man. Despite these changes, men defended this diverted path, claiming that it still allowed them to enjoy their youth and strive for manhood.

In chapter 2, I examine the experiences of young men from Western Kenya who left home and traveled the colony working for wages from the 1920s to the early 1950s. Leaving home and earning wages led to tense negotiations among male generations. Sons viewed their newfound financial and spatial independence from kin as a chance to rearticulate age and gender. They enjoyed themselves in new ways, including buying Western clothes, drinking alcohol, and trying out new dance styles. Many fathers and chiefs disapproved of such cultural deviance and tried to prevent them from going back out to work. Other young men returned home with their wages, prepared to contribute to the household. For their part, provincial administrators and labor officers encouraged, and sometimes outright compelled, young men to live and work beyond their fathers' households. Wary that boys picking tea far from home might weaken elder authority or ignite international outrage, the elder state trod carefully. It drafted child labor laws, carried out workplace inspections, and investigated families' complaints of runaway sons.

The elder state did not encourage every avenue young men took to earn an age. In chapter 3, I follow the lives of young men living and working on the streets of Nairobi, the capital city of the colony, from the 1920s until the early 1950s. On this urban frontier, young men eked out livings in the legitimate urban workforce, the black market, and the criminal underworld. Street life afforded young men new ways to form masculinities, bonds with age-mates, and relationships with seniors and juniors beyond kinship. The British tried to restrict young men's urban migration, believing that town life made them undisciplined and uncontrollable. Municipal authorities rounded up the underemployed or homeless, magistrates charged them with vagrancy, and police repatriated them home. Repatriation became the elder state's first, furtive step to inculcate in young men alternate, colonial models of appropriate mature, masculine behavior.

In chapters 4 and 5, I turn to the elder state's efforts to define and punish perpetrators of the most serious crimes through corporal punishment and institutionalization. Corporal punishment was a widespread, age-specific practice in the colony. Both African communities and colonial courts relied heavily on physical violence to punish boys. The young found caning terrifying and painful, and they conceptualized corporal punishment, whether meted out by parents or colonial officials, as part of a broader effort by adults to discipline their immaturity. Magistrates also institutionalized the most serious young offenders in approved schools. I trace the methods staff used to transform hardened house burglars and recidivist vagrants into obedient subjects. They drew on the latest techniques developed in Britain and the United States, such as vocational training and rigorous work-time discipline, as well as the very local practices of male circumcision and age grading. Young men rejected and reappropriated these efforts as they went about their own journeys toward adulthood behind bars. Some parents even negotiated for and demanded from colonial officials the incarceration of their delinquent sons.

By the 1940s, inadequate education, chronic underemployment, and debilitating poverty pushed men's plans for marriage and adulthood further into the horizon. In their frustration and confusion, they turned to violent protest. In chapters 6 and 7, I narrow the focus of the book for a moment to examine the Mau Mau war and the brutal British counterinsurgency of the 1950s. Mau Mau was one of many violent uprisings led by young men during the colonial period, yet it offers historians a useful case for how men argued over age and competing masculinities. The war became a new means for young Gikuyu to express their masculinity, lay claim to maturity, and capture the mobility that had eluded them. Their efforts ran aground against the violent, surging tide of the British counterinsurgency. A handful of influential British officials—in concert with conservative loyalists as well as Christian elite Gikuyu—identified Mau Mau as a conflict about age-relations. Together they framed Mau Mau as a form of juvenile delinquency and the failure of elders and the state to adequately discipline them. Their solution to Mau Mau led to a dramatic expansion of the elder state, in which the British sought to wield generational authority more forcefully, quite literally certifying young men's maturity in return for their acquiescence.

This work began at the Wamumu Youth Camp, built by the department of community development in 1955 to "rehabilitate" nearly two thousand Mau Mau detainees under the age of eighteen. In chapter 7, we visit Wamumu, where camp staff tried to unmake the masculinity of former Mau Mau insurgents, infantilizing them as undisciplined boys. Then, using circumcision rites, education, sports, propaganda, and job placement, they reimagined them as mature, disciplined subjects. Wamumu became a state-sponsored rite of passage aimed at defeating Mau Mau and entrenching the state's authority through age and gender. But the elder state did not stop at Wamumu. In the late 1950s, officials believed they faced a colony-wide "youth crisis." The issues that had driven the Mau Mau generation to war remained unresolved: underemployment, lack of education, poverty, political disenfranchisement, and racial inequality. Officials feared that they faced a new, rising young generation of frustrated insurgents. And so the elder state tried to piece together a youth service, massive in scope and size compared to those found in other colonies. The Wamumu program was distributed throughout Kenya in approved schools for young offenders and in hundreds of newly built youth clubs serving tens of thousands of poor young men and women in the countryside.

As the sun set on the British Empire, officials lamented the failure of this new network of institutions they had built for the young. Yet the elder state found new life in the postcolony, and age became a powerful tool of the state in newly independent Kenya. In chapter 8, I show how young men demanded action from Jomo Kenyatta and other politicians whom they had carried to power. In response, Jomo Kenyatta, the first president of Kenya, created the National Youth Service and preserved late colonial programs and rhetoric. Through the elder state, Kenyatta and the first generation of Kenyan leaders recast themselves as political elders tasked with leading a young nation of young citizens. In fact, they brought the elder state to fruition, institutionalizing maturity and masculinity as essential tools of statecraft. Young men became instruments of the elder state to build a fledgling nation and perpetuate a single generation's grip on power—one that would last nearly as long as colonial rule.

1 ⇌ An "Arbitrary Line"
Male Initiation and Colonial Authority

IN THE CHILLY MISTS of Meru in August 1919, tempers flared white-hot. Reverend R. T. Worthington, of the United Methodist mission, had stormed a nearby village flanked by a gang of mission converts. He had come in search of a certain schoolboy who had left his lessons to undergo initiation. The boy's leave had long ended, and the reverend wanted him back in the classroom. Village elders protested as Worthington broke into the seclusion hut, where the young man lay recuperating from his circumcision, and took him back to the mission. Fuming, the elders assembled before district commissioner A. E. Chamier and informed him that the Meru community would not tolerate Worthington's incendiary behavior. Worthington had done the unimaginable: remove a still-healing initiate from the moral instruction that took place during seclusion, from the lessons critical to his understanding of his new station in society.[1]

Trying to temper the elders' fury, Commissioner Chamier promised to investigate the matter. Tensions simmered for days. When Chamier finally confronted Worthington, he accused the reverend of "high-handed action."[2] Worthington retorted that Meru initiation lasted two months and disrupted mission education. He had merely retrieved a student whose lengthy initiation put eighteen precious months of schooling in jeopardy. Incredulous, Chamier replied that if two months could undermine a year and a half of Western education, it indicated "a certain ineffectiveness about mission training." For Chamier and the village elders, the reverend had violated

Meru custom, interfered with one of the most pivotal moments in a young man's life, and, worst of all, disregarded elder authority. For Worthington, Meru custom, initiation, and elder power were obstacles hindering his student's salvation and study.

Young men's initiation and coming-of-age ignited intense deliberations about the messy, overlapping frontiers of familial, missionary, and colonial authorities. To resolve such arguments like the one in Meru, the British investigated, with the help of African intermediaries like chiefs and interpreters, when men came of age and became independent of their seniors. To discover, define, and demarcate a precise moment when a young man was no longer beholden to his elders—an age when he was free to leave home to work, join a church, or attend a school—became one of the first steps in the formation of the elder state.

In their pursuit of an identifiable moment from which they could extrapolate young male agency, British administrators, missionaries, and ethnographers found male initiation. With its graphic rituals and intense interaction between young and old, male initiation became a focal point in British explorations of African age. They came to view initiation as the pivotal moment in a young African man's life, the significance of which continued and deepened as he aged. Initiation, which often included genital circumcision, transitioned boys into young men and set them on paths toward adulthood. Initiation also served as a process of concentrated socialization through which older generations imparted the life lessons essential to becoming masculine. Above all, initiation exposed the British to the intense negotiations among generations and the inequalities between young and old. They came to believe that the principal thought on boys' minds was to become men, while elders sought to control the boys' youthful energies.

Unlike female initiation and circumcision, which the state and missionaries tried to suppress, the British tampered with male initiation to meet the demands of a settler colony.[3] In partnership with chiefs and village elders, the British manipulated initiation to discipline young men and push them into the wage labor market. They modified the frequency of male initiation, lowered the age of circumcision, shortened the length of seclusion, and restricted the activities of warriors. More and more boys, at earlier and earlier ages, became men. In much the same way as during the female circumcision controversies that rocked Central Kenya, colonial officials tried to become practicing elders, making generations of matured, male bodies to strengthen state authority. As for the young men who faced the knife, they forged ahead into an age of altered rituals and uncertain meanings focused squarely on enjoying their youthfulness, achieving masculinity, and dreaming of the joys of elderhood.

PARENTAL PARAMOUNTCY

When Reverend Worthington retrieved his still-healing pupil from seclusion, he reignited a long and storied debate about the relationships between African families, missionaries, and the colonial state, as well as their overlapping claims of over the young. From the very beginning, missionary activity in East Africa tested not only the religious convictions of African communities but also the relationships between young and old. Some of the very first converts to Christianity were the very young who found meaning in the new faith, safety from a father's abusive hand, or relief from destitution and slavery. In the 1860s, only a few years after establishing a mission in Zanzibar, Roman Catholic missionaries had sixteen children staying with them, some of whom had been enslaved in Nyanza near Lake Victoria and then ransomed out of slavery. The priests viewed themselves as alternative fathers and these former child slaves as the future of missionary work in the region.[4] By the late nineteenth century, a growing abolitionist impulse and fledgling colonial administration opened more spaces for interaction between the newcomers and young East Africans.[5] Hundreds of young slaves bound for the Indian Ocean trade found themselves emancipated from their captors by agents of the British Empire. British expeditionary forces freed young captives from caravans crawling coastward while naval patrols boarded slaving vessels at sea. The British then turned many of them over to Christian mission stations like Freretown in Mombasa or the African Asylum near Bombay.[6]

In 1898, famine swept from the shores of the Indian Ocean inland to Lake Victoria. On the coast alone, an estimated forty thousand children perished.[7] The destitute found refuge at mission stations. Many of the young people who arrived at stations like Freretown represented a different form of bondage than those captured in previous decades. During the famine, desperate parents made heartbreaking decisions to keep their children alive by exchanging them, especially girls, for food and livestock with neighboring families who fared marginally better. These temporary arrangements, known as pawnship, ensured a child's survival but could also slip into slavery.[8] A year into the famine, a series of pawnship and kidnapping cases attracted the attention of British authorities. The assistant collector of Rabai, H. B. Johnstone, uncovered what he believed to be a network of child slavery. Kamba traders bought children in German Tanganyika and sold them in exchange for livestock to Duruma families across the border in the British East Africa Protectorate. The Duruma then took these children to the coast and sold them for profit. In this way, traders exchanged young people multiple times as they gradually drove them coastward for sale and shipment.[9] Whether these children had been pawned by parents or kidnapped by slavers, the British could not tell. For them, pawnship was nothing more than slavery. Concerns about pawnship continued long after the famine. In 1912, and again in 1917, officials issued warnings that Gikuyu children had been seen traveling with non-Gikuyu adults; and if anyone should see this, they must investigate immediately.[10] As the British conflated pawnship and slavery, they forced some parents to circumvent colonial authority and turn to Christian missions for help.

During the famine, Freretown fed and housed as many as one thousand "orphans," many brought there by parents who could no longer feed them.[11] As the missions accepted these young people, they participated in the practice of pawnship with African parents. Caring for freed child slaves, pawns left by their parents, or young converts drawn to a new faith forced missionaries and the colonial state to explore and define the boundaries of authority over African young people. What right did the British have to hand young people over to missions without parental consent? What right did missions have to keep emaciated pawns or emancipated slaves if parents or kin wanted them back? At what point must missionaries and officials consider what young people wanted?

These questions compelled the chief secretary of the protectorate to send out his district commissioners in April 1914 to ascertain when the young became independent of their elders. The chief secretary prefaced his request by writing that he was "strongly of the opinion that native minors of both sexes should remain under the control of their parents during the period of their minority and that they should not be permitted to leave that control without express sanction."[12] In short, the British colonial state and its African intermediaries should not allow children to leave their families. But if commissioners could determine a definitive moment in which children came of age, then the state might allow them the freedom to leave home and attach themselves to a mission station, join the ranks of the tribal police, or work on a settler's sisal farm.

As field reports trickled in, it became clear that no two ethnic communities along the coast were exactly alike or two district commissioners in agreement. The district commissioner of Mombasa did not even bother to ask local intermediaries. Rather, he felt that the Indian Penal Code, from which the protectorate took its laws, sufficiently fixed the end of male childhood at fourteen years of age and the end of female childhood at sixteen. Bending to African custom, he argued, merely weakened the penal code, thereby "rendering inoperative" imperial rule of law.[13] Other commissioners, eager to dabble in a little ethnographic research, did pose the chief secretary's question to local elders. The commissioners at Shimoni and Rabai learned that among the Nyika, puberty and marriage determined the transition from childhood to adulthood, and this usually occurred between the ages of fifteen and nineteen. The Rabai commissioner added that coming of age did not depend solely on the age of a boy or a girl, but rather the wealth of his or her family. Well-to-do fathers could marry children off at an early age, usually at fifteen, while poor parents withheld marriage, sometimes until nineteen or older. Colonial taxation, he noted, had forced parents to marry children earlier so that they could use dowry to pay off their taxes. Both commissioners saw a young man's coming-of-age as highly adaptable to economic conditions. Given this flexibility, they felt that boys should be allowed to leave home at any time, as long as they had parental consent.[14]

The commissioner at Malindi offered a much different perspective. He argued that an African child "does not come of age in our sense of the word," nor was there a precise moment when parents relinquished authority over children. The commissioner at Njale concurred. No young Giriama, he argued, was ever independent of his or her elders. Strict generational control ensured that no child at any age left his or her parents behind without consulting them first. Both men believed that parental consent and unbending generational authority lay at the heart of African social life. If the chief secretary wanted young people to ever be truly free of their elder kin, then the colonial state would have to draw an "arbitrary line."[15]

Despite these differences of opinion, a consensus formed around four significant points. First the commissioners believed that African boys did in fact come of age, though the timing depended on the community's fortunes and customary practices. They also identified initiation and marriage as the two most pivotal moments in a young man's life, precise markers differentiating childhood from adulthood. Initiation graduated boys into manhood and an interstitial space before adulthood that introduced a host of new responsibilities. Marriage matriculated them into adulthood as they began their own families. Third, commissioners sanctified parental authority as essential to controlling young men who had left childhood but not yet settled down into adulthood. Finally, they positioned the state as the guarantor of the rights of parents over their children, of the rights of the old over the young.

Once the district commissioners' reports were in, the final word fell to their superior, provincial commissioner Charles Hobley. Hobley argued that young African men and women might come of age through initiation, but they never really became independent of family life and generational authority. Girls, he argued, merely passed from the control of one male, the father, to another male, the husband. As for boys, marriage provided the pivotal moment of independence; yet, even then, they remained beholden to their fathers and the new families they created. To reject the "definite duties toward his clan and family" because he "wanders off permanently to a Mission or a town" put a young man at risk. "He may become automatically detribalized," Hobley warned, "and cannot according to native law claim to come back and participate in the division of the family wealth at his father's death."[16] To allow a young African man to stray from his age-defined duties so he could join a mission or enter the migrant labor market might, Hobley argued, unravel the entire structure of generational authority and African social life.

For Hobley, the authority of fathers over sons, of parents over children, and of seniors over juniors was an essential component of African and colonial order. The task of his provincial administration was to preserve generational authority. Hobley stressed that as "the question of control of the family is so fundamentally connected with the whole organization of an African tribe, I would strongly urge [. . .] that each case be dealt with [. . .] by the District Officer, the matter being mutually arranged between the guardian and the other party."[17] District authorities, with their knowledge of local norms, must partner with parents and elders to maintain the harness of generational authority to which the young were yoked. To favor the Indian Penal Code or any other non-African legal structure over the authority of parents and elders, to even imagine a scenario by which young men were free of parental responsibility, risked detribalization. And yet Hobley and some of his commissioners ignored the creativity and contingency in the institutions of age and family life that allowed parents in time of crisis to pawn a starving daughter or send a son to a Christian mission for education.

The district commissioner's findings and Hobley's caution were also refracted through their own ideas about age, ones that had undergone very recent renovation back in Britain. Between the late nineteenth and early twentieth centuries, the British embraced the idea, drawn from biologists and burgeoning fields of social science like child psychology, that a distinct phase of the life course existed between childhood and adulthood, one marked by growing independence. Words such as *adolescent, juvenile,* and *youth* became first scientific and then cultural ideas, created so they could be studied, understood, and ultimately controlled. By 1914, a vast literature describing the age between childhood and adulthood had been published, and new legislation to regulate it had been passed in Britain, Europe, and the United States.[18]

The young, especially men, were characterized by a near limitless energy as well as an inability to cope with their rapid physiological and psychological development. Yet when all that kinetic, unstable energy was bottled up or misdirected, it led to indiscipline, delinquency, and rebelliousness. This potential for disorder made young men all the more fascinating and frightening to social scientists and reformers, leaving girls well outside their scholarly field of view. When young men succumbed to this baser nature, it was often because they lacked firm familial discipline and had come into contact with destabilizing influences outside the home. This interstitial period between childhood and adulthood quickly became associated with all manner of socioeconomic ills: poverty, urbanization, and criminality, as well as a breakdown of the family, of tradition, and of an idyllic, rural past.[19]

Yet this new age could also be "the new 'raw material' of the future [and] a potentially awesome power."[20] Channeled and controlled by the state, young men could build nations, expand empires, and reinforce racial and national superiorities. For the British these had been hard-won lessons learned on the battlefield of Southern Africa. Stunned by their near failure in the Second Boer War, the British witnessed the possibilities of imperial collapse and national weakness.[21] Emerging from the besieged town of Mafeking, the so-called savior of the British effort against the Boers, Robert Baden-Powell, returned home with a solution to British anxieties: the mobilization of the young.[22] As Baden-Powell encouraged his readers in *Scouting for Boys*, "We must all be bricks in the wall of that great edifice—the British Empire—and we must be careful that we do not let our differences of opinion on politics or other questions grow so strong as to divide us. We must still stick shoulder to shoulder as Britons if we want to keep our present position among the nations."[23] Young men became a means to reinvigorate British masculinity, militarism, imperial purpose, and racial superiority. Years later, during World War I, ideas about age and youth were on the tips of tongues the world over as European nations channeled the energies of young men with deadly design. Tens of thousands of bright, young Britons possessed by romantic, nationalist fervor charged up and out of muddy trenches carved into the cratered fields of France. This no-man's-land became the crucible by which young Britons could test their manhood.[24]

In Kenya, colonial officials saw something of what they had lost back home in Britain: the comforts of pastoral hearth and home and the social controls of patriarchs and elder kin. They also worried that they had brought with them those same destabilizing forces that had driven British families to cities, broken them apart, and then released uncontrolled, undisciplined young men and women onto the streets. And so they had to be vigilant and guard against the unraveling of African family life that could in turn weaken indirect rule. They seized on local institutions, like male initiation, which they imagined to have been imbued with unquestioned elder patriarchal power—ignoring, perhaps intentionally, the argument and flexibility embedded in African age-relations. After the 1914 investigation, the elder state still had much to learn. Over the course of colonial rule, the British continued exploring initiation, marriage, and the liminal period in between and then tried wielding the power of generational authority themselves.

FACING THE KNIFE

Five years had passed since coastal administrators affirmed parental authority, and still Meru district commissioner Chamier had to defend the rights of fathers to initiate their sons from a missionary willfully violating local custom. What bothered Chamier most was not that Worthington had kidnapped a schoolboy from seclusion, but that he had also performed circumcisions at the mission without parental consent. The reverend did not simply remove one student from seclusion; he removed many of his faithful from initiation altogether. Reporting to his superior, provincial commissioner H. R. Tate, Chamier argued that this constituted a serious breach of African cultural life. He conceded that mission-sponsored male circumcision had also taken place in nearby Nyeri and Fort Hall, especially among Gikuyu at Roman Catholic missions. But its wider availability did not change the fact that the missions had converted one of the most climactic moments in an African's social life to its own purposes. By offering circumcision at his mission, Chamier feared that Worthington detached young people from the collective, generation-forming experience of initiation and robbed them of the customary knowledge they learned in seclusion.

Chamier's anxieties arose from his belief, which he shared with many other colonial officials at the time, that initiation was one of the most important moments in a young African man's life. Accounts of initiation among the different ethnic communities of Kenya consumed page after page of early colonial field reports and ethnographies, much of it filtered through the sieve of elder Africans, young often-uninitiated interpreters, and scraps of hearsay meticulously collected by the authors themselves. The theater of initiation—with its elaborate adornments worn, dances and songs performed, genital circumcision endured, and secrets of seclusion withheld—excited the wildest imaginations of colonial newcomers. This ethnographic exploration and interpretation, what Katherine Luongo has called the "anthro-administrative complex," empowered the British to use initiation, especially genital circumcision, as the not-so "arbitrary line" that marked the water's edge of parental authority.[25]

However, colonial investigations like the one conducted in 1914, and dozens of ethnographic studies, did not offer a clear, inert image of African coming-of-age. Rather, they provided officials with a frustratingly blurred snapshot of community practice set in motion by local and global encounters. Consider John Middleton's frustration as he wrote about Gikuyu social institutions in the early 1950s. Rather than conduct his own research, he tried to synthesize a host of older ethnographies. To his consternation, he found that when considered together, none of the early anthropologists—Routledge, Hobley, Cagnolo, or Kenyatta—presented a consistent, unified narrative of Gikuyu initiation.[26] While he rightly attributed the problem to variation in style and region, the ethnographies Middleton used spanned five decades. He had failed to consider that initiation changed over time and never embodied a fixed, original form in the first place. What the Routledges observed in 1908 should have differed from what Kenyatta's age-group experienced in 1913 and what Cagnolo witnessed in the 1930s. Anthropologists were frustrated not just by shifting initiation practices but also by the secrecy with which communities held these rituals and their meanings. In fact, the oaths binding former initiates from sharing details of their time in seclusion still hold to this day.[27]

Several ethnographers tipped their hats to the flexibility of male initiation and changes already set in motion, sometimes set off by the ethnographers themselves. Even though William and Katherine Routledge conducted one of the earliest studies of Gikuyu social life, the initiation ceremonies they observed were already adaptations to Gikuyu interaction with the Maasai and the coastal slave trade.[28] One of the Gikuyu assistants working for the Routledges during their 1908 fieldwork had postponed his initiation to aid in their research. Later, when he informed them that he had to leave their employment to undergo circumcision, they tried to convince him to stay. He flatly refused, telling them that his elders had threatened to prevent his initiation altogether if he postponed it again.[29] The Routledges were not alone in relying on uninitiated interlocutors. Around the same time, Alfred C. Hollis learned to speak Nandi from two "small boys" he met in Nairobi—one a Nandi, the other a Kipsigis. They stayed with him until he had learned the language and then returned home.[30] Some of Hollis's very first information about Nandi life and language came from the mouths of mere babes living far from home.

Some of the young men with whom early ethnographers worked had undergone circumcision but not yet completed initiation, and thereby remained but boys in their elders' eyes. Shortly after World War I, as Gerhard Lindblom made yet another fruitless attempt to witness Kamba circumcision ceremonies (he had been denied repeatedly), he noted that a growing number of Kamba men returned for their second circumcision at very old ages. Although they had been physically circumcised, they had forgone their time in seclusion to work for the government as soldiers and police.[31] In the 1930s, John G. Peristiany also relied on a circumcised yet uninitiated Kipsigis interpreter named arap Chuma. In his ethnography, Peristiany recalls that Chuma had gone to Nairobi when he was very young and had been circumcised by a European doctor. When he returned, elders allowed him to marry and settle down, but they never let him forget that he had not been initiated in the proper Kipsigis fashion. "He is constantly made to feel that, unless he is initiated, he will not be considered as really one of them." During his stay, Peristiany encouraged arap Chuma to complete his initiation.[32]

In each of these cases, ethnographers had engaged with elders through uninitiated boys or those initiated in an atypical manner. Young men, boys even, had willingly altered their initiation to take advantage of the new possibilities opened up by the colonial encounter. The British "discovered" African coming-of-age just as young men adapted its practice and form to changing colonial circumstances. Moreover, the choices these young intermediaries made in their own transitions to manhood complicated their ability to accurately translate the meanings of African customary practice, especially rituals they themselves had not yet experienced. What chief or village elder would choose to reveal such secrets to an uninitiated boy like the Routledges' interpreter or a man who had forgone his time in seclusion like arap Chuma? As the Gikuyu proverb goes: "Mûici na kîhîî atigaga kîeha kîarua," or "He who steals in the company of an uncircumcised boy will live in fear until the boy is circumcised."[33] And if elders chose to share their knowledge through the medium of the uninitiated, an act of adaptation of their own, then the conversations that formed these early ethnographies took place through a generational prism refracting what information elders chose to provide uninitiated translators and what information the boys thought important for European ears. Perhaps the very importance of initiation and age-relations in these early ethnographies was a by-product of exchanges ethnographers had with boys for whom these very issues were the principal thoughts on their minds as well as the minds of elders who found themselves engaged in tense age-infused negotiations with boys elevated far above their station.

These ethnographic missives record a form of historical theater immortalizing performances between African informants and intermediaries as well as European investigators. While they do not offer historians accounts of precolonial forms of initiation or age-relations, they provide an abstraction and a means of identifying how Africans articulated coming-of-age and how agents of colonial rule witnessed it at a particular time. These ethnographies, as well as discussions between colonial officials and African intermediaries, identified several crucial characteristics of coming-of-age that underwent dramatic change during the colonial encounter.

First, male initiation practices marked the physical and psychological transition from childhood to manhood. Before and long after the colonial period, the majority of African communities in Kenya practiced some form of male initiation. These varied in ritual practice, most notably the presence or absence of genital circumcision. Despite ritual diversity, initiation stood as one of the most significant moments in an African man's life. The Routledges argued that for the Gikuyu, events like marriage and death "hold but a small place . . . compared to that greatest of all ceremonies whereby the boy becomes a man and the girl a woman."[34] Likewise, initiation was a pivotal moment in the lives of young Kamba, Gusii, Kipsigis, Maasai, and Nandi.[35] While Luo boys did not traditionally undergo circumcision, they did experience rituals that transitioned them out of childhood.[36] Plans to initiate a boy depended on several factors. The well-being of the entire community determined when initiation occurred. Drought, famine, or war could postpone or even accelerate initiation. If conditions permitted, the decision fell to the eagerness of a future initiate and the consent of his father. A boy had to want it, and when ready, he approached his father. Only a father could secure "the satisfaction of all a boy's longings and ambitions."[37] A father's consent often depended on his ability to afford the necessary accoutrements of initiation, such as livestock, alcohol, food, and gifts.[38] A father's status also changed once he had initiated his firstborn. He or his age-group as a whole moved upward into a more advanced age with its own new privileges and responsibilities. While a father could postpone his son's initiation, he could deny neither his son's nor his own ambitions for too long.

FIGURE 1.1. African child sitting in front of house, n.d. Photo courtesy of the Melville J. Herskovits Library of African Studies Winterton Collection, Northwestern University.

Prior to and in the earlier years of colonial rule, boys' initiations occurred at some point in their late teens through their mid-twenties. Kamba boys were a notable exception; they experienced circumcision before puberty, around the age of five, but did not complete initiation until much later.[39] Preparations took many months. Fathers had to accumulate capital and consult elders. Mothers had to prepare food and alcohol. Boys had to visit relatives to announce initiation, procure the necessary adornments, and perform songs and dances. In the days running up to initiation, Gikuyu and Meru boys worked themselves to the point of exhaustion dancing and singing songs. Wachira Mwaniki, a Gikuyu from Nyeri circumcised in 1936, remembers that the songs emboldened the spirits of the boys who were about to face the knife.[40] In Kiambu, David Chege recalls that the words differed two decades later, but the spirit of the songs remained the same: "Let me be allowed to go and get circumcision, I am old enough to face the knife!" "In our family we have never seen anyone shed tears!"[41]

Before sunrise, Gikuyu and Meru initiates traveled to a nearby stream where they disrobed and stood immersed in chilly waters. After some time, the boys emerged and sat along the bank or in a nearby field where a large crowd had gathered to watch. The boys dug their heels into the cool earth, pushed back against the supportive hands of their sponsors, and fixed their gaze skyward as the circumciser walked, ceremonial knife in hand, down the line, cutting each of them with two swift strokes.[42] At the same time of day, but much nearer the shores of Lake Victoria, Gusii boys underwent a remarkably similar ordeal.[43] Among pastoralist Kipsigis and Maasai, initiation also included intense ritualized violence, such as passing through gauntlets of stinging nettles and frightening tests of honesty and endurance.[44] Bravery in the face of searing pain was a common element in genital circumcision. A boy who struggled or cried out endured mockery and humiliation. In these moments, no boy could flinch or cry out in pain. Facing the knife prepared initiates for the courage and discipline expected of them when they became warriors.

The second element emphasized by ethnographers and colonial officials was a period of intense instruction and socialization. Following circumcision, young men entered a period of seclusion, usually in a home built by their sponsors at a fair distance from their villages. These special houses went by a variety of names: the Gikuyu called them *githunu* or *thingira*, the Meru called them *gichee*, the Kamba *thomi*, and the Nandi and Kipsigis *menjo* or *menjet*. Despite their disparate names, their role in initiation was twofold: to protect and to educate the initiates while they healed. During seclusion, new initiates learned the codes of conduct of the community and expectations of becoming warriors, husbands, and eventually fathers and elders. Seclusion ensured that once physically reborn as men, their minds kept pace. Given its importance, male communities shrouded seclusion in secrecy. Before young men emerged from seclusion, their elders bound them to oaths of secrecy. These oaths frustrated ethnographers who knew little about what went on in the menjo, which ultimately pushed them to emphasize the public rituals surrounding genital circumcision over the more private affairs of the seclusion hut.

This was especially the case for Kamba initiates. Several years separated their genital circumcision from their second, great circumcision. Around the age of twelve, though boys from poor families could be twenty or older, initiates left home for the thomi. There they hunted, solved riddles, defended against mock Maasai cattle raids, and confronted their fears.[45] When the young men returned home from this second circumcision, they had taken yet another step toward adulthood. After facing the knife, young Gikuyu men convalesced for a week or two in the githunu. While they healed, their sponsors, elders, and even older siblings visited to instill in them important lessons.[46] They informed the boys that they were "not a child any longer, be very brave, and don't play with uncircumcised boys or girls."[47] Moreover, "they have gone to another stage from childhood to adulthood, behave well, respect men and women when you meet them on your way, greet them with respect and move aside to let them pass."[48] It reminded them that while they were no longer children, they were still expected to obey their elders.

The seclusion of Kipsigis and Nandi initiates was one of the longest in Kenya. After circumcision, boys stayed in a special hut known as the menjo, constructed far from the community, where they healed.[49] Here, according to men of the Chuma and Sawe age-groups, the most important aspects of initiation occurred. While recuperating, special elder instructors lived with them, teaching them the laws of the Kipsigis people as well as physical combat. As Anthony King'etich Rotich, a member of the Sawe age-group, recalls, "They were taught everything a Kipsigis needed to know so that he became a man; and when he came out he was now a man, and he was no longer a boy."[50] Another Sawe, Jonah Kiprono, concurs: "We learned about war, handling spears, bows, and arrows, and we were also taught about the behavior expected of a man."[51] This time offered them the opportunity to "forsake childhood traits and behave like an adult."[52] Several Kipsigis men carefully distinguished their time in the menjo—and not simply their circumcision—as making them men and preparing them for adulthood.[53]

Emerging from seclusion, young men entered into new sets of relations with one another as well as with their elders and junior followers.[54] The crucible of initiation forged a cohesive generation, which shared a special bond governed by strict codes of intragenerational conduct. Gikuyu young men exiting their brief period in seclusion took an age-group name, usually a remarkable, contemporaneous event connecting the group to a moment with historical significance.[55] When circumcised in 1936, Wachira Mwaniki's age-set was named cindano (needle) as well as pia (Kenya Bus Service). Pins and needles had just shown up in Nyeri marketplaces, and the Kenya Bus Service had begun operation in Nairobi.[56] Young men and their age-groups were bound together not only by their initiation and seclusion but also by the historical circumstances in which they came of age and the history they would make together.

Young men left seclusion only to remain in an interstitial period, between childhood and adulthood, of varying lengths of time. Instead of becoming adults, they became warriors of varying degrees of seniority. Gikuyu young men left seclusion to become junior warriors of a mumo, a set of youths. Over the next six or so years, they spent their days dancing, singing, and devoting themselves to military activities.[57] Their time as warriors became a way to "divert their excess energies and their strength to more profitable channels, such as raiding Maasai stock, and thereby enriching the family."[58] Out west, Maasai and Samburu initiates became moran and lived apart from the community in separate compounds known as *manyattas*, out of which they trained, prepared stock raids, and enjoyed the luxuries bestowed upon them as warriors. Communities who had to defend against Maasai moran raids, such as the Kipsigis and Nandi, prepared their own young warriors fresh out of the menjo for raids and counterraids of their own.[59]

Third, African communities experienced and British officials understood coming-of-age as a series of intense generational relationships. Each step in the journey from initiation to seclusion and on into warriorhood depended on young men's relations with older generations.[60] Pastoralist communities such as the Kipsigis, Nandi, Maasai, and Samburu organized generational life around age-groups created at periodic intervals, which formed a progressive, cyclical pattern of advancement. The decision to initiate a new group of boys into junior warriors depended on the willingness of elder men to make way for the new generation. Among the Kipsigis, elders decided to start a new age-group every fifteen years or so, each with its own name.[61] During the next fifteen-year cycle, boys would be initiated into the newest age-group. Eventually, this group would be closed, giving rise to yet another one, pushing all other age-groups upward along an ever-moving axis of age and time.[62] Consider Thomas Kisigei, a Kipsigis living near Sotik; he claims to have been one of the last initiates into the Chuma age-group. He faced the knife in 1947, during the solar eclipse that passed over southern Kenya.[63] At the moment of his initiation, the Chuma group closed its doors to new initiates. As Thomas and his fellow Chuma, who had been initiated years before, entered junior warriorhood, the age-group that had once occupied that position, known as Maina, also moved upward, becoming senior warriors. To make room for the Maina, the group that had once been senior warriors graduated into elderhood.

Creating and closing age-groups required all men to acquiesce to change — but not always willingly. Occasionally uninitiated Kipsigis or junior warriors struggled, sometimes violently, to get the generation above them to relinquish their position. Movement upward through Maasai society was not automatic either. Junior moran had to prove their value to and respect of their elders to progress to positions of senior warriorhood and beyond. This was often accomplished through violent outbursts of indiscipline and direct challenges to the authority of elders. Rebelliousness was an essential component of the Maasai system of age-graduation.[64] To signal that they, too, had the grit and guts to endure initiation, Gikuyu boys performed endless dances of a distinctly loud and militant manner until parents became so annoyed that they gladly consented to initiation.[65] However, these "rituals of rebellion" never materialized into full-scale generational revolutions whereby the young permanently overturned elder authority.[66]

Finally, ethnographers and colonial officials fixated on the power elders had over the young and the intense stratification among generations. Elder men and women demanded obedience, service in time of conflict, and legitimacy of their authority. They decided when and how to initiate sons and daughters.[67] They wielded the ritual violence of the circumcision knife. They conducted the lessons in seclusion. They held the keys to maturity and future elder power. Acquiescence and complicity were as much a part of age-relations as disobedience and rebellion. Kenyatta forcefully argued that among the Gikuyu, the youngest generations were without doubt subservient to elder groups.[68] For the Maasai of Matapato, Spencer argues that "delay and denial" were "built into the system. It is elders who . . . cultivate the popular awareness of the process of time, and hence the perception of time itself, and of maturity among younger men and women."[69] Although young men enjoyed an egalitarian spirit within their age-group, "to acquire a sense of being a Maasai, is to enter into this premise of age inequality from the bottom rung and ultimately to have a role in perpetuating it as one climbs upward."[70] Whether Maasai or Gikuyu, young men were "suspended somewhere between boyhood and full adulthood," and while they enjoyed their youth, they also held on to the promise that one day their elders would help them fulfill their ultimate dream of adulthood.[71]

This promise, this elder-sponsored path toward adulthood, was sometimes very explicitly expressed to young men. After a Meru boy's circumcision, he returned to his father's homestead. There his father greeted him and announced: "My son, as I have agreed to allow you to be circumcised, I also pledged to get you a wife. My son, I pledged to you a sword, spear, club, and shield for use when going out to fight. My son, I pledged you an ewe and heifer for your in-laws."[72] No clearer statement could have been made regarding the stakes of a disciplined, obedient coming-of-age. A Meru father said, in the starkest of terms: "Respect me and obey me, and I will prepare you for manhood." Gikuyu fathers, John Lonsdale argues, "worked for their sons, earning the next generation's bridewealth [, and] juniors, children, and clients, were expected to give obedience in return."[73] Mothers worked for their sons, too, as did sisters, whose marriages fetched the dowries that would be reinvested in a brother's marriage.[74] In many ways, the entire family labored to ensure that a son matured and started his own family. During colonial rule, and perhaps long before, boys reached manhood and young men reached adulthood through their willingness to accept their families' efforts, and, if need be, the families exerted a little pressure to help them get there.

As British officials and missionaries came to understand and imagine the cultural significance of circumcision and seclusion as well as the politics of age-relations, they looked for ways to manipulate these forces. Their pursuit to harness the energies of young men and possess the authority of elders had profound implications for the African experience of colonial rule. To alter initiation practices or the time in seclusion; to tip the delicate scales in favor of one generation over another; to subsume the power of generational authority into the state or mission station altered how young men spent their youth, expressed masculinity, and strove for maturity.

DRAWING ARBITRARY LINES

When Reverend Worthington began circumcising young converts in Meru, he participated in a long-standing practice among missionaries in Kenya. Missionaries did not initially advertise themselves as purveyors of an alternative form of initiation, nor did African parents and elders imbue them with any authority on the matter. That did not prevent them from assisting with initiation, even if unintentionally. In 1909, Reverend V. V. Verbi, of the Church Missionary Society station at Wusi, noted, "My medical knowledge had been useful [and] many circumcision cases have been brought to me."[75] The reverend became so successful in aiding parents whose sons and daughters suffered infection that local circumcision operators complained to him that he was stealing their profits. Converts also pressured missionaries to permit the practice and persuaded them to carry it out at the stations.[76] Those who had been orphans, outcasts, or emancipated slaves would have had few alternatives to receive initiation and looked to their new religious community.[77] Together, missionaries, parents whose children suffered from botched circumcisions, and orphans took the first steps in connecting missions to the powerful cultural work of initiation. In doing so, they introduced new frontiers along which ideas about and relationships of gender and generation could be tested.[78]

Yet some missionaries like Reverend Worthington took this first step further. Worthington saw his role in circumcision as a way to replace the lessons learned in seclusion with those in the classroom. He argued that Meru elders and district commissioner Chamier did "violence to the convictions of those of our number who wish to undergo the ceremony under Christian influences."[79] His converts had the right to choose where they became men and women and to whom they turned to circumcise them. If they chose his mission, then Worthington felt no obligation to send them home. He was merely accommodating the desires of his flock, Christianizing African initiation to bring it under his supervision.[80] This became a common strategy among Catholic and Protestant missionaries. They simply offered to circumcise converts or allowed them to return home for circumcision as long as they did not dance, sing, or enter seclusion. For members of the mission, to forgo the rites accompanying initiation carried a weighty stigma. Many of those "boys who have been circumcised at [the] hospital are hated by their people because they did not go through the old customs."[81]

Worthington positioned schooling as a "vital" and transformative moment in a child's life, not unlike initiation itself. "It is unjust to extract a child from mission education," Worthington argued, and "no break in education at such a vital time in the child's life should occur." Each in their own way, African initiation and Western religious education socialized the young and transformed boys into masculine, productive members of different sets of communities. However, for missionaries like Worthington, months of dancing, feasting, gift giving, and lessons in customary practice were a diabolical distraction from Bible study, literacy, and vocational training. These activities did not produce the kinds of masculinity or morals he wanted from his schoolboys. In much the same way as Methodist missionaries in South Africa, Worthington saw African initiation and Christian baptism as "both rituals of reproduction" and an "uncompromising choice between the past and the future, benighted damnation and enlightened salvation."[82] Eventually, his flock would have to choose. And when schoolboys chose to return home for initiation, they reminded missionaries of the limits of their authority and the need for a firmer hand—or, in Worthington's case, at the very least, a kidnapping.[83]

Meru district commissioner Chamier could not have disagreed more. The Meru, he believed, were not hostile to education, but rather merely "bitter" that missionaries and government interfered with custom. In his letter to provincial commissioner Tate, he argued that "if respect for a missionary is only to be obtained by violent interference with tribal customs, the price is in my opinion too high to pay."[84] The district commissioner echoed the words Hobley had uttered five years earlier: the colonial state must respect African customs—at least the ones the British recognized— and maintain the authority of parents, elders, and chiefs or pay the ultimate price of detribalization.

Chamier was disheartened when provincial commissioner Tate weighed in on Worthington's activities in Meru. Tate acknowledged the importance of initiation in the transition from childhood to manhood. He had, after all, dabbled in a little ethnographic research of his own a decade earlier as district commissioner in Kiambu. There he spent considerable time investigating the significance of initiation and cataloging a history of Gikuyu age-group names.[85] However, Tate replied to Chamier that initiation should not jeopardize the far more vital endeavor of teaching a "rising generation [to] master their desires and impulses and to order their lives in a manner not only conducive to their eternal salvation but also more agreeable to civilised standards."[86] In Tate's view, missionaries and colonial officers had partnered in a broader civilizing project, and African parents had to realize that "neither Missionary Societies nor Government will undertake the training of boys and girls unless the latter are to remain under their care *in statu pupillai* [sic] for the period of completing their education." Tate's vision of the colonial encounter and its relationships to male coming-of-age and generational authority marked a dramatic shift in policy outlined by Hobley only five years earlier in 1914. Tate laid out the position of the colonial state and missions vis-à-vis African young men and parents in the starkest of terms. When a father handed his son over to a priest or principal, willingly or unwillingly, he relinquished his authority and, by extension, his right to socialize, initiate, and discipline his son the way he saw fit. Missionaries and government officials might allow his son to return for initiation, but they were under no such obligation.

Worthington's siege of a seclusion hut exposed two competing visions of the colonial state. Chamier saw the state as a conservator of the African customs and institutions that buttressed indirect rule. Tate saw the state as a catalyst of the civilizing mission, encouraging Africans to leave the reserve, convert to Christianity, and learn a trade. Each man had served in the Kenyan provincial administration for over a decade and yet found themselves, at least on this issue, in a battle for the soul of the colonial enterprise: Was its task the protection of "native paramountcy" or the moral uplift of its subjects? In some ways, Chamier's conservatism would claim the 1920s and 1930s. Bruce Berman argues that the interwar provincial administration was a paternalistic, "conservative apparatus of control," a "guardian bureaucracy" driven to stabilize and control the social and economic forces it had set in motion.[87] Two of the most important institutions men like Chamier sought to protect were tribes and chiefs. "Obviously tribes could not be allowed to disintegrate," as Brett Shadle nicely puts it. "Chiefs without tribes were not chiefs, and with neither chiefs nor tribes Indirect Rule, and colonial rule altogether, would collapse."[88] Nor could customs like initiation be questioned when they were so central to establishing a sense of place and legitimizing authority within a community.

However, missionaries like Worthington and social reformers back in Britain shook provincial administrators like Chamier from their dusty conservatism, forcing them to live up to the lofty goals of the civilizing mission. The battle over female initiation, particularly circumcision, was one of the most spectacular examples of colonial officials and chiefs pushed to tamper with African cultural life in the name of moral uplift. In the 1920s, several religious organizations in Kenya and parliamentarians in London pressured officials to limit and then outright abolish female circumcision.[89] In response, the Central Province administration worked with local councils of chiefs to gradually alter female circumcision. Changes were small at first. Officials issued warnings that they would prosecute anyone who forced a girl to undergo circumcision against her will. They also ordered chiefs to reduce the amount of time communities spent initiating their children and lowered the age at which girls underwent initiation.[90] Officials feared that girls faced the knife far too late in life, typically after reaching puberty, which encouraged them to have sex before marriage and abort unwanted pregnancies. The provincial administrators hoped that earlier initiations would prevent premarital sex, pregnancies, and abortions, which represented moral decay, looming demographic collapse, and future labor shortages.[91]

Families resisted these changes. In Kiambu, chiefs complained that when daughters began menstruating before the agreed-upon period of initiation, families clandestinely circumcised the girls themselves.[92] The local council backed away from the limitations, permitting female circumcision throughout the year. In Meru, when faced with similar resistance, officials and chiefs aggressively enforced their rulings. When an uninitiated girl was discovered pregnant, police rounded up girls in the area and forcibly circumcised them.[93] These campaigns robbed families of the right to initiate girls as they saw fit, and put the district officials in the position of enforcing the very custom they were meant to eradicate.

As the decade wore on, administrators continued to press local councils on female circumcision, families continued to bring girls before the knife as before, and Gikuyu political activists seized on these changes to attack the colonial state and its chiefs. In 1929, the Church of Scotland Mission, the African Inland Mission, the Salvation Army, and other religious organizations called for the end of female circumcision and compelled their congregants to forsake the institution. Most administrators in the districts, who had already done much to alter the practice of female circumcision, were reluctant to push the issue any further. Provincial commissioner E. B. Horne felt the policy toward female circumcision should be one of "masterly inactivity."[94] The ban infuriated the Gikuyu. In droves, congregants abandoned the most outspoken missions and established their own independent churches and schools. They also flocked to the Kikuyu Central Association, whose leadership had successfully turned the ban into a political lightning rod. Talk of a ban was quickly silenced, and the state retreated from many of the alterations it had made to female circumcision. The British had dabbled in welfare and moral uplift and was met with a ferocious response, sowing the seeds of future political discontent.[95]

All the while, as the most outspoken missionaries sought an end to girls' circumcisions, they quietly carried them out on boys back at their mission stations. Control over young men's genitals never aroused the same political furor. Neither the state nor missionaries tried to ban male circumcision, such a thing was simply unimaginable. Susan Pedersen has argued that the British hesitated to ban male circumcision in Kenya because they were unsure how they would then handle the issue of Jews and Muslims living in their colonies.[96] But British comfort with male circumcision was not simply an issue of policy—it was a very intimate and personal one. Ronald Hyam has shown that by the end of the nineteenth century, circumcision had become vogue among well-to-do Britons, the very class responsible for running the empire. By the mid-1930s, about two-thirds of upper-middle-class men were circumcised.[97] This had not always been the case, though. For centuries, the British and Europeans used circumcision as a marker of paganism, savagery, and sexual deviance in Jews, Muslims, and Africans. Circumcision also played into the horrors Britons endured out on the edge of empire. In 1780, hundreds of British soldiers were taken captive after the state of Mysore soundly defeated the British East India Company. Their Muslim captors forcibly circumcised them, shocking the British public. Removing the captives' foreskins stripped them of their Christianity and Britishness and became an emblem of national humiliation and emasculation.[98] A century later, the British inverted the humiliation of circumcision on the Indian subcontinent into a badge of masculinity and imperial robustness. Medical officials encouraged circumcision among officials in India to promote health and cleanliness as well as to legitimize their manliness and right to rule.[99]

Officials in Kenya left behind no record of the status of their foreskins, but if Hyam is right, then a few provincial administrators might have been circumcised and more comfortable and sensitive to its cultural significance. Either way, provincial administrators recognized male initiation as an essential part of African masculinity. Dependent on the labor of young men and the power of elders to fuel the colonial economy and maintain law and order, male initiation became an unquestioned necessity.

Male initiation became a critical component of colonial authority akin to the reification of customary law, reliance on local chiefs, and enforcement of taxes and compulsory labor. In coalition with local elders, the British sought to exert authority over young men through the process of initiation. The provincial administration adapted male initiation to push newly made young men into the labor market and control their behavior. They manipulated and regulated coming-of-age by changing the timing and length of initiation, seclusion, and warriorship. As was the case among missionaries, the elder state's work with African initiation practices began in small, unexpected ways. In the early years of the protectorate, medical officers performed a few circumcision procedures strictly out of concern for a male patient's health.[100] In addition, officials at the Kabete Reformatory for young African offenders held "careful discussions" in 1916 about offering circumcision to inmates on a voluntary basis.[101] Discontinued, reformatory officials later revived the program in the 1940s when too many inmates escaped for initiation.[102] By 1947, announcements were made in Meru and Nyeri informing local leaders that government medical officers would offer circumcision to Gikuyu boys once a week, free of charge.[103] Only a small number of young men volunteered for these state-sponsored circumcisions. Beyond occasionally offering an alternative, medicalized form of circumcision, the colonial state had a much broader influence on male initiation.

Across the colony, British administrators entered into delicate negotiations with communities to adjust male coming-of-age to meet the necessities of settler colonialism. Their first order of business was to refashion junior warriors, made obsolete by British conquest, into wage laborers. In early 1920s Central Province, district commissioners met with Gikuyu, Meru, and Embu elders to regulate and limit but never outlaw male circumcision. In 1920, only a year after provincial commissioner Tate had consented to missionary meddling in their schoolboys' initiations, his replacement, D. R. Crampton, ordered district officials to persuade chiefs to shorten male initiation. According to Crampton, this was to be done to steady the flow of Gikuyu labor. "One of the reasons why this change has been advocated is that the present period of convalescence of able-bodied workers, who undergo circumcision, could be done away with and a larger supply of labour be consequently available."[104] The British believed young men spent too much time thinking about and participating in initiation-related events. They wanted a pool of able-bodied laborers with their minds firmly fixed on earning wages.

In Fort Hall and Nyeri, elders agreed on two major changes. They consolidated ceremonies into a single, large celebration for boys living in a location, and they shortened the length by limiting dances and the period spent in seclusion. They rejected requests from the district commissioner to limit initiation to one week, instead agreeing to one or two months. Chiefs sitting on local councils looked favorably on limiting initiation. In 1920, the Fort Hall local council noted that the long length of initiation ceremonies "hang[s] up the output of labor seriously during the three months, and they would get into trouble over it."[105] A few years later, the Kiambu council claimed that "a large number of ceremonies . . . was most unsettling to labour and as things were at present a native so inclined could attend one ceremony after another to the detriment of his work."[106] The year before, Governor Northey had issued his circular on the mobilization of African labor by any means necessary. Neither district commissioners nor chiefs, who were responsible for labor recruitment, wanted their efforts hampered by lengthy initiation festivities.[107] When a community spent months preparing for and recuperating from initiation, provincial administrators felt such energies could be put to use in more "productive" ways.

In Rift Valley Province, a similar negotiation began among colonial officials and Kipsigis and Nandi elders. Unlike Gikuyu initiation, Kipsigis and Nandi boys required several years to complete the process. Throughout the 1930s and 1940s, Kipsigis elders negotiated with provincial administrators to shorten the time young men spent in seclusion. According to Peristiany, the form of initiation he witnessed in the 1930s had already been shortened compared to previous generations.[108] Those initiated into the Chuma age-group from the late 1920s to 1947 acknowledged that their stay in the menjo had been shorter than that of previous generations. Thomas Tamutwa noted that his initiation took only six months rather than the two years his father had experienced.[109] The change had come from the chiefs and "the elders accepted it, and so did the people."[110]

Both government and missions argued that these changes stabilized Kipsigis education and labor. The principal of the government school in Kabianga argued in 1945 that Kipsigis boys who left school for a year of initiation were "retarded on their return, and if leave is refused, their minds are not thereafter concentrated on their school work." About 22 percent of initiated Kipsigis attending Kabianga School had been "medically circumcised" as opposed to "tribally initiated."[111] Although the rate of school attendance among Kipsigis was much lower than in other communities like the Gikuyu or Luo, these 22 percent attested to the reality that more and more young men experienced a modified initiation. The Kipsigis Sawe age-class initiated during the 1950s experienced the most change to their time in the menjo. Sawe schoolboys underwent initiation during their December recess, which lasted about a month.[112] Those who did not attend school experienced a much longer period of initiation. Kimeli Too, John Kiptalam, and their cohort of friends in Kabianga, near Kericho, went to work on the tea estates rather than school. They spent a year in the menjo, compared to the month experienced by boys attending the government school.[113] In the same location, young men could experience very different lengths of initiation depending on whether they herded livestock, picked tea leaves, or attended school.

Labor and education were not the only factors pushing Rift Valley communities to shorten their periods of initiation. The heavy presence of Kipsigis and Nandi in the military also raised concerns regarding the length of seclusion. In 1941, the district commissioner of Kapsabet alerted the provincial commissioner that the Nandi Chumo (or Juma) age-group was about to undergo initiation. He warned that uninitiated Nandi serving in the King's African Rifles would have to be given leave so they could return home for initiation, or they would become "disgruntled."[114] Worse still, they would likely stay home well beyond the two weeks afforded them by the military, thereby interfering with the colony's preparedness. "Circumcision is the most important event in the life of a Nandi," he argued, "and it cannot simply be ignored, and is now becoming the principle [sic] thought on their minds to the exclusion of everything else." The military rejected the commissioner's proposal for extended leave. Those soldiers who left the service for initiation would either face charges of desertion or forfeit their time in seclusion. Soldiers struggled more than most to balance the cultural demands of household and community life with the rigors of regimented military service.[115]

Across the colony, the shift to earlier initiations of much younger boys also played a role in maintaining law and order. Ethnographers of the Gikuyu claimed, with near unanimity, that boys had been initiated in the past between the ages of fifteen and eighteen.[116] Louis Leakey, one of the most active chroniclers of Gikuyu custom, stressed that elders told him circumcision could not take place before the age of seventeen.[117] Over the course of colonial rule, the age of male Gikuyu initiates fell to around thirteen or fifteen, even younger in some cases.[118] By the mid-1930s, chiefs in Central Province complained that boys faced the knife far too early.[119] Farther west, the age at which Kipsigis boys underwent initiation also fell dramatically. Groups that came of age just after the turn of the century, such as Nyonge, were initiated at twenty to twenty-five years of age.[120] But by the time Chumo and Sawe initiates entered the menjo in the 1930s and 1950s, they were only in their mid-teens.[121]

When British conquest ended the reign of warriors, fathers no longer needed to wait for their sons to physically mature so that they might defend the community or raid for livestock. Colonial rule had enabled willing families to initiate their sons at an earlier age and push them into the labor market so that they might earn enough wages to pay tax, fulfill compulsory labor requirements, and add to the family income. Moreover, the British hoped that young laborers would be more pliable to employer demands. In the 1930s, H. E. Lambert, who would later write on the subject of Gikuyu social institutions, was asked by the chief native commissioner about foreseeable problems with early male circumcision. According to Lambert, late-age initiation had dangerous psychological effects on young men. The results, to Lambert's thinking, took the "form of mental stultification, sexual aberration [as well as] imbecility and criminality." The older the initiate, Lambert mused, the more restless and violent he became to gain access to the rights and responsibilities associated with adulthood. Earlier initiations, he argued, might prevent boys from future indiscipline.[122]

In addition to shifting the timing of initiation and shortening seclusion to encourage young men to labor, colonial officials used initiation to discipline their behavior. Among pastoralist communities like the Kipsigis, Maasai, Nandi, and Samburu, junior and senior warriors had not dissipated as quickly as they had done among the Gikuyu or integrated as easily into the colonial police and military as the Kamba.[123] Warrior moran continued to meet, dance, raid for cattle, and occasionally irk district administrators. The rituals of rebellion that made moran manly and worthy of warriorship had become liabilities. Armed with a maturing understanding of the progress by which generations succeeded one another, district officials sought to turn the graduation of age-groups to their advantage. They forcibly and prematurely transitioned young moran out of warriorship and into settled lives as adults, reverse engineering rituals of rebellion into a punitive regime.

From the turn of the century until World War I, moran had worked well with the British. They grew wealthy in cattle by raiding and skirmishing with neighboring communities the colonial state had pacified. But by the 1920s, having suffered debilitating cattle epidemics, land alienation to European settlers, and forced relocations, Maasai relations with the British soured. Throughout the 1920s and 1930s, burdened by fines for stock theft and pressures of forced labor orders and education, junior moran participated in a series of violent outbursts directed at the colonial state and its intermediaries. Maasai elders, fearful of further uprisings and retaliation by the colonial state, purposefully shortened the period of junior warriorhood following circumcision. They activated the initiation of new age-groups much earlier to force troublesome groups of moran out of junior status and into premature adulthood. By the late 1930s, Maasai boys were not simply circumcised at a younger age but also remained active moran for only a short time. Moreover, warriorhood became a privilege, not a right, dictated by whether young men obeyed and met the expectations of elders and district officials.[124]

The provincial administration overseeing Samburu areas used similar techniques to rein in the activities of warrior Samburu. Over the course of colonial rule, an "alliance of convenience" developed between elders and administrators.[125] From the 1920s onward, district commissioners tried to prevent Samburu moran from cattle raiding and murdering neighboring Turkana warriors by imposing collective fines on livestock and confiscating weapons. In 1936, district commissioner H. B. Sharpe, frustrated by continuing raids, demanded that elders activate the initiation of a new age-group to push the current moran into early maturity. The move also sent a message to the incoming age-group that such could be their fate if they, too, disobeyed the colonial state. Sharpe's ultimate aim: keep the number of moran low, keep them young, and keep them under constant threat of losing their right to warrior status.

According to Peristiany, colonial officials in the 1920s ended the Kipsigis ceremony by which age-groups transitioned upward because they did not want young men gathering together with weapons. While the ceremony itself was ended, the administration, in conjunction with elders, continued to initiate new age-groups to discipline young warriors. In the late 1920s, "disheartened" Kipsigis elders hastily inaugurated the new Chuma group to pass the disorderly young men of the Maina age-group into premature adulthood.[126] Elders halved what would have been a seven-year period of junior warriorship for the Maina. Nandi elders also closed the period of Maina initiation early when junior warriors became a nuisance to the district commissioner.[127]

Having succeeded in experimenting with the ways boys experienced initiation, district officials and chiefs were caught off guard by unintended consequences. Once boys of tender years faced the knife, they suddenly had access to the rights and obligations of men. Even H. E. Lambert, who had argued for early initiation, warned that circumcising younger initiates might lead to an entire generation of boys claiming the privileges of adult men.[128] Early initiation produced initiates sometimes younger than thirteen claiming the right to have sex, drink alcohol, leave home in search of work, and, more terrifying still, expecting the right to marry, accumulate livestock, and own land. The provincial administration had strayed from its supposed conservative principles, reengineering African cultural life to push young men into the labor market and punish their behavior. Elders and the British began to worry that they had accelerated the very socioeconomic uncertainties they were meant to slow down.

CONCLUSION

"The spirit of manhood in the youth," wrote Jomo Kenyatta in his ethnography of the Gikuyu, "has been *almost* killed by the imposition of imperialistic rule."[129] The pacification of Kenya, the introduction of Christianity and Western education, and the recruitment of young men into the labor market had transformed how young men spent the liminal period between initiation and marriage—almost, at least. The "spirit of manhood" had not been snuffed out entirely. It simply found expression in different ways. The men who experienced the changes instigated by the elder state defiantly declared that their coming-of-age had been no different than their forefathers'.

When asked how his initiation compared to those who had come before him, Thomas Tamutwa bluntly replied: "It was the same."[130] John Kiptalam Tesot concurred, "The teachings in the menjo remained the same," despite the period being shortened. "We all traveled the same road," he said.[131] His friend and neighbor Daniel Langat recalled that "life was the same; there were no differences in the way our grandfathers, fathers, and we lived as young men."[132] Looking back to that time, many men argued that in spite of such dramatic changes, the core values of initiation remained unchanged. When pressed further to explain how elders could instill, in such young boys, the knowledge necessary to become men in such short periods of time, many admitted that elders had indeed sacrificed some aspects of initiation. Elders had abandoned certain practices such as traveling to the homesteads of kin to exchange gifts and training for military combat.[133]

But, as many men acknowledged, just as they gave up some aspects of initiation, they also gained new ones. "It was the same" because they had also found meaning in the new possibilities opened up by the colonial encounter. They "all traveled the same road" because these new possibilities reinforced the lessons of seclusion or allowed them to continue expressing their manly mettle.[134] Those men who endured shorter initiation ceremonies to attend school argued that religious and educational instruction augmented the moral lessons of initiation. Anthony King'etich, who attended the Kabianga government school where about 22 percent of his classmates had been medically circumcised, firmly stated that "instructions in schools and churches were in tandem with what the menjo teaches, so what they don't get in the menjo they get in schools."[135] Schoolboys became warriors of a different class, armed with literacy and vocational skills rather than shields and spears, prepared to do battle in the labor market rather than in livestock raids. Those who faced the knife early and then left home to work for wages discovered the possibility of earning their own currency, paying their own dowry, and starting their own households—with or without the help or consent of fathers. The manipulation of initiation practices by the elder state encouraged young men to reconsider, in very familiar ways, how they earned and expressed age and gender.[136]

But boys and young men also found this new terrain littered with new obstacles. The colonial encounter had introduced new actors who claimed authority over them. Chiefs, missionaries, schoolteachers, and a host of other government officials joined fathers and elder kin in an effort to control the activities and behavior of young men. In 1927, the acting governor of Kenya, Edward Deuhaur, warned that young schoolboys and migrant laborers "undoubtedly enjoy the immunity given them from tribal restraint, the opportunity afforded them of mixing with their seniors and of seeing something of town life." Yet he also warned that young Africans found themselves ensnared in a tightly controlled disciplinary regimen: "They are surrounded by sanctions of every description from early youth."[137]

These sanctions had been the product of intense arguments begun at the very start of the colonial encounter like those between the Meru elders, Reverend Worthington, Commissioner Chamier, and the schoolboy who chose to sit in seclusion instead of school. In their effort to identify, mediate, and reify the boundaries of parental and colonial authority, the British blended the two together. The elder state, in this instance provincial administrators and chiefs, expanded and legitimized their tenuous authority by accessing the power of age they believed inherent in African communities. Manipulating male initiation became one of the first and most potent ways the elder state exerted itself—all in an effort to direct and discipline the energies of young men. Over time, young men adapted these changes to meet their own goals of proving their masculinity, enjoying their youth, and eventually earning their maturity.

2 ꙍ "I Wanted to Make Something of Myself"

Migration, Wage Labor, and Earning an Age

THERE WAS SIMPLY no precedent for it. In 1917, before the bench of the Mombasa resident magistrate stood ten-year-old houseboy Izaji Mamuji and his employer, Mzee bin Ali. They were at odds over a contract.[1] The case perplexed Chief Justice Robert W. Hamilton and Judge George H. Pickering of the high court. At issue was whether a child had the right to enter into and abide by a contract. Izaji worked as Mzee bin Ali's houseboy in Mombasa, earning three shillings a month plus clothing and food. No colonial law had been written in regard to whether an African as young as ten had control over his own labor. The 1910 Master and Servants Ordinance, which laid out rules for apprenticeships, offered little assistance. A contract for domestic service was not an apprenticeship. So they turned to English common law. Drawing on a 1911 order-in-council, Hamilton and Pickering ruled that a contract could be upheld if the work benefited the boy. In Izaji's case, they claimed it did and ruled that his contract should stand. Crown counsel disagreed. Izaji's contract was void because the boy's father had the right to disavow the contract. No one should tamper, counsel argued, with the power of a parent over a son's labor. Izaji Mamuji v. Mzee bin Ali exposed the early elder state's uncertainty as to where the authority over a young African's labor lay. Three years before, provincial administrators along the coast had mediated the struggle between parents and missionaries, and now the judiciary grappled with tensions between parents, employers, and sons-turned-employees. Hamilton and Pickering granted a young ten-year-old boy agency over his own labor, while Crown counsel warned of the potentially destabilizing effects of weakened parental authority.

The case of Izaji Mamuji v. Mzee bin Ali lay nestled between the 1927 correspondences of labor inspectors and district officials in Western Kenya.[2] What was it doing there, a decade out of time and miles out of place? Officials in the western districts had dredged up the case file looking for guidance as to their role in the migration of young men out of the reserves and onto the tea, sisal, and other estates scattered across the colony. A decade might have passed, but provincial administrators and labor officials still fretted over whether boys had a right to their own labor and whether the state and parents had any say in the matter.

Despite its anxieties, the elder state worked tirelessly to push, and sometimes coerce, young African men into the wage labor market. In Western Kenya, between the 1920s and early 1950s, the recruitment of young African men to work on settler estates intensified negotiations among the young, their elders, recruiters, employers, and the state. Recruitment became one of the most common and successful means of drawing young men into the labor market. As recruiters reached into African homesteads, provincial administrators began to fear that putting young men to work far from home might weaken generational authority or awaken international outrage. Provincial administrators and their colleagues in the labor and medical departments tried to exert some control over the rush for African labor in Western Kenya, but more often than not, their actions accelerated the process. Throughout the period, the elder state did just enough to silence criticism from the metropole and muffle the concerns of parents worried about migrant sons. It created labor laws specifically for young people to define who could and could not work based on age, to curtail the abuses of the recruitment system, to inspect workplaces, and to ultimately fine the worst employers. Regardless of these regulatory efforts, the colonial state never seriously questioned young men's decisions to work. As sons and fathers debated the merits of migrant labor, the British sided decisively with young men entering the colonial economy. As a result, the elder state swung back and forth between regulating the welfare of young laborers while pushing them into the labor market.

Young men were themselves the greatest catalyst for the migration of labor out of Western Kenya and into settler estates, agricultural industries, and towns. Age and gender figured prominently in their decisions to leave home, work for wages, and then spend their hard-earned shillings. They viewed their mobility, financial independence, knowledge, networks, and distance from elder surveillance as new ways to enjoy their youth, rethink manliness, and come of age. Their migration and work instigated intense arguments with their age-mates and elders. Sons viewed their newfound financial independence and distance from family as a chance to express their growing senses of manhood in new ways outside of kinship. This cultural deviance attracted the ire of fathers and elders who nervously contemplated a future in which younger generations had abandoned their villages and forgotten their familial responsibilities. Yet some sons did return home, often with earnings in hand, willing to contribute to the household or rely on fathers to purchase livestock on their behalf. Some boys used their time as migrant laborers to indicate their readiness for initiation and manhood. Migrant labor complicated arguments within households, but it did not always erode the significance of age-relations. Above all, it provided yet another interface for the elder state to enter into and weigh in on debates about age-relations with African communities.

"RAWEST AND MOST IGNORANT OF YOUTHS"

The principal directive of the colonial state in Kenya was to ensure the profitability of the settler economy and produce goods that nourished Britons and their empire. The British were in search of able-bodied men to fill an ever-expanding list of occupations: carpenters and clerks, policemen and postmen, house servants and field hands. To fill these posts, the colonial state levied its authority, often violently, to pull African communities out of subsistence and push them into the wage labor market. At first, most Africans resisted the lure of paltry wages, miserable working conditions, and travel far from home. But gradually, tens of thousands, most of them young men, entered the workforce. After absorbing the infrastructure of the Imperial British East Africa Company in 1895, the British forcefully exercised their authority inland. They did so in part by constructing a railway connecting the main coastal port city of Mombasa to ivory traders near the shores of Lake Victoria.[3] To build the rail lines, the British imported thousands of laborers from British India and conscripted many young men from surrounding communities. Scouting ahead of the railway, the British drove columns of young African soldiers and porters on expeditions of conquest. They established forts along the future path of the railway, secured alliances with agreeable local leaders, and subjugated unenthusiastic ones.[4]

Rail lines and conquests were costly, and the British sought a way to make the territory profitable. Parts of the colony were incredibly fertile, especially along the Rift Valley. Prior to the turn of the century, communities like the

Gikuyu, Kipsigis, and Maasai had used the soil to their advantage. Their herds and farms prospered. They sold their surplus foodstuffs and livestock to traveling Swahili caravans, slave traders, and eventually the colonial state. And as these communities thrived, families expanded out into the frontier, founding new households, farms, and herds.[5] Rather than rely on the expertise of these local agriculturalists and pastoralists, as they had done in Gold Coast and other colonies, the British transformed Kenya into a settler colony. Beginning in 1902, they encouraged European and white South African émigrés to settle farms and grow cash crops. Colonial surveyors segregated the landscape, carving out the choicest portions for European settlement and then confining African communities to reserves.[6] Settlers were then offered thousands of acres of the most fertile land near Nairobi stretching north and west into the Rift Valley. Those African families, especially the Maasai, Gikuyu, and later the Kipsigis, who had lived in areas alienated to European farmers were evicted from their homes and moved onto reserves or offered a chance to remain as squatters.

Communities unaffected by settler evictions, especially in Nyanza Province west of the Rift Valley, had little motivation to permanently enter the wage labor market. Their agricultural and pastoral pursuits remained profitable and temporary; seasonal wage labor paid taxes and supplemented incomes. British officials lamented the intransigence of would-be African laborers. In 1907, director of agriculture A. C. MacDonald complained that "the native . . . will only engage himself for a month or at most two. If the work is not to his liking he may take himself off quietly at the end of a week."[7] And even if an African laborer fulfilled his contract, he then "returns to the Native Reserve to spend a ten or eleven months holiday and the farmer has to take on a fresh batch of the rawest and most ignorant of youths, when ground has to be cultivated, seeds sown and crops harvested." These "raw, ignorant youths" proved a hindrance to MacDonald's ideas of efficient agricultural production. They came untrained, earned just enough to purchase livestock, and returned only when they ran out of money.[8] In order to make labor more regular and permanent, officials like MacDonald believed the state had to pry open the reserves and draw out African labor with a firmer hand.

Steadily, the number of Africans working away from home grew from 5,000 in 1903 to 120,000 in 1923.[9] Part of this change reflected several strategies the British employed to draw out labor. First, they relied on the heavy hands of local chiefs, often only recently installed themselves, to compel young men into the labor market. Eager to secure their political positions, African chiefs traveled from village to village rounding up laborers by any means necessary.[10] Under pressure from chiefs, fathers often turned to their children to fulfill compulsory labor demands, which, when discovered by missionaries like Archdeacon Owen, embroiled British authorities in international scandal.[11]

Second, British officials turned to taxation. The hut tax required married men to pay for the number of homes in their compounds. It targeted the wealth of older men who might send their young male dependents into the labor market and then use their wages to pay the tax. Officials also introduced the poll tax, targeting young, unmarried men over the age of sixteen.[12] Almost immediately, district officials struggled to determine who was sixteen years of age and eligible to pay. They examined would-be laborers for circumcision to determine whether or not they were old enough to work. The same generation of provincial administrators who pressured families to initiate their sons at a much earlier age also used male initiation to determine whether those same young sons should pay the poll tax. By the 1930s, parents and even some chiefs complained that boys faced the knife too early, ended up on the tax register, and then had to work at too tender an age.[13]

A third strategy was the continued eviction of families off their land. Before World War I, European emigrants settled on grazing lands used by the Maasai and farmland tended by Gikuyu. In the interwar years, as land seizures spread west, Kipsigis and Nandi also lost their lands to British war veterans and large agricultural firms. Many African heads of household, especially among the landless, chose to move onto European estates as squatters. Squatters spent part of their days tending a settler's livestock, cash crops, or household. In exchange for their labor, squatters gained access to plots of land where they grew their own foodstuffs and grazed their own herds. An entire squatter family, including young sons and daughters, balanced work between their household and that of their employers. Before and during the interwar years, squatting was an attractive, profitable arrangement, so much so that poor, landless young men in the reserves sought out work as squatters.[14] With their profits, they expanded herds and even hired laborers to increase production.[15] In the Gikuyu reserves, some of the first to set off for European estates were landless tenants who had worked the farms of their wealthier Gikuyu neighbors. Others saw the estates as a means to escape burdensome taxation, compulsory labor, and tense familial relationships.

While many African families settled into work as squatters, others entered the wage labor market as seasonal migrants.[16] After their own crops had been planted and harvested in the reserves, they traveled to settler estates and hired themselves out on temporary contracts. Rather than bring their families with them, these employees left home alone or with a few male kin and worked for a short while. Once their contracts expired, they either signed up for another or returned home. Many estates used a combination of squatter and migrant labor. During the interwar years, a growing number of settlers and large-scale agricultural industries began relying more heavily on migrant contract labor. Settler estates located near African reserves could rely on short-distance commuter labor. European farms in areas without nearby African settlements, especially the sisal industry, required workers brought from farther afield. Moreover, larger British agricultural firms had been attracted to Kenya to produce cash crops like sisal and tea. These firms purchased vast tracts of land, invested heavily to expand production, and intensified demand for larger numbers of African migrant laborers, especially during the harvest season.[17]

By the 1920s, African curiosity, compulsory labor drives, taxation, evictions, and a growing list of labor laws alone were not enough to meet the demands of large agricultural industries and more sure-footed settlers. In response, a fourth means of drawing young African men into the labor market reached new heights: professional and private recruitment. The networks of recruitment that developed in Central, Rift Valley, and Nyanza Provinces relied on a coalition of interests: the creative strategies of ignominious recruiters and employers as well as the emerging desire of young men to earn a wage. The elder state tried to exercise some control over recruitment and mitigate the scandal that resulted if Britons discovered young Africans were spirited away to work in sisal mills—all the while encouraging the young to leave home and work.

"SCOURING THE DISTRICTS"

Recruitment became one of the most influential techniques to draw out African labor in Kenya. From their earliest years on the coast, the British recruited laborers to work on clove plantations in Mombasa and Zanzibar.[18] As the railway wound its way through Central Kenya, and forts and farms bloomed along the route, European and Asian recruiting agencies scoured Kamba and Gikuyu villages for young men. In 1908, the colonial state ordered that recruitment should be left largely to market forces—a combination of settler demand, recruiter persuasion, and African curiosity.[19] Wary to be seen compelling Africans to work directly for private enterprise, British officials hoped professional recruiters would fill the void. And they did. From 1913 to 1914, an estimated 74 percent of Africans out working had been recruited.[20] By the end of World War I, the vast majority of young men in Machakos, Kitui, and Kiambu had engaged with a labor recruiter.[21]

Yet the British were wary of throwing open the gates of the African reserves to unregulated privateers. The Master and Servants Ordinance created the position of labor agents: individuals or firms appointed to serve as middlemen between recruiters and employers. In theory, labor agencies eased the burdens on provincial administrators by issuing recruiter permits, recording the number of men leaving the districts, and protecting the reserves from being overrun by too many privateers. For their part, district and labor officials tried to systematize recruitment by creating labor camps where recruiters had to bring laborers for inspection before sending them to employers. In reality, labor agencies often participated in recruitment and colonial officials did not cope with the sheer number of recruiters operating in and laborers traveling out of the reserves.

Nowhere were officials more inundated by recruiters and recruits or more aggravated by abusive recruitment practices than in 1920s Western Kenya. As labor demands reached new heights after World War I, all eyes turned toward the reserves of Nyanza and Rift Valley Provinces. By 1923, 75 percent of registered recruiters in the colony operated out of Nyanza Province.[22] Around the same time, communities out west had become more receptive to seasonal migrant labor. Although the creation of reserves ended their ability to expand their holdings, less land had been taken from them than from their Maasai and Gikuyu neighbors. Families of Kipsigis, Luo, or Gusii had little reason to leave their reserves to become squatters on European estates. Instead, households sent out their boys and young men to work in the hopes that their income would supplement household wealth and pay taxes. Most young men went out confident they could still rely on one day inheriting their fathers' farms and herds.

Before World War I, thousands of young recruits passed through the Kisumu labor camp. Linked by rail and road to Mombasa and Nairobi, the camp served as a base of operations for labor agents and recruiters. Young laborers were forwarded from the camp by train or lorry to employers in Kericho, the White Highlands, Nairobi, and as far as the sisal estates near the coast. Between January and March 1914, more than four thousand African men passed through the camp—this during the recruiting off-season when men usually stayed home to harvest their own crops.[23] Africans despised the Kisumu labor camp. The journey was arduous and, for a few, fatal. Many arrived at Kisumu with sleeping sickness, malaria, and other diseases. Fearful that recruiters would load the sick or dying onto cattle cars and send them out east, British officials required that all laborers undergo medical examination. Africans resented the intrusive exams, unexplained vaccinations, and detention in overcrowded conditions. Worse still, if they were declared unfit, they were expected to return home on their own. Of the four thousand men who passed through the camp in the first three months of 1914, medical officers denied work to nearly six hundred.

District and labor officials saw all this as a success. By 1919, the chief native commissioner noted that because of the system, the government registered most labor coming out of the region and outfitted them with work passes. Nyanza recruitment was a vast improvement, he argued, over practices in Coast and Central Provinces. But by the mid-1920s, the strings colonial officials pulled to control Nyanza recruitment frayed. High on their list of complaints: the rising number of underage Africans passing through the Kisumu labor camp. In March 1925, the assistant district commissioner inspected the 10:30 a.m. train out of Kisumu. On board he found "a number of uncontracted *totos* [children]" being forwarded to employers by the Kavirondo Labour Bureau and John Riddoch, both successful labor agents in Nyanza. At the labor camp he found a further thirty-four boys, all of whom were sent home. In July of that same year, labor inspector P. de V. Allen informed the chief native commissioner of a growing number of Nyanza boys working at railway fuel and ballast camps and on sisal estates in Thika and Fort Hall. Allen worried that they lived in squalor, earned too little to feed themselves, and might drift to towns and slip into criminality. A month later, at a labor camp along the new Thika-Nyeri rail line, the district commissioner of Fort Hall found fifteen Gusii boys, all between the ages of twelve and fifteen, working construction. To his astonishment, all of them carried proper registration and passes.[24]

Despite these complaints, it was only when young laborers died, when parents complained, or when girls went out to work that officials scrambled to investigate and promise reforms.[25] In 1926, labor officials traveled to Thika to investigate the deaths of eight young employees of British East Africa Fiber and Industrial. They interviewed two twelve-year-old Gusii boys named Mugire Kyamukia and Obuya Nyarang—the only survivors. According to the boys, a fellow Gusii named Petro had recruited them back home. Inspectors knew Petro all too well. He worked for the Kavirondo Labour Bureau in Kisumu. The bureau's labor agents, Messrs. Yates and Mackey, were notorious in Nyanza for their flagrant disregard of regulations. Mugire and Obuya admitted that they had undergone neither medical inspection nor registration before boarding the train. A month after their arrival, eight of their coworkers fell ill and died. Fortunately, Mugire and Obuya had been taken to the hospital in time. When questioned later, Mackey took responsibility for his recruiter Petro, but argued that once the boys arrived at the sisal estates, whether they lived or died was none of his affair.[26]

FIGURE 2.1. Extracting sisal fiber, n.d. Photo courtesy of the Melville J. Herskovits Library of African Studies Winterton Collection, Northwestern University.

FIGURE 2.2. Sisal in Kenya. A view of the interior of the Machakos sisal factory showing the brushing, grading, and baling sections, n.d. Photo courtesy of the National Archives, Kew.

The strategies of men like Mackey and Petro revealed to the British, in the starkest of terms, just how little control they had over the flow of labor out of Nyanza. Professional recruiters hired African subcontractors who knew the country, spoke local languages, and understood local custom. Many subcontractors sought out young men, often relatives, from their own villages.[27] When these men ran afoul of district authorities, recruiters like Mackey and Yates simply argued that their subcontractors had hired relatives; what transpired had been a voluntary family decision, not recruitment. Recruiters also let their subcontractors take the fall for breaking recruitment rules by paying fines or spending a few days in jail. Recruiters used other tactics to circumvent the authority of district officials. When medical officers rejected a batch of boys, recruiters put them on the train anyway or drove them by foot to different labor camps. In September 1928, officials discovered that recruiters eluded the Kisumu labor camp by taking boys up to North Kavirondo District, where medical officials were less stringent. Recruiters also mixed boys into larger groups with older men, in the hope that government officials might be unwilling to check each and every individual.[28]

Officials loathed recruiters like Mackey and Yates. The commissioner of South Kavirondo described them as "ex-convicts, defaulting debtors, dipsomaniacs, or men of straw" who should not be allowed to "roam about or to live in the heart of a Native Reserve for the purposes of recruiting."[29] The commissioner in Kisii complained that his town was swarming with recruiters who fought among themselves and created an unseemly spectacle that did not go unnoticed by the African community. Recruiting, he argued, opened the door to a "host of undesirables who will compete with each other for labour and [stop] at nothing to get it."[30] Recruiters revealed European weakness, corrupting the image of respectable authority district officials had worked tirelessly to create.

Yet when the government had the opportunity to stop the recruitment of boys, it did very little. In 1927, the provincial commissioner of Nyanza Province visited a medical officer in Kisumu to observe the procedure for examining would-be laborers. While there, he watched three batches of boys arrive and undergo examination. The recruiters informed the commissioner that two batches would go to coffee estates in Kiambu and Fort Hall, the third to the Donyo Sabuk sisal estate in Thika. After looking over the recruits, the medical officer determined that the average age of one group was about seven. All of them were approved for work and loaded onto a waiting train.[31] The most powerful colonial official in Western Kenya had just observed the inspection of Africans as young as seven and their transport to work hundreds of miles from home. There was no record of his outrage—only his silence—as the boys boarded the train.

Agents of the colonial state sometimes actively participated in recruitment. African chiefs often assisted recruiters in their search.[32] Raphael Ndai, who grew up in North Kavirondo, recalls that chiefs would call young men to his homestead with promises of sugar and caramel. Once assembled, Raphael and his age-mates were told to line up. The chief inspected them and took the tallest boys aside. During one particular recruitment drive, Raphael's elder brother was among them. He was taken to Kisumu by foot, vaccinated, loaded onto a train, and sent to the sisal estates.[33] Whether chiefs coaxing boys with candy or British officials standing by as medical officers approved boys for work, the elder state found itself implicated in the very recruitment process it claimed to regulate. As detestable as they found recruiters like Yates and his ilk or as dirty as they got their own hands, the British did exercise some measure of authority over recruitment. Labor agents, professional recruiters, and subcontractors still brought most young men to labor camps for inspection, registration, and transport. And British officials still had some power to turn unsuitable workers away, fine recruiters, or revoke contracts.

By the late 1920s, employers began to bypass the system of professional recruitment. In 1926, John Riddoch warned district officials that employers had begun hiring private recruiters, who answered to no colonial regulation.[34] The depression-era economy of the 1930s pushed employers, especially larger tea and sisal firms, to look for cheaper labor and more efficient methods of recruitment. By hiring privateers or turning their own laborers into recruiters, estates looked to extend their influence directly to African communities, sidestepping labor agencies, camps, and inspectors. In 1928, African Highland Produce even hired a former colonial labor inspector, Ernest McInnes, to organize its recruiting system. The Kenya Tea Company, run by Brooke Bond, paid its employees to return home and offered incentives for bringing back relatives.[35]

Private recruitment made it easier for many young men to find work. Recruiting offices began to appear in trading centers across Western Kenya. Boys from nearby villages easily walked to these offices and boarded transport directly to tea or sisal estates.[36] Lazaro Weke recalls meeting a recruiter in the trading center of Awendo in South Kavirondo District. Rather than walk the hundred miles to the Kisumu labor camp, Lazaro boarded a bus with several other boys, which then traveled from town to town picking up more would-be laborers until it finally reached Kericho. Abiathar Opudo also remembers recruiters driving from village to village, asking children and young men to work.[37] The tea estates contracted Asian bus companies to run routes through the western districts. This system of free transportation, paid for by employers, created a two-way connection between the estates and the villages. No longer did boys and young men have to make the arduous trek by foot to major towns like Kisumu only to be stripped, prodded, and vaccinated by medical officers or turned away by district officials. The buses encouraged African employees to go home after their contracts ended and return with young kin in tow.[38]

While private recruitment was more expensive for the estates, it stabilized the ebb and flow of labor. When business was good in the late 1920s, private recruiters increased the number of Africans brought to the estates. The tea estates in Kericho boasted that their recruiting infrastructure allowed them to call up ten thousand boys and young men from South Kavirondo District alone.[39] During the depression, when demand for labor fell, the estates could limit free transportation, tightening the spigot. Private recruiting also released the estates from government regulation. The provincial commissioner of Nyanza freely admitted that private recruiters "scouring the Districts in search of Labour" required no permit and brought no one in for registration or medical inspection.[40]

Private recruiting still relied on coercion and exploitation. Young men who grew up in Western Kenya at the time recall that as they tended their fathers' livestock, recruiters approached them and promised candy and money.[41] Christopher Achar, who lived near the Awendo recruiting office, remembers being told by recruiters, who were always local people, that they were going bird hunting. Boys eagerly and unwittingly boarded buses bound for Kericho, only to end up picking tea rather than hunting birds the same day.[42] But not all young men who went out to work were coerced, and for many of those who were, migrant wage labor became a profoundly important part of growing up.

"CHANGE IS NATURALLY, ABHORRENT TO ALL OF US"

As young men went out to work in the 1930s and 1940s, British colonial officials, especially those in the provincial administration and labor department, struggled to define the role of the elder state. Beginning in the 1930s, the district and labor officials tried to intervene more frequently in the lives of young wage earners. They crafted laws specifically for young people, defining who could and could not work based on age. They tried to curtail the abuses of the recruitment system. They inspected workplaces and fined employers who allowed the young to work too closely to machines or underground in mines. They returned home thousands of young people when they ended up in town or their parents complained.

However, forces outside the colony instigated many of the elder state's efforts, which nearly always coincided with scandalous stories of exploitation in the British media or pressure for the colony to align itself with changing metropolitan and international labor standards. Throughout the 1930s, the Colonial Office, needled by the League of Nations and revelations that Kenya did not meet the empire's international commitments, forced the colonial state to reexamine its labor policies. But district and labor officials never seriously questioned or prevented young men's decisions to work. Rather, they did just enough to silence their critics and prevent further scandal. Any blossoming of state labor regulations in the 1930s was short-lived. World War II grabbed the attention of Britain and her empire, and colonial officials in Kenya and employers leveraged the war effort to stifle new regulations.

The elder state's first major effort to legislate the labor of young people came in 1933, with the Employment of Women, Young Persons, and Children ordinance (EWYPCO). Long overdue, the ordinance put Kenya in line with conventions that the International Labor Organization had passed thirteen years previously. The ordinance had little impact on the vast majority of young workers; instead, it regulated their work at night, in factories and mines, or aboard ships. Children under the age of twelve could no longer work alongside machinery or in mines. Mines and other industries could hire young people between the ages of twelve and eighteen as long as they kept a register of their names. The ordinance also established fines between £2 and £5 for employers who broke the new rules.[43]

The EWYPCO also opened up, ever so slightly, two new means for the colonial state to control the labor of young Africans. First, it pushed the British to define more precisely who was and was not too young to work. By prohibiting children under the age of twelve in industry, the British took a major step in creating an acceptable minimum age for work. Twelve also corresponded with the efforts of provincial administrators to lower the age of male initiation. The ages in the EWYPCO were not simply the application of the International Labor Organization standards but part of a broader endeavor by the colonial state to release children around the age of twelve into the labor market under the cover of colonial law and African custom. Second, the EWYPCO required industries to keep records of their young employees, a requirement they would try to extend to the entire underage labor force by the end of the 1930s. In fact, registering the young became a central feature of the elder state's efforts. In 1937, the chief native commissioner and the chief registrar of natives wanted young people to carry their own registration certificates, or work passes.[44] By forcing young men to obtain their own *kipande* work passes, officials hoped they might finally find a way to track the number of young people who were out working, prevent the children of tender years from working, and appease parents who did not know or approve of where their sons had gone.

As these ideas circulated the lower rung of the colonial administration in Kenya, scandal consumed the Colonial Office over Kenya's continued reliance on the labor of children and young people. The man who struck the match was Archdeacon W. E. Owen of the Church Missionary Society. Owen had long been an outspoken critic of colonial labor practices, especially compulsory labor in Nyanza Province. His letters and newspaper articles routinely exposed the Colonial Office to criticism.[45] In May 1938, in the pages of the *Manchester Guardian*, he condemned the recent passage of the Employment of Servants Ordinance in Kenya. The ordinance, Owen argued, was further evidence of the colonial state's exploitation of young Africans. Chief among his complaints: the ordinance permitted anyone ten years or older to enter into a labor contract. He argued that allowing children to work resulted in empty schools, villages desperate to find missing children, and estates overrun by underage drunks. Owen appealed to Britons' own uneasy history with child labor. "Must African children go," he wrote, "through the same mills of tragic experience, as did many in England?"[46] It was, he argued, a moral stain on Britons and their glorious empire.

That summer, two more editorials from Owen appeared in the *Manchester Guardian*, 109 letters from angry citizens arrived at the Colonial Office, and scores of inquiries were made by agitated ministers of Parliament.[47] On the floor of the House of Commons, secretary of state for the colonies Malcolm MacDonald faced a barrage of questions.[48] MacDonald promised a full and speedy inquiry—to be handled by officials in Kenya. In the meantime, the Colonial Office remained vague in its response to Owen's editorials. To deny his claims or point out inaccuracies might lead to further scrutiny. Assistant undersecretary of state for the colonies J. J. Paskin warned that "we are not in a position to deny it without providing him with a handle for widening his agitation to over all the colonies in which there are similar or lower minimum ages."[49] The Colonial Office library had recently discovered that the minimum age in Kenya was the same in Nigeria, Gold Coast, Sierra Leone, and three other territories. The age was even lower in Malaysia and British Guiana. If the press were to find out that this was a systemic problem across the empire, the Colonial Office's woes would only escalate.

Meanwhile, the governor of Kenya, Robert Brooke-Popham, hastily assembled a committee to allay concerns back in Britain. The committee consisted of only four members, most of whom were retired colonial officials. The chair, E. B. Hosking, had served as Nandi district commissioner and chief native commissioner before retiring in 1938. Joining him were H. R. Montgomery, who had ruled the Coast as provincial commissioner until his retirement in 1936; and S. V. Cooke, the former district commissioner of Lamu, whom Montgomery had forced out years earlier. Both men were of "decided and generally opposite opinions."[50] Once out of the service, Cooke had become a member of the Legislative Council and often spoke out for African rights. Rounding out the group was R. G. M. Calderwood, a Presbyterian missionary for the Church of Scotland Mission.

Committee members fanned out across the colony to visit agricultural estates, goldfields, factories, and other businesses. At each stop, they met with government officials, settlers, and associations representing the major industries. They also met with Archdeacon Owen. And just as he had feared, their final report tried to extinguish the flames that consumed the Colonial Office back at home. In their report, the committee acknowledged that they found African boys common fixtures of working life in the colony but not a trace of girls. They characterized boys' working conditions as "almost without exception good."[51] They found little wrong with their work on sisal farms or cotton ginneries, though they were alarmed by a number of boys working in mines. Their only criticism came with the work of young men in towns like Nairobi, which they believed led to "consorting with undesirables" and "becoming detribalized nonentities."[52]

The committee reaffirmed that wage labor among young Africans was an accepted, unquestionable principle. Without compulsory education, they argued, work had its advantages. No "mill of tragic experience," as Owen had put it, existed in Kenya. Having defended the practice of encouraging young Africans to work, the committee then tried to silence its critics with a series of proposals to amend the Employment of Servants Ordinance. Their recommendations included raising the minimum age from ten to twelve, restricting the recruitment of young Africans to private recruiters rather than professional agencies, and ending penal sanctions for underage workers.[53] Deftly, the committee responded to each of Owen's main criticisms while still maintaining the necessity of underage labor.

In December, Governor Brooke-Popham announced a new draft amendment to the Employment of Servants Ordinance. The amendment required all young people to obtain an underage version of the despised kipande work pass. Employers also had to keep a register of all underage employees, and the colonial administration could cancel those contracts if inadequate working conditions were discovered.[54] Unmoved, Owen viewed the recommendations as a promising yet inadequate start.[55] Before he could launch any further critiques, the attention of the British public, the British government, and the colonies shifted dramatically to growing tensions in Europe. All eyes lay on the movement of German troops into Eastern Europe rather than the movement of young men in and out of their reserves. The outbreak of war in Africa and Europe swept the issue of colonial labor practices from the headlines and postponed passage of the amendment. Yet, throughout the 1940s, the Colonial Office continued to fret that someone might discover nothing had been done, and when the war ended, they would be engulfed in yet another scandal.

In Kenya, labor officials spent much of the war thinking about how to issue these new work passes to the young, with farcical results. In November 1939, the government approved a proposal to provide every employee under the age of sixteen a nickel wristband, which would serve as their work pass. According to the registrar of natives, A. E. T. Imbert, a boy interested in finding work would visit his district officer, from whom he would receive a registration certificate and a metal container to store it, free of charge. He would also be given a nickel wrist bracelet stamped with his registration number and the initials JUV. The district officials would fasten the bracelet together on the boy's wrist with a sheep punch.[56]

A great deal of effort went into their plan to shackle Kenya's entire under-age workforce. Officials spent time deciding whether the bracelets should be made of nickel, finished brass, or copper. Estimates had been drawn up by companies for the price of the metals and production of the boxes and the bracelets. The labor superintendent had collected one thousand wrist measurements of Luo boys to give the registrar's office a more precise estimate of just how much metal they would need. But all this hustle and bustle came to a screeching halt in April 1940, when the Crown counsel's office informed the registrar that the Colonial Office was likely to frown on "the permanent clamping of this kind of bracelet on the wrist of an African juvenile." Not to mention that the new Employment of Servants Ordinance had called for a "disk" not a "bracelet."[57] Back to the drawing board officials went, busily imagining just what a kipande disk should look like and how might they prevent children from losing them. Should they use string, leather straps, or metal chains to hang the disks around their necks? In less than two years, more than £1,000 was poured into the search for the perfect juvenile kipande. In July 1940, the chief native commissioner abruptly announced that the government's main priority was registering the young men conscripted into the military, not their younger kin sent by lorry-load to pick tea.[58]

In London, the Colonial Office waited anxiously for Kenya to amend the EWYPCO and the Employment of Servants Ordinance.[59] In September 1942, members of the Colonial Office discussed the reasons why nothing had been done. Henry Moore noted that the colony was suffering from a shortage of metal for the disks and chains to fasten them. Granville Orde-Browne, who had some experience with labor issues in East and Central Africa, argued that in Kenya there was simply not the same objection to the labor of young people as elsewhere in the empire, and, therefore, bringing the law into force lacked any urgency. But in the end, the Colonial Office decided that the approaching coffee harvest could not be disrupted and that any intervention must wait.

Back in Kenya, talk of nickel disks suspended by nickel chains from the necks of young Africans disappeared. Registrar of natives G. Wedderburn had returned from leave in 1942, irked to find waste and wild ideas consuming his department. He outright rejected the need for a separate system for young people when the state could simply use the same procedures for registering adults. In a letter to the chief native commissioner, Wedderburn outlined what the registration of young laborers should look like: Kilonza Nyamai, a boy under the age of sixteen from Kitui, goes to see his district officer accompanied by a parent or guardian. There, he obtains a registration certificate like any other African, bearing his name, tribal particulars, and fingerprints. "He then becomes KTI.1556501 Kilonza Nyamai which number he will retain for life."[60] If a boy like Kilonza had no guardian, then the district official could stand in his kin's stead. When he turned sixteen, he would return to the same office to exchange his certificate for the adult variety. Wedderburn's system required no shackles or necklaces, simply the same kipande work pass that so many adults despised and burned in protest.

Without fail, when word broke that the government would begin registering all laborers under the age of sixteen, the Kenya Tea Association vigorously voiced its irritation.[61] In January 1943, the association met with the labor department to dissuade it from registering the more than sixty-five hundred laborers under the age of sixteen working on its farms. The association argued that "with a large number of their European staff on Active Service [in the war], and with a shortage of material, [its members] are producing tea in quantities of more than 60% over normal pre-war production figures."[62] If the British wanted to maintain those incredible levels of wartime production, then they would have to abandon any attempt to register their young employees. In short, "the free flow of labor from Kavirondo [Nyanza Province], at present ample for the greatly increased production necessary for the war effort, would be greatly impeded and all but stopped."[63] Tea production in Kericho would grind to a halt as thousands of youngsters trekked back home simply for a slip of paper. Worse still, the association worried that once home, parents and elders would not let the workers return again.

FIGURE 2.3. A labor inspector's job takes him beyond the city factories and shops to places like this sisal estate with its mill, n.d. Photo courtesy of the National Archives, Kew.

Plans to register laborers under the age of sixteen died in that very meeting. "Change," the association argued, "is naturally, abhorrent to all of us." Yet it would have been feasible to provide lorries, fuel, and drivers to transport sixty-five hundred young laborers back home. It had been done the year before, but in the opposite direction. In 1943, over four thousand laborers, mostly under the age of sixteen, had been brought to Kericho to work. But any effort by the colonial state to bring the Employment of Servants Ordinance into effect would "have the most shattering effects on output."[64] To justify their decision to abandon any effort to register young laborers during the war, colonial officials took the Kenya Tea Association at its word: that none of its sixty-five hundred workers were under the age of twelve and that it offered adequate provision on its estates in the form of schools, hospitals, sport, housing, and food.[65]

In February, when the Colonial Office prodded the colony yet again, Governor Henry Moore firmly replied that no action would be taken. He had "received long and reasoned protest" from the Kenya Tea Association and the Sotik Settler's Association, who had expressed sympathy for the new regulations—if only they had lived in "normal times." To register underage laborers in the midst of the war "would completely disorganise their labour forces and seriously jeopardize their production programme."[66] Rather than wait out yet another harvest season, the governor requested that they simply wait out the war. And so thousands of boys continued to pick pyrethrum blossoms, cure coffee beans, and sweep sisal fibers throughout the war, in conditions and for wages that had not changed since the 1920s.

OF GOATSKINS AND *SHUKAS*

For all the money and manpower exerted to compel the young to leave home and labor, employers ultimately had to wait until young men found something of value in it. Boys and young men did not simply choose to work; they made decisions about the kinds of work they wanted, where they would labor, and how much money made it worth their while. And from the very beginning of colonial rule, some willingly sought out wage labor as an alternative to tending a father's livestock. By the 1920s, more and more young men were interested in doing so.[67] The decision to work outside a father's household was never easy and never made alone. Young men discussed leaving home to work with their age-mates, elder siblings, and parents. Consider the different paths of Thomas Tamutwa and Kimeli Too, both Kipsigis men born twenty miles apart in 1932. They came to wage labor in very different ways and had very different relationships with their fathers.

A son's decision to labor could ignite intense negotiation in a household. Thomas Tamutwa struggled to get his father to understand why he wanted to leave home. Thomas desperately wanted to go to school.[68] But his father refused. Who, he asked Thomas, would tend his livestock? As Thomas's father knew well, the labor of sons and daughters reproduced the wealth of their fathers and enabled them to learn the skills to one day produce their own wealth.[69] Many African men who grew up during the colonial period described their boyhood, and the boyhood of their forefathers, as enriching social work among age-mates that formed the backbone of their socialization into a set of reciprocal, respectful obligations with their seniors.[70] Nearly every ethnic community in Kenya, prior to and in the earliest years of colonial rule, put their sons to work looking after livestock. A father might start his son off with a kid goat, and as the boy proved capable, he graduated to larger animals. Each morning at sunrise the boy woke up, threw his goatskin blanket over his shoulders, took porridge, and headed for the grazing fields with his father's herd. There he met other boys, they mixed the herds, and then spent the day watching the livestock, hunting, playing games, and wrestling. If they were caught ignoring the herd by a passerby, they would be beaten. At sunset, the boys separated the herds and returned home. They took their supper and spent the evening by the fire listening to stories told by their elders and readying themselves to start again the next day.

Thomas's father could not understand why his son did not want to enjoy the labors of childhood as he had done. Thomas pressed the issue, sneaking away to join his friends at school. "He would beat me at the mention of a school, asking me who I would leave the goats to, the cattle to. He would flog me whenever I mentioned school." Thomas's frustration and fear of his father's firm hand finally got the better of him. "He beat me until I decided to run away," he said. Thomas fled to the Kericho tea estates "to escape the constant caning."[71] Working the tea estates during World War II offered Thomas an escape from his father's violence and obstinacy.

In the struggle between Thomas and his father, the rebellious, uncircumcised son won out. Thomas had access to a network of age-mates who had already made the decision to work, with or without their fathers' consent. When asked why he ran away to the tea estates rather than the classroom, Thomas replied, "I went to Kericho because that is where everybody went. The whites had employment opportunities at the estates. There are my age-mates who were already there and would brag that Kericho was where the action was. My age-mates would teach me the ways of Kericho whenever they visited home."[72] Thomas's decision to travel to Kericho in search of a wage embodied what district and labor officials as well as European settlers had hoped would happen. Young employees would go home and recruit their peers. Thomas ultimately made his decision to earn a wage through the intimate, everyday coercions built into childhood relationships and peer pressure, as well as the complicated relationships between fathers and sons.

After working for several months, Thomas returned home wearing a new *shuka*, a blanket made of red cloth with multicolored patterns worn by the Maasai, and carrying six shillings in savings. His father was overjoyed to see him, and even more impressed by the money the boy handed him. "He loved me a lot for that. Even my mother! I had my shuka on and gave them six shillings."[73] With the money, Thomas's father bought him a goat and sheep. Many men from Kipsigis and Luo families recall that their fathers bought livestock for them with the savings they brought back—down payments on bridewealth and a household of their own some day.[74] Young men found that if they returned home, their wages often fundamentally changed their relationships with their parents.

As parents saw the benefits of a wage-earning son, they eventually came around to the idea of their sons working far from home.[75] Before Thomas set out to start another contract, his parents took him aside and asked him "to work and not squander money, but to save and bring more."[76] Well into the 1940s, a father's household remained for many a primary investment in the future. Many young men also saw their wages as part of a familial responsibility and an investment in their own futures. A father still worked for his son, accumulating wealth in livestock and increasing currency that would one day provide the young man with a wife, land, and a future. Sons also now worked for themselves, playing a more active role in their own financial destinies. Savings symbolized hard work, discipline, and masculinity. How a young man spent his wages could showcase his growing maturity.[77]

And as the crucible of work made young men feel more mature, they developed confidence in their skills and an awareness of just how valuable they were to the colonial and household economies. They left employers in search of greener pastures. They moved up into more skilled, more highly paid positions, and a new, younger generation of boys replaced them herding a rancher's livestock, picking tea leaves, or sweeping sisal factory floors. Thomas Tamutwa recalls that he worked on the tea estates for three years, and in 1946 he left for Molo, where he worked as a herdsboy, which brought the added benefit of having milk at meals. "I felt I was old enough to venture further, so I sought work in Molo for I would drink milk," and he would earn ten shillings a month, ten times his previous wage.[78]

For his industriousness, Thomas was rewarded with the greatest of gifts — his initiation into manhood. In 1947, at the age of fifteen, Thomas was initiated into the Chuma age-group, the last group of young boys to do so. He faced the knife far earlier than some of his age-mates. Thomas's initiation was an acknowledgment by a once-resistant father that wage labor had made his boy a man. Within a generation, age-relations could integrate, though not always smoothly, the new possibilities of colonial rule. Yet some youthful rebellion was required first. If it had ended there, then Thomas might never have faced the circumcision knife at home, left to labor as a wayward, uninitiated boy. But the return of the prodigal son to his father's homestead showed respect and obedience as well as the value of his labor — traits worthy of manhood.

Kimeli Too, born the same year as Thomas but initiated a year or two later, tells a different story of how he came to leave home. From the very beginning, his decision to work was an easy one, made in concert with his father. Kimeli began working at the Bureti Tea Estate as a farmhand in 1948, shortly after his initiation and seclusion that admitted him into the Sawe age-group. He earned six shillings a month, about average for a man his age in the tea industry at the time. Working for Bureti made practical sense: the estate was a short commute from home, and his father also worked there. Kimeli's decision was affected by the same choice his father had made years earlier. Kimeli's father made his livelihood as a migrant wage laborer. He was likely among the first or second generation of Kipsigis to leave home to work on the tea estates. Kimeli recalls that his father lived on the estate for twenty-five years. "He would come home over the weekends for family visit. At times he would make impromptu visits during weekdays and then rush back the following day early in the morning."[79] His father's decision had paved the way for his son to do the same as an acceptable alternative to tending livestock at home. Kimeli could not say whether his father had struggled with his grandfather over the decision, but it is clear that his father's choice to earn a wage had made it an acceptable possibility for Kimeli.

Kimeli's decision to join his father at Bureti Tea also coincided with his initiation. Kimeli decided to work "because I wanted to make something of myself. Just staying idle at home when you are grown up would make you look like a fool."[80] His initiation had transitioned him into a "grown-up," and wage labor became a way to actualize his newfound maturity and masculinity. Unlike Thomas, who saw his labor as the reason to become a man, Kimeli saw it as a fulfillment of his maturity. He then proved it every month when he brought the five shillings he had earned to his father. "I would keep my earnings and bring it to my father. Once the savings were enough, my father would buy cattle." In the Too family, migrant labor had become the norm rather than a mark of cultural delinquency. Kimeli need not argue with his father over the value of hard work and a wage. And his father believed that Kimeli, recently initiated into manhood, would have the discipline to bring home part of his wages. Kimeli had nothing to prove; his father had nothing to fear. Yet, as a result, Kimeli was initiated a year or more after Thomas Tamutwa. The young man who had followed the rules and obeyed his father faced the knife long after the wayward son. Despite these differences, both Thomas and Kimeli had not strayed too far beyond the behavior their elders expected of them.

Not all young men returned home, however. Some stayed out on the estates, moving from contract to contract. Out on the migrant labor circuit, a young man could lose track of time and ultimately a sense of where he had come from. Among former young Luo migrants, stories abound of boys escaping the estates only to get lost on the way home, eaten by wild animals, or, worse, captured and assimilated by the Kipsigis or Maasai. Those who had to sojourn the farthest to find work carried fear-filled memories that they had traveled so far they might lose their sense of kinship in the process of trying to become mature men. Parents worried too. When a son did return home, the boy was not so subtly warned that if he went out again, he was expected to come back. Thomas remembers that his parents made it clear they expected future installments of capital. "They would ask me for money, but I also felt it was my obligation to provide for them. How could I earn and visit home empty-handed? My father wouldn't have liked it."[81] And if he happened to squander his wage and return home with nothing, he would be beaten.

Some of the first young men to leave home to attend school, join a Christian mission, work for a wage, or travel to towns tried to alleviate their elders' concerns. In 1928, the Kikuyu Central Association (KCA), a political organization of young Gikuyu elites like Jomo Kenyatta, began a vernacular journal called *Mwigwithania*, meaning "one who makes people listen (and agree) together" or "the reconciler."[82] Many of is members, like Kenyatta, had been the culturally dissident youths of their generation. In the journal, KCA members discussed the news, translated biblical passages, and shared Gikuyu proverbs. One of the most common parables shared in *Mwigwithania* was that of the prodigal son, who left his father, squandered his inheritance, and returned seeking forgiveness.[83] Throughout the journal, KCA readers encouraged their young prodigal audience to go home or at least remember their responsibilities to their elders. Yet the Old Testament story is also known as the parable of the two sons. While the younger son enjoyed his youth, the elder son remained at home, obedient and disciplined. And while he had not lost his inheritance, he bristled at the notion that his father had never celebrated his respect for elder authority as he had celebrated his brother's return. Perhaps *Mwigwithania*'s authors and readers in fact pitied the thankless life of the herdsboy who stayed home, ever toiling beneath the watchful eye of his family, inexperienced in the youthful adventures beyond the village.

Migrant work was for many a thrilling adventure. Young men did all kinds of work during the colonial period: herding cattle on the Delamere ranch, picking tea leaves for the Brooke Bond Tea Company, sweeping the manufacturing floor at Ziwani Sugar, and digging for gold at Bwemba Gold Mines across the border in Tanganyika. It was typically unskilled work, or at least work for which young men had the requisite skills. A boy's first job often mirrored the kinds of tasks that he had done for his father or that suited his physical attributes. Young Kipsigis or Nandi boys found work herding livestock and milking dairy cattle because these duties fell within the skill sets they had learned at home. Likewise, European settlers actively recruited them to pick tea and pyrethrum because their height and "nimble fingers" made them efficient harvesters.[84]

However, employers also de-skilled complicated production processes, just as they had done in Britain, so that younger workers could complete smaller, simpler tasks. Uncoupling skill from labor, employers could hire young people, whom they paid much less than adults, and reduce their production costs.[85] The sisal industries, major recruiters in Western Kenya, routinely de-skilled the manufacturing process of sisal fiber so they could hire the young. At Taveta Sisal and Teita Concessions, young laborers harvested sisal leaves on the farm and brought them into the factory. Adults ran the sisal through a decorticator machine to separate the fiber and the flesh, known as tow. The young then transported the fiber outside to dry and swept the machine and floor to pick up any small leftover pieces.[86]

Many African men look back fondly at the work they did growing up. Those who left home and found work on European estates remember the monotonous grind of getting up each morning, preparing a breakfast of porridge, reporting to work, taking a break for lunch, heading back to work again, and then retiring for dinner—only to do it all over again the next day.[87] "At the beginning," Thomas Tamutwa recalls, "it was hard work, but once you were used to it, it was quite easy."[88] Once they disciplined their minds and bodies to the pace, it became easier to focus on other things like their social lives. In the evenings tea pickers would play games with one another or tell stories around the fire. Herdsboys stepped away from grazing cattle to fit in a little high-jumping and wrestling.[89] Migrant labor became as much a social affair as it had been back home, as well as an important part in forming relationships among age-mates and reimagining masculinity.

During the 1940s, estates began to offer more opportunities for young employees to enjoy themselves after hours. High wartime demands pushed companies like Kericho Tea and Brooke Bond to open schools, organize open-air cinema nights, and build football pitches. In 1943, Kericho Tea had sixty-five hundred young men between the ages of twelve and sixteen working on its estates. Estate managers had to find ways to keep their young employees occupied. Too many were already falling into drunkenness, smoking, and drug use.[90] Football was especially popular, and employees formed teams to represent their estates against rival teams from nearby companies. Boys were also attracted to the schools. Daniel Langat managed to work his way up to standard three before he returned home. But because classes were voluntary, many young men received only a smattering of instruction. Kimeli Too recalls that he went to classes on and off and did not learn as much as he would have had he gone to a proper school. Work and football came above arithmetic.[91]

Age-relations with older employees were also integral to young men's working lives. Older men often supervised younger workers. They set quotas for the day and made sure they were met. In the evenings they ate with the boys and watched over them at night. Depending on the size of an estate, these older supervisors could handle just a few boys or several hundred.[92] Even though they worked far from home, young employees still lived under the watchful eye of elders. Thomas Tamutwa recalls that these old men "were quite gentle." He adds, "If I was respectful, then I could live with him as long as it took . . . but if I made a mistake, then I would just be disciplined. If I confessed, then he would pardon me and life would continue."[93] Age-defined codes of conduct remained intact in the workplace, and employers often used young people's respect for elders as a means of ordering work and play. When young men required more intense discipline, white supervisors stepped in with more drastic forms of punishment, such as reducing a worker's pay or corporal punishment.

Not all young men found work to be a social or even enjoyable part of their coming-of-age. The experiences of young Luo men, whose families lived far from the estates, differed considerably from the experiences of Kipsigis employees, who could return home more easily. Lazaro Weke and Christopher Achar remember the relentless, exhausting work and complete lack of social life.[94] For some young Luo men, the work was so isolating that they deserted their contracts. Work was indeed hard, and boys sometimes lost their fingers, limbs, and lives in the grinding gears of the colonial economy. They also encountered and struggled against profoundly unequal, exploitative labor relations. In July 1942, labor officer J. H. B. Murphy inspected the farm of Mrs. A. G. O. Hodgson in North Nyeri. Mrs. Hodgson had a small farm — about twenty acres of pyrethrum, five acres of oats, and a herd of three hundred shorthorn cattle. Young men made up a third of her forty-one-person workforce. When Murphy interviewed Hodgson's herdsboys, they complained that their wages were too low. They demanded that Murphy advocate on their behalf, and by the time the inspector left, the boys had renegotiated their wages up to eight shillings per contract with food rations.[95]

The following year, an urgent request came to the labor office from the Government Flax Mill in the Uasin-Gishu District — the workers had gone on strike. Labor commissioner P. de V. Allen rushed out to inspect the factory. When he arrived, he discovered that nearly half the workforce was made up of young Luo under the age of sixteen. Much to Allen's surprise, the boys had led the strike. They informed Allen that they were being cheated out of their food rations. According to their contracts, they were supposed to be getting two pounds of mixed meal rations, a pound less than in past years, along with salt, sugar, and meat or groundnuts. When he weighed the meal ration, Allen discovered the boys were indeed being shortchanged about three ounces. Allen informed the young strikers that sadly no more rations were available. Furious, the boys replied that there was plenty back home in the reserve. The state broke the strike. No record was made of whether the boys deserted their contracts.[96]

Tens of thousands of young men took these sorts of risks to earn a wage. When asked why, they almost always brought up money, even though they earned dramatically lower wages than adults. A boy could expect to earn at most half as much as an adult. In 1938, chief registrar of natives A. E. T. Imbert estimated that Africans under the age of sixteen earned about four shillings a month, which could include food and lodging.[97] The young could find ways to earn much more. Jobs in towns like Nairobi offered substantially higher wages. As early as 1919, the chief native commissioner admitted that farm boys could earn twice as much by working in Nairobi.[98] Some boys also capitalized on the skills they learned at school. Abiathar Opudo, who grew up in Homa Bay in the 1930s, decided to abandon his schooling and find a job.[99] His basic literacy and arithmetic skills piqued the interest of an Asian firm transporting produce across Lake Victoria. Abiathar became a bookkeeper at the age of twelve, recording the firm's profits and calculating how much the porters would be paid. He earned twenty cents a day. Likewise, Wachira Mwaniki left his school in Kiambu in 1940 to work as a domestic servant for a pyrethrum farmer in Kinangop, a decision that devastated his mother. He earned 120 shillings per month, an astronomical sum compared to the wages his age-mates earned picking pyrethrum blossoms just beyond the kitchen window.[100]

Even a handful of shillings a month meant a great deal to boys who had only recently herded goats. Wages dramatically altered young laborers' self-perceptions as men as well as their ability to project notions of manhood to one another, parents, and kin. When asked to recall the very first thing they bought for themselves, Gikuyu, Kipsigis, and Luo men who left home to work for wages in the 1930s and 1940s — in a near unanimous chorus — mentioned clothing.[101] With their wages, they abandoned the goatskin blankets of their boyhood and adorned themselves with new styles of clothing. During the war, Thomas Tamutwa earned a paltry sum of one and one-half shillings a month weeding, pruning tea bushes, and mowing grass. Despite his low wages, Thomas bought a shuka. "Being able to wear a shuka, while I had a goatskin," Thomas recalls, "is what attracted me to Kericho."[102] He bought the shuka at an Indian canteen for one shilling, nearly an entire month's wages. "I felt so proud," he says. Buying and wearing a shuka marked a personal milestone. After WWII, both Terer arap Korir and Daniel Langat, who grew up in the same village in Kabianga, went to work at the Chamji tea estate for five shillings a month. With their earnings they both bought shukas for about fifty cents apiece. Terer recalls, "I felt so proud because it didn't feel cold anymore."[103]

Clothing, whether shukas or trousers, also came to represent a young man's growing sense of masculinity, which when displayed earned him respect back home. When young migrants returned to their villages emblazoned in bright red shukas, they attracted the notice of their age-mates. David Bett remembers his friends admiring and approving of the new clothes he wore when he returned from the tea estates. Shukas, he recalls, "were the most fashionable then and people liked them a lot," and "[my friends] treated me with respect and admiration. This made me feel quite great."[104] Boys wearing shukas also piqued the interest of girls. Dominic Gaga, who grew up near Kisii, spent a substantial portion of the wages he earned picking tea in Kericho on clothes and, as he described them, shoes that made noise. After his contracts expired, he returned home, put on his clothes, and strolled through the village, certain he felt the female gaze fixed on him.[105] Wachira Mwaniki, who lived in Kiambu and Laikipia, remembers one particular shirt called *hariri*, Kiswahili for "silk," that caught the eyes of potential lovers. "There were some shirts in fashion which when dancing would fill with air like a balloon, and it was lovely."[106] Silk shirts tucked loosely, billowing in the wind, inflated the egos of young men who had the capital to wear them.

Wages and the commodities they bought differentiated migrants from village boys wearing goatskins and students wearing uniforms. They worked to translate their commodities and their time away from home into displays of growing maturity and manliness. Some, like Dominic Gaga, believed that the "boys in the villages feared them because they were independent, whereas the boys on farms at home were still dependent on their parents."[107] Being a migrant laborer and controlling his own wage granted Dominic a sense of independence, or at least the perception of independence. Five shillings per month for picking tea or herding dairy cattle was hardly enough for a young man to go his own way. Wachira, who made considerably more as a domestic servant, argued that his wage meant that he "could buy nice clothes and dress just like adult youths."[108] Clothing made Wachira feel more mature but did not necessarily make him more mature. While brightly colored shukas, gleaming black shoes, and silk shirts might have gotten the young men lovers, clothing did not pay a bridewealth or build a household.

While parents and elder kin overlooked a few shillings for clothing and candy, they tried to subvert young men's efforts to express manhood in ways they deemed inappropriate. Alcohol was one new privilege that young men enjoyed, much to the displeasure of parents, elders, and colonial officials. As early as 1910, officials in Kiambu complained that young Gikuyu men were drinking too much and causing a ruckus.[109] By the 1920s, the colonial state had developed laws to prohibit the use of alcohol among Africans, but to no avail.[110] At local native council meetings across Central Province, chiefs bemoaned the behavior of young men who drank. Communal labor became difficult to organize with young men drunk or hung over. They spent their money on liquor rather than paying their taxes. They also took to fighting and injuring one another.[111]

For chiefs and parents, alcohol was not the problem. Alcohol was a necessary component of social and political life underpinning the success of initiations, marriages, harvests, and religious ceremonies.[112] The problem was the new ways in which it was consumed and commoditized. In a letter to the Nyeri council in 1935, Chief Nderi recalled that in the past, "young men did not drink. The old men forbade [it]. Now the country is changing for the worse because drink is bad. In olden times there was no sale."[113] For Nderi, the problem was twofold. First, young men took part in a right once limited to older generations. Their command of wages granted them access to something they should not have. Second, Chief Nderi scolded his fellow council members for profiting off the sale of alcohol. Throughout Central Province, chiefs invested heavily in sugar mills and the production of alcohol. In Fort Hall, Chief Kangethe hosted dance parties where he charged fifty cents for homemade brew. The parties had grown so popular that even Luos from nearby European estates attended them.[114] Chiefs sold alcohol to young men and then profited off their wages and drunkenness. By allowing alcohol to be bought and sold to young men, stripping it of its ritual meaning, the chiefs confused the privileges and authority of elderhood as well as weakened the boundaries between generations.

In the minds of chiefs and district officials, drunkenness and indiscipline were age-defined problems—with age-defined solutions. From the late 1920s until the 1940s, local councils prohibited certain age-groups from drinking. Yet banning young men under the age of twenty-five, as they did in Nyeri, or limiting permission to drink to "senior warriors," as they did in Embu, failed miserably.[115] The young continued to buy alcohol and dance the night away while chiefs continued to sell it to them. Local efforts to resurrect and reify age-old, age-specific prohibitions merely accentuated their ineffectiveness and weakened their authority over the young.[116]

The 1950s played out much like the two decades before. District and labor officials continued to feel pressure from superiors to avoid the scandal of young men working in "satanic mills." They continued to complain of "pirate lorries" sailing the reserves, shanghaiing the young from their homes while the young parleyed with recruiters and employers to find work without the consent of parents or the elder state.[117] And a few enthusiastic officials continued to concoct wild schemes to bring recruitment and registration under some control. Offstage, away from the theater of shackling young laborers with sheep punches, the elder state worked tirelessly to preserve the flow of young labor out of the reserves. The labor department and provincial administration did inspect workplaces to pluck out boys they deemed too young to work, identify atrocious working conditions, and fine disreputable employers. Yet their main aim was to satisfy the demands of the settler economy, and they did so by encouraging boys to stake their manhood on earning a wage by making migrant labor an acceptable way to come of age.

And young men did much of the work for the elder state. In the earliest years of colonial rule, many resisted pressures to leave home and work, but by the 1920s a growing number were answering the call of recruiters and employers. Boys and young men quickly realized they could leverage their wages, experiences, and access to new ideas and commodities into expressions of masculinity. Certainly, migrant labor created conflict within the households of Western Kenya and elsewhere in the colony. But many young men and their elder kin argued productively about valuing work outside the household, about investing it back into family fortunes, and about incorporating it into existing ideas and practices of growing up.

Not all parents approved, and they made their outrage known to chiefs and district officials. The elder state shared these fears with parents as many young men labored in ways threatening to colonial law and order, especially urban labor. Not all young men labored in the way the colonial state desired. Thousands of young men left home for trading centers and towns where they participated in casual labor, black marketeering, and theft. They threatened the property of the non-African community, flagrantly rejecting the racial boundaries established by the state. They preyed upon and disrespected their fathers and elders, who, unable to control them, sought out the elder state for assistance. The elder state responded with institutions to discipline the young and transform them into mature subjects—while being drawn ever deeper into arguments about age and authority.

3 ⤳ "I Saw a Paradise"

Growing Up on the Streets of a Colonial City

IN AUGUST 1925, Ogayo sat before labor inspector Ernest McInnes, recounting his harrowing search for work that had taken him from his village of Karachano to the bustling town of Kisumu to the capital city of Nairobi. Word had spread in his village, Ogayo explained, that a certain recruiter in Kisumu would find boys work.[1] Looking to earn a wage, Ogayo left for Kisumu. When he arrived, he sought out a representative of the recruiter, who took him to an open-air, overcrowded labor camp near the railway station. Five days passed and Ogayo continued to wait. Finally the recruiter, a European named Mr. Yates, approached Ogayo with work in Mariakani, a town near Mombasa that was home to several sisal factories. Mr. Yates, one of the most infamous recruiters in Western Kenya, was frequently under investigation for operating without a license and for being in breach of recruitment procedures.[2] According to Ogayo, Yates "put me in the train [but] gave me no ticket. He left saying he was going to get me blankets and *posho* [food]. I waited, but he did not return and the train left."[3] Ogayo traveled with twelve other boys, part of a larger "batch" of thirty-six who had all pressed their ink-stained thumbs onto contract number 544/25 and boarded the cattle car. They had only a vague idea where they were headed, but they were all hopeful that when they arrived, they would work.

At the Nairobi station stop, halfway to their destination, the stationmaster inspected the cars. When he spotted Ogayo, he asked the boy for a ticket. Yates had not given him one, and when he failed to produce it, he was arrested. As police escorted Ogayo out of the station, the twelve other boys with whom he had traveled disembarked and disappeared into the crowd. As for Ogayo, he was on his way to see labor inspector Ernest McInnes. To McInnes, Ogayo was just another example of Mr. Yates's unscrupulous tactics, his administration's failed recruitment policies, and a city teeming with young African migrants. To Ogayo, the labor inspector was yet another obstacle hindering his search for work. After answering McInnes's questions, Ogayo asked that he be allowed to travel onward so he might fulfill the contract he had agreed to do. "I wish to go to Mariakani and work. I have no blanket, no *posho* [food], and no money. I know that *totos* [children] are not supposed to work like men, but the white man at Kisumu informed me that I should obtain lighter work than the men."[4] Ogayo knew the colonial state frowned on what he had done. Children should not work like men. But he also made clear his fear and frustration. The labor recruiter's negligence had left him destitute and in police custody in a town he did not know. McInnes ignored his request and ordered him repatriated back to Karachano.

But this is not just the story of Ogayo's misfortune. This is the story of those twelve other boys, who eluded police and dissolved into the bustling, crowded station. The archival record does not reveal whether they were ever caught and returned home or if they eventually made it on to Mariakani. Far more likely is that these twelve boys took up residence in the shantytowns of Nairobi, staying with relatives or joining bands of street boys. This is Ogayo's story in the sense that he was denied the right to work because colonial officials feared what might happen on account of his age and gender—if he had gotten off that train and become a town dweller. The moment the train stopped in the colonial capital and the stationmaster boarded his car, Ogayo was transformed from a potential productive young laborer, a pillar of the settler economy, into a threatening crack in the colonial order, an unproductive boy in an urban space.

While colonial officials encouraged the rural migration of young men to labor in colonial industries, they tried their utmost to restrict their movement and their lives in towns. Unlike agricultural migrant labor, town life sat along the edge of what the British deemed productive and disorderly. They superimposed their own troubled history with urban life onto their young African subjects, conflating town life and criminality with age and masculinity. The British feared that towns like Nairobi unmade mature men. They believed that African boys who came to town uncoupled themselves from elder authority, lived in abject poverty, descended into criminality, and grew up ungovernable. Town was no place for young men—or at least too many young men. Yet even the youngest street boys had their uses,

unloading vegetables at market or passing notes between a British adminis-
trator and an African sex worker. Not all young men living and working in
Nairobi pickpocketed passersby or sold stolen goods on the black market.
Young dockworkers, railway apprentices, domestic servants, street sweepers,
and rickshaw drivers, among others, were all allowed in town as long as they
carried their kipande work passes and had a place to stay. Municipal authorities directed much of their ire at the small number of young men whom they
deemed up to no good—idle, unemployed, and homeless. Throughout the
colonial period, a few thousand street boys, a mere fraction of the urban
African population, claimed a disproportionate presence in the elder state's
imagination.

For those often-homeless young men accused of idleness, the streets of
towns like Nairobi became sites of new possibilities. The town opened up
alternative frontiers along which they forged their futures. Many street boys
did not come to town simply to search for work; rather, they left home to
escape the discipline of elders or the poverty of broken homes. On the streets
they joined others around their own age, coordinating the crucial and often
dangerous quests for food, money, security, and territoriality. These pursuits
became new ways to earn masculinity and maturity, often outside of rural
homesteads and kinship networks, which they then poured back into their
relationships with street mates. These boys were an essential ingredient of
cosmopolitan urban African life—loading goods onto lorries or helping
launderers wash clothes, all in exchange for a few shillings or permission to
sleep out on the veranda.

When their numbers grew too large or crimes too noticeable, municipal officials rounded them up, charged them with breaking vagrancy laws
and township bylaws, and then repatriated them back to their reserves.
Over the years, the elder state repatriated tens of thousands of young
people at a tremendous cost. Rather than wait and arrest them for theft or
burglary, municipal authorities simply criminalized being young, male,
and seemingly idle. They were arrested not for any particular action or
behavior but for their presumed propensity for immaturity and criminality. Repatriation became one of the elder state's most common methods
of controlling the migration of young Africans and preventing their criminality. The state also tried to augment parental and elder authority, reat-
taching urban migrants to their rural homesteads. Returning boys home
was a reminder that they belonged in their fathers' homesteads and that
the elder state aimed to keep them there at considerable cost. Through
repatriation, the state took yet another step in using age to order the uncertainties of colonial rule.

In May 1901, Commissioner John Ainsworth rounded up twenty "young boys" whom he found "wandering about Nairobi . . . without parents or any proper home."[5] At the time, Nairobi barely boasted five thousand residents and looked more like a frontier railway outpost than a town.[6] Five years earlier, Nairobi consisted of Fort Smith and a campsite along the river where traders rested after the arduous twenty-five-day trek from the coast. Ronald Preston, the man who brought the rail line up from Mombasa, described the future capital of Kenya Colony as "a bleak, swampy stretch of soppy landscape, windswept, devoid of human habitation of any sort, the resorts of thousands of wild animals of every species."[7] And still, at least twenty young men had taken the opportunity to travel there in 1901, in search of work or curious to see the dusty trading center with the train that rolled through it.

Ainsworth arrested the twenty boys for being young and idle as well as for lacking parental supervision and housing. Ainsworth made no recorded attempt to ascertain where they had come from, why they had come to Nairobi, or whether they actually had homes, parents, or kin elsewhere in the protectorate. Rather, he sent them to the Church Missionary Society station in Mombasa, some three hundred miles away. Ainsworth and Reverend Burt of the mission had corresponded in the past about the growing number of young people coming to Nairobi and had struck a deal whereby the mission would accept them. Just as the British had done with emancipated slaves and pawns only a few years earlier, they now handed would-be young town dwellers over to mission stations.[8] The arrival of twenty boys in Nairobi and their removal by Ainsworth marked an early urban colonial encounter and a point of origin, one in which young African men ventured to colonial towns and, when discovered, were promptly turned away by colonial authorities. The fate of these twenty boys had been sealed when Ainsworth determined that they had no employment, parental supervision, or places to stay. They were an early manifestation of Nairobi street boys, though the capital had just one dusty main road at the time. Their only crime had been to cross paths with Ainsworth, who believed they lacked productive purpose and therefore surely had disruptive intent.

Age and town life occupied prominent, interconnected places in the British colonial imagination. The British viewed the colonial city as a site of social and spatial dislocation, a modern and thereby foreign ecosystem in which Africans encountered the dark and twisted undergrowth of Western life and lost themselves to individualism, poverty, and criminality. "The average native," Kenya's chief native commissioner observed in 1919, "when he leaves his reserve is, for the time being, no longer subject to his former re-straints." "Unless," the commissioner warned, "he is guided and controlled and also instructed as to his responsibilities it is hardly to be wondered at that numbers of these people should act in an irresponsible manner."[9] These "former restraints" of which the commissioner spoke were, of course, the moral authority of elders, the social obligation of kinship, and the politi-cal power of chiefs—the imagined foundations of African age-relations and British indirect rule. Of all their African subjects, the young were seen as the most susceptible to the effects of town life.

As the chief registrar of natives, who was routinely frustrated by hav-ing to keep track of young people migrating to towns, warned a few years later: "Once a juvenile leaves his reserve of the custody of his parents or guardian . . . in course of time he develops into an anonymous personality wandering from place to place in the Colony and eventually, by the time adulthood is reached he becomes that more or less pitiful object a 'detrib-alised native.'"[10] The registrar had no doubt boys could reach adulthood during their tenure in town, but this was not the kind of maturity officials should want for their young subjects. Town life replaced the proper sociali-zation and discipline boys received back home in the reserves with that conducted in back alleys and shantytowns. Migration and street life made young men aimless, anonymous, and ungovernable. Drift and detribaliza-tion quickly "turns to delinquency" and "irritability of temper and an in-ability to concentrate or to sustain mental and physical effort."[11] Officials feared that street life transformed disciplined herdsboys, schoolboys, and tea harvesters into grubby panhandlers, petty thieves, alleyway gamblers, and belligerent drunks.

The belief that town life had retrogressive effects on young Africans was only partially rooted in racialized colonial ideas about the nature of African social and rural life. These anxieties also stemmed from how the British understood their own historic encounter with town life back home.[12] In Britain and Europe, throughout the nineteenth and early twentieth centu-ries, fears about urban crime, vagabondage, and delinquency among young people ran rampant in the academic and popular presses, drawing on new ideas about urbanization and the dichotomy between tradition and moder-nity.[13] Drawing on theories like urban degeneration, many scholarly writers came to believe that urban life eroded domestic households, conservative cultural norms, and self-restraint, especially among the young. As Charles Masterman wrote in *The Heart of the Empire*, boys met "with bad com-panions" on the streets and found "delight in spectacles like that of a man being dragged to gaol or of a drunken quarrel, which can only degrade their character, and encounter nothing but what fosters and appeals to their animal nature."[14] A contemporary of Masterman, the infamous social Darwinist Alfred Marshall, argued that children who were swept from the thresholds of their homesteads into the streets of London suffered from stunted physical and mental capacities.[15]

The city did not produce the modern man but rather devolved him down the great chain of being, stripping him of his class and racial identity.[16] When visiting Manchester, Alexis de Tocqueville remarked that "civilisation works it miracles, and civilised man is turned back almost into a savage."[17] Borrowing the metaphor of savagery, John Shaw, when writing of vagrants he met at a nineteenth-century London mission, compared them to "the wildest colony of savages, transplanted by an act of conjuration from the centre of Africa."[18] Much closer to the center of Africa, in Kenya, members of the 1932 crime committee described idle African town dwellers as "the native counterpart of the 'hooligan,' that objectionable feature of the larger towns of England."[19] The city at the heart of an empire metaphorically transformed white Englishmen into Africans; meanwhile, its colonial counterpart out on the frontier conjured Africans into poor white Englishmen. In the British imagination of the late nineteenth and early twentieth centuries, town life was an unnatural consequence of capitalism and modernity—one that they brought with them to far-flung corners of the empire.

Notions of picturesque rural life were also important to colonial ideas about age and urbanization. Unlike the British countryside, towns like London, Manchester, and Liverpool possessed none of the social forces necessary to bind young people to a deferential social order. In towns there were no obstinate fathers, nagging mothers, nosy neighbors, or parish constables on patrol.[20] A romanticized rural life also lay at the heart of the colonial encounter in Kenya, not simply because officials believed Africans to be a rural people bound by a strict social and generational order, but because hundreds and later thousands of European settlers had come to re-create the vestiges of a lost white man's countryside in a new-found black man's land.[21] Both the colony and its people were idealized through the prism of an imagined rural and traditional British past. The idle young man in Nairobi reaffirmed historic British insecurities about modern life, unsettled colonial certainties of African rural and generational order, and threatened future designs to re-create Britain's idyllic, rustic past in Kenya.

FIGURE 3.1. Nairobi, n.d. Photo courtesy of the Melville J. Herskovits Library of African Studies Winterton Collection, Northwestern University.

"LIFE WAS GOOD"

British officials described the migration of African boys and young men to towns as a form of wanderlust, a reaction to the supposed tedium of village life and herding livestock. They often imagined Gikuyu boys standing atop the ridges of Kiambu District in awe of the glittering sun-lit rooftops of Nairobi at noon or the flickering fires at night. And like moths to a flame, they came. But rather than the push of village-induced boredom or the pull of town life's bright lights, young people came to towns looking to labor, escape household crises, or experience a little adventure. In the first two decades of colonial rule, Mombasa and Nairobi attracted a growing number of would-be African workers. As Asian and African laborers laid rails across the heart of the East African interior, they sealed Mombasa's fate as a port of call for imperial trade and African wage labor. They also established supply depots along the route. Some grew into trading centers; others became outposts of European settlement; and one in particular, Nairobi, became the seat of colonial political power.

As early as 1909, the government noted that "many thousands" of Africans traveled to Nairobi and Mombasa in search of work and returned to their homes with their earnings to pay taxes and invest in livestock.[22] There they found employment as domestic servants in European, Arab, and Asian households; as street sweepers and junkyard scavengers for municipal government; and as apprentices for carpenters, tailors, and the railway. These jobs often offered better wages than those on settler farms and in smaller towns. The native commissioner estimated that by 1919, town wages were nearly 100 percent higher for rural young people. This disparity, he argued, had led to a disquieting level of migration.[23]

By the early 1930s, the colonial state came under pressure both from within its own ranks and from the Colonial Office to curb the employment of young people in towns. The deputy registrar in Nairobi reported that recent inspections carried out by his office revealed "considerable employment of children," some as young as twelve, in domestic service. He called on the district commissioner to restrict the access of young workers to Nairobi. "I do not think it could be argued," he wrote, "that the sight of those mud caked little *totos* is very edifying or that their employment under such insanitary conditions is a good thing."[24] The Colonial Office also demanded that the administration adopt child labor laws to match those recently passed in Britain. In 1933, the colony complied with the Employment of Women, Young Persons, and Children Ordinance.[25] Although the ordinance was one of the most detailed in British Africa, it did little to create an infrastructure to inspect and penalize employers reliant on the urban labor of young African men.[26]

What began as twenty boys in May 1901 became thousands by the late 1940s. During the war, more casual laborers were needed in Nairobi and Mombasa to work the railways, docks, and burgeoning industries. And African laborers responded, beginning a renewed, intense period of rural-to-urban migration during and after the war. By 1946, the population of Africans living in Mombasa reached fifty-seven thousand—tripling since 1931. In Nairobi, an estimated seventy-seven thousand Africans, 15 percent of whom were under the age of sixteen, crammed themselves into inadequate housing offered by colonial authorities or made due in the shantytowns. Their numbers had doubled during the war alone.[27] And a decade later, well over a quarter of Nairobi's African population was under sixteen.[28]

In much the same way as girls and young women, boys turned to town life because their home lives had become too difficult to bear.[29] Household crises took on many forms: from poverty and hunger to abuse and disobedience to intense, complicated disputes within polygamous marriages.[30] The tensions that arose from these strained economic and personal relationships within households had a significant impact on the nature of urban migration. Sometime in the late 1940s, James Karanja Kariuki's life on the streets of Nairobi began because of a bitter rivalry between his father's wives. Conflict in the Kariuki household arose, James explained, because his father's family was large and well to do. His wives and sons vied for his favor—often at one another's expense. "You see there is always a big problem when the family is big," James explained, "when each person wants this and that, and some do not want their dad to help where necessary . . . such problems normally occur in such a home."[31] He left his father's home in Kiambu after a terrible argument with his brothers, one ending with a threat on his life. After his first night on the streets of Nairobi, he tried not to look back.

Other young men came to town fleeing physical abuse and memories of parents lost. Born in the interwar years, Harry Kimanji spent his childhood on a European estate in Elburgon near Nakuru. His earliest memories were of picking pyrethrum blossoms with his mother to supplement the family income. She was paid by the weight of her harvest and so Harry's help contributed significantly. The work for such a small boy was exhausting, but each morning he went to the fields. He remembers that his father died while he was still very young. "He had married my mother when he was already too old." Shortly after, Harry's mother died. Orphaned, he went to his uncle's farm in Kiambu, where "life was very difficult, tough, and very bitter." A severe man, his uncle put him to work taking care of his younger cousins, washing their clothes, and fetching water. "I was not given enough food and was worked like a slave. I could not complain because if I did, I would be chased away, and I had nowhere to go. I had to persevere." Sometime after World War II, Harry decided to "run away from them, and go to Nairobi and become a street boy."[32] Around the same time Harry decided to leave home for Nairobi, Gabriel Kahugu Muchahi's mother also passed away, and his father's other wife became responsible for him. According to Gabriel, she abused him, and he, too, fled his father's home in Kiambu to Nairobi.[33]

For some young men, their urban migration and misbehavior were sources rather than consequences of family crisis. Born during the war, Samuel Uiru Kaguara grew up in a village near Ndenderu in Kiambu, not far from Nairobi. Several years after the war, Samuel started making trouble for his parents. "They really wanted to help me as a loved son, but there came a point when I joined a peer group at school that showed me how to go to Nairobi."[34] Boys like Samuel often traveled on the recommendation or in the company of other boys. Word circulated among young people that there was something on offer in towns that they could not find at home.

Peer pressure often prevailed over the desires and discipline of parents. Before Samuel met up with his friends and ventured to Nairobi, he would steal a few shillings from his parents, usually five or so. They frequented the Marigiti vegetable market and used their stolen start-up capital to "buy fruits and anything else." Five shillings "was a lot of money then," nearly an entire month's wages for boys picking tea in Kericho. Whatever produce they did not eat themselves, they sold to passersby. It was enough to score a profit and enjoy one's self, Samuel recalls. "Life was good."

Each of these men understood that the mere act of traveling to town or the behavior that led them there had contravened their parents' hopes and expectations. Looking back, Gabriel Kahugu admits, "My dad advised me to love going to school after herding animals, but I used to disobey those rules and go to Nairobi."[35] For many young men like Samuel and Gabriel, town life was an act of indiscipline, a breach of parental authority, and, as they would quickly realize, a violation of colonial law. Historians have argued that like British colonial officials, most adult Africans viewed towns as "social and political problems rather than . . . productive or cultural opportunities."[36] Africans who traveled to towns like Mombasa, Nairobi, and Kisumu during the colonial period did not view themselves as permanent urban residents. Even by the 1960s, only about 8 percent of Kenyans lived in towns.[37] They straddled urban and rural life. Each morning, girls and young women flooded into town markets to sell foodstuffs, skins, and cookware until they returned home in the evening.[38] Young men traveled into towns regularly, too, though their stays often lasted longer as they searched for work and fulfilled labor contracts. Eventually, many of them would return home too.

The temporality of town life was often a result of its hardships. Towns quickly dashed the hope of better wages, decent living conditions, and education. Urban housing for Africans was largely a self-help enterprise. In Nairobi, Africans had developed six settlements in and around the railway depot by 1910.[39] Rather than assist African migrants with urban planning and sanitation schemes, the colonial government took to periodically demolishing them.[40] The destruction of African homes did little to discourage migration and aggravated the housing crisis. Housing conditions in towns like Mombasa, Nairobi, and Kisumu were among the worst in the colony. In the smaller towns of the Rift Valley, European and Asian employers were more willing to provide housing to their employees and their families, easing many of the pressures that Africans experienced in larger towns.[41]

In Nairobi, the government made a few attempts to construct residential areas for African railway workers and municipal employees. In 1922, it designed its first African location, known as Pumwani.[42] But serious efforts by municipal officials to organize and improve African housing began only after World War II. By then the level of migration to towns and the increasing number of urban-born Africans strained already overcrowded locations. Twenty-eight percent more people lived in Pumwani than the recommended number.[43] Compounding the housing crisis, wages failed to meet rising costs of living. In 1939, a bag of maize meal cost five shillings; by 1948 the price had skyrocketed to twenty-nine shillings.[44] Many turned to the informal economy for survival. Moreover, a lack of urban educational facilities worsened prospects for those born in or leaving for towns. In 1931, government schools in the town educated about 1 percent of its urban population, with only six schools servicing 1,770 students.[45]

The young also experienced town life temporarily. For Samuel Uiru and Alan Kanyingi Ngugi, life in Nairobi did not start out as a permanent adventure. Instead, they and their friends played truant from school, walked to town, and wiled away the day spending their parents' money and causing a bit of mischief. By nightfall, they returned home, slept in their own beds, and slipped out early the next morning.[46] This was especially true of Nairobi. Enveloped to the north by the Gikuyu reserves, Nairobi attracted boys and young men from Kiambu, Fort Hall, and other nearby districts close enough to reach town by foot or a short lorry ride. Much the same could be said for Mombasa. After the war, many of the young men arrested in town for vagrancy and other bylaws came from nearby Digo and Teita-Taveta. While by no means within a day's walk, most of the street boys arrested in and removed from Mombasa represented a local or regional migration.[47]

The pattern of urban migration among young people in the postwar Rift Valley Province was more diffuse and diverse. In Nairobi and Mombasa, colonial authorities returned young men to nearby districts. But in the largest Rift Valley town of Nakuru, young repatriates were sent to homes much farther away, including Eldoret, Kiambu, Kisumu, and Nyeri.[48] Other boys arrested in Nakuru were sent to smaller nearby trading centers such as Ol'Kalou, Elburgon, Londiani, and Gilgil. Rift Valley Province lacked a central urban hub like Nairobi or Mombasa, consisting instead of several smaller trading centers. Furthermore, the presence of hundreds of thousands of squatters and migrants living and working on European estates complicated the urban migration patterns of young men. A Luo boy wiling away the hours in the Nakuru town center might have doubly strayed from home. Arrested in Nakuru, municipal authorities had to decide whether to return him to his workplace, a settler estate in Mau Summit, or to his home of origin, a village outside of Kisumu.

Although life in town was temporary for most African young men, either by choice or by colonial design, sometimes urban migration became more long-lasting. The permanence of town life could be a gradual process. While wandering Nairobi alleys in search of food or swiping fruit from Mombasa markets, young men lost track of time. Day slipped into night, and it was easier to stay in town than to return home. And after a while, Samuel Uiru recalls, "you never went home."[49] For those escaping domestic violence and poverty, like Gabriel Kahugu, there was no other choice: "For me, I couldn't go home after the beating [from his relatives] because even home was worse."[50]

When darkness fell, street boys sought shelter. They squeezed inside culverts, staked out corners of building sites, and lay on the backseats of junkyard cars.[51] The verandas of Asian and African homes were also a common place to lay a weary head. In the late 1940s, Peter Mwarangu and many of his fellow street boys found shelter beneath the awnings of homes in Pumwani, one of Nairobi's oldest African neighborhoods. "Pumwani had houses which were built in such a way that there was a veranda in between," Peter says. He and his friends negotiated deals with the women who owned these homes to sleep there at night. "Those women were friendly because they could send us to fetch water [and] wash clothes for them."[52] These women were powerful players and patrons in Pumwani. Many had come in their youth and remembered their own transitions to permanent town life. They had begun laundries, breweries, and brothels out of their homes and within a generation became landlords. They were the center of social and economic life not just in Pumwani but also elsewhere in Nairobi, and many street boys found themselves in the orbit of these successful women.[53] Life in Pumwani and the shantytowns of Nairobi could also be entertaining. While municipal authorities claimed that African locations were rife with poverty, overcrowding, crime, and political unrest, many African residents recall lives of joy and leisure. By the 1940s, Pumwani teemed with bars, billiard halls, dance halls, cinemas, music venues, tea parties, and boxing matches.[54]

As boys had fun and forged new networks, town life quickly became a much more permanent affair. The longer they stayed, the more intimate they became with the town's physical and economic geography and in turn the social geography of their relationships with one another and the colonial state. Their movements and behavior within towns came to threaten the presumptions of colonial town life the government held so dear. A tiny population of boys and young men very quickly became a menace to the elder state.

Urban planners, police, and municipal authorities ordered towns in Kenya to maintain the semblance of a racialized order and obscure the contradictions that lay within. Even as a ramshackle railway outpost, Nairobi ordered urban life around race. In 1905, the Land Committee for the East Africa Protectorate directed housing in Nairobi to be separated along racial lines.[55] And as one early visitor noted, the "sticky morass of the subordinate railway quarters" and the "palatial residences of the Railway officers" had "awakened a sense of injustice in the hearts of the men that no plausible speech [could] eradicate."[56] While Nairobi was to be a settlement for whites and a seat of political power, it was also a commercial hub requiring African, Arab, and Asian laborers.[57]

From the 1920s onward, Nairobi was divided into several racially and commercially defined zones. In the town center, situated beside the railway station, lay the district commissioner's office and a rapidly growing commercial sector. To the south and the southeast, town planners reserved space for Nairobi's slowly developing industrial sector. Residential real estate lay to the north. Areas to the west of Nairobi, such as Karen and the Ngong Hills, were reserved for Europeans. Parklands directly north of the town center became home to the Asian community. Finally, to the east, municipal authorities isolated the sprawling makeshift, self-help shantytowns that African laborers had built themselves.[58] In Nairobi, urban planners made concrete the racial stratification and segregation at the heart of settler society. Even in towns with European and Asian populations, such as Nakuru, Naivasha, Nyeri, and Kisumu, these same principles operated on a much smaller scale.[59] Yet young people living on the streets did not view fences of sisal, stone, and steel as obstacles; rather, they resurveyed the racial topography, drawing together aspects of everyday town life that were never meant to meet.

Those young men who remained more permanently on the streets quickly integrated themselves into preexisting groups of young men.[60] Although he slept alone on his first night in Nairobi, James Karanja met up with a group of twenty-five boys the next day with whom he became "good friends."[61] He became part of a group of young men who operated out of Westlands, Mathare, and Muthaiga in the late 1940s. Having established himself with a group, he quickly learned that there were others, and that they, too, staked claims on different parts of town. "There were some areas," James recalls, "[to] which you would not dare go, because those boys controlling there were fully grown, and would not let you interfere with their area. Also you could not play with certain trash bins on which other boys depended for food. So it was a matter of you searching for food from free areas [and] then bringing it back to your kingdom."[62] In short, there were rules of generational engagement a new street boy needed to learn and obey.[63] As they did back home in the countryside, boys and young men organized themselves into a hierarchy of groups based on age. Which group you joined depended on your age, and which territories your group claimed depended on where it sat along the generational hierarchy. The youngest street boys stayed together and respected the territory and authority of older groups. In their new urban environment, young men reappropriated the meanings and expressions of age to organize their lives and activities on the streets.

Boys also constructed for themselves geographic rules of engagement, enclosures that could not be crossed without permission and open urban fields where they could meet and interact freely. According to former street boys, the largest, most bountiful free zone was the town center, where they all rummaged for food in alleys behind hotels and restaurants early each morning. Downtown was a dangerous place, though, where they risked exposure and arrest. In the late 1940s and early 1950s, Gabriel Kahugu remembers that certain hotels and restaurants baked bread in the evening, and by morning he would find broken or misshapen loaves that had been thrown into the trash. Some garbage bins yielded rich pickings, like day-old meat.[64] Young men did not restrict their foraging to downtown Nairobi; they also pillaged trash bins in Asian residential areas like Ngara and Parklands. "We used to borrow food from the Asian homes and trash bins."[65] The morning scavenge was the most important part of the day. After all, "no one was cooking for you," so "food for that day was the only concern."[66]

Afterward, some groups of boys headed to the river on the outskirts of town. The streams of the Nairobi River Basin were an integral part of street life. Some boys, like Harry Kimanji, took the food they had found to Mathare River, while others, like Gabriel, used the Nairobi River at Kipande Road. At the water's edge they rinsed off the food they had found, cleaned the cooking pots and utensils they had collected, and prepared their meals. The riverbank also provided them a place to rest, bathe, and transform themselves into respectable town dwellers. At the river, "[you take] a shirt like this one, and you take soap, and you wash and put it on, and you look like somebody."[67] The river water washed away filth and provided the boys a means to achieve some measure of respectability. Their food might be a little rotten, their cooking pots might be stolen, their shirts might be secondhand, but they could all be washed. Along the river, boys participated in household duties and behaviors that affirmed their self-sufficiency .

Food was not the only thing on the minds of these young scavengers. They filled their days with schemes to make a quick shilling. Harry Kimanji and the other boys with whom he traveled collected usable items like pots, pans, soap, and clothing they found in trash bins. They cleaned up the merchandise and took it to the African areas where they sold what they could to hawkers. "We were just selling whatever we got. You go and wash them, when they're clean you go back to town or Majengo [a quarter in the Pumwani slum in Nairobi]." Looking back, Harry admits it was not the most profitable venture. Sometimes they found nothing of value to sell, and even when they did, they had to sell it at a "throwaway price."[68]

Other street children found more lucrative means of earning income—theft. Gabriel Kahugu and his friends did not just take food from the trash bins of Asian homes; they also stole clothing from laundry lines and anything else they got their hands on. They then "sold them to other ethnic groups at Ziwani [a neighborhood where government employees lived], like Luos and Luhyas, who worked for the government and had money and could afford to buy those clothes."[69] It was a simple operation that exploited the relative wealth of government-employed Africans. James Karanja's group operated a more elaborate scheme. He recalls that older boys in his group would break into Asian workshops and steal tools and car parts. They would hand off the stolen goods to younger boys, like James, who would travel across town to the industrial area where they would sell them for ten cents an item. This sort of burglary required greater planning than petty theft from laundry lines or parked cars. Older boys with more experience handled nighttime break-ins, while their young accomplices had the more dangerous task of traveling with stolen goods during the day. The boys operated with a clear understanding of the colonial legal system. If caught, younger boys received more lenient punishment—it was the difference between an inconvenient repatriation order for the young or painful strokes of the cane and imprisonment for the old.

Money was of central importance to young people on the streets of colonial towns, and casual labor and theft allowed them to expand their material horizons and served as a means to invest in future opportunities. According to Samuel Uiru, by nightfall "you had to make sure you had enough money, capital to buy other things in the market the following day."[70] To succeed on the streets, street boys of the late 1940s and early 1950s saved and invested their profits. Yet saving was tricky given the dangers of the streets, especially older boys or rival groups. As Peter Mwarangu argues matter-of-factly, "There were no banks or post offices. You had to think wisely where you could save your money."[71] One common method of saving money was to sew coin shillings into the waistbands of trousers. However, street boys did not simply squirrel away and reinvest, they also enjoyed their earnings. Money allowed young men on the street to forget, at least temporarily, about their daily struggle to find food. James Karanja recalls that pockets full of change "were happy moments because we went to the restaurant proudly and ordered food because we had money and because the food was sold so cheap."[72] To saunter into a restaurant or tea shop was a step up from rummaging through alleyway garbage.

Their earnings also gave them the opportunity to circumvent the moral norms to which they may have been held at home under the watchful eyes of parents and kin. The black market in postwar Nairobi offered Africans inexpensive access to cigarettes, alcohol, and drugs like khat and *bhangi* (marijuana). It was on the streets where many young men had their first encounter with drug use. According to Harry Kimanji, it was peer pressure within his group that got him started. "The problem was that we lived with other people, so you had to live with what they were doing. We would buy *bhangi* [and] illegal brews like *busa'a* and *changa'a*."[73] Many bought their brew from women in the African areas of town.[74] Even in smaller towns, mere trading centers during the colonial period, young men also succumbed to pressure from their peers. Of life in late 1950s Gilgil, a small town on the road from Nairobi to Nakuru, James Ng'ang'a recalls that it had "a lot of influence of the peer group and copying what other boys were doing, you would think it was good." At the age of ten, like his elder brother before him, he "started . . . smoking, drinking alcohol, and that naughty behavior entered into me."[75]

According to some former street boys, smoking and drinking were not in and of themselves bad things. "It made someone's mind rise, and one would see the sky going around. You feel very happy and see that you are enjoying it."[76] Yet, as Harry Joseph and others admitted, alcohol and drug use often proved the catalysts for risky behavior. In late 1940s Nairobi, drinking and marijuana made Harry and his friends aggressive. They fought among themselves and harassed and abused people in the streets. They also attracted the attention of police and were arrested. This reckless behavior brought the possibility of ending young men's tenure on the street. In a world where secrecy and camaraderie, along with theft and subterfuge, preserved young men's abilities to live beyond the authority of the state and their elders, drugs and alcohol often cast an unwanted light on the shadows in which they lived. Many former street boys vigorously refute the idea that they spent their days drunk and high.[77] It let their guard down—something that got them arrested, or worse.

FIGURE 3.2. Group of natives and rickshaw, Nairobi, n.d. Photo courtesy of the Melville J. Herskovits Library of African Studies Winterton Collection, Northwestern University.

The presence of hundreds of unemployed African youths pilfering vegetables at the market and picking pockets at the train station, as well as drinking, smoking, and gambling in alleyways, was an affront to colonial security and sensibility. Yet it was not their visible lives on the streets that municipal authorities and non-African town dwellers feared; it was their less visible, potentially criminal dealings—the things the state did not know.[78] Each time clothes were stripped from laundry lines behind Asian homes in Parklands, trash cans were pillaged outside European compounds in Karen, or car parts were stolen from a mechanic's shop on Canal Street, Nairobi residents were reminded of the municipal government's failings and the ease with which young Africans breached the racial segregation of the city. What colonial officials and non-Africans decried as detribalization or delinquency was merely young men's exploitation of new urban possibilities and the state's inability to survey, map, and control their capital city.

Decades before young men like Harry Kimanji, James Karanja, and Gabriel Kahugu set foot in Nairobi, municipal authorities had come under pressure from non-African residents to protect their personal property and secure the racial boundaries of towns like Mombasa and Nairobi.[79] As early as the turn of the century, colonial authorities in Mombasa and Nairobi had managed urban migration as well as law and order by removing unemployed Africans from towns or forcing them to labor. By 1920, this practice, known as repatriation, became the state's official policy for banishing the unemployed from town, and, in theory, to prevent detribalization and delinquency. Repatriation came to form one of the cornerstones of the elder state's efforts to turn back the urban migration of the young. By casting out the young, municipal authorities tried to preserve the careful choreography of urban segregation and their own authority.

REPATRIATING THE YOUNG, PRESERVING ELDER AUTHORITY

Commissioner Ainsworth's May 1901 roundup of twenty boys for "wandering" idly through Nairobi was an early form of control that colonial authorities came to depend on over the next six decades. The British crafted a host of legal regimes to restrict young men's access to towns by periodically removing them to prevent a settled urban life. Municipal bylaws, employment identification, registration procedures, and vagrancy ordinances all endeavored to sweep the streets of unwanted young, predominantly male, Africans. These laws did not prevent the migration of young men at their rural source but ensured that once they had arrived in town and did not find honest work, their stay would be temporary. Young men convicted of violating these urban ordinances would be repatriated back home to the countryside, back under the authority of their kin and chiefs. In this way, municipal authorities promoted a constant circular and cyclical pattern of urban labor migration to ensure that urban labor demands were always satiated but the human excess was washed away before it resorted to criminality.[80]

Vagrancy laws were one of the first assaults on African town life. In 1898 and 1902, Mombasa and Nairobi each adopted vagrancy acts calling for the arrest of anyone "asking for alms or wandering about without any employment or visible means of subsistence."[81] Even before spaces like Nairobi could be defined as urban, colonial authorities sought to criminalize African access to them. Those the police suspected of vagrancy were arrested without a warrant and, if convicted, imprisoned for up to three months. While incarcerated, vagrants labored for eight annas per day (the equivalent of half an Indian rupee or less than one British shilling) until enough money had been saved to send them back home.

Early vagrancy laws made no distinction between adults and young people, and as officials quickly found a growing number of young Africans in their custody, they had to decide whether to incarcerate them in prison alongside adults or find an alternative solution. In 1907, Governor James Hayes Sadler wrote a letter to Lord Elgin, secretary of state for the colonies, recounting his colony's difficulty in implementing Kenya's vagrancy laws, especially with respect to the young. He complained that the police kept in check the migration of underemployed Africans to towns with periodic sweeps of African locations and arresting "all whom they find without a visible means of subsistence." Unfortunately, he argued, this process failed to distinguish between vagrants and criminals as well as young and old, and, therefore, many idle young people went to jail where they associated with hardened adult criminals.[82]

In a note that followed the governor's letter, the problem with the colony's vagrancy laws was underscored as part of the much larger problem of mobile young Africans. "There is a large number of juvenile vagrants in this country and it is a matter of extreme difficulty to know how to deal with them, the reason being in many instances they either have no parents or have been removed from the district where they were born and do not know whether their parents exist or not."[83] In short, too many young men wandered into towns, and colonial authorities had no idea where they had come from or what to do with them. The only recourse available was the Vagrancy Act of 1902, under which the punishment for vagrancy was imprisonment and forced labor. Almost as soon as authorities passed the vagrancy law, they began looking for alternatives to incarcerating young urban migrants. In 1907, Governor Sadler proposed the construction of a reformatory for young offenders. When the reformatory opened its doors a few years later, it provided only temporary relief. The number of young vagrants and more serious offenders arrested for housebreaking or assault quickly outstripped the institution's limited space. As a result, magistrates reserved the reformatory for only the colony's most serious young offenders. Corporal punishment offered another alternative to imprisonment, but, yet again, magistrates tried to restrict the pain of the rattan cane to thieves and more troublesome young men. The British could also have continued sending young vagrants to mission stations, as John Ainsworth had done in 1901. Once more, the number of young people rounded up in Nairobi and other towns forced officials to face the reality that missionaries could take in only so many.

Struggling to find a suitable punishment that fit the severity of vagrancy, municipal authorities turned to roundups and repatriation orders. Rather than caning, incarcerating, or forcing young Africans to labor, magistrates ordered them removed from town and returned to their reserves of origin. Repatriation became official policy in 1920 with the passage of the colony's revised vagrancy ordinance. Under the 1920 ordinance, any adult or young person found wandering or residing in a space such as a veranda, outhouse, or vehicle without the owner's consent could be arrested for vagrancy.[84] The new ordinance also became one of the earliest colonial laws in Kenya to differentiate punishment based on age. Officials detained adult vagrants until they found employment for them. If an offender refused to labor, then he was imprisoned. If work could not be found, then he was repatriated. Young people under the age of sixteen were to be immediately repatriated back to their families. Any young man charged with returning after repatriation or recidivist vagrancy received corporal punishment.[85] Throughout the 1920s, only a hundred or so Africans were arrested for vagrancy each year, and even fewer were under the age of sixteen. In 1928, of the seventy-six Africans charged with vagrancy, officials identified only one as under the age of sixteen.[86]

Magistrates used repatriation not only to punish young vagrants but also as part of a punitive package for all sorts of crimes. In 1931, the chief native commissioner acknowledged that "after the award of corporal punishment of a juvenile, the police further charge the offender with vagrancy, and the court orders him to be repatriated to his reserve."[87] In that year, 268 young people under the age of sixteen were caned and some repatriated home afterward. Caning and repatriation became a popular marriage of punishments. Boys and young men sentenced for serious offenses such as theft punishable with caning also found themselves cast out of town. Moreover, the labor department and municipal authorities in Mombasa and Nairobi often worked together to rid each town of underemployed young laborers. The police swept through African shantytowns, sometimes weekly, arresting any young men they encountered who appeared unemployed or failed to produce a work pass. The labor department and criminal courts would then share the workload, splitting the number of cases between them.[88]

Magistrates did not simply use vagrancy laws to rid towns of young people; they also relied on a host of municipal bylaws. In Nairobi, bylaw 557 served as a supplementary vagrancy regulation but with a temporal twist: any African found without residence or remaining in town for more than thirty-six hours could be repatriated.[89] The Mombasa municipal board also created bylaws and petitioned the governor to impose stricter vagrancy rules like those in Nairobi. By the late 1920s, despite its dependence on casual labor, especially along the docks, Mombasa also began its own sweeps and roundups.[90] In smaller towns like Kisumu, Nakuru, and Eldoret, similar bylaws were on the books regarding violations that ranged from loitering on traffic islands to misusing bicycles—all in an effort to increase the number of offenses for which young Africans could be arrested and repatriated.

By the 1930s, as the depression settled over Kenya, town life grew too difficult for many Africans to bear. Between 1929 and 1935, wages fell by 40 percent and demand for labor in towns and on agricultural estates declined.[91] Family networks back in the reserves became crucial safety nets, and many town dwellers and squatters decided to return home until the economy improved. By 1933, the ministry of health estimated that 8,824 Africans had vacated Nairobi since the outset of the depression.[92] And yet the colonial state dramatically increased its use of repatriation orders. In 1932, the chief native commissioner noted that 1,002 adult and juvenile vagrants had been rounded up in Nairobi, an increase over previous years.[93] Indeed, during the depression, despite falling African residency, municipal authorities continued to complain about the migration of young people to towns, whether to seek employment or to escape rural poverty.[94]

While only a few young men had been arrested for vagrancy and then repatriated throughout the 1920s and early 1930s, this dramatically changed by 1938. By then, repatriation had become the second most common form of punishment for those under the age of sixteen. Around this time, officials began preparing registers of all young offenders brought before colonial courts. Drawing on the registers available for 1938 and 1939, magistrates charged and sentenced 1,534 young men under the age of sixteen.[95] The registers reveal that vagrancy accounted for 12 percent of the cases. Coupled with cases involving municipal bylaws, the full legal regime developed to restrict African access to towns represented about 28 percent of total offenses committed by young offenders in 1938 and 1939. The registers show that in the midst of the depression, when African migration to towns had receded, municipal authorities made a major push to remove underemployed young men.

The 1938 and 1939 registers also reveal the kinds of young people arrested by police. Vagrancy was the crime of an idle male. Police arrested few young women for vagrancy, and the courts did not repatriate a single female in the late 1930s.[96] Only a handful of girls passed through the courts, charged mainly with theft, then fined or released with a warning.[97] Despite the presence of women on the streets of colonial towns, magistrates did not remove them in the same ways they did young men.[98] To municipal officials, an urban girl on the street proved more productive and less dangerous to urban order than her male counterpart.[99] A street girl hawking her wares represented a particular kind of threat—a sexual, moral one—that often attracted the ire of African men more than it did the colonial state.[100] Chiefs sitting on local councils and the growing number of predominantly male ethnic associations, including the Kavirondo Welfare Association, Luo Union, Kipsigis-Nandi Union, and Kikuyu General Union, closely monitored the girls and women who traveled to towns. Political organizations like the Kikuyu Central Association also railed against women's migration to, as well as their labor and leisure in, Nairobi.[101] When families inquired with chiefs or members of these associations about the daughters' whereabouts, these groups dispatched men to town to find them and return them home. These African-initiated repatriations, which occurred only rarely, could take on sensational, scandalous proportions. Girls in town would be confronted, stripped naked, made to wear a burlap sack, and then paraded through their home village before jeering, sneering crowds.[102] Associations repatriated urban women to humiliate them into staying in the reserves. Yet they also used these violent, sexualized confrontations to reexert waning male authority over women who had profited from town life.[103]

In addition to the gender of those brought before the courts, the registers also recorded their ages. The average age of those young men repatriated by courts for vagrancy and violating other municipal bylaws was about thirteen. Thirteen fell well below the upper limit of sixteen the vagrancy act had set or the much older average age of those sentenced to caning or institutionalization in a reformatory. Whether or not the boys were actually thirteen — magistrates and medical officers continually struggled with assigning ages to young offenders — the courts saw fit to categorize them as such. For magistrates, thirteen became an appropriate age and a clear marker for a repatriation order. If a medical officer or magistrate decided a young man was around the age of thirteen, then he should be sent home to his family. If he was older, say, between the ages of thirteen and sixteen, then he required harsher punishment meted out by the state. Laws governing access to urban spaces and repatriation subdivided young people, defined gradations of age, and assigned them levels of criminal responsibility. Magistrates sent the youngest offenders home in an effort to preserve parental authority, or at least give it another shot. For older boys, those over the age of thirteen, they should have known better. Their parents had clearly lost the disciplinary upper hand, and the elder state had to intervene.

During World War II, officials relaxed their control of migration and the urban lives of young Africans in an effort to meet the demands of a wartime economy.[104] Municipal authorities and labor officers fretted over rapid urban growth during the war, especially among those between the ages of twelve and fifteen earning extremely low wages as urban casual employees.

Financial constraints compounded officials' anxieties and hampered their ability to continue sweeps and roundups in the African locations during the war. Paying for young repatriates to take the train or lorry back to their homes drained already low municipal and labor office coffers. Such were the realities of a colony pressed into the service of war and struggling under a growing budget deficit.[105] In 1941, when native affairs officer T. C. Carlisle decided another roundup of underemployed youths was needed, he received a curt message from labor commissioner P. de V. Allen: "I must point out, however, that I do not agree to just a round-up and then giving them a free ride home. I have no money in my repatriation vote for joy rides for juveniles."[106] Paying for transport had become too burdensome. As a result, many magistrates began cautioning or discharging young offenders brought before them on vagrancy and municipal bylaw charges. In the years shortly before the war, over three hundred juveniles were released with a mere slap on the wrist, roughly 20 percent of young offenders.[107] In 1945, 21 percent of young vagrants were simply released. Police officers saw the "visible" signs of idleness on young African faces, arrested them, and escorted them to court. But magistrates could not cope with the numbers brought before their benches, nor could municipal authorities pay for their repatriation home. As a result, hundreds were simply issued warnings and released back onto the streets.

Accompanying the rapid growth of the African urban population in the 1940s was a fear among non-African town dwellers that crime and disorder had also increased. By the early 1950s, "scarcely an issue of the *East African Standard* . . . did not contain articles, letters to the editor, and editorials complaining about the rising number of assaults and robberies taking place within Nairobi."[108] Municipal authorities began openly discussing what they believed to be an intense, organized criminal element in towns. African affairs officer Thomas Askwith believed that a state of "lawlessness" in Nairobi was the handiwork of underemployed Africans, many of them young men.[109] African town life and the perception of rising African criminality, coupled with fear and outrage among urban non-African populations, spurred municipal authorities into action. Unshackled by the financial constraints of the war, colonial authorities began to dramatically expand their methods for dealing with young town dwellers.

After the war, the colony introduced the Removal of Undesirable Natives Ordinance in 1946. The ordinance was a temporary measure, legalizing the removal of any African who had spent time in prison or had lived in Nairobi less than three years.[110] Such legislation sought to remove only the most recent arrivals to Nairobi and other towns. Two years later, the British amended the vagrancy ordinance to include far harsher punishments than it had in the past. Under a 1948 revision, adult vagrants were to be either forced to work immediately or repatriated. For young men under the age of sixteen, the new ordinance established more rigorous forms of punishment. Boys charged with repeated vagrancy faced caning or imprisonment for up to six months followed by repatriation.[111] For the first time, a young person convicted of idleness, homelessness, or underemployment could be beaten or imprisoned. Larger and more frequent roundups were undertaken, and the number of young people arrested and removed from towns across Kenya increased. After the war, the colonial officials resumed recording and submitting annual registers of young offenders convicted and punished by the courts. These figures clearly illustrate a renewed focus by police and magistrates to remove the young from urban centers and return them to their reserves. Repatriations doubled from before the war, and more and more repatriates were beaten before being returned home. Between 1946 and 1947, in the midst of another "cleanup," repatriations reached their peak—1,309 young men were removed from towns that year.[112]

For young men repatriated from Nairobi in the late 1940s and early 1950s, police sweeps and roundups barely register in their memories of street life. When asked how many times police had arrested him during his time on the streets, Gabriel Kahugu responded, "Many times, I can't even remember how many times."[113] Samuel Uiru also lost count but recalled that after being sentenced to repatriation, "when we reached Kiambu or Kirigiti, we were expected to go home, but instead of going home we went back to Nairobi."[114] In the midst of searching for food, earning a few shillings, and enjoying illegal brew, the presence of police, magistrates, and repatriations was but a passing inconvenience in the lives of Nairobi street boys. When the labor commissioner described repatriation as nothing more than "joy rides for juveniles," he had not been too far off the mark. To many magistrates and labor officers, the practice of rounding up young Africans, clogging up courts, and transporting them by lorry to their rural homes seemed like a colossal, costly failure.[115]

Even some African chiefs and headmen, the very figures of elder authority that repatriation sought to reify, considered the practice a failure. At a Kiambu local council meeting in 1932, Chief Koinange complained that repatriation made chiefs look weak. If they could not even keep children at home, then to what did their authority amount? He proposed requiring villagers to spy on their vagrant neighbors and turn them in if they went missing.[116] In some ways, Koinange and his fellow chiefs wanted provincial administrators to provide them with the kind of authority practiced in rural England's historic battle with vagrancy. In England, repatriation had depended on the ability of rural communities to root migratory young men to their home parishes. The success of English repatriation had not simply relied on vague municipal laws, massive police roundups, and transport out of town. Beginning in the seventeenth century with the Poor Law and Settlement and Removal Act, local parishes in England were required to punish young vagrants or find them work. Critics of the parish system argued that the poor laws transformed the countryside into a lucrative prison in which young men were rounded up by posses organized by local officials and passed from parish to parish.[117] Of course, in rural Kenya, chiefs and district commissioners had neither the financial nor the logistical capabilities to turn African reserves into a system of poor relief and migration control. Yet this did not stop Chief Koinange from requesting similar powers for himself and his fellow chiefs.

At a meeting of the Meru local council, chiefs discussed prohibiting young men under the age of sixteen from leaving the district. Too many, they complained, traveled to towns like Nairobi. During the meeting, Chief Ngentu asked the district commissioner, not without some incredulity, whether the state actually had the power to bring children back who had left without parental consent. The commissioner responded, perhaps sheepishly, that the government did indeed have such power.[118] The meeting minutes did not mention whether Ngentu asked the follow-up question: If the state had such power, why not use it? Whether a rural chief or municipal officer, each understood that in the reserves, trading centers, and towns of Kenya, no effective, sustainable solution to the migration and street life of young men had been found. For every lorry-load of young vagrants departing towns across the colony, there were an equal number returning by foot for free.

By 1950, the number of repatriation orders subsided, but this lull in the removal of young town dwellers did not last. In the face of growing organized and violent criminal activity in Nairobi carried out by gangs of young men like the Anake a Forty and the connection between these groups and growing violent unrest in Central Province, officials relied on repatriation more than ever.[119] After declaring a state of emergency in 1952 to combat what the British believed to be a Gikuyu anticolonial insurgency, which they called Mau Mau, municipal authorities used roundups and repatriation orders more than ever.

CONCLUSION

The streets of Nairobi and other towns and trading centers of Kenya provided boys and young men new spaces to come of age. And while the elder state encouraged young men to work in town, it saw those who did not have enough work to occupy their time as a danger to colonial rule of law. When the presence of young people on the streets of Nairobi grew too noticeable, when parking boys pestered European town dwellers, or when the number of burglaries in Asian homes rose, municipal authorities activated vagrancy and bylaws to evacuate towns of potential young ne'er-do-wells. As long as the streets seemed clear and those cleared returned home, albeit temporarily, a smooth veneer was bonded over the issues of race, urban growth, rural crisis, and colonial dependence on African labor.[120]

Repatriation served a myopic, short-term urban strategy, which allowed the elder state to respond to the ebb and flow of African migration to colonial towns. Repatriation also provided the state with an ability to circumvent its own constraints. Periodic sweeps, roundups, and repatriations were less costly than social programs and urban reform. Above all, repatriation marked yet another step by the elder state to define coming-of-age. Growing up was, for the elder state, to be a rural experience. Municipal authorities reaffirmed the power of parents and kin over the young, reifying the kind of generational order they imagined existed between boys and their elders. The practice never needed to function perfectly; it needed only to provide families with repeated opportunities to exert discipline over their sons. However, young vagabonds were one thing—recidivist thieves, house burglars, and murderers were quite another. And as young men seriously tested the boundaries of acceptable behavior, the elder state had to craft new, more intrusive ways to control them.

4 ⤺ "The Old Way . . . the Only Way"

Corporal Punishment and a Community of Disciplinarians

> *The Cat must go, and we must search*
> *For milder substitutes*
> *Since neither English cane nor birch*
> *Our local climate suits*
> *A weal upon a dusky skin*
> *Would be the worst of blots;*
> *The weapon needed must be thin,*
> *And free from joints or knots.*
> *Altho' our aim is to deter*
> *Our convicts when we've got 'em,*
> *Our consciences are tenderer*
> *Than any native's bottom.*[1]

ON 15 MARCH 1931, when he should have been in class at the Indian School, Amritlal Monji took his father's motorcycle without permission out for a spin along Nairobi's Canal Street. Joyriding through town, the thirteen-year-old was arrested by police and held at the station until his father made bail. The next day, he and his father went before resident magistrate Frederick Gamble, who read aloud the charges: driving a motorcycle without a license, permit, or silencer to reduce noise pollution.[2] The typical sentence for traffic offenses like these was a fine. Magistrate Gamble turned to Amritlal's father, Hirji, a local mechanic, and asked if he was willing to pay his son's fine. He was not. Hirji's refusal to pay put Gamble in a legal conundrum. Fining young men was common enough in Kenya, but under the penal code, failure to pay resulted in imprisonment. Without Hirji's help, Amritlal would surely face prison time. Rather than risk the boy's possible imprisonment, Gamble ordered him caned. Since the colony's earliest years, magistrates had loathed sending young people to prison. Behind the bars of a Nairobi or Mombasa jail cell, officials feared that adults instructed young inmates in criminal craftsmanship and loose morals, stripping them of their innocence and initiating them into a malformed quasi-adulthood.[3] Instead, Gamble ordered the boy to receive four strokes for each offense, a total of twelve—the maximum penalty for anyone under the age of sixteen.[4] The sentence was to be carried out that day, as soon as the guards could escort Amritlal to the Nairobi prison.

Corporal punishment was commonplace in Kenya. European settlers bruised houseboys and harvesters with steel-toed boots. Schoolteachers "broke" pupils' backs to mold their minds. African chiefs conducted forced labor to the cadence of the *kiboko*.[5] African fathers raised walking sticks to absentminded herdsboys. And colonial magistrates sentenced thousands of young Africans to caning for crimes like bicycle theft and breach of contract. In Kenya and elsewhere in Africa, as young Africans and Asians like Amritlal came into contact with Europeans, the diversity of individuals and institutions laying claim to disciplinary violence expanded. The colonial state relied on corporal punishment to broadcast its authority, often in military barracks, schools, courts, and penal institutions.[6] Colonial courts were especially devoted to physical violence as a method of discipline and an alternative to imprisonment, fines, or other forms of punishment.[7] Courts in many British African colonies, from native courts in Northern Nigeria and Uganda to magistrate courts in Gold Coast, sentenced offenders to corporal punishment.[8] In colonies with white settlement, like Kenya and South Africa, a "cult of the cat" formed to humiliate disobedient African chiefs, establish racial hierarchies, and emasculate male sexuality to salve fears of black peril.[9] Moreover, the use of the *kiboko* in Kenya and the similar *sjambok* whip in South Africa were common methods to coerce and discipline male African laborers.[10] Corporal punishment became an "essential pedagogical tool" of the colonial encounter, teaching through physical violence.[11]

African parents and elder figures also relied on corporal punishment to correct immaturity, negotiate boundaries between generations, and exercise senior authority.[12] It separated men from boys and adults from children, situated them on opposing sides of the kiboko, and established the authority of one over the other. While fathers and elder menfolk in Kenya relied on a diverse disciplinary repertoire to correct the behavior of young men, corporal punishment was a common feature of growing up in African societies.[13] As T. Dunbar Moodie argues for South Africa, "Being beaten was a completely normal part of growing up male."[14] So, too, was it normal for African males coming of age in colonial Kenya.

Colonial rule brought young men under the watchful eyes of a wider community of disciplinarians. Those with the right to beat a boy, once exclusively African parents and communities, began to include missionaries, schoolteachers, employers, chiefs, and the colonial state. Each of these disciplinarians considered physical violence an appropriate form of punishment for young males. In fact, corporal punishment of the young was not a distinctly "colonial" or "African" form of punishment, it was also used in Britain and much of the world in the early twentieth century.[15] In Kenya, it linked an ever-expanding network of African and non-African adult actors and institutions wielding physical violence in competing yet complementary ways, all in an effort to exert authority over young men.

Colonial courts and domestic households were two of the most common settings in Kenya of this age-defined and gendered form of physical violence. Prior to the 1920s, colonial courts began curtailing the use of judicial corporal punishment on African adults. However, caning became one of the principal methods of punishing crimes, such as theft, committed by males, mostly Africans, under the age of sixteen. A review of 10,410 cases of juvenile caning, collected for the years 1928 through 1955, reveals how magistrates used corporal punishment during this period. The registers provide a wealth of information such as where young men were caned, why they were caned, and how often they were caned. African men who felt the crack of a court-ordered caning recall the physical and psychological pain as well as the procedure and formality, rendering it both intimate and impersonal. They also readily admit that it did not affect their long-term behavior. Those same boys strapped to a caning form by order of colonial courts had also received ineffective blows from fathers' walking sticks at home. Those men who experienced corporal punishment both at home and by the elder state often juxtapose them. They do not claim that the performance and execution of state-ordered caning and familial beatings were the same. Yet they recognized that both relied on physical violence to confront their delinquency. No matter the setting or the hand holding the instrument of pain, they understood that the actions of the elder state and elder kin were part of a broader network of adult authority aiming to punish their wrongdoing and reexert control over them.

After his trial, Amritlal Monji was escorted to the Nairobi prison, where he received twelve strokes of the cane. At the time of Amritlal's sentence, corporal punishment was one of the most common ways the state disciplined young male offenders. That year, Amritlal was one of 192 young men beaten by order of the court. Physical violence as punishment was one of the hallmarks of East Africans' encounters with Europeans. In the late nineteenth century, missionaries, explorers, and traders whose caravans crisscrossed the region used violence to keep African porters moving. Ewart Grogan, who later settled in Kenya, flogged porters who stole supplies as he traveled near Rwanda in 1898. When thirty others tried to desert him, he took out his rifle and shot at them.[16] Lashes from a kiboko whip, blows from the butt of a rifle, and outright murder on the caravan roads of East Africa gradually turned to the violence of British conquest after the turn of the century. Marching westward along the main road linking Uganda to the coast, the British, alongside African soldiers and Maasai auxiliaries, raided and harried communities into submission: burning villages, pillaging livestock, and beating those who stood in their way.[17]

To keep soldiers in line, British officers relied on corporal punishment. Commanding officers viewed flogging as a necessary tool to forge Africans into weapons of war. A soldier in the King's African Rifles could receive up to twenty lashes, or worse, for even the slightest mistake during training.[18] Magistrates, provincial administrators, African chiefs, and Muslim judges also used physical violence to discipline laborers, punish criminals, and assert their tenuous authority in the early years of colonialism. Under the laws governing the East Africa Protectorate, the Indian Penal Code allowed "wide-reaching" use of corporal punishment, and the 1897 Native Courts Regulation permitted magistrates to sentence Africans to up to one hundred lashes.[19] Corporal punishment had very quickly become the state's "ordinary corrective" for "delinquent natives."[20]

Physical violence was also a part of everyday life on the estates and in the homes of European settlers. The white community in Kenya remained perpetually critical of the state's capacity to ensure its safety. Settlers often took matters into their own hands. Their brand of frontier justice was especially brutal; they "understood the value of a well-placed punch or crack of the *kiboko*. Violence helped them control Africans, and bolstered prestige."[21] They viewed the public spectacle of beating their domestic servants, cooks, and field hands to be as natural as a parent disciplining children. Infantilizing Africans in this way, settlers used age to permit them to beat anyone they wished, no matter how old. They camouflaged their extralegal use of violence as a normal part of race and age-relations.[22]

Kenya could be a place of unspeakable violence—but not without limits. As soon as the protectorate sanctioned corporal punishment, it curtailed it. In 1897 and again in 1902, secretary of state for the colonies Joseph Chamberlain ordered all territories to submit annual returns of corporal punishment for Parliament's perusal. Chamberlain worried that the colonies would become too dependent on an inexpensive disciplinary tool that, if used too liberally, might result in costly, scandalous exposure.[23] Officials in the East Africa Protectorate complied, submitting detailed registers of adult and juvenile corporal punishment. When Colonial Office staff found irregularities or illegalities in the registers, they badgered magistrates to sentence offenders more carefully.[24] The protectorate's attorney general and chief justice also reviewed such cases and warned magistrates about troublesome rulings. Collecting and reviewing registers did not, however, prevent painful sentences carried out months before or the embarrassment the Colonial Office suffered when truly gruesome floggings came to light.

And flogging scandals did indeed rock the protectorate prior to and shortly after World War I. In each grisly case, a settler had beaten an African employee to death, often demanding other white and African employees to assist him. Although found guilty, the floggers' sentences were woefully inadequate.[25] These cases prompted the Colonial Office to further press the government in Kenya to reform its legal codes and restrict its use of corporal punishment. Pushing back, officials in Kenya refused to abolish corporal punishment, but they did place it under greater scrutiny. In 1905 and again in 1911, the protectorate's high court sent circulars to magistrates and provincial administrators, who also served as judges in the districts, warning that corporal punishment must be reserved for only the most serious or exceptional cases. A year later, the high court stripped district commissioners, African chiefs, and Muslim judges of their ability to sentence anyone to a flogging.[26] This was not the case in other parts of colonial Africa, where traditional authorities like Ovamboland kings and headmen used corporal punishment to punish the crimes of young men.[27] Of course, the rulings in the East Africa Protectorate did not stop some chiefs or provincial administrators from occasionally using physical violence to maintain order in their districts.

In 1913, Governor Henry Conway Belfield introduced further restrictions, outlawing the birch rod, cat-o'-nine-tails, and whip in favor of the rattan cane.[28] Rattan, a type of palm resembling bamboo, had long been used in South and Southeast Asia for corporal punishment because of its flexibility and durability. Kenya began importing rattan canes from India where they were manufactured to certain specifications. The governor ordered two different canes produced for the colony, one for adults, which was forty-two inches long, and another for young people, which was shorter and thinner.[29] As the courts banned government officials from punishing offenders with whips and birch rods, the term "caning" became common parlance for corporal punishment. Even the Kiswahili word *kiboko* came to refer to the rattan cane rather than the animal-hide whips of the past. The cane and the kiboko became synonymous with corporal punishment. Today, when Kenyans speak of corporal punishment or their memories of it in the colonial past, they use the words *kiboko* and *caning* interchangeably.[30]

The restrictions established by the high court and Governor Belfield had a remarkable effect on the number of court-ordered floggings in the protectorate. Between 1911 and 1912, 778 Africans were beaten by the state with the birch rod or cat-o'-nine-tails, about 7 percent of the 10,974 Africans convicted by the court. The following year, after the restrictions went into effect, the rate of corporal punishment in the courts dropped to 346, a mere 4 percent of the 8,418 Africans convicted.[31] Yet the courts never questioned whether "violence was illegitimate in the colonial project, but rather how much violence could or should be used—or how much violence could be used without creating a scandal."[32] Nor did they tackle the violence that took place in workplaces or on settler estates.

Ever so slowly, though, debate emerged within the colony over the effectiveness of corporal punishment, a debate that would ultimately push the flogging of adults aside in favor of its use on the young. Just such a discussion occurred among the members of the 1923 Native Punishment Commission, whose purpose was to review the array of punishments that could be inflicted on Africans. Its members included Governor Northey, Chief Justice Barth, several other officials, and members of the settler, religious, and Asian communities. The commission agreed that corporal punishment should remain on the books in the colony; however, there was some disagreement as to whether it was effective. Those in favor argued that it allowed the state to work around its own inadequacies, which included a lack of prisons. They also believed caning was "inexpensive, that it is summary, that the native is a child and should, therefore, be punished as a child and that it is effective."[33] They argued further that African laborers and criminals would rather be flogged than fined or incarcerated. "It is a matter of common knowledge and everyday practice in the Colony that a native given the choice of going before a Magistrate or accepting a thrashing from his master for some detected offence will often choose the latter, and cheerfully undergo it without any loss of self-respect, or of the esteem of his fellows."[34] Dissenting members of the commission argued that corporal punishment had a morally deleterious effect on convicts, magistrates, and prison officials. Others questioned whether Africans could even be "flogged to a higher morality."[35]

While the commission debated the future of adult caning, it never questioned the necessity of using it on the young. All the committee members believed the rattan cane was a suitable disciplinary instrument for young offenders under the age of sixteen; that the young could in fact be "flogged to a higher morality." The commission went so far as to make recommendations on the size of the cane, the number of strokes, and procedures to be followed in cases involving young people.[36] In the years following the commission, the number of adult canings ordered by the courts continued to decline, while the caning of young offenders increased. A year after the report, the number of young Africans receiving corporal punishment surpassed the number of adults for the first time.[37] Between 1905 and 1925, the state relegated adult caning to the margins of the penal system, reserved for male sex offenders, unruly prison inmates, and the occasional undisciplined soldier. Meanwhile, the rattan cane quickly became the centerpiece of the elder state's efforts to punish young male Africans under the age of sixteen.

Historians have rightly argued that the persistence of corporal punishment in Kenya and elsewhere in colonial Africa lay in the virulent racism that underwrote colonial rule.[38] Europeans believed Africans were mentally underdeveloped and therefore must be punished like children. There can be no doubt that such racism reverberated through rattan. Yet these ideas also underscored the belief that corporal punishment was an age-specific form of discipline, one ideally suited for the young. African children were, after all, still children regardless of their race. And when the young committed crimes, British officials believed that the cane was an ideal punishment.

The growing reliance on caning in Kenya was not simply part of Britons' pursuit of racial superiority; rather, caning had a long, storied place in their judicial system. Physical violence against the young was an integral part of British juvenile justice and schooling. Even as the flogging of adults in British prisons declined after the Whipping Act of 1861, as well as of soldiers twenty years later, the young continued to be beaten by the state.[39] British magistrates used corporal punishment to discipline those they believed to be beyond parental control.[40] An officer of the court wielding a birch rod assumed the role a parent seemed unable to fulfill. Moreover, rather than sentence young Britons to long terms in government-run reformatories or continual visits from probation officers at the expense of taxpayers, a swift, salutary stroke of the cane was believed cheap and effective.[41] Although the number of young people receiving corporal punishment in Britain shrank, it was not until 1948 that Parliament finally abolished its use on young offenders. Caning died a slow death in the Western world. It was not a premodern form of punishment banished by high-modernist methods of discipline to far-flung imperial territories.[42] The birch rod was not abandoned in Britain until 1998.[43]

Back in Kenya, by the 1930s, 80 percent of all court-ordered canings involved young men. Moreover, between 1932 and 1948, more than 40 percent of all juveniles convicted by colonial courts were sentenced to corporal punishment.[44] After World War II, the rate of juvenile corporal punishment nearly doubled as the state responded to rising levels of crime, migration, urban overcrowding, and rural unrest. Hundreds of juvenile canings became thousands in the 1950s as district commissioners in Central Province used their enhanced powers under the state of emergency to beat Gikuyu young men suspected of participating in what they believed to be an anticolonial uprising known as Mau Mau.[45] Over the course of colonial rule, thousands of boys and young men felt the crack of the cane. And each year, as more and more African young men were beaten by the state, corporal punishment came under greater government surveillance, sentences became proceduralized and medicalized, and statistics were recorded and scrutinized.

THE CHARACTER OF CANING

Once resident magistrate Gamble ordered thirteen-year-old Amritlal beaten, the case was destined for a unique bureaucratic afterlife. A clerk would be required to add Amritlal's name, age, offense, and sentence to a register of all judicial canings that involved offenders under the age of sixteen. By the end of 1931, Amritlal was twenty-fourth on a list of 192. Magistrate Gamble's name, the location of the court, and the attending medical officer would also be recorded. The clerk would then post the register to London for review by the Colonial Office where Amritlal became a carefully scrutinized statistic. His caning eventually became one of 10,410 cases reported to the Colonial Office between 1928 and 1955.[46] The Colonial Office perused these cases for irregularities, mistakes, and whiffs of scandal. When they discovered them, they pushed the government in Kenya to be more mindful of its errors. Yet the details in these registers reveal how colonial magistrates used corporal punishment and age to discipline young offenders.[47]

First, judicial caning in Kenya was a gendered form of punishment. In Kenya, as in Great Britain, a male state differentiated between male and female bodies and the forms of punishment those bodies could receive.[48]

Caning was simply not suitable for girls. When it occurred in the empire, controversy stirred. In 1914, two African women from Northern Nigeria were stripped and beaten in public by order of the colonial administration.[49] When word reached London, the Colonial Office complained and officials in Nigeria defended their decision, claiming that corporal punishment of women was a customary practice in that part of the colony. Of course, the Colonial Office never questioned the use of corporal punishment, merely its application to a woman's body. Few Britons wanted to see a woman stripped, strapped to a caning form, and flogged at home, much less hear about it taking place in public in the empire.[50] For colonial officials in Kenya, issues of gendered respectability and physical differences between female and male bodies mattered less than the different forms of power exerted over them. For the state to order the caning of girls betrayed the gendered authority of fathers and husbands, a responsibility the elder state dared not question.

The names of African girls were very rarely entered into court registers of young offenders in Kenya. From 1938 to 1939 and then 1945 to 1950, there were roughly 6,494 cases of young Africans that came before the colonial courts, especially the juvenile court established in Nairobi after World War II. Of these, only forty-two were girls.[51] Unlike Nigeria, magistrates and police in Kenya did not bring African girls before the courts as juveniles.[52] This does not mean that African girls were free of delinquency or exempt from prosecution. The colonial state defined female and male maturities differently. For African girls, womanhood arrived with reproductive maturity and then marriage, signified in some communities by initiation.[53] As for boys, the colonial state often defined maturity by labor discipline and submission to law and order. It is possible that many girls and young women were tried as adults. When colonial magistrates did discipline young women—often for crimes like prostitution, beer brewing, and hawking—they were punished with fines or returned to their families in the countryside. Fines and repatriation represented a dual assault on a young woman's economic and spatial mobility and an attempt to augment the patriarchal power of fathers and husbands. Debates about the control of girls, their behavior, and their punishment fell most often to elder men sitting on local councils.[54]

In addition to gender, race played a role in corporal punishment. The vast majority of young men caned by the colonial state were Africans, and only a handful of Arab and Asian young men received corporal punishment. Amritlal Monji was part of a small cohort of Asians caned during the colonial period, and his experience would ultimately differ in some ways from those of African young men. In very rare cases, magistrates sentenced young European offenders to caning.[55] Most young European males encountered corporal punishment at school. There, the sons of settlers and colonial officers were subject to the same form of discipline as students in African and Asian schools. Use of the birch rod by headmasters and prefects at the Prince of Wales School and other European schools in the colony continued well into the 1940s.[56] However, the disparity between the numbers of Africans and non-Africans subjected to court-ordered physical violence illustrates that the rattan cane was indeed an instrument of racialized violence.

Age mattered in corporal punishment cases too. From 1928 to 1955, British colonial magistrates reserved the rattan cane for young men they believed to be around thirteen years of age, around the average age of circumcision. Thirteen was well below the upper legal limit of sixteen provided for under the penal code. Corporal punishment became a way to define age, a method to punish boys on the cusp of manhood. It allowed magistrates to separate out those for whom the sharp shock of pain might still serve as a deterrent from those too young to possess an understanding of right from wrong or those too old and incorrigible.

Yet determining whether or not an offender was sixteen or thirteen at the time of the crime was virtually impossible. Most Africans did not track their numeric age along the Christian calendar, and, therefore, neither the young man nor the magistrate presiding over the case knew his precise biological age. Furthermore, colonial officials had no tried-and-true way to determine African age to a legal certainty. Various tests were devised to do so, from searching for armpit hair in the 1920s to X-rays of molars and epiphyses in the 1950s.[57] A more common method to determine age was to examine for genital circumcision among boys whose communities practiced it during initiation. Some magistrates requested medical inspections to certify whether offenders had been circumcised, then used this information to determine the age, as well as the type and severity of the punishment. However, relying on circumcision was unreliable. The introduction of Christianity and education, the spread of hospitals and dispensaries, and the intervention of provincial administrators had lowered the age of male circumcision. Some magistrates understood this and boasted that they rarely requested the assistance of a medical officer, preferring to simply eyeball the young offender's age.[58] Yet circumcision and medical inspection did provide a little evidence with which magistrates performed some educated guesswork.

Boys even used their foreskins to get themselves out of trouble. In his memoir of growing up on a European settler's estate in Rift Valley, Muga Gicaru recalled being rounded up by police at the local market. Under suspicion of burglary, Muga and several men were taken to a local police station. Muga watched as police interrogated and then beat two of the men with a kiboko. As Muga looked on, the other men with whom he had been arrested quietly encouraged him to use his age to get out of being beaten. "Say you are a boy," they whispered. "Say you are uncircumcised . . . too young to carry a pass." When the police officers called Muga into the interrogation room, he walked straight up to them and dropped his trousers. "Before the white officer and his colleagues had time to say anything, I let them see exhibit number one to confirm that I was uninitiated. This was conclusive evidence! I was a boy, and as such I was no subject to pass laws. The only word I said was 'mtoto—boy.'"[59] The policemen exchanged glances and ordered Muga to leave and not get caught loitering again. Muga had learned a valuable lesson from his Gikuyu cellmates: age mattered to the elder state, and nothing proved a young man's age better than having faced the knife. Unfortunately for Muga, his cheek earned him a single lash of the kiboko before he left—for the audacity of exposing himself to a white man.

Male, African, and around the age of thirteen—this was the typical portfolio of those offenders most often caned by order of the colonial state. In addition to their gender, race, and age, they shared similar criminal vitae. If in fact magistrates relied on a single dominant feature to sentence a young man to corporal punishment, it was the type of crime an offender committed rather than his age. The traffic charges against Amritlal were relatively rare among Africans. A young African male zipping through Nairobi on a motorcycle would have certainly been charged with more than failing to produce a permit. In the early 1920s, the rattan cane was most commonly used for a variety of labor-related crimes such as absenteeism, desertion, and failing to carry a work pass.[60] But by 1928 and until 1952, nearly 60 percent of young men sentenced to caning were convicted of crimes against property. Young thieves made up 43 percent of all court-ordered juvenile canings, while thefts by domestic servants represented about 11 percent and stock thieves nearly 5 percent.[61]

The connection between convictions for theft and sentences of caning was, in part, influenced by the ways in which magistrates differentiated the severity of certain crimes and the limited number of punishments at their disposal. The three most common forms of punishment for juveniles during the colonial period were repatriation, corporal punishment, and incarceration in a reformatory, later known as an approved school. Prior to World War II, first-time offenders or those committing minor offenses like trespassing or traveling to towns were often cautioned and discharged. After the war, as juvenile migration to towns like Nairobi and Nakuru increased, magistrates used repatriation orders more frequently. Young men convicted of more serious crimes, such as murder, rape, and habitual housebreaking, were institutionalized. Caning fell between slaps on the wrist, free rides home, and years of incarceration. Given the limited space at approved schools and the perception among colonial officials that repatriation was a costly, colossal failure, corporal punishment became an indispensable, alternative form of punishment.[62]

The state's shallow punitive repertoire became a rallying cry for magistrates and officials in Kenya. To them, corporal punishment was a necessity amid the financial and logistical constraints of colonial rule. In 1939, when Malcolm MacDonald, secretary of state for the colonies, joined the long-standing Colonial Office tradition of trying to convince Kenya to abolish corporal punishment, Chief Justice Joseph Sheridan indignantly replied: "Abolish it and one would ask what alternative is there available for offences not of a serious nature. Imprisonment is unsuitable if only for reasons of undesirable association with those imprisoned for serious crime [and] detention in an approved school for a period of three years may be an excessive punishment."[63] In Sheridan's view, without caning, punishment in Kenya was either too lenient or too severe. Magistrates had taken an approach to corporal punishment similar to that of their counterparts in other corners of the British Empire. In late nineteenth-century India, magistrates explained away their reliance on caning as the result of the paucity of juvenile-specific punishments at their disposal.[64]

Just as the type of punishment reflected the seriousness of a young man's crime, so, too, did the severity of his caning. From 1928 to 1955, magistrates showed little creativity in their sentences. The average beating of a young offender was seven strokes, which remained remarkably consistent over time. Two houseboys stealing two fountain pens twenty years apart were likely to receive the same number of strokes. Magistrates did sentence some types of theft to harsher penalties than others. Stock thieves and house burglars received an average of nine strokes. Minor offenses, not involving theft, usually resulted in the lightest canings. Train station beggars, alleyway gamblers, and unlicensed Lake Victoria trout fishermen, to name a few, received six strokes or less.

The relationship between the severity of the crime and its corresponding punishment underscored the seriousness with which magistrates and police took crimes against property. In the words of one police commissioner, housebreaking was "perhaps the most definite criminal act of all."[65] Although most arrests during the colonial period were for minor offenses such as restrictions on labor and disorderly behavior, police and magistrates consistently focused their efforts on preventing and prosecuting burglary and stock theft.[66] At the heart of concern about housebreaking lay the fierce anxieties of the colony's propertied class, namely European and Asian families. Almost immediately after their arrival, European settlers demanded that the Kenya police protect their personal property and security.[67] In response, the police mainly serviced areas of European settlement and investigated crimes against property.[68] Magistrates, too, did their part to alleviate European fears. They reserved their most painful punishment for young men who threatened to tear the thin veil separating personal space, wealth, and security suspended between Kenya's multiracial communities.

The influence of European settlers on the nature of corporal punishment grows when considering the physical and legal geography of caning. Between 1928 and 1933, one-third of all juvenile canings originated in courts in Rift Valley Province, especially Nakuru, Naivasha, Eldoret, and Kitale — all major areas of white settlement.[69] The municipality of Nairobi contributed a further third of all juvenile corporal punishment during this period. After World War II, Rift Valley continued to contribute the most juveniles sentenced to corporal punishment, followed closely behind by Central Province. It was not until the 1950s during the state of emergency and the military campaign against Mau Mau that Central Province, especially Nyeri District, overtook canings in the Rift Valley.[70]

While most young men sentenced to flogging went before courts in Rift Valley and Nairobi, they also shared a similar legal geography. A majority of caning sentences emanated from resident and first-class courts. Resident magistrates held court in the larger towns of Kenya, such as Nairobi, Mombasa, Nakuru, Naivasha, and Eldoret, and oversaw cases from the surrounding area. First-class courts, often presided over by provincial administrators, handled cases in more rural areas of European settlement, such as Kitale, Kapsabet, and Kericho.[71] The prevalence of juvenile caning cases in these courts reveals that many of these cases likely involved young men arrested in towns and trading centers where they were most likely to meet non-African populations and police. The presence of white settlers in a particular area greatly increased a young African's probability of being caned when brought before a magistrate. Arrests made in areas of white settlement and Nairobi represented nearly two-thirds of the total number of young people sentenced to judicial caning in Kenya.

Most settlers took matters into their own hands. They shunned the courts, raising their fists and cracking the kiboko to punish crimes committed on their property. They valued corporal punishment because pain matched, in their eyes, the severity of a young man's offense: failures to labor well, observe authority, or respect personal property. Only a few settlers and employers turned to the courts to settle crimes that had occurred in their homes, businesses, or fields. Caning as punishment for labor indiscipline on settler estates served the immediacies of capitalism well. Repatriating undisciplined laborers to their home villages or incarcerating them for three years in an approved school jeopardized labor contracts and required employers to find replacement labor. On tea, coffee, pyrethrum, and sisal farms, juvenile labor was a cheap yet prized resource. Pain was a swift, expeditious form of urban and frontier colonial justice. A negligent herder or thieving servant could be caned and back in the grazing field or kitchen by midafternoon.

PAIN AND PROCEDURE

When the guard arrived at the courthouse, he loaded Amritlal Monji onto a van bound for Nairobi prison. Once they arrived, he led Amritlal into a room where three men waited: chief prison officer Partridge, sub-assistant surgeon Siriram Thind, and an unnamed African prison guard. Each man had a different role in the procedure. Partridge oversaw the caning, Thind certified whether the boy was medically fit to receive the strokes, and the African prison guard carried out the sentence.[72] In the room, Amritlal noticed a table, a towel, and a long, thin brown stick. The instrument was made of rattan, three and a half feet long, and three-eighths of an inch thick. It was designed to inflict pain. If Amritlal had not felt fear before, he certainly did now.

Partridge instructed the young man to take down his trousers and bend over the table. Amritlal could not, would not, do it. The officer called four African prison guards to seize him, remove his trousers, and hold him down prostrate against the table. Struggling against the guards, Amritlal felt the towel, cool and wet from antiseptic, draped over his buttocks. He heard someone step into position behind him, then the whistle of rattan slicing through the air, and finally the crack as it struck him. After the searing pain of twelve strokes, the wet towel was removed and the four guards eased their grip. Partridge ordered him to pull up his trousers and leave the prison quickly or he would receive another five.[73]

Amritlal's encounter with the cane bore a striking resemblance to the memories of Africans who experienced corporal punishment as young men during the colonial period. After fleeing the violence of an abusive uncle, Harry Joseph Kimanji became a street boy in late 1940s Nairobi. He spent his days rummaging through garbage bins for food, stealing clothes hanging on the line to dry, and sleeping in culverts. Nairobi police arrested him many times, but it was after his second arrest that he first encountered the cane. "They told me to lie down on the table, and then caned me on my buttocks. They would not beat you on your ankles because they did not want to harm you, they beat you on the buttocks, which would grow swollen, but they would be fine."[74] He received five strokes and was released back onto the streets, only to be arrested, tried, and caned on two more occasions. During his third beating, officials applied a wet towel and salt to his backside, which were used to "make more pain." Gabriel Kahugu and Peter Mwarangu, streetwise contemporaries of Harry Joseph, also found themselves hauled before the court and sentenced to corporal punishment in Nairobi. Both men lost count of the number of times they had been arrested and sentenced to corporal punishment, but each remembered being "laid on our stomachs, and beaten on our buttocks."[75]

The canings of Amritlal, Harry Joseph, and thousands of other young men were harrowing experiences marked by physical and psychological pain. For some offenders, the pain of the cane was enough to correct their behavior, if only temporarily. James Ng'ang'a recalled that the pain from his caning in 1950s Gilgil was so great that for a time, he returned to school and obeyed his parents. He and his friends "feared the pain."[76] But after a while, he resumed playing truant from school, smoking cigarettes, and harassing young women. Indeed, the potency of caning should not be overestimated. Harry Joseph recalled that despite numerous canings, it never severely wounded him or made him bleed.[77] Moses Nyatia, who grew up in Nyeri and experienced court-ordered caning in the 1950s, recalls that "you felt pain, but after a while the pain disappeared, so you wouldn't mind."[78]

Although painful, canings were also private and highly regulated procedures, offering no public spectacle of African humiliation from which the state drew its authority. Both corporal and capital punishments had been moved indoors, away from the gawking eyes of spectators.[79] The notion of private, violent punishment arose in late nineteenth-century Europe and North America as governments began to view public executions and floggings with certain embarrassment.[80] In colonial Africa, the public nature of capital and corporal punishments worried British officials, who recognized the contradiction between public displays of state violence and the civilizing mission.[81] Concealing the cane and muffling the sounds of suffering, the colonial state declared it a modern, "humane" punishment. Magistrates and other officials went to great lengths to regulate and isolate the location where the young were beaten. Back rooms of prisons and police stations were common sites of judicial caning.

Specific rules were to be followed during a sentence. In many but not all sentences of corporal punishment, three individuals had to be present: a prison or police official, a medical officer or surgeon, and a prison guard.

The relationships between the purveyors of corporal punishment exemplified the hierarchical and segregated nature of colonial rule. And, in a perverse way, these canings evoked a distorted multiracial community coming together to exercise discipline over unruly young men. The man endowed with the most power, the white prison officer, served as a witness and record-keeper; though, in the earliest days of colonial rule, he would have carried out the flogging himself. Yet, even as a bystander, the caning of another man could have a deep effect on an official's psyche. In the early days of colonial rule, Henry Seaton, who had served as a district official in the East Africa Protectorate, witnessed the flogging of an African prisoner at the Kismayu prison in Jubaland, modern-day southern Somalia. He had been brought to the prison by one of his fellow assistant district commissioners on a procedural matter. In an attempt to reduce the severity of corporal punishment, the chief justice had recently recommended that all new magistrates witness a caning before having to mete it out themselves. As Seaton watched his colleague strike a prisoner twenty-four times, he found himself overcome with emotion:

> I felt sickly and beastly—so sick and so beastly, I could not think clearly. Was it right? Could it possibly be right to do such a thing? I forgot that I'd been beaten, that the head of my prep. school had taken a delight in wielding a cane on my bottom and on that of many another boy. At that moment I felt convinced that sudden rage could be the only possible extenuation for the crime of causing pain. When blood was cold, as ours was, such punishment smacked of torture. No wonder the [chief justice] had issued that circular.[82]

Simply bearing witness to a caning could twist an official's stomach, maybe even remind him of the pain he had felt as a chastised schoolboy back home. Present, too, was a surgeon, most often an Asian, who provided specialized services by inspecting the boy and his wounds to determine whether or not a sentence should continue. The dirty work, one with its own psychological repercussions, fell to the African prison guard, striking the offender again and again. The most powerless person in the room, the young, typically African offender, witnessed representatives of the colonial community coming together to exert discipline over him.

As a result of these procedures, officials came to believe that the caning of young men represented a merciful, compassionate form of discipline. Henry Seaton came away from the flogging he witnessed in the Kismayu prison wondering "if a single High Court judge in England had ever seen the cat in operation," and knew "that that punishment, worse than what I had just watched, was inflicted in English prisons."[83] Because Seaton had witnessed and later carried out such brutality, he believed he understood it more clearly. His counterparts in Britain knew nothing of the violence to which they subjected offenders, and, therefore, its practice in British prisons was an even worse infliction than in East Africa. This idea reemerged throughout the colonial period, as officials defended the practice from an increasingly irked Colonial Office. In 1945, commissioner of prisons Heaton observed several juvenile canings and argued, "I have witnessed the infliction of corporal punishment with all the instruments enumerated above and I have no hesitation in stating that in my opinion the instruments in Great Britain are far more severe in their application than the 'school boy' instruments used in this Colony."[84] Heaton's comparison between Kenya's rattan cane and Britain's birch rod tried to reverse the perception that punishment in the colonies was more brutal than in the metropole. Heaton claimed that the colonial efforts to proceduralize corporal punishment—limit the strokes, regulate the cane's size and shape, require the presence of a medical officer, and carry it out discretely—made it more humane than its British counterpart. These arguments became fixtures of the colonial state's numerous attempts to deflect criticism and resist efforts by the Colonial Office to abolish the punishment.

In 1950, secretary of state for the colonies Creech Jones made yet another attempt to encourage the colonies to abandon the cane. The secretary argued that with the exception of the British Commonwealth, "the greater part of the civilized world has found other methods."[85] In Kenya, a commission established to review the use of corporal punishment disputed the secretary's circular. The commission reported "the difference in severity to be so marked as to merit a different nomenclature referring to caning in Kenya as *chastisement*, to distinguish it from judicial corporal punishment as was commonly understood, for example, in Britain."[86] Ultimately, the best defense of caning in Kenya was to rebrand it.

Despite colonial claims about procedure and compassion, caning was a deeply personal, intimate experience. Gabriel Kahugu recalls that "the strokes were painful because after the beating, one of the white men applied salt that would hurt the bruises."[87] What Gabriel believes to have been salt could have been antiseptic, which was commonly used by medical personnel to prevent infection after canings.[88] The medicinal intent of the "salt" was lost on Gabriel, irrelevant in light of the additional suffering a white man caused. Corporal punishment was a personal, painful encounter with the state, made manifest by a white man rubbing "salt" into fresh wounds. As private, procedural, and medical as the state tried to make corporal punishment, the violence of the cane remained an intense physical and psychological demonstration of colonial power.

CANE AS CUSTOM

At 6:30 in the evening, Hirji Monji watched his son stumble through the door of his Canal Street home and called for Dr. Mackinnon, a well-known physician in Nairobi. Mackinnon inspected Amritlal and found "long linear scars with severe subcutaneous hemorrhages on both buttocks." The boy could neither sit nor stand. The doctor concluded that "a considerable amount of energy [had] been applied in administering the twelve strokes."[89] When word spread of the caning, it caused a sensation within the Asian community. The Indian Association sent a letter to the chief secretary condemning the government's brutality. On Sunday, 22 March, the *Kenya Daily Mail*, an Asian newspaper published out of Mombasa, ran a letter to the editor from Amritlal's father. In the letter, Hirji claimed that it had been Gamble who had refused to let him pay his son's fines and allowed African prison guards to touch and beat his boy. It was a clear case, he argued, of racial discrimination.[90]

An investigation began. Resident magistrate Gamble vigorously defended himself. "The allegation of racial discrimination on my part hardly calls for comment," he argued, "but it may be interesting to observe that I ordered a European child to be caned for an identical offence committed in respect of a motorcar."[91] The prisons department reviewed the caning and noted that officials had followed standard procedure, adding that the boy had not bled, and an Asian prison guard, not an African, had beaten him.[92] In May, the clipping from the *Kenya Daily Mail* reached the desk of Lord Passfield, secretary of state for the colonies. After reviewing the Kenyan penal code, Passfield argued that despite Gamble's assertions, his legal gymnastics were illegal. The penal code allowed caning to be used only in lieu of imprisonment, not in lieu of payment of a fine. In short, the boy's inability to pay a fine, and his father's refusal, had no bearing on the case. Amritlal should never have been beaten.[93] Passfield ordered a review of caning in the colony.

Little came of Amritlal's case. Lord Passfield's call for an inquiry merely perpetuated the policy of reviewing annual returns and highlighting irregularities long after wounds had healed. Yet, unlike the majority of young men caned by the colonial state, Amritlal had the advantage of his father's fury, literacy, and, above all, connections to the Indian Association. Hirji Monji publicized his son's pain and communicated his outrage to the highest levels of the Colonial Office. Most parents in Kenya remained uninformed or uninvolved in the courtroom proceedings or caning of their sons. Moreover, if they opposed the court's ruling, few had the ability to publicize their anger as Hirji Monji had done. Judicial corporal punishment rarely involved parents or kin; it was an encounter between young men and employees of the state.

At first glance, caning represents a contradiction in the way the elder state punished young men. Repatriation and cautionary slaps on the wrists left discipline in the hands of fathers and elders. At most, the elder state made an effort to return young offenders home to face, it hoped, parental and chiefly authority. In serious cases like burglary and assault, cases in which magistrates believed parental authority had failed, the elder state assumed full responsibility for young offenders, incarcerating them in a reformatory. The rattan cane occupied an interstitial space between the two, between augmenting parental, generational authority and sidelining it in favor of Western methods of punishment. This was the source of Hirji Monji's outrage: the colonial state had claimed his parental prerogative to punish his son, in a way unbefitting of his son's race.

In the case of Amritlal's caning, the elder state came into unanticipated tension with the Hirji household, unforeseen because many British officials believed that corporal punishment was a normal, familiar way to punish the young. Yet it was also something, they believed, that African elders understood and used on their own children; it was an African tradition as much as a British one.[94] Some Africans played a role in perpetuating this view. During a review of corporal punishment in the 1950s, Chief Waweru of the Nairobi African council argued that beating boys was "customary" among African peoples and "acted as a deterrent."[95] Along the Coast, Muslim sheikhs invoked the use of corporal punishment in sharia to promote its continued use. From this, British officials presupposed that caning was an easily communicable form of discipline that both they and members of a multiracial Kenyan community understood.[96] Unlike imprisonment, corporal punishment was not necessarily an imposition of Western disciplinary practices on African communities.

Some African intermediaries claimed that corporal punishment was a historic, traditional form of discipline. It certainly had a place within African households during the colonial period, and possibly long before. Whether parents were Gikuyu squatters in Central Province, Kipsigis herders in the Rift Valley, or Luo artisans in Nyanza, they sometimes relied on physical violence to punish their children.[97] According to Augustine Ruto, who grew up in Sotik District, "The old way of disciplining children was the cane; the only way. So, if you do not cane a child then you are not teaching."[98] Even though Augustine had been born in 1938, he understood corporal punishment as an old form of discipline, one linked to the socialization and education of the young.

At home, and in the village, boys could be beaten for a wide range of misdeeds. Most men who grew up in the 1930s and 1940s recall that corporal punishment most often came following their failure to properly herd livestock. The list of possible violations was long. A boy who slept while the herd grazed, a boy who encouraged bulls to fight, a boy who let cattle stray into a neighbor's farm, a boy who allowed herds to mix, or a boy who lost a goat or a sheep could all be beaten.[99] Children could also be given corporal punishment for fighting too fiercely with one another or stealing from parents or neighbors. A father's surveillance knew no bounds in the village and grazing fields. Kinfolk and neighbors had the right to strike any child they saw misbehaving. "Anybody could punish you whenever you committed a mistake. Everyone had the right to discipline a boy."[100] The discipline of young men was a community responsibility. In some cases, a boy who received a few strokes from a passerby could expect a second set from his father when he arrived home. Word in the village spread quickly.

Nevertheless, corporal punishment had limits at home. Fathers did not sport cat-o'-nine-tails, rattan canes, or other instruments specifically designed for punishment. Instead, they reached for the nearest switch.[101] Among the Maasai, some spaces were off-limits to elder authority, especially the manyatta, where warrior moran lived together. As Waller argues, Maasai elders sought to remove moran from their manyattas and return them to their fathers' homesteads, where they could be more easily disciplined.[102] In addition, some men claim that a beating could last for some time and the strokes could be "innumerable" or "many, up to twenty times."[103] Gabriel Kahugu, a former Nairobi street boy, bitterly remembered the painful blows from a prison guard, but these were sufferable compared to the physical and emotional pain he experienced at the hands of his father before fleeing to Nairobi.[104] Punishment at home could be a violent affair. Colonial restrictions and procedures for caning had no jurisdiction in a father's household.

Furthermore, men recall that corporal punishment was an age-specific punishment. After a boy's initiation, they argued, corporal punishment ended. Especially among those communities practicing male circumcision, a father or elder could not beat an initiated young man. Facing the knife bravely had earned him that respect.[105] Instead, to punish the initiated and circumcised, "your words would be the cane."[106] Young men were expected to display a greater level of self-discipline after initiation, and, in return, adults drew from a less violent reservoir of punishment. In much the same way, British magistrates often relied on male circumcision to determine whether an offender should be caned. However, the practice and ideas about initiation, age, and discipline became increasingly ambiguous during the colonial encounter. Children were initiated earlier and earlier. Their time in seclusion in which elders instructed them in codes of conduct shortened or, in some cases, disappeared.[107] Elders began to question whether such young initiates were equipped with the ability to weigh right and wrong. Whether fathers and elders breached past disciplinary norms and resorted to beating undisciplined young men after they had been initiated is not known. But if there was uncertainty over age, initiation, and discipline, then it is possible.

The disciplinary power of fathers and kin shifted the farther their sons traveled from home or the more wealth they accumulated in their work. Although many young men believed they might have eluded the authority of parents and chiefs, they quickly encountered new disciplinary regimens. The arrival of missionaries, settlers, police, and colonial courts dramatically expanded the settings in which corporal punishment occurred. One of the first encounters young men had with corporal punishment outside their homes was in school. Headmasters relied on physical violence to maintain discipline in their classrooms. John Osawa recalls that he and other boys were caught between violence at home and school. Boys often attended school, he argued, because they grew bored of herding livestock and fed up with their fathers' floggings. Yet, when they faced the cane at school, they promptly returned to the grazing fields only to cause mischief there, earn a beating, and wind up back before the headmaster yet again.[108] They found themselves trapped between competing yet complementary disciplinary regimens.

Living on or near European estates also offered boys and young men a whole host of opportunities to cause mischief and run afoul of settlers and police. Moses Nyatia recalls that living near Europeans in Nyeri had its pleasures and pitfalls. As a child, "we herded our animals around this area which was occupied by white families. We would steal their children's bicycles and toy pistols and ate fruits from their yards." Moses and his friends would then ride the bicycles around town, and when spotted by police, would be arrested and caned. "We were caught and given strokes at the police station, three strokes each, and then we were released."[109] Estate supervisors and owners often beat young migrant laborers or the children of squatters.[110] On the tea estates of Kericho and Sotik, "when the settlers came, cases of wayward children were reported to the authorities. Complaints were made to the district commissioner, and the children would be caned and released to their parents."[111] On a farm in Molo, Siamba Maina recalls a time when some sheep went missing from the flock he was hired to herd. Police came to the farm and caned him and another herdsboy. "We were just caned to scare us into telling the truth."[112] Less serious mischief could result in a farm manager escorting a boy to his office and caning him without involving the police.[113] Christopher Achar recalls that on the African Highlands estate, children were flogged with a cane as wide as a pencil and as long as his arm, and they only ever received four or five strokes.[114] Colonial rule had dramatically expanded the community that claimed the right to discipline African young men. What had once been the purview of parents, kin, and neighbors grew to include schoolteachers, farm managers, and employers.

Chiefs sitting on local African councils, desperate to exert some authority of boys and young men in their districts, repeatedly asked the colonial state to reinstate their authority to use the rattan cane in local courts. Rebuffed each time, chiefs resorted to persuading parents to more freely beat their sons, even for minor offenses, to improve discipline.[115] Although they had no legal authority to cane the young, chiefs and village elders sometimes took the law into their own hands, often at the behest of parents or victims. According to Wills Opiyo Otondi, who served as a headman in Nyahera, chiefs in the 1940s and 1950s would often take it upon themselves to arrest unruly young men, cane them, and scold their parents.[116] In some cases, a young man's family bypassed chiefs and elders and approached British police or probation officers directly. A self-described young gangster living in Gilgil just prior to independence, James Ng'ang'a frequently defied his parents and played truant from school. He eventually ran afoul of police while riding a stolen a bicycle. His parents came to the station and informed police officers, "Our child has become too much; you can do what you wish with him."[117] He was beaten thoroughly, and, afterward, his parents escorted him home. Some frustrated parents appealed to the state when the "normal way to discipline children" no longer worked.[118]

Most parents did not rush to district commissioners or chiefs to handle their mischievous children. Some elders argue that parents never took young people before district officials, keeping punishment strictly within the community.[119] Likewise, opponents of court-ordered corporal punishment, such as Nairobi city councillor Gikonyo, argued that the cane was the exclusive right of parents over their children, not of the colonial state.[120] Nevertheless, with the rattan cane, the elder state had inserted itself into a crowded field of disciplinarians. Whether a resident magistrate in Nairobi, a farm manager in Kitale, a schoolteacher in Maseno, a chief or elder in Siaya, or a father in Kiambu, corporal punishment had become a shared instrument of generational order. British magistrates elevated it to a principal form of punishment in the colony and considered it an effective, communicable method of legitimizing and exerting the authority of the elder state.

CONCLUSION

Over the course of colonial rule, magistrates used the rattan cane in particular ways, reserving it for certain gendered age-groups, offenses, and locations—all in a broader aim to exert authority over younger generations. Just as young men felt the crack of the cane in colonial prisons, so, too, did they feel it at home. Reserved for the young and uninitiated, fathers used physical violence to correct the behavior and labor of sons. As the young found new ways to make mischief, parents increasingly turned to corporal punishment. Boys found themselves part of an ever-expanding colonial community prepared to use violence to discipline them during colonial rule. Corporal punishment provided a mutually reenforcing method of age-defined discipline shared by adults, Africans and non-Africans alike, forming a network of authority figures over the young. Coming-of-age was, at times, a violent experience for young African males. Despite the elder state's numerous attempts to cast judicial caning as a limited, civilized punishment—more akin to chastisement—it remained a painful, humiliating encounter for thousands of young Africans as well as a few Europeans and Asians like Amritlal Monji. Some Africans, beaten by fathers and kinsfolk, remember such domestic violence as a normal part of growing up, while others recall it with bitterness. A father's walking stick and a prison officer's rattan cane might not have corrected their behavior then, but they etched indelible memories of pain and power. Not all of Kenya's underage offenders experienced the brutality of rattan, however. When punishing the colony's most serious offenders, the elder state introduced a new method of discipline: institutionalization. Within the walls of the reformatory, later known as the approved school, the elder state set out on its own, away from the influence of other adult disciplinarians, to reform and reimagine immature young offenders into mature, manly subjects.

5 ⇌ "Jaili Watoto,"
the Children's Jail
Reforming the Young Male Offender

KEREN WALKED INTO the Githunguri police station in early April 1954 with a problem: her son, Kanyingi. The boy had just returned home, having left without warning days before. No sooner had he arrived than he broke into a neighbor's home and stole twenty shillings. For Keren, this was the final straw. Decades later, Kanyingi still remembers this moment, the capstone on a history of wandering and pilfering. She had said to him, "I can't deal with you! I can't . . ." And so, Kanyingi recalls, "she took me to the police station."[1] The stress of raising a thirteen-year-old vagrant and thief had taken its toll. Keren informed the police of Kanyingi's theft and recounted his laundry list of misdeeds. For years, Kanyingi had awakened at dawn, slipped out of her home, and walked to nearby towns and trading centers. When he visited Nairobi, he swam in the river with other street children, stole bread from hotels, and loitered by storefronts. By nightfall, he strolled through his mother's door, only to leave again the following morning.[2]

Keren had not always struggled to control her son. As a midwife for the medical department at the Githunguri Health Center she earned a decent wage, which provided her children with adequate though cramped housing and school fees. Kanyingi believes his disobedience began when his father became a doctor at the center and took on a second wife. His father's decision to celebrate his material success by expanding the family and exhibiting his emerging maturity drove Kanyingi's parents apart. After the divorce, Keren struggled to balance her job, the needs of her three children, and Kanyingi's growing delinquency.[3] By April 1954, Keren decided that she could no longer control her son, and so she turned to the elder state. Kanyingi's case fell to assistant probation officer K. E. Kibachia, who interviewed both mother and son. Keren informed the probation officer "that Kanyingi is [a] quite disobedient and dishonest boy" who played truant from school and ran away.[4] Kanyingi recalls being very forthcoming with the officer, going so far as to tell Kibachia that he was interested in becoming a mechanic or blacksmith. During the trial, Kibachia recommended that Kanyingi go to an approved school where he would receive discipline and vocational training. The magistrate agreed and sentenced the thirteen-year-old to five years.

The approved school, first known as the reformatory, was one of the elder state's oldest, most forceful interventions in the punishment of young African men. Whereas repatriation and caning represented prescriptive efforts to prevent further delinquency, the approved schools were treatments of last resort for recalcitrant young offenders. They marked the final disciplinary destinations for thousands of young Africans determined by colonial courts to lay beyond parental authority. Approved schools locked inmates and the elder state into three to six years of intense engagement and investment. An inmate could spend part, if not most, of his coming-of-age within the confines of an approved school arguing about age and manhood with his carceral age-mates and the elder state.

Approved school inmates represented only a fraction of the tens of thousands of young men removed from towns or caned by court order, but they experienced a far more intense interaction with the elder state. They encountered a disciplinary regimen that studied them. Approved schools were colonial observatories where staff collected a wealth of data on inmates: age, physical and psychological development, sexual behavior, education, religion, family history, and criminal history, to name just a few categories. This data informed the state about African age and gender, and, with it, staff tested different methods to inculcate in inmates "acceptable" age-defined, masculine norms. The British understood the schools in much the same way as local initiation practices: sites of transformation that initiated the young, physically and psychologically. From its humble beginnings in 1907 until the 1930s, staff concentrated their efforts on discipline through hard labor and vocational training. From 1934 until the late 1950s, they promoted self-discipline through controlled social interaction such as sports, military drills, and competitions. These different methods blended the state's understanding of local age-relations with global ideas about institutionalization and reform.

What began as a single reformatory in 1907 grew to seven approved schools incarcerating nearly seven hundred inmates at the end of colonial rule in 1963, with plans for two more in the future. Compared to the rest of colonial Africa and the British Empire, and in spite of the pressures of indirect rule on a shoestring, the administration in Kenya created an impressive system of juvenile institutionalization. The approved school was an ambitious, early experiment to assess the state's potential to affect the development and welfare of young Africans, a project historians typically attribute to the "developmentalist" state of the post–World War II era.[5] Long before the 1940s, the work done behind approved school bars represented a long-standing idealism and firm faith in the power of the state to produce better, more respectable, disciplined subjects. But it was a faith that regularly faltered. The approved schools often failed to live up to these lofty ideals.

No matter the method, no matter the bold idealism, the success or failure of the approved schools depended on the inmates—what they made of and made with the different strategies staff brought before them. Young offenders used the elder state to make themselves men. According to ex-inmates of Kenya's approved schools, incarceration provided them an opportunity to observe the elder state too. They tested its coercive capabilities and considered the kind of masculinity offered.[6] Their daily lives did not amount to mere resistance or acquiescence; rather, the boys forged for themselves moral and economic worlds within the barred windows of their dormitories. During their sentences, friendships were formed, academic and vocational lessons were learned, mischief was made, bodies were used for sex, and age-relations were re-created. As did their captors, some boys came to view the approved schools as spaces of physical and psychological training infused with ideas about masculinity and maturity—a possibility to be exploited. Other boys rejected the schools outright, spending their days battling staff and planning their escape.

Approved schools were not isolated islands of punishment. By the 1940s, parents and a host of other adult authority figures were drawn into discussions with the state over how to best discipline wayward boys. After the war, British and African officers of the newly created probation service investigated an offender's history and filed detailed reports to magistrates. They visited and interviewed the suspect as well as his family, neighbors, schoolteachers, employer, and chief. From these conversations and their own observations, probation officers recommended to magistrates whether a young man should be institutionalized. By reviewing such reports, historians glimpse the qualities probation officers looked for when deciding the fate of a young offender: a family's wealth in livestock, a household's cleanliness, a mother's marital status. These qualities also reflected a probation officer's biases. How did a young, educated male African probation officer measure a father's wealth and authority? How did a female British officer decide whether a single mother was able to control her son? The triggers that set a boy's institutionalization in motion reveal what characteristics these members of the elder state looked for in their search for immaturity and criminality. The probation reports also show what parents and other community members thought of a suspect and what they had to say to the elder state. Probation officials frequently found themselves thrown into the middle of family squabbles or as witness to a village's fury over a recalcitrant thief. In some cases, parents admitted that they had lost control of their sons and petitioned the elder state to discipline them. A sentence to an approved school became a tense conversation between African families and the elder state, together trying to reassert generational authority over the young.

THE FACES OF DISORDER

In 1907, the first governor of the East Africa Protectorate, James Hayes Sadler, wrote to the Colonial Office requesting funds to build a reformatory. In his letter, he argued that in Africa, as in England, towns attracted young people who looked for work, slipped into idleness, and then descended into criminality.[7] The protectorate, he noted, possessed too few legal procedures and punishments for offenders. The Vagrancy Act was particularly unhelpful. It required officials to imprison or to compel all vagrants, regardless of age, to labor. Sadler did not want to prosecute and punish the young in the same way as adults. Without a reformatory, he believed, adult prisoners corrupted younger cellmates. He viewed criminality, like many late nineteenth-century contemporaries, as a contagion, and prisons as vectors for its transmission.[8] Once infected, a boy who had previously committed no crime other than idleness would succumb to the life of a career criminal.

The Colonial Office approved Sadler's request. Construction of the reformatory began at Kabete, just north of Nairobi. Kabete was and would later become the site of several institutions at the forefront of the state's efforts to develop its administrative and commercial capabilities as well as train a skilled African workforce. Next door to the reformatory, the state built its experimental agricultural station, later known as the Scott Agricultural Laboratory, where staff studied the local climate, pest-control measures, and cash crops such as tea and coffee.[9] The laboratory also trained African agricultural personnel. Down the road, the department of education built the

Native Industrial Training Depot in 1925 to train African artisans. The depot took the best and brightest from surrounding mission schools and taught them trades like carpentry, masonry, blacksmithing, and tailoring, skills in high demand by European settlers.[10] Two years later, Kabete became home to Jeanes School, a department of education experiment to train African teachers in the hopes that they would bring better sanitation, schooling, and agricultural techniques back to their reserves.[11] The Anglican Church Missionary Society also had deep roots in Kabete, where it established the Alliance High School in the same year as the Jeanes School. Alliance, a secondary school offering literacy and vocational training, ultimately graduated many of Kenya's African elite.[12] By the 1920s, Kabete had become a site of concentrated colonial innovation; the reformatory had been there from the start.

As Sadler drafted plans for the reformatory, he invested his protectorate in a global experiment in reforming serious young offenders through government-run institutionalization. In the late nineteenth and early twentieth centuries, ideas about the transformative role of government intervention in the lives of young people flourished in the West. In 1854, Britain began transferring young offenders to government reformatories.[13] In 1908, a year after Sadler's petition, the Children's Act established a justice system solely for young people in Britain.[14] The British sought to reform young people rather than punish them, fueled by a firm faith in the power of the state to orchestrate the "social reconstruction" of young offenders.[15] These ideas quickly traveled the sinews of empire. In 1876, British India passed an act establishing reformatories. On the African continent, Kabete was one of the few government-run reformatories. Cape Colony opened Porter Reformatory in 1882. Sixteen years later, the Egyptian government, with a long history of juvenile institutionalization, also built a reformatory along the lines of those in Europe and the United States.[16] Other British colonies in Africa resisted efforts to establish government-run reformatories. Until the mid-1940s, Gold Coast and Nigeria relied on the Salvation Army to institutionalize young offenders.[17] At the time, Sadler's opening of the Kabete Reformatory in 1907 was an extraordinary achievement in British Africa.

More surprising than its existence was the speed with which the protectorate acted and the financial resources it set aside to build and operate Kabete. Within a year of Kabete's opening, Sadler tasked the director of agriculture to run it and directed medical officers to routinely inspect the inmates. In his first circular of 1909, the protectorate's principal judge encouraged magistrates to begin sentencing repeat offenders to the reformatory.[18] In its first year, Kabete held twelve boys, some as young as six years old.[19] Admissions to the reformatory grew gradually in its first two decades. Between 1912 and 1914, magistrates had sent fifty-eight young offenders to Kabete. By the 1920s, fifty or more new inmates arrived outside Kabete's gates each year.[20]

Captain W. H. Wood, superintendent of Kabete during the 1920s, improved record-keeping and amassed detailed information on the inmates. These records chronicled Wood's practical efforts to maintain a well-ordered institution. Yet his record-keeping also allowed his staff to carefully study how to improve the institution. They observed inmates' health and growth, identifying outbreaks of infectious diseases or malnutrition as well as recording the meals inmates ate, down to the very ounce.[21] This data collection represented early experiments in colonial incarceration. How many boys could be packed into a dormitory? How little and what kinds of food did they need to survive? How much labor and discipline could they endure until exhausted?

These early reports also archived information regarding whom the courts imagined as the faces of serious colonial disorder. As soon as Sadler proposed Kabete, he sparked a flurry of discussion as to who could and could not be held in a reformatory. The opening of Kabete marked a critical moment in the colonial state's long-standing struggle to imagine, define, and categorize African age. At first, magistrates simply applied Britain's Children's Act of 1908 to establish the appropriate age for inmates. In 1910, Justice Hamilton declared that no one under the age of nine or over the age of eighteen could be sentenced to a reformatory. In addition, their sentences could not last longer than seven years or less than three years.[22] By 1922, Kabete staff complained that magistrates committed inmates too old to serve out the length of their sentences.[23] Chief Justice Barth adjusted the age restrictions, ruling that no inmate over the age of sixteen could be sent to the reformatory, and anyone who turned nineteen years old during his sentence must be released. The change ensured that every inmate served his full, three-year sentence.[24] Like Hamilton before him, Barth relied on existing British law as an instrument to resolve the ambiguities of African ages, which officials had few methods to ascertain with legal certainty.[25] Those who were nine years of age were too immature to benefit from the curriculum or be held fully responsible for their criminal activities. The age of nineteen marked the start of adulthood and the end of the reformatory's purpose. These boundaries located inmates in an interstitial space between childhood and adulthood and reimagined them as immature, undisciplined boys. The reformatory could then remake them into mature, disciplined men. This differentiation imbued the reformatory with transitive properties, much like initiation.

Gender and race became important ingredients in reformatory life. From 1909 until the late 1950s, no girls were sentenced to government-run reformatories. The reformatory was a masculine space. It reflected the belief among colonial officials that African girls and women must remain under the authority of fathers and husbands as well as broader European ideas that females were not as inherently delinquent as males.[26] In Nigeria, no girls were incarcerated at the Enugu Approved School in Lagos; and in South Africa, girls were held in a special dormitory of the Female House of Correction in the Cape Town jail.[27] The reformatory also remained, by and large, an institution for punishing Africans.[28] Only a handful of Asians and Arabs, and the stray European, joined the African inmate population. And when Asian and Arab young offenders did arrive at Kabete's gates, they rarely remained long. Their families frequently petitioned for early release or complained that their sons would be converted to Christianity or forever shamed by incarceration. In cases such as these, the state released the offenders, often on the condition that they be voluntarily deported to India.[29]

Last, the reformatory incarcerated the colony's most serious young offenders. Governor Sadler's original vision for Kabete had been to prevent incarcerating young vagrants alongside adults. But by the late 1920s, most Kabete inmates had been convicted of theft and housebreaking rather than urban idleness.[30] Their other common crimes included murder, manslaughter, and sexual assault. This shift reflected a change in the colony's methods of punishment. The new vagrancy ordinance of 1920 had directed magistrates to repatriate young people to their reserves rather than incarcerate them. This freed them to use the reformatory for the worst of the worst. Kabete was the end of the line, and staff had only a few short years to refashion the inmates into mature, disciplined men.

LEARNING THROUGH LABOR, 1920–1934

From the moment it opened until the mid-1930s, labor and vocational instruction defined the reformatory project. Inmates worked on the experimental farm next door, testing whether coffee, tea, tobacco, and other plants would thrive in Kenyan soil and yield rich profits for European settlers. In 1912, the director of agriculture began training the boys in trades such as carpentry and masonry; and a year later, after the boys requested courses in reading and writing, he hired an African schoolteacher for academic coursework.[31] During a visit in 1916, Judge Hamilton was "astonished at [the inmates'] intelligence and keen desire to learn as well as the results arrived at by the native teacher's unsupervised efforts."[32] Other visitors, like acting provincial commissioner Traill, frowned on the work at Kabete. "At present," he complained, "the Reformatory compares most unfavourably with either the average prison or the Machakos Industrial School. . . . I cannot consider that herding stock and planting cabbages are the occupations in which they ought to be engaged."[33] That Traill even uttered the reformatory's name in comparison to Machakos Industrial School, a well-known government-run technical training program, revealed his higher hopes for Kabete. He expected reformatory officials to offer the same level of rigorous instruction to hardened offenders as to mission-educated apprentices in vocational schools. Traill's comments begged the question: Did officials envision Kabete as a prison for young offenders, a vocational school, or something in between?

In its early years, the reformatory never achieved the level of instruction found at programs like the Machakos Industrial School or the Native Industrial Training Depot. Yet its mere association with such institutions underscored that colonial officials viewed the reformatory as a unique disciplinary space distinct from adult prisons and vocational schools. Superintendent Wood, who ran Kabete in the 1920s, envisioned labor and education as disciplinary tools to reform, rather than punish.[34] Under Superintendent Wood, the reformatory blended disciplinary and vocational curricula well into the mid-1930s. He exerted considerable effort to improve the quality of technical instruction at Kabete. He hired a British carpentry instructor to teach inmates to build tables, chairs, filing cabinets, doors, and window frames for the government. He hired his inmates out to nearby European estates. Wood expanded training to include blacksmithing and tailoring. He even arranged for the inmates to assist the young apprentices at the Native Industrial Training Depot. Inmates who showed little aptitude for vocational training worked on a two-hundred-acre farm growing food for the reformatory or for sale at market.[35] Kabete inmates became a part of the local economy: fixing farm equipment, building furniture, and growing food, all while using their profits to offset the cost of their incarceration.

Entangling punishment, labor, and technical instruction at the Kabete Reformatory reflected much broader colonial aims. The development of a semiskilled artisanal class became a means of alleviating fluctuations in the labor market and producing a cadre of skilled laborers to build the very infrastructure of colonial administration. In the waning days of the nineteenth century, the British encouraged mission schools to forgo literary instruction in favor of vocational instruction. In 1911, the department of public works built a training program, which would later become the Native Industrial Training Depot, for young men, some as young as twelve years, to continue rudimentary education in carpentry and other trades they had received at missions. These young men would form, officials hoped, a class of apprentices and artisans who would compete with more expensive Asian labor.[36] In its earliest incarnation, the reformatory was part of this effort to transform wandering herdsboys and young delinquents into wage-earning laborers. As a result, some of the colony's worst offenders experienced training reserved for only a handful of young men and the stuff of mere dreams for the rest of their well-behaved peers.

The use of labor and vocational training as a means to discipline and reform young offenders was not unique to the Kabete Reformatory nor Kenya Colony. In the reformatories and borstals of Britain and the United States, vocational education was an essential instrument of reform. Kabete officials took cues from racialized American educational theories and practices tested at institutions like the Hampton and Tuskegee institutes, which provided African Americans with agricultural and vocational training.[37] In postemancipation America, educational reformers like Thomas Jesse Jones believed manual semiskilled labor, as well as education through memorization and rote, best suited African Americans. On both sides of the Atlantic, Americans like Booker T. Washington and Thomas Jesse Jones, as well as Britons in Kenya like Joseph Oldham, believed this form of education could be modified and applied to meet colonial labor demands.[38]

When Thomas Jesse Jones visited Kenya in 1924 as part of the Phelps-Stokes Commission touring British colonial educational institutions, he remarked that Kenya had surpassed its neighbors in terms of vocational instruction. Jones believed that "nowhere has the whole system of civilization been dropped so suddenly and completely into the midst of savage races as here. It is a situation that may well give pause to missionaries and officials alike, for it has within it the seeds of an unprecedented development or an appalling disaster."[39] To Thomas Jones and the committee, the degree to which the colonial state offered and hundreds of young African men responded to vocational training marked either a glorious phase in colonial custodianship or a ruinous end to empire. In short, Kenya had the makings of a colonial utopia inhabited by disciplined, contented wage laborers, or a colonial nightmare haunted by half-civilized trade unionists demanding independence.

At Kabete, officials believed their work fell into the former category. No one at Kabete expected every ex-inmate to obtain a job fixing plows on European estates or building dispensaries for public works. Yet they hoped many would return home, apply the skills they had learned, and improve the countryside. Wood argued that the success of reformatory training and reformation could be seen in the reserves, where "many square and iron roofed houses are springing up, whilst draining appears to receive attention and gardens are laid out in a much more workmanlike manner."[40] Likewise, in Britain and parts of continental Europe, instruction at reformatories often harkened back to an "idealized rural past" aimed at stemming the tide of migration, urbanization, and industrialization.[41] They also spoke to a certain kind of male domesticity. Building iron-roofed homes and orderly farms was not just masculine work—it was the work of fathers and husbands. Although Wood never used the language of domesticity, fatherhood, or family life to describe the outcomes he hoped for Kabete's inmates, these were often implicit. The expectations were that ex-inmates would find work, build homesteads, marry, start families, and ultimately pass down to their children the sense of discipline they had learned behind bars.

Yet, in Kenya, as in Britain, labor discipline and incarceration served contradictory purposes. On one hand, the reformatory was a corrective for the modern influences that had caused indiscipline. It provided skill sets for rural development, such as building irrigation ditches, installing iron roofs, and tending orderly English gardens. With these skills, former Kabete inmates were expected to return home and tend rosebushes rather than steal bicycles. On the other hand, Kabete encouraged now semiskilled young men to leave their rural homes, seek out higher wages, and circumvent the authority of elder kin and the state. If they could not find work, they might inevitably return to crime. As Abosede George argues, ex-inmates of the Enugu Approved School found that the "novel skills cultivated in the institution preceded the markets for them" in postwar Nigeria.[42] Enugu's shoemakers had no choice but to return to Lagos to find individuals with the interest in and the wealth to buy a pair of new European-style shoes. Back in Kenya, colonial officials feared that vocational training, urban migration, wage earning, and criminality reinforced one another in a vicious cycle leading to "detribalization," the unraveling of African traditional life; or, as Thomas Jesse Jones had put it, the "appalling disaster."

As such, the curriculum at Kabete came under growing scrutiny. Beginning in 1928, the commissioner of prisons, C. E. Spencer, made moves to push Wood out and incorporate Kabete into the department of prisons. Spencer criticized Wood for staggering reconviction rates. Between 1925 and 1928, 181 boys had been discharged, and, according to Spencer, 100 of them had been reconvicted. Spencer's attack had less to do with Kabete than with Superintendent Wood. Several of Wood's projects had become publicly embarrassing to the administration. In 1930, Wood's agricultural program had exhausted half of Kabete's two hundred acres of cultivable land. An agricultural officer had to instruct Wood in the rudimentary agricultural techniques he was supposedly teaching his inmates, such as crop rotation.[43] That same year, the treasury investigated a work order issued by Wood to build a house for a man named Douglas Cooper at the cost of £700. Wood charged Cooper only £325 and requested that the treasury pay the remainder. Irked, the treasury demanded an explanation. Wood admitted that the work of Kabete's apprentices was so inadequate he could not charge the man in full.[44] Following the investigation, the Nairobi district commissioner demanded Wood's suspension, the treasury requested stricter accounting, and the governor expressed his displeasure with Kabete's management.[45] At no time did officials question the value of the reformatory; instead, Spencer and the prisons department assumed responsibility for Kabete in 1934, ushering in a new era for the inmates.

RETHINKING THE REFORMATORY, 1934

As Spencer and the treasury planned the ouster of Superintendent Wood, a committee on crime convened in 1932 to study rising levels of lawlessness in the colony, especially in Nairobi. For a start, the committee believed that improved policing techniques had created more criminals, which magistrates then had to punish.[46] "The manufacture of criminals," committee members argued, "involves the State eventually in greater expenditure than does the proper application of preventative and remedial measures to potential criminals in infancy."[47] Instead, the committee argued, the state should focus on prevention and reform. In this endeavor, the committee stressed the potential of the Kabete Reformatory. Members acknowledged that Kabete had succeeded in disciplining its inmates, keeping them healthy and training capable artisans. Despite this success, Kabete failed in other ways. The reformatory remained "rather of the nature of a prison than a school, that there is little, if any, reformation, and quite inadequate education." To underscore its point, the committee noted that "it is indeed known among Africans as the *jaili watoto*."[48] The committee believed that this derogatory language illustrated a failure of the state to portray Kabete to its African subjects as a place of correction, education, and welfare. Kabete needed rebranding.

And so, one committee begot a second that was tasked with studying the treatment of young offenders in England with an eye to applying such techniques in Kenya. The chair of the second committee, S. H. La Fontaine, who had served as colonial secretary and provincial commissioner of Central Province, left for Britain a few months later.[49] During his stay, he toured the infamous borstal at Feltham and several reformatories run by philanthropic and missionary societies. He made special note of how staff considered an offender's crimes and home conditions. He appreciated Britain's system of institutional specialization: reformatories for young offenders, borstals for older inmates, and industrial schools for "care and protection" cases like vagrants and orphans. La Fontaine also took lengthy notes on the curricula of the institutions, especially Feltham. Feltham divided its inmates into houses, each with their own color and housemaster, and competed against one another through sports. Those who behaved were promoted along a hierarchy of grades that carried privileges like cigarettes and camping trips. La Fontaine's tour of British juvenile justice institutions confirmed his belief that similar policies could be adapted to Kabete. He wrote that Africans "possess in underdeveloped form many of the qualities which go to make up the average European lad," yet their "plastic nature" and "natural respect" for European values overrode these "underdeveloped qualities."[50] Thus, reformatory work in a colonial setting, La Fontaine argued, could be more gratifying than in England because young Africans received the benefits of European tutelage while the European reaffirmed his superiority.

La Fontaine toured Feltham and other institutions for the young just as the British overhauled its juvenile justice system. In 1933, Parliament enacted the Children's and Young Persons' Act requiring courts in England and Wales to consider the welfare of children and young people, remove them from undesirable conditions, and arrange for their education. The act shifted focus from punishment to welfare.[51] As the British Parliament drafted the 1933 act, the League of Nations pressed the Colonial Office to encourage similar laws in the empire.[52] The Colonial Office circulated a draft bill among the territories nudging them to do so, but officials in Kenya needed no prodding. In anticipation of La Fontaine's report, they had already begun drafting an ordinance similar to the 1933 act. In fact, officials in Kenya were far more receptive to the input of the Colonial Office and application of British methods of incarceration than other colonies. Nigerian officials were uninterested in recommendations from London, dismissing Western reforms as inappropriate for young African offenders.[53]

The next year, Kenya enacted the Juveniles Ordinance, which made major changes to how the colonial state conceived of and handled young offenders.[54] The ordinance required Kenya to create a juvenile justice system similar to the one in Britain. It required police and magistrates to consider an offender's "welfare" and "care and protection."[55] The ordinance also called for a probation service to investigate whether young offenders required the state's care and protection. This proposed welfare-oriented relationship between the state and young people had far-reaching effects on the

Kabete Reformatory, now renamed an approved school, and its inmates.[56] Under the Juveniles Ordinance, the government had to develop three types of approved schools. Class one approved schools, operated by Christian missions, would hold children under the age of fourteen in need of "care and protection." Class two and class three approved schools, run by the government, would incarcerate serious offenders between the ages of fourteen and eighteen.[57] In addition, a newly formed probation service would investigate cases, make recommendations on sentencing to magistrates, and oversee aftercare programs.[58]

The ordinance redefined the approved school as a site of protection rather than punishment. No longer content to merely discipline its inmates and prepare them for lives as semiskilled artisans, the approved schools aimed to prevent future indiscipline by preemptively protecting those it deemed most at risk. Considering the welfare of an offender joined labor discipline as the chief preoccupations of approved school staff. The changes ushered in by the Juveniles Ordinance required police, probation officers, and magistrates to more aggressively pass judgment on a young man's past and present and then wield greater authority over his future prospects.

FOSTERING SELF-DISCIPLINE, 1935–1955

In 1935, the Kabete Reformatory became an approved school designated for older inmates between the ages of sixteen and eighteen, roughly equivalent to British borstals like Feltham. Two years later, the government built a second approved school at Dagoretti, a few miles west of Kabete, for younger inmates under the age of sixteen.[59] The colonial state also turned to the Salvation Army for assistance in operating two class-one approved schools at Nairobi and Malakisi in North Nyanza. The new approved schools also came under new management. After years of criticizing the work of Superintendent Wood, the department of prisons finally got the chance to operate Kabete and Dagoretti. The new commissioner, J. L. Willcocks, well versed in the academic literature on reforming young offenders, dove into his new role managing the approved schools. In one of his first acts, he hired W. H. L. Harrison as the superintendent of Kabete. Harrison had been a former employee of the borstal service in Britain.

Together, Willcocks and Harrison shifted the focus away from labor discipline to new methods of behavioral modification being tested in Britain and the United States. In his 1935 report for Lord Hailey's survey on Africa, Willcocks laid out his vision for Kabete and Dagoretti. He argued that in the reserves, young people experienced "ignorance, dirt, an early acquaintance with sexual matters" bearing "frequent witness of orgies of drunkenness" and "exploits of stock thieves." In the towns, they associated with "the scum of the native locations and the worst types of the Indian artisan and petty trader, many of whom, doubtless, have a close acquaintance with the inside of prison."[60] Willcocks's views on an inmate's criminality stemmed from two ideas circulating in Britain and the United States at the time. First, social reformers and penologists had begun to focus on environment as a key factor in juvenile criminality. Alexander Paterson, who ran British borstals in the 1930s and later visited Kabete Approved School, argued in his book *Across the Bridges* that a young south Londoner's surroundings—domestic life, neighborhood associations, and access to resources—determined his propensity for crime.[61] Second, social scientists began to consider the inner, psychological traits of young people. Scholars in the burgeoning field of child psychology argued that the young experienced a period of rapid emotional and physiological growth and thereby a proclivity for indiscipline and pliability when led astray.[62] Together these external and internal forces—an unsettled environment and an unhinged young mind—explained why so many young men in Britain took up lives of crime.

Yet these same two forces could also reform the young. If a boy had been twisted by poverty, abuse, and criminality, then introducing him to a new environment might undo the damage done. The plasticity of a young mind also meant it could be reforged straight and narrow. Willcocks believed that the "average African juvenile . . . is an imitator, a hero-worshipper and plastic stuff for the moulding and it is for these reasons that environment during his formative years must play a large part in shaping his future conduct of living."[63] Like Paterson writing in Britain, Willcocks surmised that if the state provided an alternative environment of stability and rubric for sound moral conduct, then African young men would learn self-discipline and, upon release, resist the very temptations to which they once succumbed.

This new vision of the approved school rejected the old aims of the interwar reformatory where industry had been the instrument of reform. Prisons officials believed that the early reformatory's focus on vocational training had actually encouraged ex-inmates to move to urban slums looking for work, aggravating detribalization and increasing the chance they might slip back into criminality.[64] Moreover, learning through labor served little purpose in a depression-era economy. In the early 1930s, the economic crisis had crippled the building trades, forcing the government to halt the number of projects undertaken. Government also ended its insistence that missions teach vocational training for grants-in-aid.[65] Between 1930 and 1935, the colonial economy shed thousands of jobs, in sectors from the railways to the coffee and tea estates. Wages also plummeted. An average African laborer earned 40 percent less in 1935 than he had five years earlier.[66] The necessity of training skilled, better-paid masons and mechanics ended during the depression. Willcocks and Harrison feared that to give a boy a vocational education and then release him with the expectation that his training would lead to a job when none existed ensured that many ex-inmates would inevitably return to lives of crime. They had to alter their message to inmates. Approved schools were not apprenticeships; they were sites of reformation and maturity making.

Following Paterson's lead, vocational training became the first casualty of the new approved school curriculum. The program adjusted vocational courses to train handymen not artisans, and academic classes to teach newspaper readers and letter writers not interpreters and telegraphists.[67] In the absence of vocational training, Willcocks and Harrison focused on breaking down inmates to their "individualized" form, then rebuilding them with a "spirit of social solidarity."[68] To accomplish this, they introduced the house and grade system that had inspired La Fontaine at Feltham a few years earlier.[69] Each inmate joined a house and wore the house color on his uniform. Within the houses, inmates were organized into a hierarchy of grades. Those who had been at the approved school for three months or less entered at grade one. Grade one offered no privileges and strict discipline. With good behavior and hard work, inmates earned promotion to grade two, which earned them a new shirt, football twice a week, and relaxation of discipline. Those with stellar records climbed the ranks to grade three and enjoyed more freedom and family visitation. Grade three inmates also earned one cent per day, which they could spend on sugar, soap, and sweets from the canteen.[70] The grading system created a reciprocal relationship among inmates and staff. If inmates acquiesced to the demands of the school, then their lives and rank improved. The new program also relied on the readiness of inmates to control one another, fostering solidarity but also sowing competition. At the top of the grade system sat house captains and leaders whose behavior communicated the qualities superintendents demanded of the other inmates. House captains and leaders also invested in a successful, well-ordered house, encouraging their fellow inmates to expose misconduct in order to climb the graded ladder.

From 1938 until the end of the war, the boys at Kabete and Dagoretti responded to the new approved school curriculum with growing disobedience. Staff recorded more incidents of indiscipline each year than actual inmates. Some inmates turned to everyday forms of obstruction: disobeying staff, lying, refusing to work, and leaving the approved school for an afternoon only to return by evening. Others tried to escape. Escape attempts, regardless of their success, became the most common form of indiscipline at Kabete and Dagoretti. About 17 percent of the inmate population tried to escape between 1934 and 1950. One popular method of escape was feigning an illness and being sent to hospital in Nairobi; slipping past nurses was far easier than evading Kabete warders.

To punish escapees at Dagoretti, the officer in charge, Kennison, perverted the house and grading system, with violent, horrific results. After recapturing an escapee named Nyaa Kingola Mvaa, Kennison handed the boy over to his fellow housemates to mete out punishment. Nyaa's escape attempt had cost his house badly. With good behavior and strong showings at sporting events, each house earned marks. At the end of each week, the lowest-ranked house would receive the worst jobs for the following week. As punishment, Nyaa "was beaten with sticks, punched, kicked and generally manhandled and finally made to lie down with his face on the ground and a heavy metal implement used for moving earth, weighing 140lbs., was placed on his back by two or three boys and left there for approximately half an hour."[71] Four days after enduring such cruel and unusual punishment, Nyaa died in hospital of congestive cardiac failure and crush syndrome. Crush syndrome occurs when the body goes into shock and kidney failure following a massive blow to the skeleton and its muscles. It is typically found in victims of collapsed buildings and cave-ins. There were no consequences for the inmates, who had murdered Nyaa with a 140-pound weight; nor Kennison, who had allowed boys of no more than sixteen years of age to choose a fellow inmate's fate.

Although his superiors had no direct evidence, Kennison knew what the boys were up to; an investigation at Dagoretti revealed that he routinely allowed the inmates to resolve their own disputes with violence. Staff at Dagoretti disclosed to investigators one telling episode. Inmates from the Kabete Approved School had come to Dagoretti to put their artisanal skills to use building a new dormitory. During their stay, they stole several articles of clothing from Dagoretti inmates. Unwilling to be bullied, "the Dagoretti boys then proceeded to beat up the Kabete boys and although they were smaller, they were in greater numbers."[72] It took a Kabete staff member to stop the fight before it got out of control. Kennison had stood by and watched the entire episode. Dagoretti's officer in charge relied on a dangerous combination of peer pressure, competition, and violence to encourage the inmates to maintain order. These acts of violence betrayed the kind of self-discipline Willcocks and Harrison had hoped for years earlier and the care and protection mandate of the approved schools.

Staff struggled to wrest power back from inmates who had manipulated the approved school to meet their own needs. Those desires included commodities obtained through an informal economy. An entire black market economy emerged within the approved schools. Boys punished for theft or possession of banned items accounted for nearly a quarter of all incidents of indiscipline at Kabete and Dagoretti between 1936 and 1950. Although the inmates had access to on-site canteens, they created an entire network of informal exchange among themselves, staff, and the outside world. Staff routinely found the inmates in possession of cigarettes and money. The boys stole some of these goods from the approved school stores, but the vast majority smuggled them in with the help of staff or their connections on the outside. After the war, officials canceled visits to the Catholic church because inmates used Mass as an opportunity to "traffic" in goods. The superintendent also complained that African staff took "the line of least resistance" by permitting the possession and sale of unauthorized items as a way of "currying favour with the boys."[73] That adult African staff deemed it necessary to curry favor with hardened young criminals whom they were paid to punish illustrates just how far the inmates had seized the initiative.

The boys also challenged the heteronormative masculine codes of conduct that staff struggled to instill in them. Many of the men with whom I spoke who had spent time at Kabete or Dagoretti freely admitted that the inmates had sex with one another; though, they added, it did not happen very often. Regardless of the frequency, sex happened. In an all-male space dominated by teenage boys, sex was a necessity—it brought inmates pleasure and companionship, making their incarceration a little more bearable.[74] Sex and sexual violence were also exercises in power. Young men used seduction and conquest to work out age-relations, express their manhood, and establish seniority. Patrick Njoroge, an inmate at Dagoretti and Kabete in the mid-1950s, recalls that sex usually occurred between inmates of different ages. Older boys would initiate sex with younger inmates whom they could pressure more easily, often in the toilets or during trips outside the school grounds.[75] An older inmate used his seniority to claim the right over another inmate's body, whether it was given willingly or not. Young men hardened by the mean, hypermasculine streets of Nairobi were also known to take what they wanted from naive country boys.[76] Their lives in the shantytowns of Nairobi had prepared them to accept sex with other men as part of their masculinity. "Country boys," though, were by no means ignorant of sexual play with one another, especially prior to their initiations. Out on the grazing fields, uncircumcised boys participated in sexual games in front of or with one another.[77] According to some former inmates, an entire sexual economy developed inside the approved schools. Those boys incarcerated long enough to have steeled themselves against hunger pangs used that self-discipline to extract sexual favors from boys desperate for a little extra at mealtimes. Kanyingi Ngugi remembers that new inmates at Kabete, who were not used to the quantity of school rations, often exchanged sex for food.[78] An inmate with a reputation for being "gluttonous" became an easy target for older boys looking for sex. When a boy suddenly gained a little weight, the others knew he was offering sex.[79]

Publicly, approved school staff viewed sex or other acts of "gross indecency" among inmates as a profound failure of their efforts to exhaust bodies and discipline minds.[80] As early as 1913, Chief Justice Hamilton complained that inmates slept together in the same bed. "[That] such a state of affairs should be permitted to exist in a Government institution for the reforming of boys' character needs no comment," he wrote.[81] Two decades later, officials at Kabete seemed befuddled when inmates kept contracting gonorrhea and syphilis despite sleeping in dormitories with barred windows, locked doors, and watchmen at the gate.[82] Rarely did staff see fit to record cases of sodomy, gross indecency, and rape. Between 1936 and 1955, only fifty-two inmates were punished for sexual indiscipline.

Privately, some staff breached the heterosexual norms they were meant to enforce. Officer Kennison was never disciplined for the death of Nyaa, the inmate crushed by his housemates, because at the time he was facing prosecution for having sex with one of the Dagoretti boys. What relationship Kennison had with the inmate is unclear, though the chief secretary's office referred to it as "revolting and of the usual kind."[83] It is also unclear what he meant by "the usual kind." Was it the typical kind of sex act in which two men might engage; the usual sex that went on in the approved schools; or just the type that went on between British officials and African young men? Although investigators believed the boy, they cited a lack of evidence to bring Kennison to trial—he was fired instead.

The efforts of Willcocks and Harrison to foster a certain kind of self-discipline floundered. And perhaps there was no critique of their curriculum more pointed than what came from the near death of ex-inmate Francis Nyoka Dafu. In December 1940, a letter arrived on the desk of the commissioner of prisons recounting the struggle of Francis and other former approved school boys. Francis worked for the locomotive department in Tanga, a job secured for him by Kabete's superintendent. Fortunate to have a job straight after release, Francis still struggled with his meager wage of twenty cents a day—nowhere near enough to pay for rent, heating fuel, clothing, and food. He had so much trouble budgeting with very little money that he

FIGURE 5.1. Kabete Approved School dormitories, now abandoned. According to staff at the newer, nearby Kabete rehabilitation school, these were built during renovations in the 1950s. Photograph by the author.

became malnourished and quit his job. The unknown author of the letter found Francis near destitution and wrote on his behalf to the commissioner: "When their time is finished they are sent out into the world, a world of which they know nothing to fend for themselves. They have never had to buy their own food or clothes. . . . Debt is likely to follow or as in this case ill health and there is a good chance of recidivism if the lad gets into bad company."[84] The author argued that inmates knew only an approved school economy in which they exchanged good behavior and hard work for food. Fostering self-discipline did no good if it failed to prepare ex-inmates to survive in the world beyond the approved school.

Some of those ex-inmates who returned to lives of crime stood boldly before colonial officials to condemn the inadequacies of the curriculum. In 1952, twelve-year-old Mwangi Macharia escaped from Dagoretti, only to be arrested by police months later for stealing clothing from a car in Nairobi. At his trial, Mwangi informed the magistrate that he escaped because "he wanted more lessons in reading." He then warned the magistrate that "he would not remain at the Approved School unless he was taught to read."[85] That same year, sixteen-year-old Mwariki Githenge told officials that he had escaped from Kabete "because he was not taught a trade he wanted."[86] Mwangi's, Mwariki's, and Francis's frustrations lay in the approved school's abandonment of education and preparation for life after reform.

With each escape, disregarded order, theft, and sexual act, the boys of Kabete and Dagoretti rejected the schools. In the waning years of his tenure as Kabete superintendent, Harrison began to see clearly the inadequacies of his changes.[87] He had stripped the approved school of what inmates had valued most—education—and thereby their confidence in the elder state. The elder state had broken the reciprocal arrangement it had struck with young offenders since the 1920s: accept colonial authority, abandon indiscipline, and the state will provide education and skills that could be leveraged on the outside to earn an age. By 1945, the new commissioner of prisons, D. C. Cameron, lamented that the approved school had become nothing more than an "asylum."[88]

The war years were even harder on the inmates and staff than the depression. The British military had temporarily taken over Kabete for use as a prisoner of war camp, forcing the department of prisons to cram more than two hundred boys, ages seven to twenty-one, into the woefully small Dagoretti facility.[89] In response to the asphyxiating conditions, inmate indiscipline exploded. Weathering the wartime conditions, approved school staff simply battened down the hatches by tightening their grip with stricter discipline, more frequent canings, harder work detail, and, in extreme circumstances, transfer to adult prison.[90] By the early 1950s, the department of prisons aggressively restarted the education programs at the approved schools. The return of vocational training at Kabete and Dagoretti represented a postwar push for development-minded planning in British colonies. In the devastating wake of World War II, the Colonial Office hoped to strengthen its imperial holdings, infusing them with development projects—more roads, dams, airports, hospitals, industrialized agriculture, manufacturing—in an effort to strengthen Britain's reconstruction back home. This meant getting Africans, especially returning ex-soldiers, back in the classroom and back to work in skilled jobs. The same went for approved school inmates. In 1951, Commissioner Cameron boasted that "big strides were made [at Kabete] in this direction," and the approved school now offered vocational courses "based on modification of those at the KTTS [the old Native Industrial Training Depot]."[91] A few years later, Dagoretti's younger inmates received improved academic training, including reading, writing, and arithmetic, with a smattering of basic vocational training.[92]

FIGURE 5.2. Kabete Approved School workshops, now abandoned. In the workshops pictured here, inmates learned mechanics, blacksmithing, and sign-writing. Photograph by the author.

Many of the inmates at the Kabete and Dagoretti approved schools welcomed the return of academic courses. Kanyingi Ngugi experienced first-hand the postwar merger of once-competing curricula. He spent most of his adolescence incarcerated at Kabete learning to read and write in Kiswahili, studying mechanics and electricity, and achieving an advanced level of education compared to most Africans his age.[93] He claims that he received an education he later used to become a mechanic, get married, buy a homestead, and achieve the measure of a man. He also was careful to stress that at Kabete he found the discipline his mother had so hoped the elder state might provide when she turned him in on that fateful day in April 1954.[94]

AUTHORITIES ENTWINED

Although the merger of education and self-discipline profoundly altered the approved schools after World War II, it was the creation of the probation service that brought about one of the most significant changes to the juvenile justice system in Kenya. Called for under the Juveniles Ordinance, the probation service began with a small staff—a single European officer and two African assistants working out of Nairobi. Led by Colin S. Owen, the service made vast improvements in the quality and quantity of its staff and expanded its operation to Kisumu, Kericho, and Mombasa. Between 1946 and 1954, the probation office handled hundreds of cases.[95] Senior probation officers, like Colin Owen and Mary Kenny, were usually British, while most of the assistant probation officers were African. The African assistants were usually given cases involving offenders from their own ethnic communities. Investigations typically involved an officer interviewing an offender and then traveling to his home to speak with parents, neighbors, chiefs, and even teachers and employers. Afterward, they filed reports in which they recommended to the magistrate what kind of punishment the young man required. These reports offer historians a rich and lengthy paper trail, revealing intimate details of young offenders' lives and relationships with family as well as the elder state's anxieties, preoccupations, and biases. In the Kenya National Archives, I found 381 of these probation reports collected together involving serious offenders sentenced to Kabete or Dagoretti.

What these reports make clear is that probation officers were influential interlocutors, the eyes and ears of the elder state. Through probation officers, the state could peer into African households and listen in on family arguments. Likewise, young offenders, parents, and communities communicated their desires and anxieties directly to the state and pulled it into their often-heated conversations. Drawing on what they saw and heard, the probation officers passed judgment on young men and their families. Their reports did not reflect the realities of a young man's life but the tales probation officers told to make a case, secure a conviction, and, above all, justify the need for the state to intervene. The reports reveal what features British and African probation officers looked for to explain a young man's delinquency, a parent's powerlessness, and a homestead's inadequacy. Sometimes families did probation officers' work for them, boldly requesting that the state institutionalize a boy in an approved school or at least discipline him in some way. In such cases officers needed no stronger evidence to secure a boy's sentence.

One of the most common judgments probation officers passed on African families was the condition of their household. In over 35 percent of the 381 cases, a boy's home was described at length. Probation officers commented on the number of cattle or acreage of land a father owned, the size and quality of the homestead, and the family's wealth, or the lack thereof. "Dirty" households reeking of poverty and immorality were clear-cut cases for institutionalizing a boy for the sake of his welfare. In late September

1952, eleven-year-old Peter John Uzice was brought before the Nairobi district commissioner's court on a "care and protection" order under the Juveniles Ordinance. Police believed Peter had been sexually assaulted. Colin Owen assigned the case to Mary Kenny, one of Kenya's most active probation officers. Kenny's investigation revealed that Peter lived with several of his ten siblings in a two-room home in Eastleigh, a Nairobi slum. Peter's sisters operated a brothel out of the home, and he worked passing messages between his sisters and their clients. He occasionally engaged in sex work himself. Kenny also learned from the family that Peter had recently been gang-raped by three young Asian men.[96] Peter's four-year sentence to the Dagoretti Approved School was not a punishment but an indictment of his household. Rather than sites of punishment, probation officers used the approved schools as sites of refuge, believing that Peter Uzice and other sons of prostitutes, abusive drunkards, or destitute parents should come of age in the care of the elder state.

Probation officers also scrutinized the health and the marriage of an offender's parents. In nearly every report filed between 1947 and 1954, they used the age of parents to determine whether or not an offender should be incarcerated. Consider the case of Wahuria Gitwaria, a fourteen-year-old boy charged with stealing in Nairobi in 1953. When the African assistant probation officer visited his one-room home in Dagoretti he met his poor, very elderly parents. In his report, the officer noted that "the accused had no proper persons to take care of him. His parents are very old, and unable to exercise powers on the boy [. . .] in this way the boy is able to do anything in his powers."[97] Simply having elderly parents, too mature to exert physical discipline, sealed Wahuria's future. He spent the next four years in an approved school. The wealth and robustness of a father weighed less on the minds of probation officers than his relationship with his wife or wives. The absence of a parent, whether through separation, divorce, or death, provided magistrates compelling evidence to institutionalize an offender. Roughly 36 percent of the cases involved boys who came from households in which one or both parents had died.[98] Officers also took note of whether or not parents had divorced or separated, a further 13 percent. Probation staff argued that boys who came from these sorts of "broken homes" lacked the discipline and control that they believed a two-parent household provided.

In one particularly heart-wrenching case, probation officer S. J. Moore investigated Ngungu Mbogo, a ten-year-old from Kiambu charged with theft. When asked why he stole, Ngungu replied that he wanted to go to the cinema and buy food. He also cheekily asked Moore to cane him quickly so he could leave. Instead of caning him, Moore traveled to

Ngungu's home and met his mother, Nyambura Karioki. According to Nyambura, after marrying Ngungu's father she had grown unhappy and fled her husband's household with her infant son. Her husband demanded she return Ngungu or pay back the dowry. Penniless, Nyambura had no choice but to return her only child to her estranged husband. To raise the 450 shillings to repay her bridewealth and recover her son, she cared for the children of others. Several years later, money in hand, she returned to her husband's homestead and paid her debt. But Nyambura's troubles had only just begun. As soon as Ngungu was old enough, he began leaving home, associating with bad company, and playing truant from school. Nothing would deter him, not even corporal punishment. After fighting for so many years to reclaim her boy, she relinquished custody of him yet again, this time to the colonial state.[99]

The trial of Ngungu and the tribulations of Nyambura represent a far more complex situation than a probation officer marshaling evidence against a poor, divorced single mother and then unilaterally deciding what was best for her delinquent son. The case also reveals a conversation between Moore, Nyambura, and Ngungu, one with important consequences for the approved schools. Probation officers often discussed the best way to discipline an offender with families and communities. Of the 381 probation reports between 1947 and 1954, officers had conversations with families about their relationships with the offenders and how the boys should be disciplined in 160 instances, roughly 42 percent of the time. In this way, probation officers became a new interface between families and the elder state. African parents and kin—like Nyambura and Kanyingi's mother, Keren—communicated their frustrations to probation officers and even made recommendations or requests of their own.[100] These 160 cases make clear that many parents and kin came to view the colonial judicial system as an alternative or supplement to their own disciplinary efforts, and that the elder state wanted and used this to justify taking custody of their sons. Approved schools became part of intense deliberations between parents, probation officials, and the wider community to determine who would discipline the young.

In about a third of these 160 conversations, African families and neighbors spoke with probation officers about whether they were willing or able to assist young offenders. Some parents eagerly wanted their sons back home and still had faith in their own disciplinary power. If parents vigorously defended a son's character and promised to look after him, then magistrates often released offenders back into their parents' care. In 1951, Michael Bwile stood before a magistrate in Kericho charged with breaking and entering. Despite the seriousness of the crime, Michael received only two years probation.

The outcome of his case hinged on a conversation between Michael's father and the probation officer, E. S. Oluseno. According to Oluseno, he "interviewed his father Joseph Oloo at Railways Landies Lumbwa with regard to his son's behavior [. . .] his father informed me that Michael has been a very good boy since his childhood, and is very sorry for what Michael has done."[101] A father with a good job at the railways and willing to testify to his son's good character, and an offender with no previous convictions, offered Oluseno and the magistrate an easy case for probation. After arguing with the state, some parents retained authority over their children — if they chose to exercise it.

But in the majority of the 160 cases, fathers and mothers, to varying degrees, ceded disciplinary power of their children to the elder state. They did so in several different ways. First, a few parents simply refused to assist their sons. These parents declined to take their boys back, forcing magistrates to make the decision on their own. Refusal could have been an expression of frustration with past disciplinary failures or acceptance of colonial authority. Second, many families freely admitted to probation officers that they had lost control. To acknowledge the failure of their own authority exposed their frustration with and agony over sons who had repeatedly committed crimes or left home without permission. In 1951, the father of Toho Kareithi informed assistant probation officer D. J. Kituri that his son had been "very bad at home," preferring to spend his days loitering about Nairobi.[102] Toho had a lengthy criminal record, including nine previous convictions for which he was caned seven times. Weary of his son's mischief-making, Toho's father admitted that he could do nothing to control his son. Kituri then used this conversation to justify his recommendation that Toho spend the next three years in an approved school.

Finally, a few parents requested, sometimes adamantly, that the state intervene. In sixty of the 160 cases, about 37 percent, parents, family, and members of the community specifically asked the probation service to punish a young offender. Some parents, like Kanyingi's mother, Keren, vaguely requested that some form of discipline be administered. Others suggested that the officer send their sons to an approved school. In thirty-five instances, the reports indicated that a family or community member asked the officer to incarcerate the offender at Kabete or Dagoretti. A further eleven agreed to institutionalization in an approved school when the probation officer brought it up during the interview.

These thirty-five exasperated kin requested approved schooling out of frustration with countless shillings spent on unattended schools, compensation to neighbors for stolen property, and restless nights waiting up. For these parents, the approved school had become a punishment of last resort. The father of Kihio Kibanjwa was one such parent. In 1947, Colin Owen paid a visit to Kihio's father in Thogoto after the boy had been arrested for housebreaking and theft. Owen quickly sized up the father: he was a veteran of World War II, owned a farm of "good size and well looked after" with several cows and goats, and made sure his family members were "well provided with the necessities of life."[103] Owen found nothing lacking in this African homestead. But Kihio's father bitterly complained to Owen that the boy had caused him considerable trouble. Beginning in 1943, Kihio began stealing from the neighbors, forcing him to pay three hundred shillings in compensation. He had even petitioned the magistrate in Kiambu to incarcerate Kihio in an approved school, a request that had gone ignored. On Owen's and the father's word, the magistrate incarcerated Kihio at Kabete.

It was not just parents with whom the probation service conversed about institutionalizing young men. In thirty-four of the 160 cases, just over 20 percent, probation reports gathered information from neighbors, chiefs, and employers—a much broader network of authority figures. In April 1952, after discovering his son Mathenge had stolen a bicycle, Kamau turned him over to Nakuru police. Probation officer S. J. Moore traveled to Kamau's homestead, located on the estate of a British settler named Mr. Dawson. Kamau worked as a squatter on Dawson's farm. In a peculiar twist, Dawson had served as the superintendent of the Kabete Reformatory prior to World War I. After he retired, Dawson invited several former Kabete inmates to work as squatters on his farm—one of those ex-inmates was Kamau. During his interview with Moore, Dawson lamented Mathenge's behavior and claimed that he had tried everything to get the boy to behave. Dawson believed Kamau, a drunk whose violence had chased away four wives, unraveled his efforts with the boy. Dawson also noted that Mathenge had a keen intellect, a knack for mechanics, and might respond well to vocational training. Based on the father's request for discipline and an employer's recommendation, Mathenge became a second-generation Kabete inmate.[104]

That Moore included Dawson's comments on how Mathenge might benefit from vocational training at Kabete pushed conversations between probation officers, families, and community members beyond simple debates about punishment. Certainly most fathers and kinsfolk pressed the probation service to punish boys like Mathenge and Kihio because they required more aggressive discipline. Yet families had other reasons for requesting approved schooling that were intertwined with ideas about their sons' future maturity. They, too, saw the approved schools as spaces where immature boys might be transformed into productive, mature members of their family. When the assistant probation officer for Kisii District, H. J. Wanguche, visited the home of fifteen-year-old Guta Isoe, he got an earful from family members eager to send Guta to Kabete. As the probation officer explained the nature of Guta's theft to his father, the old man announced that "he did not care and that the government could do whatever it wished with his delinquent son." After the old man's performance, other family members informed the officer that everyone did in fact care and wanted the boy "sent to the approved school [. . .] because when he came out he would be able to earn a lot of money."[105] Guta's elder brother "insisted on saying that Guta should be sent to an approved school where he had heard that people learn all sorts of trades, and that when Guta would come from there he could make the best 'fundi' [carpenter]."[106] Many other parents viewed the approved schools and their vocational curriculum as a disciplinary regimen that possessed the power to turn recalcitrant delinquents into mature young men with the potential for future material success.

Over the din of parents, siblings, neighbors, chiefs, employers, and the elder state, the voices of young offenders were rarely recorded in the probation reports. The vast majority of young men did not want to come of age locked away in Kabete or Dagoretti. They lied, gave aliases, covered for one another's stories, escaped from custody, and even tried to fight their way out of police stations. But for 381 of them, they wound up in an approved school nonetheless—subject to the authority of the colonial judicial system with the backing of some in the colonial community. Yet sometimes probation officers and magistrates heard the concerns of the boys, and in these cases, the approved schools served as sites of legitimate care and protection. In late April 1952, S. J. Moore brought Ngige Kimani, who had been arrested for stealing money from his employer, back home to his father in Naivasha. Ngige's father was not happy to see his son. He informed Moore that his son "had been disobedient and had run away from home."[107] Ngige enjoyed a more welcome reception from his mother, who pushed gifts of sweet potatoes in Moore's hands for returning the boy. Despite the warm homecoming from his mother, Ngige requested that Moore send him to an approved school. "The boy himself complained of harsh treatment by his father, that his father expected him to go without clothes. . . . He is keen to go to the Approved School but not keen on being put on probation unless he can keep far away from his father."[108] Whether his father's abuse extended beyond refusing to buy him clothes, Ngige feared the man enough to insist that Moore send him to the approved school. Moore thought the boy best put on probation, possibly swayed by his mother's sweet potatoes. But the magistrate saw it differently, sentencing Ngige to three years of training at an approved school. As rare as Ngige's case might have been, his voice was heard and played a part in his institutionalization.

Make no mistake, probation officers relied above all on the original criteria for which James Sadler had opened the Kabete Reformatory in 1907: punishing serious crimes like housebreaking and theft committed by boys who had previous convictions, bad character, and even worse associates. Yet the probation service opened up the approved schools and elder state to broader conversations with Africans about an offender's well-being and indiscipline, a family's authority and dysfunction, and the state's role in household struggles. They also served to legitimize the elder state's own growing authority over the young.

CONCLUSION

Within the world of the approved school, the elder state tried to mold young criminals into colonial subjects, instilling in them labor productivity, self-discipline, and maturity. Approved schools became tense, masculine spaces that entangled British officials and young male Africans in debates about acceptable expressions of masculinity and mastery of one's self and surroundings. British officials drew their plans from globally circulating ideas about incarceration and reform, such as experimenting with work-time discipline through vocational training. They also relied on their understanding of local ideas about discipline, such as initiation, competition, and hierarchical age-grading. Some inmates rejected these methods outright, choosing to resist or escape their institutionalization. Many others used the training and discipline to chart their own futures, very literally wielding the tools of the approved school to come of age. Beyond approved school walls, African parents and kin played powerful roles in the incarceration of sons and siblings. A few African families openly and forcefully requested that the elder state institutionalize their children. For parents like Kanyingi's mother, Keren, jaili watoto was no pejorative joke. It was a last chance to reassert authority over deeply loved yet dangerously immature boys by harnessing the power of a very willing colonial state.

However, the success of the approved schools and boys-made-men like Kanyingi hinged on the days, weeks, or even months after release. Many ex-inmates slipped back into lives of crime, whether by choice or desperation. As for Kanyingi, nothing could have prepared him for the crisis he encountered outside Kabete's gate. While on leave from the approved school, granted for good behavior, a man approached him, thrust a gun in his hand, and asked him to deliver it to someone in Kiambu. Kanyingi knew this man to be Mau Mau—a Gikuyu fighter who had taken up arms against the colonial state. On his way to Kiambu, Kanyingi was shot by police, taken into custody, and detained. His effort to actualize the training he received at Kabete ended prematurely. He would spend the next several years locked away in a vast system of detention. All around him, Mau Mau fighters engaged colonial forces in bloody battles across Central Province in search of a means to articulate their own senses of age and manhood. As they did, hundreds of families flocked to the approved schools in search of refuge for their children.[109] Amid the violence of the 1950s and its aftermath, the approved schools would undergo their most dramatic overhaul yet. And their importance to the elder state's efforts to discipline young offenders, and now cope with thousands of recalcitrant young fighters and refugees, would take on a desperate urgency.

6 ⮑ "In the Past, the Country Belonged to the Young Men"

Freedom Fighting at an Uncertain Age

YOUNG SOLDIERS RETURNED TO KENYA from far-flung battlefields in the years following 1945, scarred but alive, pockets full of severance pay. In the blink of an eye, money ran low, anxieties ran high, and their war became survival on the home front. The old possibilities to which their forefathers had access had been denied them: accumulating livestock and raiding for cattle or clearing the forest frontier and tilling the soil. The new possibilities of the colonial encounter, like migrant wage labor, education, and town life, no longer guaranteed the material success they could pour into making themselves men. Regardless of their biological age, many men felt trapped in a prolonged, liminal period between childhood and adulthood, between initiation and marriage. As they wrestled with this uncertain age, many turned to violence.

Across postwar Central Kenya, young Gikuyu men smoldered with anger and anxiety. In the White Highlands, squatters faced empowered white settlers, who demanded household heads increase family work hours, reduce livestock holdings, and expel young sons.[1] These young squatter sons-made-migrants traveled the estates and towns of the Rift Valley looking for work and finding few jobs, stagnant wages, rising costs of living, and others who shared their discontent. From the White Highlands to Olenguruone, migrants and squatters began protesting these hardships, joining political parties like the Kikuyu Central Association and the Kenya African Union, and taking oaths of unity and collective political action.[2] The young men sitting idle in the tea shops of Rift Valley towns advocated for more radical, militant local politics. Oaths became aggressive and violence an accepted means of political expression. Reform of oppressive colonial policies was no longer enough; they called for the end to colonial rule altogether. The most militant struck at settlers and the state, maiming livestock, burning down buildings, raiding police stations for munitions, and killing settlers' relatives and loyal African employees. Terrified by trusted houseboys-turned-terrorists, settlers expelled more than one hundred thousand Gikuyu squatters from their farms.[3]

Exiled squatters and migrants returned to the reserves of Central Province to find kin embroiled in their own conflicts. Overcrowded homesteads, over-taxed farms, and underemployment had radicalized young Gikuyu in the reserves too.[4] They directed their ire at chiefs and well-to-do families, whom they blamed for manipulating labor and landrights to grow rich, for enforcing onerous colonial regulations, and for supporting the female circumcision ban. Moreover, a growing number of schoolboys had to abandon their studies because they could not afford tuition or secure places in secondary schools. Even the independent schools, built and run by local Gikuyu communities, could not satisfy the demand for education.[5] In 1949, the Beecher Report, commissioned to reform Kenya's woefully inadequate education system, dashed the hopes of parents and pupils. Rather than expand education, the report recommended limiting African access to secondary schools and the number of independent schools.[6] Education had never seemed so far out of reach. Those who did graduate found fewer opportunities for employment despite their advanced degrees.

In the colonial capital, too, places to earn a wage and lay a weary head were scarce, though ways to spend precious shillings were not. In Nairobi, more so than elsewhere, radical politics drew strength from desperate living conditions and criminal gangs like Anake a Forty, which organized labor strikes and employed violence to "bring the wheels of government to a standstill."[7] By late 1952, militant Gikuyu had aggressively spread oathing throughout Nairobi, Central Province, and Rift Valley Province.[8] As oaths proliferated and grievances festered, unrest increased throughout the region. The British came to believe they faced an organized, widespread anticolonial insurgency among the Gikuyu, one they called Mau Mau.

Historians call Mau Mau many things. Some imagine it as a nationalist struggle led by Western-educated intellectuals with clearly articulated political motivations. Others argue that Mau Mau was a class-based peasant uprising. And still others have searched for religious as well as gendered explanations for the violence.[9] Mau Mau's decentralized origins, loose organization, broad aims, and rural and urban character, as well as regional variation, contributed to many competing interpretations. That is perhaps why so much has been written on Mau Mau. It certainly meant many things to many different Gikuyu. Rather than an organized movement with coherent motivations and goals, Mau Mau was more akin to a series of intense, often violent, arguments within the Gikuyu community and between the Gikuyu and the colonial state. What, then, did young Mau Mau men argue about? As Luise White and John Lonsdale show, they argued about their age and masculinity and how, in the midst of crippling poverty and racial discrimination, they were meant to become mature men.[10] Regardless of variations in class, education, region, or religion, a vast majority of those who participated in Mau Mau were young men.[11] Surveying former fighters in Kiambu District, Greet Kershaw estimated that more than 80 percent had been under the age of twenty-five and half had been below the age of eighteen.[12] Formed by and fed off the fury of the young, the meanings inscribed in Mau Mau became tightly intertwined with debates about age and gender.[13] A major front in Mau Mau's war was resolving what fighters identified as an increasingly prolonged, uncertain age in which their manly mettle went untested and their desire for adulthood hung forever on the horizon. Through the efforts of Gikuyu, young and old, Mau Mau created and rallied a generation of warriors—regardless of their biological ages—to resolve this ambiguity. Mau Mau became a new possibility through which they might earn an age.

The British responded to Mau Mau by declaring an eight-year state of emergency in October 1952, and launching a brutal counterinsurgency campaign that killed thousands and detained over 150,000 men, women, and children in a vast network of detention camps.[14] Colonial officials, settlers, and missionaries also argued about the origins and aims of Mau Mau. Among a small but influential group, age and gender played a critical role in how they explained the crisis. They coalesced around the view that Mau Mau represented the inherent indiscipline of young men and the total disintegration of elder authority—sentiments shared by Gikuyu chiefs who had long decried the withering of elder patriarchy as well as conservative, loyal Gikuyu.[15] In the past, both Gikuyu elders and the elder state had failed to exert adequate control over younger generations. To rein in these reckless young men, they proposed a program of rehabilitation. Rehabilitation pushed the state to intervene in the lives of young men more forcefully than it ever had before, posing as an elder and ushering young Mau Mau into manhood once and for all.

Yet these plans were, for a time, put on hold. In the early years of the emergency, colonial authorities pursued confused, contradictory policies toward young suspected Mau Mau. Conflating youth and rebellion, they rounded up a diverse assortment of young Gikuyu: hardened forest fighters, Nairobi street boys, orphans, and refugees. They were all suspected Mau Mau. Not until 1954 did the elder state make a concerted effort to implement the program of rehabilitation by separating the detention of Gikuyu into two parallel paths based on age. In one, Gikuyu over the age of eighteen experienced extraordinary hardship. In the other, young men encountered the elder state, which offered rehabilitation and an alternative path to manhood and maturity, but for a price.

FINDING MEANING THROUGH MAU MAU

The young Gikuyu men who took oaths and joined Mau Mau drew from a deep reservoir of grievance that had defined their coming-of-age. For most Mau Mau, their war and the British counterinsurgency coincided with their ritual initiation. For their older compatriots, who had already undergone initiation but had not yet achieved a sense of adulthood, Mau Mau served as a second, alternative initiation; one that might end their prolonged youthfulness. Regardless of their biological age, they imbued Mau Mau with meanings about maturity, masculinity, and generational mobility. The experience of Waruhiu Itote, the man who became the Mau Mau leader General China, evokes the anxieties over age that compelled many young Gikuyu to resort to violence. During the war, Waruhiu served in the King's African Rifles in Burma. He watched white men being picked off by Japanese snipers and commiserated with African American soldiers who opened his eyes to other worlds of racial inequality and solidarity. At war's end, Waruhiu returned to his father's homestead with one thousand shillings for his service. There he grew idle; and after some time, his father summoned him. Waruhiu's mother poured them honey beer. His father suggested that they lay their life savings on the table. Whoever had saved the most kept everything.

Mulling over his father's request, Waruhiu thought, *How on earth could the old man have saved up [more than my severance pay] from his herd of scrawny goats?* And so Waruhiu

> gaily slapped my one thousand shillings on the table. Itote [my father] was looking steadily at me, not speaking. He took the damp-smelling bundles of notes from Wamuyu [my mother] and handed them to me. Quietly he suggested I should start by counting them.

> When I had reached three thousand shillings there was still much more to come. I did not know where to look. . . . What was worse was that my wife and my mother had both been present to witness my shame. *Like a small boy*, I said that I wanted to relieve myself. I went outside and walked, or rather ran, the five miles to Karatina where I took a train to Nanyuki. . . . I was safe from any shame there, forty miles from home.[16]

That night, Waruhiu's father laid bare his embarrassing immaturity. Yet Waruhiu was no small boy. In his mid-twenties he had faced the circumcision knife, married, brought a child into the world, and fought a war. Although Waruhiu possessed many of the characteristics of manhood, his social and economic place within his family suggested otherwise. He remained but a boy compared to his father. A herd of scrawny goats had made a man, not a white man's war. Waruhiu had not expected to be elevated above his father's station, yet he rightly hoped that initiation, marriage, fatherhood, and soldiering half a world away might make him a measure of a man. They had not; and, like a child, Waruhiu ran away from home, determined to return to his father's homestead a prodigal, successful adult.

The Kenya to which Waruhiu returned was filled with thousands of others who had discovered their paths to maturity littered with seemingly insurmountable obstacles. Like them, Waruhiu traveled from Nyeri to Nanyuki to Nairobi, and at each stop he found his efforts to earn a living obfuscated by racial discrimination.[17] Others sought education as the path to a better life. They, too, had their hopes crushed. Former schoolboy Kiboi Muriithi took the oath and joined Mau Mau because "the price of my education was beyond my father's reach [and] from the classroom I went on to the land, back to our two tiny acres. And each day, as I worked, I worried about the future. I vowed that any move to expel the White man would receive my support."[18] Waruhiu's and Kiboi's visions of the future were entangled with their fathers' fortunes. The elder Itote's success became a burdensome model that Waruhiu could not achieve. The elder Muriithi's failure to afford Kiboi's school fees rendered his son's future uncertain. Looking back, former Mau Mau fighters like Waruhiu and Kiboi positioned their decisions to join Mau Mau alongside their arguments with their fathers over an unrequited age. As John Lonsdale argues, part of the postwar crisis for young Gikuyu lay in the realization that the possibilities older generations had once accessed to gain wealth, maturity, and a sense of manhood no longer worked for them. More crippling still, new possibilities like soldiering and schooling failed to bring them any closer to matching their fathers' fortunes or overcoming their fathers' poverty.[19] Mau Mau became an alternative, violent means to earn a sense of manhood and maturity. Oaths of unity, reclaiming lost lands, and driving out the British might resolve the burdens of an uncertain age, which had made boys of men.

They were the Mau Mau generation, an age-group fused together by the frustrations of collective immaturity.[20] And, like any age set, many experienced their induction into Mau Mau with the same sense of gravity they had felt, as children, when they faced the initiation knife. Some former fighters explicitly considered the moment they took the oath as a second initiation ceremony.[21] In his darkest days as a fighter, Kiboi Muriithi's mind often returned to the Mau Mau oath he took at the age of twenty-one. "As I shivered that night, alone in the depths of the forest, without jacket or coat, and hungry, my mind went back to how it all began. To that day in Nairobi when, as a callow, frightened youth I was tricked into taking the oath of allegiance to Mau Mau. The oath was the watershed of my life. It marked the beginning of manhood."[22] Muriithi's oath represented a second initiation of sorts. If his first had failed to place him on a path to successful adulthood, then the oath offered him a new or supplemental initiation from which he could begin again. That Mau Mau could, in the imagination of some young men, reactivate the process of manhood and replicate the crucible of adulthood made it a rite of passage.[23]

Elder Gikuyu involved in or sympathizing with Mau Mau also viewed the oaths as pivotal moments in age-relations and an opportunity to exert a little generational authority. After taking the oath, Gucu Gikoyo received a lengthy lesson from the elders who oversaw it, explaining his obligations to Mau Mau and the whole community. Once they finished, he left the ceremony only to be approached by an old woman who took him aside and said, "I want you to know that in the past the country belonged to the young men; for it was they that fought for and defended it. I should like you to realize that we are getting old and that the land of our forefathers has been grabbed from us. If you wish to let it go and condemn your children to slavery, that is your affair."[24] With bitterness, the old woman recounted a Gikuyu history entangled with generational tension. In her version of the past, she and her age-mates had been victimized twice over. The land on which their forefathers toiled, as well as the warriorhood their forefathers enjoyed, had been stolen. To right these wrongs, she called upon young men like Gucu to join Mau Mau, reclaim their sense of warriorhood, and restore their lost lands. Her words also carried shades of regret, of youthful transgression. If the country once depended on the strength of the young, then the young had failed to defend it. The old woman reasserted her role as an elder by restoring Gucu's responsibility to defend his community, rearming him and readying him for battle.

Gucu's encounter with the old woman underscores the significance of junior-senior relations in activating Mau Mau violence. The organization of Mau Mau, whether in Nairobi slums, Central Province villages, or the Aberdares forest, involved "elders," or Gikuyu men whose leadership or self-promotion enabled them to presume the title. Some former Mau Mau fighters recall an "elder bureaucracy" that organized Mau Mau activities.[25] If the oath had offered Gikuyu an alternative form of initiation, then it also organized Mau Mau around a hierarchy of age. Karigo Muchai was one such member of an "elder bureaucracy." He had served in the war as a driver in Somali, Ethiopia, and Burma. Like Waruhiu Itote, he returned from the front with high hopes, only to find that "the life I returned to was exactly the same as the one I left four years earlier: no land, no job, no representation and no dignity."[26] By 1953, Karigo had taken the oath and served on a committee of "elders" in Kiambu District. These "elder" committees organized oathing campaigns, raised money, distributed supplies, and recruited potential soldiers. When members disobeyed their authority, they meted out punishment. In September 1953, when Mau Mau general Gitau Kali disobeyed the committee by attacking police posts without authorization, the "elders" sentenced him to fifty strokes and hung him by the wrists from a tree for an hour.[27] The use of corporal punishment by "elder" committees to discipline fighters, let alone Mau Mau generals, is striking. Some Mau Mau, especially those who had served in the British military, would have understood corporal punishment as a normal form of discipline.[28] Yet many Mau Mau had never served and would have been unfamiliar with military discipline. Instead, they came from communities where elder men could beat only uninitiated boys. To have faced the knife, taken the oath, and then endure a beating from "elder" bureaucrats would have been deeply humiliating.

In the rushed effort to craft a chain of command, Mau Mau members fabricated a confused generational hierarchy and wielded age-defined instruments of discipline. Karigo Muchai explained that members of the council on which he sat called those Gikuyu who took the most militant oaths îhîi. According to Karigo, a kîhîi means an "'uncircumcised youth' or simply 'son,' but during the revolution it was used to refer to men who had taken the Batuni Oath."[29] The word îhîi was also, and remains to this day, a pejorative term for "boys." To call a man a kîhîi is to question his masculinity and maturity, to infantilize and belittle him. But to call a man who had just taken an oath to die for the cause of Mau Mau a kîhîi became a way for the leadership to reinforce its authority and reduce him to the role of subordinate. Separating the men from the îhîi became a means of creating an age-defined chain of command.

Mau Mau reimagined and reimposed an age-defined order on the struggle by using familiar ritualized generational practices like initiation, disciplinary instruments like corporal punishment, and relational categories like "elder bureaucracy" and îhîi. Freedom from the ambiguity of their age meant clarifying the structure of Mau Mau and their relationships with one another in terms of age. Yet these efforts did not always transmit themselves clearly. More often than not, ideas about age and age-relations were confused by and confusing to many Mau Mau participants. When some fighters finally met their Mau Mau "elders," they were stunned to discover men barely older than themselves. Ngugi Kabiro, in his mid-twenties, worked hard to assist in oathing ceremonies, thereby earning him "a certain respect by the elders," which earned him still greater responsibilities until he ran afoul of their rules.[30] Caught buying and smoking European cigarettes, Ngugi was hauled before a "Mau Mau court." Mau Mau leaders had issued a ban on European goods like beer and cigarettes—a position deeply unpopular among fighters. When he arrived at court, Ngugi found nothing more than a room full of "Gikuyu youths" armed with pistols and very stoned.[31] The youths sentenced him to twelve strokes and a fine of two hundred shillings. Ngugi describes it as a scene of topsy-turvy generational rules: young men beating another young man as though they were elders. Confusion not clarity ruled in the courtroom where Ngugi protested this absurd perversion of age. Submitting to "elder bureaucracies" irked Joram Wamweya. Joram fumed that elders made him and his fellow fighters wait at "intolerable lengths" for a taste of the action. Young men prepared to fight, only to be delayed by elders. "At times, young men lost patience and rebelled," Joram recalled, "sometimes even manhandling the elders."[32]

The age-infused meanings young Gikuyu ascribed to Mau Mau changed as the war intensified. Faced with a mounting British counterinsurgency campaign, Mau Mau forces found themselves outgunned and isolated deep in the forests of Central Province. An estimated twenty thousand Gikuyu fighters died in combat and tens of thousands more were captured and detained by British forces.[33] Hard-pressed by such losses and short on supplies, Mau Mau leadership compelled young men to take the oath.[34] Desperate times called for desperate measures. Expanding its ranks quickly and violently meant oathing new recruits who might not share in the same political convictions or ideas of how to use the uprising to make themselves mature men. Those conscripted into Mau Mau's ranks were much younger than those who had joined at the start of the emergency.[35] Many of these new young recruits had yet to feel the initiation knife or the frustrations of an unfulfilled age.

The Mau Mau war had begotten a second, younger generation of uniniti-ated boys who came of age amid the violence, made desperate by schools closed, jobs lost, homesteads burned, and loved ones murdered.[36] Joseph Gikubu took his first oath while he attended a Kiambu primary school. He admits that he did not fully understand the consequences of this oath at the time. He was simply too young. Yet Joseph remembers viewing it as the start of a separate education into something bigger than himself.[37] According to Nicholas Kinyua, himself an unmarried young Mau Mau, he oathed many uninitiated boys in Nyeri. They could be relied on, he argued, to obey their parents.[38] But trusting the uninitiated carried risks. Some Mau Mau believed that older boys who had not yet undergone initiation talked too much, lacked discipline, and proved unreliable agents. Nicholas Kinyua recalled a Gikuyu proverb warning: "Mûici na kîhîi atigaga kîeha kîarua," or "He who steals in the company of an uncircumcised boy will live in fear until the boy is circumcised."[39] Woe to the Mau Mau fighter whose life de-pended on talkative, uncut îhîi.

Although the youngest Mau Mau might have lacked the maturity to artic-ulate the struggle in the same way as their older compatriots, they still drew meanings from the conflict in terms of age and gender. Simon Kariuki's ten-ure as a Mau Mau fighter began when his school closed and Home Guards dragged his parents from their home on the charge of oathing neighbors. He and his siblings never saw them again. Seeking vengeance, he joined a Mau Mau gang that traveled between Nairobi and the Aberdares, transporting supplies and escorting new recruits to the forest.[40] He equated his activi-ties as a fighter with the black-and-white films brought to him by colonial mobile cinemas, especially American westerns. He described his Mau Mau tenure, which included killing policemen, as "just like a game; just like the cinema. I did the same thing as in the movies."[41] Emulating the masculine bravado of cowboys became one of his enduring memories of the struggle.

For others, their struggles looked suspiciously like juvenile delinquency. Joram Wamweya had taken the more militant oath well after the declaration of the state of emergency in late 1953. As Mau Mau, he and his friends spent their days planning raids on local shops, complaining about "elder bureau-cracies," and smoking marijuana. One day, Joram decided to plan a daring daytime raid on a local Asian shop in Limuru. His friends "applauded the idea" and declared that "it was time our [village] proved it had brave young men."[42] The next morning, Wamweya and his gang held up the Asian trader but managed to steal only a few watches because they were so thoroughly and embarrassingly stoned. Despite being in his mid-twenties, an act aimed at proving his manhood exposed Joram's dangerous immaturity. This was not Mau Mau; this was thuggery. While Simon's and Joram's experiences lacked the politicized character of other fighters', their struggles were no less dictated by making themselves manly.

REHABILITATING FATHERS' FAILURES

As Mau Mau fighters argued about age and masculinity with one another, they found themselves in heated debate with other Gikuyu who flatly refused to join the uprising. Early on in the conflict, the community fractured. There were those who actively supported and joined Mau Mau, those known as loyalists who rejected the oaths outright, and those who tried to avoid choosing a side or slipped—sometimes rather easily—from one side to the other. Some of the most infamous acts of violence during the war occurred among Gikuyu.[43] Indeed, the emergency began in October 1952 after Gikuyu assassins murdered Chief Waruhiu of Kiambu for his outspoken oratory against Mau Mau. Several months later, Mau Mau and loyalists clashed in the town of Lari, battling over local political disputes and massacring innocents.[44] Above all, the Home Guard epitomized a divided community. Made up of young men recruited by the British to hunt down Mau Mau, the Home Guard symbolized the material rewards of siding with the colonial state.[45]

Age became a way for Mau Mau and loyalists to belittle one another and challenge the legitimacy of one another's positions. In battle, the Mau Mau and the Home Guard hurled abuse at one another, calling each other îhîî, or uncircumcised boys, over the eerie silence of reloading weapons. They each tried to emasculate the enemy and invalidate their competing quests for maturity. Loyal chiefs and headmen took the language of age a step further, beyond mere name-calling. They positioned Mau Mau fighters as delinquent, disobedient children. Chief Muhoya called on Mau Mau to "go back to your ordinary life of obedience to your parents."[46] Other loyalists argued that Mau Mau had begun when "young people started to ignore their parents' advice and got into filthy things." In loyalist eyes, Mau Mau was child's play brought on by the rebelliousness of the young and the inability of the old to keep them in line.

Among some conservative Gikuyu, Mau Mau represented a broader crisis of generational authority. Several influential British colonial officials and European settlers shared this interpretation of Mau Mau with their loyalist allies. They also believed that age and generational relations lay at the very foundation of the conflict, and so, too, the blueprint for its defeat. Just as Gikuyu argued over Mau Mau, the colonial state and the European settler community argued over competing visions to define and defeat Mau Mau. Settlers coalesced around a racialized view of the conflict, especially those who felt most at risk living on Rift Valley farms surrounded by Gikuyu squatters. They saw Mau Mau as a race war for control of the colony's future. The colonial state's response to Mau Mau must be brutal and uncompromising.[47] Other members of the white community countered this extreme settler position with their own explanations.

A coalition of settlers like Michael Blundell and Louis Leakey, reform-minded government officials like Thomas Askwith and Colin Owen, and religious leaders like Joseph Oldham supported the idea of a multiracial Kenya in the not-so-distant future. If Africans continued down the enlightened paths of Christianity, education, and modernity, then they might one day have a place at the governing table. They believed Mau Mau represented the failure of some Gikuyu to fully embrace these goals, the desperate scream of a society suspended in painful transition between tradition and modernity. In their psychological anguish, Mau Mau cut a bloody path back the way it had come.[48] They also laid blame on the colonial state for allowing economic grievances to fester.[49] This interpretation dominated official narratives about the crisis.[50] Its dueling languages of barbarism and the specter of communism became the official explanation of the uprising and justification for the counterinsurgency. But buried in this unfolding narrative lay a hidden yet powerful supplementary narrative about age.

To augur their official position, the colonial state sought the advice of Dr. J. C. Carothers, a retired psychiatrist who had worked in Kenya for years as director of Mathari Mental Hospital in Nairobi. Called out of retirement to diagnose Mau Mau, his task was to ground the ideas of Leakey, Askwith, and Blundell into cold, hard social science. His report, *The Psychology of Mau Mau*, legitimized the notion that Mau Mau was a symptom of profound psychological shock brought on by an incomplete transition to modernity but also severed age-relations. Carothers argued that Mau Mau emerged just as the "supportive and constraining influences" of Gikuyu culture fell.[51] Gikuyu had once taken moral nourishment from the authority of elders and the certainty of an age-defined hierarchy. Drawing inspiration from ethnographic research like Otto Raum's *Chaga Childhood*, Carothers claimed that authority lay in initiation rituals meant to "impress upon the youths that they are still subordinate to their elders and must not attempt to step beyond their junior status."[52] However, Carothers believed colonialism had weakened elder authority. While older generations continued to socialize the young, they did so with halfhearted convictions and ever-withering rituals, leaving the young feeling detached and terrified. "The beliefs [they] learned in childhood had become inapplicable and ineffective."[53] One need only consider the Mau Mau oaths, he insisted, to see just how irreparable the rift between Gikuyu generations had become. Older Gikuyu, he claimed, still believed in the power of traditional oaths of unity. The young put little stock in them and turned to more militant, coercive oaths. They had traveled so far from past authoritative practices that they had to form new ones, escalating fear and violence to secure allegiance.[54] In Carothers's analysis, the young were looking for something, anything, to tether them to the moral world.

The same year that Carothers published his report, Louis Leakey—settler, scientist, and self-described white Gikuyu—weighed in with his own emerging history of Mau Mau. In his book *Defeating Mau Mau*, Leakey characterized Mau Mau as religion rather than psychological disease, but his views aligned with those of Carothers nonetheless, especially in terms of age. Leakey described Mau Mau as a perversion of Gikuyu religion orchestrated by "evil men" like Jomo Kenyatta who made "murderous fanatics" of the young, who had been made susceptible by poorly taught Christianity, rudimentary Western education, and the loss of venerable age-relations.[55] Gikuyu elders had few weapons left to combat Mau Mau. According to Leakey, in the past, "a youth who showed signs of not accepting these rules could be held back from initiation year after year."[56] The fear of one's elders was gone. "More and even more the young refused to listen or to learn and take advice"; and the result was "a huge body of youth who were not only without any real religion, but who were also without moral principles, and who had had no character training to speak of."[57] Mau Mau tried in vain to reclaim traditional values without ever having been taught them. To prove his point, Leakey highlighted the use of sugarcane and banana leaf archways in the first Mau Mau oath. This was, he believed, the same type of archway Gikuyu boys and girls passed through during their initiation. Leakey argued that to travel through such symbolism for a second time, to be reinitiated, could have untold repercussions. Tradition and custom in the hands of such ignorant young men had profoundly destabilizing effects—it was generational chaos.[58]

One member of the colonial administration who shared in the visions of Carothers and Leakey was Thomas Askwith, the former Nairobi municipal African affairs officer and future commissioner of the department of community development. In 1953, Askwith joined Leakey on a committee called to discuss government solutions to Mau Mau. That same year, Governor Baring sent Askwith to Malaysia to examine the colony's methods for defeating Chinese communists who had risen up against the British.

His discussions with Leakey and study of the Malaysian state of emergency deeply influenced his ideas.[59] On his return, Askwith took the reins of community development and outlined a program to defeat Mau Mau known as rehabilitation. To break Mau Mau, Askwith believed, the British had to isolate the Gikuyu and break their oaths. Government must detain anyone who had taken an oath. While in detention, Gikuyu were expected to confess and reject their oaths. They then underwent rehabilitation, a blend of hard work, technical and agricultural training, reeducation, and moral rearmament.[60] Rehabilitation was a gendered project designed specifically for men. It sought to reconstruct Gikuyu manhood by resocializing those in detention with ideas about proper, civilized male behavior.[61] A few attempts, like Maendeleo ya Wanawake (Women's Progress), were made to rehabilitate Gikuyu young women willing to renounce their oaths or side with loyal chiefs. Members of Maendeleo ya Wanawake learned sewing, cooking, hygiene, and the other trappings of modern, Western domestic life.[62]

The efforts by Maendeleo ya Wanawake were limited; instead, the state focused on rehabilitating men, and increasingly young men. In April 1954, Askwith described Mau Mau as "the problem [that] mainly concerns the young men, aided and abetted by the girls. A whole generation has disintegrated. Tribal discipline has disappeared and no adequate alternative has been established."[63] In Askwith's calculation, the colonial government had shortened initiation, promoted medical circumcision, outlawed dancing and warriorhood, and encouraged migration. The colonial encounter had also weakened parental and chiefly influence. The British had failed to offer alternative ways for the young to express themselves or augment elder authority. Mau Mau had filled those voids. Rather than yoke the young to elder power, as Leakey suggested, Askwith believed the state must replace elder discipline through rehabilitation.

First, rehabilitation had to reestablish discipline and respect for colonial authority. Askwith believed grouping young men together according to their villages, making them responsible for collective labor and behavior, and encouraging the emergence of leaders who restored their faith in one another and respect for authority would be an important first step. Second, the state had to provide young men with opportunities to express their energies. Bush clearing, carpentry, masonry, terracing, and agriculture were not to be understood as punishment but rather as natural as the human reflex. Young men were then to be given a "new faith" and "enlightenment and civics," though Askwith did not specify how faith in religion or state would be taught. Finally, rehabilitation was to replace banned extracurricular activities. A "young man aspires to display his bravery and skill," Askwith mused, and so the state must replace dancing, hunting, and warfare with schooling, scouting, and sport. Askwith's program of rehabilitation, which had been originally commissioned as a short-term means of breaking oaths and reintegrating tens of thousands of Gikuyu detainees, evolved into a long-term plan for the social reengineering of young men more audacious than anything the British had tried before in Kenya. State-sponsored discipline, labor, education, religion, and recreation would deliver a decisive blow to Mau Mau. Rehabilitation did not merely propose a new method of punishment and behavioral adjustment; it redefined the elder state's relationships with young Gikuyu.

Legitimized by Carothers's science and Leakey's reputation, and programmed by Askwith, this history of and solution to Mau Mau became a powerful, supplemental narrative to the official propaganda used to validate the counterinsurgency. This age-based explanation for Mau Mau opened up a small space for an alternative solution, one that handed the detention and rehabilitation of young men over to the elder state and split the British counterinsurgency into two pipelines: one for adult Gikuyu and another, much smaller one, for the young. Moreover, the narrative that Mau Mau was a generational crisis that could be solved by the elder state also offered the British a powerful propaganda tool to address growing criticism of its counterinsurgency. The colonial administration met Askwith's program of rehabilitation with equal parts admiration and derision. Community development and education officers as well as district commissioners supported his plans. The treasury remained dismissive. Yet events in early 1954 outpaced Askwith's efforts. The speed with which settlers evicted squatters, Gikuyu neighbors murdered one another, provincial administrators arrested suspected Mau Mau, and military operations routed forest fighters created a rapidly growing population of detainees. And as the military campaign turned its gaze toward cleansing Nairobi of Mau Mau, the number of Gikuyu in detention soared. Even as he drafted his program of rehabilitation in 1954, Askwith's plans were already being scuttled, at least for the time being, in favor of the harsher realties of punitive detention.[64]

BATTLING MAU MAU'S VAGRANT BATTALIONS

Before 1954, British officials had no coherent, formal method for handling the growing number of Gikuyu they arrested, especially the young. In the absence of official policy, contradictory strategies emerged from various corners of the state. C. M. Johnson, the provincial commissioner of Rift Valley, turned over young detainees to missions willing to take them at £100 a head.[65] The district commissioner in Nyeri sent young Mau Mau to the Kabete and Dagoretti approved schools until the superintendents discovered them oathing other inmates.[66] District officials across Central Province used corporal punishment. Between 1953 and 1955, they caned nearly thirty-five hundred young Gikuyu under the age of sixteen, an eightfold increase over the previous three years.[67] Unsure how to handle the growing numbers of young men arrested for violating emergency-related regulations, the state wielded an unprecedented degree of physical violence. Detention became the most common destination for the captured and surrendered. After their arrest, Mau Mau fighters like Joseph Gikubu, Gucu Gikoyo, and Joram Wamweya were all held in makeshift prisons run by district officials and then transferred to larger detention camps such as those at Athi River, Kajiado, and Manyani.

In 1954, several factors radically altered how the British conducted the counterinsurgency campaign against Mau Mau. First, the arrival of General George Erskine and the establishment of a war council led to a more consistent military and civilian strategy.[68] Second, the capture of Waruhiu Itote, the infamous General China, dealt a blow to Mau Mau. The intelligence he provided the British disrupted Mau Mau operations and eliminated several operatives.[69] Last, government shifted the warfront from the forests and reserves of Central Province to the streets and slums of Nairobi. Its assault on the capital netted tens of thousands of potential suspects. Overwhelmed by the numbers, the war council ordered the expansion of the detention camp system. The council also began to articulate a set of emergency policies to specifically handle and discipline young men suspected of Mau Mau. Through these policies, Thomas Askwith's program of rehabilitation was revived, ensuring a dramatically different wartime experience for thousands of young men.

Nairobi's tea shops and congested bachelor's quarters had long served as hotbeds of political agitation. The shared hardships of shanty life bound together the colonial capital's African residents, whether trade unionists, low-level government employees, casual laborers, beer brewers, sex workers, hawkers, or gangsters.[70] The more militant members of the Kikuyu Central Association (KCA), a political party that had agitated for colonial reforms since the 1920s, found fertile political ground in the capital. In 1948, the KCA began to extend the oath of unity to Nairobi residents.[71] The KCA recruited Fred Kubai and John Mungai, notable trade unionists and political agitators, to administer the oath in Nairobi. Kubai and Mungai, with the help of Bildad Kaggia, further radicalized the urban political scene, building networks to collect information, funds, munitions, and manpower for what they believed would be the inevitable conflict with the colonial state.

The war council and Nairobi municipal officials were not oblivious to the city's importance to Mau Mau. They imagined Nairobi as a limitless reservoir of supplies and radical recruits. Boys and young men visiting or living in Nairobi were indeed pulled into the orbit of organized gangs and political groups affiliated with Mau Mau. While on leave from Kabete Approved School, Kanyingi Ngugi was oathed in Nairobi, given a gun, and instructed to transport it to fighters in Kiambu.[72] Street boys like Gabriel Kahugu, James Karanja, and Samuel Uiru were swept up in the conflict. Gabriel, who had fled abuse at home in Kiambu to the streets of Nairobi, was rounded up several times during the state of emergency. Each time, police took him to the screening camp at Makadara and presented him to E. E. Jackson, the Nairobi extraprovincial district officer. Each time, she awarded Gabriel a caning and repatriation. Finally, after seeing him one too many times, she offered him work cleaning her office. She hoped a job under her watchful eye might put an end to his days foraging in garbage bins. When word of his new job spread, a man approached Gabriel and asked him to steal firearms from her office. Gabriel managed to get his hands on a handgun and hand it over to him before being arrested and brought before a deeply disappointed Jackson. For his involvement in aiding Mau Mau, she could have mercilessly sent the boy to a detention camp. Instead, she placed Gabriel at the newly opened center for Mau Mau orphans at Ujana Park.[73]

More drastic measures were needed, the war council believed, to sweep suspected Mau Mau from town. In 1954, colonial and military officials finalized a secret plan known as Operation Anvil to sever supply lines running between town and forest, and to detain suspected oath-takers. On 24 April 1954, a force of about twenty thousand men—five British battalions, one King's African Rifles battalion, and hundreds of police and Home Guard— surrounded the African areas of Nairobi and arrested Gikuyu suspected of being Mau Mau.[74] So swift were the roundups that rumors swirled of infants left crying in their cots unattended for days.[75] Over the course of four weeks, colonial forces arrested thousands of Africans, transported them out of the city in caged lorries, and held them at the Langata detention camp. At Anvil's end, more than fifty thousand Gikuyu had been screened; half remained in detention, and the rest were repatriated to the reserves.[76]

Operation Anvil gutted Nairobi of its Gikuyu population, accomplishing in four weeks what municipal authorities had tried to do for decades—the removal of the town's unemployed population, especially young vagrants. Magistrates in the juvenile court could hardly keep up with the increased caseload. After the court opened in July 1953 until April 1954, it handled 558 cases.[77] In the months following Anvil, more than twenty-seven hundred young people passed through the docket. The following year threatened to shatter even Operation Anvil's record as nearly sixteen hundred young people came before the bench in the first six months.[78] The elder state had never handled so many cases. Overburdened, the court sentenced the bulk of the boys to repatriation. During and after Anvil, the elder state relied more on repatriation to remove young people from Nairobi than at any other time in the policy's fifty-year history. And just as they had done since those early days of colonial rule, thousands of boys returned to town weeks or even days later. Anvil temporarily drained young Gikuyu from Nairobi, but the war in Central Province sent them spilling back. According to James Karanja, the capital had become a common destination for young people whose families had been displaced, detained, or murdered.[79] He experienced this sense of insecurity in the reserves firsthand. His father served as a headman to Chief Waruhiu. After the chief's assassination by Mau Mau and a failed attempt on his father's life, tensions mounted in the Karanja household. After quarreling with his stepbrothers and stepmother, James fled to Nairobi. To the war council, the persistence of boys like James underscored the social and economic upheaval erupting in the reserves as well as the uninterrupted activity of Mau Mau's urban campaign.

By mid-July 1954, only three months after Anvil, the war council became "exercised" by the number of young people remaining in Nairobi and sitting in detention. Council members believed some five thousand young Gikuyu women under the age of twenty remained in town earning money as sex workers. A further two thousand boys under the age of sixteen continued living in the capital because parents had fled to the forest, wallowed in detention, or died.[80] In response, the war council drafted an emergency welfare of children regulation in 1954, providing government with new powers over the lives of the young. The regulation granted district officials the ability to round up anyone under the age of sixteen whose parents were missing, detained, or dead. Once held by the state, young people were to be taken to religious and charitable institutions, called "approved institutions," until the emergency ended.[81]

Governor Evelyn Baring invited the Save the Children Fund to open an approved institution later that year.[82] Save the Children had some experience in handling young people during a counterinsurgency. In 1946, the fund had built the Serandah Boys Home in Malaysia as a "place of safety" for children affected by the counterinsurgency. Save the Children went on to replicate the scheme in Somaliland, Sudan, and Uganda—a wider model for late colonial British humanitarianism.[83] Thomas Askwith

FIGURE 6.1. Kenya's Dagoretti Center for Kikuyu orphans. The children leaving the entrance for a morning walk, n.d. Photo courtesy of the National Archives, Kew.

had visited Serandah during his trip to Malaysia to study the rehabilitation efforts there and had been quite taken with the project.[84] Working out of a section of the Langata detention complex, the Save the Children Fund opened Ujana Park. The center held a motley assortment of mostly boys ranging from suspected Mau Mau spies and gunrunners to Nairobi street kids and malnourished orphans; among them was the young handgun thief Gabriel Kahugu. The fund originally planned to handle only a hundred boys and girls, but after a few months the center ballooned to more than three hundred. Surrounded by the barbed wire of the Langata detention camp, Gabriel and his fellow young detainees slept in four dormitories, took meals together, maintained roads, cleaned the compound, and attended school. Sometimes, after dinner, they played football.[85]

Ujana Park and other institutions, like the Dagoretti Children's Center operated by the Christian Council of Kenya, were propaganda tools used by the British to propagate the myth that its efforts to eradicate Mau Mau included "welfare-oriented" programs.[86] The *Sunday Post*, published out of Scotland, ran a story about Ujana Park in late 1955. The headline read: "Langata 'Boys' Town." Although the center sat inside the Langata detention camp, a stone's throw away from where many Gikuyu endured brutal screenings and atrocious conditions, the article portrayed Ujana Park as no more sinister than Father Flanagan's Boys Town half a world away in Nebraska. There "a new life has begun for former Mau Mau messenger boys, dope-runners, and even some orphans." Careful not to give its audience the impression that the center rewarded young Mau Mau with luxury and pampering, the *Sunday Post* made certain to note that Ujana Park was "no scheme worked by namby-pamby types with a touching faith in human nature."[87]

Despite the propaganda, the Save the Children program was a new model of detention during the emergency. An uncomfortable marriage of state-sponsored detention and nongovernmental welfare, Ujana Park signaled that the British were willing to treat the young differently than their older fellow fighters. The detainees responded in kind. For a former street kid like Gabriel Kahugu, the camp at Ujana Park gave him the food and shelter he was lacking. The slightest kindness and sense of security left a mark; the boys felt safe, "so we felt like home."[88] Yet, as the counterinsurgency raged on, nongovernmental organizations like Save the Children grew unwilling and unable to accept more cases. None of the many nongovernmental programs begun after Operation Anvil could cope with the sheer number of young Gikuyu brought to them by colonial officials or meet the diverse needs of the state. The elder state had to take matters into its own hands.

DIVERGING FORMS OF DETENTION

The dual war fronts of Nairobi and the forests deluged already overcrowded detention camps like Langata, compelling the war council to expand its detention system even further.[89] Beginning in 1954, the British enlarged Langata so that it could hold an additional ten thousand detainees. They also built two new camps to hold fifteen thousand detainees at Mackinnon Road and Manyani, along the hot, dusty road to Mombasa.[90] From screening camps on settler farms, to transit camps in Nakuru, to work camps at Athi River, to detention camps at Manyani, well over 150,000 Gikuyu men, women, and children passed through detention during the eight long years of the emergency.[91] The Langata, Manyani, Kirigiti, and Kamiti camps held the largest populations of children and young people, dumping grounds for a wide array of young Gikuyu, from hardened Mau Mau forest fighters to Nairobi street boys.

Once detained, Gikuyu underwent screening to ascertain their degree of Mau Mau adherence. Screening teams, made up of British officers, African police, and loyal Gikuyu informants, held absolute power over the fate of thousands of suspected Mau Mau. They relied on information from brutal interrogations and hooded informants known as *Gakunia,* or "Little Sacks," to categorize detainees and determine the length and hardship of detention.[92] Those categorized "white" went home. Screeners had deemed them loyal. "Grey" Gikuyu, often oath-takers, supply runners, and spies, moved to work camps further down the pipeline. Their only path to freedom lay through rejection of the oath and then hard labor on communal projects. Hard-core or "black" detainees, those who refused to cooperate, went furthest down the pipeline to special camps where their intransigence might be loosened with harsher forms of punishment.[93]

Inside this network of camps, young people bore witness to the brutality and humiliation of screening and detention. While detained at Makadara, eleven-year-old James Karanja spent his days assisting elderly detainees who awaited transfer to Manyani. James found only "sadness" at Makadara. There this son of a loyalist headman to the assassinated chief Waruhiu came to know "what was being fought for." He watched screeners beat his fellow detainees, "beating them until some died."[94] The camp "was no joke," James recalls. "I witnessed, with my own eyes, their cries. They were saying '*tiiri*' [soil], and it was then I knew it was all about this soil." James and many other Gikuyu remember detention as a gauntlet of physical and psychological violence through which the British endeavored to break their hearts and minds.

They also suffered hunger, malnutrition, and disease. Looking back at his time in Manyani, Joseph Gikubu, only in his late teens then, remembers "the gun and fear" as well as hunger and sickness.[95] The detainees in Joseph's compound never had enough food and many developed scurvy and pellagra. Concerned about conditions in the camps, the labor department hired Dr. H. Stott to tour the pipeline and record incidents of disease and malnutrition. He estimated that among the 57,261 detainees in detention at the time, 3,700 cases of ill health occurred each week. The most common ailments were malaria, pellagra, diarrhea, dysentery, and influenza.[96] Nothing could prepare camp officials or Stott for the epidemic of typhoid that raced through the Manyani camp that same year. "We started suffering from typhoid," Joseph Gikubu recalls. "So many people died every day. There was no medicine."[97] As Joseph watched the bodies pile up, Stott counted eight hundred cases of typhoid at Manyani alone.

While detainees found life behind the wire brutal and degrading, the pipeline was no "closed universe" where "space, time and social exchange were completely organized and routinized."[98] Detention varied from camp to camp and depended on the resistance of detainees and the temperament of British officials and African warders. Even within a given camp, compounds and individuals experienced detention differently. Joseph Gikubu experienced these contradictions of the pipeline firsthand. When his chief arrested him for running errands for Mau Mau, he spent several months at the Mackinnon Road and Manyani camps. His lasting memory of Mackinnon Road was football. The camp officer in charge "liked young people," Joseph stated.[99] He selected a few from the camp population and then at four o'clock played football with them. "I could not believe it. He took us out, and we were playing football!" Yet his last memories of the Manyani camp were ones of idleness and illness. Joram Wamweya also experienced beatings and boredom at Manyani but still took pleasure in cooking, telling stories, and sharing cigarettes with his fellow detainees.[100]

For other Gikuyu, like Josiah Kariuki, detention was a continuation of their struggle for freedom.[101] Just as Mau Mau had been a crucible for maturity and expression of manhood, so, too, was detention. Hard cultural work went on behind the wire, where elders and young men carried on their age-relations with one another and strove for maturity.[102] Harry Joseph Kimanji, who had spent much of his childhood living by his wits on the streets of Nairobi, was swept up in a police raid in Starehe and sent to the Mwea work camp in 1954. At Mwea, he and his fellow detainees endured hard labor and little food. One night his compound agreed to strike for more rations. According to Harry, the strike brought up a white man from Nairobi, a "big man with his medals [who] didn't know Swahili."[103] He asked if anyone in the compound spoke English. Harry stepped forward, much to the surprise of his fellow detainees. Harry had told no one that he learned English at Tumutumu, a Church Missionary Society school, where he had been sent after one of his many boyhood arrests. For the duration of the strike, Harry served as an interpreter. He informed the official that his compound held over six hundred detainees and was due four bags of maize flour per day, not the single bag they had been getting. The official agreed and the food shortage ended. Although Harry had never participated in Mau Mau, the compound cheered his courage and contribution.

In return they offered him something just as important as food—his manhood. Despite being in his early twenties, Harry remained but an uncut boy. After the strike, they offered to circumcise him. "They said, because we have got this food through you, we will circumcise you. Will give you our food so that you can recover quickly." Where they found the knife, Harry does not recall, but he faced it bravely. "I was not given any injection like the hospital. It is only the knife." Highlighting the atypical circumstances of his initiation, his role in the strike, the lack of anesthetic, and the sacrifice of his sponsors, Harry asserts that it amplified his sense of manhood and maturity. Just what elder members of the camp made of their uncut interpreter, Harry cannot say. He remembers that three other boys were circumcised inside his compound at Mwea during his detention. Perhaps the Gikuyu warning that no secret is safe with an uncircumcised boy settled in the pit of their stomachs when Harry stepped forward to reveal his command of English.[104] The camp committee might have decided that to truly be certain of Harry's discipline and ability to keep his very valuable mouth shut, he had to be circumcised. At that moment, whether Harry knew it or not, the camp elders used initiation to exert their authority.

The presence of children and young people in detention presented problems for the elder state as well. The war council worried that the scandal of so many children and young people in detention might menace the carefully crafted image of the emergency broadcast across the globe. The last thing the war council wanted to see splashed across the pages of British and international newspapers were the faces of starving doe-eyed Gikuyu boys pressed against barbed wire. In the waning days of 1954, secretary of state for the colonies Alan Lennox-Boyd specifically inquired of Governor Baring how he was handling children and young people in detention. The secretary's letter concerned members of the war council as they watched the number of the underage detainees grow.[105] In the waning days of 1954, officials began to make a concerted effort to separate underage detainees from the adult population and hasten the pace of their release.

At Langata, camp staff constructed a separate "juvenile pen" to hold over 270 young detainees.[106] Inside the pen, assistant probation officer Geoffrey Mbugwa Kimani screened the boys and investigated their backgrounds. Geoffrey complained to his superiors that with the exception of two hours of football each day, the boys sat inactive and bored, making them headstrong and unmanageable. During the screening process, Geoffrey struggled to combat rumors that if the boys turned informants, they would be sent to Mombasa to die in the heat or, worse, be hired out as houseboys to government officials.[107] Those boys who did cooperate were repatriated home, though some Langata boys did so by giving Geoffrey false names and addresses in Kiambu. It was common for the Langata boys to tell camp officers they were from Kiambu so when taken to the district they could easily return to Nairobi by foot. Twenty-five percent of the young men at Langata had already been returned to the camp four or more times. At the Manyani camp, in early 1955, officials had also set aside a special compound for detainees under the age of eighteen. Joseph Gikubu remembers the day camp officials consolidated all young detainees in one camp: "There was too much noise from the government in Britain that there were a lot of children in Manyani, and they should not be mixed together with the grown-ups."[108] He and roughly two thousand others, abouth one-eighth of the camp's total population, were moved to the compound.

Underage Mau Mau had to be handled differently before colonial courts as well. Throughout the emergency, the British convicted 1,090 Mau Mau on meager or illegal evidence and hanged them from the gallows.[109] Yet the involvement of so many young Gikuyu under the age of eighteen in Mau Mau frustrated the colonial state's pursuit to hang as many fighters as possible. Under colonial law, no young person under the age of eighteen at the time of the crime could be sentenced to death. While the law was clear, the ages of young Mau Mau were not. In July 1954, magistrates called on the medical department to produce a field-tested method to determine the age of captured Mau Mau. Three doctors from the medical department studied ninety-five young Gikuyu schoolboys at several missions. They took X-rays of molars as well as the rounded ends of long bones in the arms and legs. They concluded that measuring teeth and bones could not determine, with a legal certainty, that a boy was over the age of eighteen.[110] A month later, lawyers in the case of Kariuki Karuma successfully used the medical department findings to prevent the boy from going to the gallows. Frustrated by inexact science, lawyers in Mau Mau cases set aside several death penalty sentences due to the defendants' uncertain ages.

Simon Kariuki escaped the death penalty due to his age.[111] On the night of his capture, British forces ambushed his gang outside Gatundu, halfway between Nairobi and the forests of the Aberdares.[112] A firefight broke out. Simon took a bullet to the arm and blacked out. He awoke in a hospital bed, shocked to discover his right arm had been amputated below the elbow. Still reeling from the loss of his arm, he was brought to court, charged with Mau Mau crimes, and sentenced to death. But looming uncertainty over Simon's age, and lingering fear that putting juveniles to death might scandalize the British public, forced officials to rethink Simon's case. A doctor examined him and declared him underage. As a result, the magistrate set aside capital punishment and sentenced him to life imprisonment. Simon went to the Nairobi prison, where the guards took a liking to the plucky forest fighter and nicknamed him *Gakono*, meaning "one-armed."

The growing bifurcation of emergency practices around age was not isolated to the detention camps of Langata and Manyani or the courtrooms of Nairobi. In the Gikuyu reserves, too, district commissioners began to differentiate forms of treatment of detainees based on their age. In Nyeri, when dozens of boys fled the military campaign raging in the forests and surrendered to Home Guard units in 1953, they were brought before district officer John Nottingham. Rather than hold the boys with older detainees, he created a separate space for them. He closed the Gatuyaini primary school, threw up barbed-wire fencing, and provided them with literacy and skills-training courses.[113] Months later, in Fort Hall District, district officers developed three "youth camps" at Kangema, Kigumo, and Kandara.[114] Anxious Fort Hall chiefs had also urged the construction of some form of detention for young men because they believed that "every child had been fully indoctrinated with the evils of Mau Mau and every teenage boy and girl was an active participant in the subversive activities of the day."[115] During their detention, the boys continued their education with teachers on loan from the Church Missionary Society and the Consolata Catholic Mission. The provincial commissioner lauded the success of these camps, claiming they had eradicated the Mau Mau threat among the youngsters. He ordered several of the boys at the Kandara camp to be hired as tribal police and those at Kangema and Kigumo to be rewarded with a year of school fees. Yet the success in Fort Hall was short-lived. The Kangema and Kigumo camps closed due to a shortage of staff and funding by the end of 1954. Kandara was raided and destroyed by Mau Mau fighters only a month after opening.

CONCLUSION

By early 1955, two separate, age-defined forms of detention emerged—one for adults, another for young people—with vastly different philosophies on how to eradicate Mau Mau. A separate, palatable method of handling young people, whether directly or indirectly involved in Mau Mau, had become a necessity that could no longer wait. In creating these two paths, the British assured that the two distinct generations of Mau Mau, which had emerged during the uprising, received very different forms of treatment. The first, older generation, those young Gikuyu in their late teens, early twenties, or older—men like Waruhiu Itote and Gucu Gikoyo—rotted in detention, worked on backbreaking communal labor projects, and hung from the gallows. They had taken up arms to resolve the ambiguities of their age. While they might have endured initiation, worked for wages, married, and bore sons, they felt suspended between childhood and adulthood. Their first coming-of-age had not made them mature men, and so they lashed out with violence to cut an alternative path through the obstacles the colonial encounter had littered before them. The second younger generation, those under the age of eighteen whose coming-of-age coincided with the violence sweeping across Central Province, entered a separate system where they encountered the elder state in the guise of Thomas Askwith's program for rehabilitation. In 1955, rehabilitation was salvaged from the wreckage of good intentions and became the cornerstone of colonial policy for young detainees. A fusion of Askwith's rehabilitation program, the war council's welfare of children regulation, and the makeshift youth schemes of Fort Hall and Nyeri formed the foundation of a new program that would profoundly alter the experience of the emergency for thousands of young men.[116] Known as the Wamumu Youth Camp, young Mau Mau fighters under the age of eighteen were about to begin an accelerated process of maturation and socialization orchestrated by the elder state.

7 ⤳ "We're the Wamumu Boys"

Defeating Mau Mau; Creating Youth at the End of Empire

As TYPHOID RACED through the Manyani detention camp, Joseph Gikubu watched two young community development officials approach his compound. The strangers stood for a moment surveying the nearly two thousand young men mulling behind the barbed wire, then they announced that everyone was to be transferred out of Manyani.[1] The two officials, whom Joseph later came to know as Geoffrey Griffin and Roger Owles, ordered the young detainees onto a train bound for Nairobi. As they boarded the cattle cars, guards handed each boy a blanket. At the Nairobi railway station, the train paused to change tracks. The boys exchanged those blankets for cigarettes with hawkers through the barbed-wire windows. Under way again, Joseph had no idea where they were headed. Suddenly the train creaked to a halt and the doors slid open. The boys stepped off the train, studying the forbidding landscape before them: rows and rows of the familiar A-frame tents of detention and then wilderness beyond. They had been brought to the southern outskirts of Embu District near the Tana River, a place "filthy and full of snakes," a place called Wamumu.[2]

As Joseph Gikubu and his fellow detainees settled into their new tents, Simon "Gakono" Kariuki wandered the Langata prison kitchen pilfering food. The self-proclaimed Mau Mau cowboy had been captured and lost an arm during a firefight with government forces. His age had spared him the death penalty. As Simon served out his life sentence, he received a visit

FIGURE 7.1. Wamumu Youth Camp detainees raise the Union Jack, possibly during the 1956 Empire Day celebration, n.d. Photo taken by Gordon Dennis. Courtesy of the National Museum of Kenya.

FIGURE 7.2. Wamumu Approved School, 1956. Photo possibly taken by Gordon Dennis during the 1956 Empire Day celebration. Courtesy of the National Archives, Kew.

from Geoffrey Griffin too. As he had done at Manyani, Griffin sought out underage Mau Mau for transfer to Wamumu. Leaving his kitchen privileges behind, Simon and several fellow inmates boarded a lorry bound for this place with a strange name.[3]

In late 1955, eighteen hundred young male detainees, drawn from detention camps, prisons, and a few nongovernmental institutions across the colony, converged at Wamumu.[4] There they encountered a unique form of detention, one that diverged sharply from adult detention.[5] Over the next few years, these young detainees underwent Thomas Askwith's program of rehabilitation. Mau Mau had arisen, Askwith argued, out of a crisis of generational authority and youthful indiscipline.[6] To crush the rising, the elder state must seize the initiative and redirect young Mau Mau's disorderly energies. Rehabilitation was also a weapon in the war for hearts and minds, not just of the Gikuyu but also of British skeptics back home. Showcasing the rehabilitation of young detainees distracted from the horrors committed in adult detention. Lengthy reports, photographs, and news stories filled the files of the department of community development and office of information. Yet Wamumu was not just an optical illusion. The officials who oversaw the detainees' daily lives were true believers in the power of the state to mold the behavior of the young—ideas they shared with social scientists and policy makers back in Britain. For them, Wamumu was a transformational space where the state made mature men and disciplined disciples of empire.

For Wamumu detainees, the camp was more complicated. Former detainees with whom I spoke had spent considerable time in the labyrinthine network of detention camps, and they all spoke of Wamumu in very different terms than those who had endured adult detention. As they shared their memories with me, they shifted from proudly explaining why they joined Mau Mau to enthusiastically describing the camaraderie, education, and jobs they earned at Wamumu. I pushed back, still waiting to hear their denunciations of British detention and the untold hardships they suffered, sentiments that had become commonplace in the shadow of a legal bid for reparations.[7] Instead, as their life histories unfolded, Mau Mau and Wamumu became complementary and sequential parts of their coming-of-age. At Wamumu, they negotiated advantageous terms of surrender, participating in rehabilitation to access the very things for which they had taken oaths and flung themselves into battle. They remade the camp into an alternative, state-sponsored rite of passage—a strange marriage of Gikuyu cultural life, colonial policy, and carceral contingency. In unconventional surroundings, with newly imagined ritual forms, the detainees replicated the most climactic moment in any young Gikuyu's life, his initiation.

Wamumu had its limits, though. The youth camp was a male space, denying the many girls and young women arrested during the state of emergency the same kind of rehabilitation. Moreover, the youth camp was designed to handle only a small number of Mau Mau suspects. By 1956, district and community development officers in Central Province awakened to the destruction they had wrought. They braced themselves against waves of young refugees and orphans whose parents were dead or detained, their villages burned or consolidated, their schools shuttered, and their search for work prohibited by movement restrictions. These officials recast the aftermath of the counterinsurgency as a "crisis of youth" that, if left unresolved, would lead to another outbreak of violence. By using the word *youth*, officials tapped into new ideas circulating in Britain, Europe, and the United States about the nature of young people and the role of the state in shaping their behavior. Their solution was to construct hundreds of youth clubs, drawing on and then exporting Wamumu's program of rehabilitation across Kenya. In the waning years of the emergency, Wamumu and the youth clubs became the backbone of a nascent youth service, one of the largest on the continent.

As an ever-increasing number of boys and young men languished in detention, the war council charged Thomas Askwith and his department of community development with creating a separate detention camp where Gikuyu under the age of eighteen would undergo rehabilitation. Finally given the green light to put rehabilitation into practice, Askwith quickly set out hiring his team. To run the camp, he chose George Gardener, an ex-sergeant in the British military who had worked in East African prisons and sat on the Scouts Examination Board of Kenya. Geoffrey Griffin and Roger Owles, both sons of settlers, mutual friends, and officers in the King's African Rifles, would assist Gardener and supervise the detainees' daily activities. Two former Kenya prison officers experienced with young offenders, J. R. Law and W. D. Bird, oversaw dozens of African police and staff who guarded and disciplined detainees. Askwith also recruited an administrative assistant with physical training expertise and an ex-headmaster of Tumutumu to handle the educational curriculum.[8] At Wamumu, Askwith assembled the most qualified staff of youth workers on the continent, with the exception of the Diepkloof Reformatory in South Africa.[9]

Construction began on Wamumu in July 1955, in a remote and expansive area in southern Embu locked between the deep purple hills of Fort Hall to the north and the Ukambani Hills to the south. It would have been an imposing scene to any boy looking to escape. Freedom lay across the crocodile-infested Tana River or through the endless flatlands of tall grass and acacia. This inhospitable landscape and the supposedly hard-core young detainees it held gave the camp its name: Wamumu. A distortion of Gikuyu and a weak double entrendre, *Wamumu* meant a "hard place for hard people," or somewhere for those caught "between a rock and a hard place." In name, Wamumu was a contradiction. Was it a detention camp where hard treatment might rehabilitate hard-core Mau Mau or a camp of last resort for victims of the war?

Despite Askwith's lengthy reports outlining rehabilitation, colonial officials, from the war council down to Wamumu staff, were unclear what the camp was meant to do. Initially, the war council intended Wamumu to house two thousand young detainees threatened by typhoid at Manyani and Langata.[10] Roger Owles and Geoffrey Griffin had been stationed at Manyani for several months separating the detainees by age, which they sometimes did by examining for circumcision. They also assessed each detainee's suitability for rehabilitation. At first, the boys did everything in their power to fool them. But gradually, over the course of two months, the youngest detainees in the compound began to approach them:

Many could not hope to control their tears. Some were stunning in their terribleness; I could hardly believe that boys so young could be so involved. Others brought the story of their arrest and of the fearful condemnations placed on them by hooded men and the like. The majority told their bits not professing innocence but just the truth, so they said. Most told of how many oaths and why and when they had taken. Details of the money they had collected, the errands they had done, the ammunition they had passed on and the oath ceremonies they had guarded came pouring out.[11]

To Owles and Griffin, these younger detainees were ripe for rehabilitation. By June, they recommended that twelve hundred detainees under the age of sixteen be transferred to Wamumu. Their older compatriots were returned to the adult compounds, many of whom ended up digging irrigation ditches at the Mwea rice scheme not too far from Wamumu.[12]

Griffin and Owles did not stop with Manyani. Later that year, Griffin visited the Langata prison in search of young Mau Mau who had escaped the gallows; there he found Simon "Gakono" Kariuki. In July 1955, five hundred of "the worst type of Nairobi 'cover boys'" were transferred to Wamumu. These included boys held at the Langata screening camp as well as welfare programs like Ujana Park and Dagoretti Children's Center. Orphans and street boys like Gabriel Kahugu, who had enjoyed the security of Ujana Park and the status of care and protection cases, were suddenly transformed back into suspected Mau Mau detainees and sent to live alongside hardened forest fighters. District commissioners in Central Province were also ordered to transfer boys held in detention camps in the reserves to Wamumu.[13] At the Kirigiti camp in Kiambu, James Karanja and Samuel Uiru, street boys turned Mau Mau suspects, both remember the day when a British official came to their detention camp and ordered all the young men to line up. He walked down the line, striking some of them on the head while leaving others unscathed. Samuel Uiru felt the sting of the official's hand and left for Wamumu. James Karanja did not and remained behind.[14] What separated some boys from years of rehabilitation at Wamumu and others from further detention was sometimes an indiscriminate blow to the head. By September 1955, in excess of eighteen hundred boys had converged at Wamumu.

This motley assortment of hard-core Mau Mau fighters, spies, and supply runners, as well as thieves, vagrants, and orphans, did not conform to the war council's original intention. These young detainees represented two distinct groups. The first group—suspected Mau Mau participants—were the vanguard in a war for maturity. Those like Simon "Gakono" Kariuki and Joseph Gikubu had taken oaths, battled for the right to be mature men, and wore their war wounds proudly. They were hard folks in need of a hard place. The second group—orphans, street kids, and young offenders—were the vandals of colonial law and order and victims of colonial violence. They were boys caught between the rock of Mau Mau and the hard place of the counterinsurgency.

The question arose among camp staff: If Wamumu was to cater to such diversity, then what form should rehabilitation take? For Wamumu's inaugural class, rehabilitation initially looked very much akin to adult detention. In the first few months, the detainees were put to hard labor, building the camp that would confine them. Each day, they turned out one thousand bricks to build staff housing, offices, and other facilities.[15] Ngugi Kabiro, who worked as Gardener's bookkeeper, recalls that the guards were brutal, often forcing Griffin and Owles to intervene. Even Gardener began to question the rehabilitative potential of Wamumu. "The school," he complained, "was very much a detention camp; hedged about with barbed wire and armed warders."[16]

Feeling betrayed by the promise of a different kind of detention, many of the detainees tried to escape or to continue the Mau Mau struggle inside the camp. On the evening of 27 September, Simon Kariuki escaped Wamumu. With one arm, he crawled through a double-strand wire fence, through askari lines, along a drain, and under the outer wire.[17] Days before, he had plotted a mass breakout with fifteen other detainees. Yet when he found himself alone in the dark with miles of wilderness before him, uncertainty seized him and he returned to Wamumu. According to Griffin, when Simon realized his comrades had betrayed him, out of cowardice or simply a good laugh, the boy marched straight up to Owles's compound, woke him up, and fingered all fifteen of his coconspirators.[18] In light of the attempted escape, Gardener suspended all work until a moat filled with wooden stakes was built around the camp. Further investigations revealed that thirty-two "hard-core" Mau Mau had not only encouraged Simon to escape but conducted oathing ceremonies, fashioned weapons, and obtained money and false documents inside the camp. Gardener conveniently deemed the thirty-two inmates too old to remain at Wamumu. In front of the entire assembly of detainees, they were beaten and returned to adult detention.[19] Simon was allowed to stay.

Watching the beatings left a mark on the detainees, and their behavior grew more acquiescent in the following months. The spectacle also affected camp officials. They began to question whether rehabilitation had ever been a reality at Wamumu. At the end of 1955, Gardener and his staff reimagined just whom they were rehabilitating. "It was agreed that, although the background of many of the boys included arson, intimidation and murder, those crimes had been committed under the stimulus of a general tribal movement, with the youth simulating their elders in a condition of genuine, albeit misguided, enthusiasm."[20] Although their criminal records were serious (sixty boys had already admitted to committing murder), Gardener believed that the detainees must not be held accountable for their actions. They were minors, mimicking elder misbehavior, manipulated by their faith in the wisdom of seniority.[21] Where the colonial state had once seen only hard-core Mau Mau, it now saw only child's play. Emasculating and infantilizing the detainees in such a way solved the practical problem of trying to rehabilitate boys of varying ages, backgrounds, and degrees of Mau Mau affiliation. It no longer mattered that some had fought in the forests while others dug through dustbins on the streets of Nairobi—they were all misguided boys, led astray by failed elder authority. Firmly setting Wamumu apart from the rest of the system of detention, and its detainees apart from the rest of Mau Mau, Gardener, Griffin, and Owles began putting rehabilitation into practice.

COLONIAL RITE OF PASSAGE

Shortly after watching their thirty-two comrades beaten and expelled, the remaining Wamumu boys dismantled the catwalks, watchtowers, and barbed-wire fences, and then built brick-and-cement dormitories, classrooms, sports facilities, gardens, and two churches—one Catholic, the other Protestant.[22] Of the two hundred warders, on whom Ngugi Kabiro blamed most of the violence, only forty remained. Amid these changes, the Reverend Dennis Hooper of the Church Missionary Society stopped by to inspect Wamumu. After seeing the camp, Hooper offered a rather twisted description of the boys' lives:

> At first sight the tall barbed wire fences enclosing the "lean-tos" of aluminum sheeting, with sentries at the gates, hold little promise of satisfactory home making. Yet an hour or two spent within that enclosure dispels the sense of restriction: the barbed wire only serves to make the community compact: the armed guards turn out to be no more sinister than college porters with routine duties. And the "lean-tos" prove comfortable if ascetic quarters for the raw material, which is sent to this village to be remade in the likeness of true *manhood*.[23]

Physically, Wamumu remained a detention camp, but Hooper quite literally reinvented it as a foundry smelting youthful "raw material" and forging it into "true manhood." Wamumu made men. Rather than a place of detention, Wamumu became something more akin to a rite of passage. The reverend wrote up his experience at Wamumu in a piece he entitled "We're the Wamumu Boys." The article then circulated to a wider audience within the missionary community, used to highlight rehabilitation to blunt the growing criticism of the counterinsurgency.

Rehabilitation at Wamumu consisted of several stages. First, the boys had to rewrite their pasts. "It was decided," Gardener wrote, "that the only realistic line of action possible was to ignore individual records and to endeavor to start each boy with a clean slate."[24] All the young detainees, regardless of their biological age or self-perceived maturity, became minors stripped of any agency in and responsibility for Mau Mau. The first step was to uninitiate the detainees, restoring the innocence of childhood. Their pasts were to be wiped clean through confession and Christian baptism. Many confessed their oaths, renounced their allegiance to Mau Mau, and provided camp staff with intelligence that could be used in the counterinsurgency. From previous experience, officials knew that the young, if handled properly, could be valuable sources of information, even key witnesses in Mau Mau trials. Following confession, some of the boys underwent Christian baptism, even if they had already been baptized at birth. While confession was mandatory, conversion was not. Only 790 detainees, less than half, became Roman Catholic or Protestant in the first year. The rituals of confession and baptism, as Louis Leakey had prescribed, absolved detainees of their sins against the colonial state.[25]

Confessing oaths and professing Christian faith bound Wamumu to the wider revivalist work being done in detention at the Athi River work camp and elsewhere. In fact, Askwith had originally wanted the youth camp built at Athi River.[26] The camp, which opened in 1953, would have been an ideal location for Askwith, as the dirty work of rehabilitation was well under way, overseen by Howard Church, a prominent revivalist and member of the Church Missionary Society; and Alan Knight, a member of Kenya's branch of Moral Re-Armament. "The program of rehabilitation," Derek Peterson argues, "was revivalism in a coercive mode."[27] At Athi River, a team of twelve revivalists preached to detainees for hours each day. If persuaded of their Mau Mau misdeeds, detainees then confessed their sins. Their confessions all too easily slipped into revelations of other personal sins committed over a lifetime and the casting of stones at others. Like Athi River, the focus of the youth camp was to be confession, absolution, and reeducation; yet

Askwith was refused the space and given land at Wamumu instead. Shortly after Wamumu opened, Athi River closed. Although Athi River lasted only three years, the rehabilitation conducted there paved the way for a much broader missionary influence, especially among Protestants, inside detention. Wamumu staff relied heavily on the expertise of these Protestant missionaries and their faithful, especially those of the Church Missionary Society at Tumutumu.

Returned to the innocence of childhood, Mau Mau men-made-boys could now undergo the next step of rehabilitation: discipline, labor, and tradition. Inventing and inculcating a sense of tradition at Wamumu became an integral part of rehabilitation. Gardener ran the camp along the same lines as the British military service and public school system. The boys were sorted into four senior houses—Grogan, Delamere, Boyes, and Lugard— some of Kenya's most infamous European settlers and one of Britain's most powerful colonial mandarins. Each house was assigned a badge with house colors: blue for Delamere, yellow for Grogan, green for Boyes, and red for Lugard. Each detainee wore a uniform of khaki shirts and shorts during the day, and a white vest with blue shorts during athletic events.[28]

The boys woke to reveille at 6:00 a.m. and assembled before Gardener for prayer. The camp flag, which the boys had embroidered themselves, fluttered above. The cluttered Wamumu standard bore the wheel of progress, the Christian cross, tools of the artisan, the torch of the scholar, and the lion of Kenya set above the motto "Truth and Loyalty."[29] The boys then listened to Gardener list the day's announcements and impart words of wisdom. He often reminded them that he, too, had been a young miscreant in his home village in England. One day the authorities sent him to the army to prove himself a man. How similar their paths had been, he used to say.[30] Classes began at 8:00 a.m. and lasted until 4:00 p.m., when the boys had the option of continuing to study or playing sports. Football, boxing, and track and field, masculine activities socializing millions of British young men, were wildly popular at Wamumu. The boys made sports an essential part of their daily routine. They especially enjoyed competitions among the houses and playing teams outside Wamumu, like the students of Kigari Teaching Training College, the inmates of Kabete Approved School, or the child laborers of the East African Sisal Estates.[31]

The boys competed not just on the football pitch; they and their houses were pitted in competition with one another. In creating a house system and posts like house prefect and school captain, camp officials believed the boys would form a sense of loyalty to their house, cast a watchful eye over the activities of the other houses, and battle one another to earn positions of personal power. An internal disciplinary regime formed within and between each house. The prefect of Boyes House drove his comrades to perfect even the most mundane tasks.[32] Peter Mwarangu recalls that even in the evenings, "you still had some other duties to attend before tomorrow. In the dormitories there was some work like cleaning here, painting here, and also competition among cleaners. The competitions were done monthly so the boy in charge of the block saw to it that the house was winning. When it was done for the night, he would turn off the lights for everyone to sleep. So it was not as free as such."[33] Only when the work was done did a prefect allow his fellow inmates to sleep. His personal position and his house's reputation were at stake. Internal hierarchies, constant competition, and ceaseless activity exhausted the boys and formed a self-regulating system of coercion at Wamumu.

When competition and exhaustion were not enough to discipline the detainees, they found themselves punished with extra work detail, caning, or solitary confinement. Most detainees at Wamumu felt the sting of the rattan cane, usually for minor offenses like laziness, theft, fighting, or having sex with one another. When a prefect or captain noticed another boy being lazy, he noted it in the offense book. Griffin or Owles would later review the book and give the offender several strokes of the cane. For more serious or repeat offenses, boys earned stints in D-block. A boy sentenced to D-block was stripped of his uniform, forced to wear a pair of black underwear inscribed with the letter *D*, and put to hard labor. He remained in solitary confinement until he agreed to behave.[34]

The use of confession, tradition, competition, and punishment certainly distinguished Wamumu from adult detention, but in many ways rehabilitation seemed nothing more than a reframing of approved school techniques, a blunt and imprecise instrument to fashion manhood. At the outset, community development had even toyed with calling Wamumu an approved school. Yet camp officials tried to establish deeper connections between detainees and the elder state that separated rehabilitation from what went on at the Kabete and Dagoretti approved schools.

Former Wamumu detainees recall that the personal relationships they formed with European and African staff set the camp apart from other forms of detention. No camp official lives on in their memories more vividly than Roger Owles, or, as the boys called him, Wamathina. Owles oversaw their daily activities, watching them from sunrise to nightfall. They listened to his announcements over the loudspeaker and felt the smack of his cane when they broke camp rules. The boys saw him as a contradiction, a source of pain and comfort, reflected in his nickname, *Wamathina*, meaning "a person full of problems."[35] It was a clever pet name for Owles. As camp disciplinarian and taskmaster, he hounded the detainees to work harder and get along with one another. To the boys, he was a wellspring of problems overflowing with commands and reprimands. He was also the man to whom the detainees most often went for help. If someone felt harassed by others or hungry, then Owles rectified the problem. Simon Kariuki recalls that the nickname had originated early on when screeners came to Wamumu to interrogate the detainees. When a screener beat one of them, it was Owles who intervened on the boy's behalf.[36] Wamathina took on their complaints, filling himself with their problems. Geoffrey Griffin was also well liked at Wamumu and went out of his way to form personal relationships with many of the detainees. While at Wamumu, Simon Kariuki continued to go by his nom de guerre, "Gakono" or "One-Armed." One day, while out on the foot-ball pitch, Griffin called Simon into the carpentry workshop. When he ar-rived, he found Griffin waiting for him with a surprise: a wooden prosthetic arm made by his fellow detainees and the carpentry instructor, Mr. Dennis. Fighting back tears as he recounted this moment to me, Simon described it as one of the finest of his life. The prosthetic and the act of kindness from his fellow detainees and Griffin began to heal a long-open wound.

To special relationships, camp officials added special events that aimed to impress upon the public the important work being done at the youth camp. At events like Empire Day, staff very literally paraded young detain-ees before cameras and onlookers to herald the defeat of Mau Mau. They also used Empire Day to impress upon the detainees their connection to something larger than themselves: the "glorious history and inheritance of the British Empire."[37] Such messaging served as a form of counteroath. On 24 May 1956, the detainees celebrated Empire Day with a parade along the main drive in front of the flagpole. Tribal police stood in their uniforms, setting "an example of discipline and smartness."[38] Next stood camp staff and house prefects. Then came the detainees, led by those who had joined the Wamumu branch of the Boy Scouts. Gardener inspected the rows, then signaled everyone to march to the sporting grounds and sit before the grandstand. "In silent concentration the great crowd listened to" Gardener, who, "in simple words, and using vivid imagery," spoke "of the rise of the Empire, the benefits that it had conferred upon its peoples, its ideals, unity, and strength. . . ." Afterward, the boys bowed their heads as Gardener read aloud the Empire Day prayer, thanking God for granting the queen "a great dominion in all parts of the earth" and bringing together "in true fellowship

FIGURE 7.3. Wamumu Youth Camp detainees on parade outside the camp gates, n.d. Photo taken by Gordon Dennis. Courtesy of the National Museum of Kenya.

the men of diverse races, languages, and customs" to bear one another's burdens and work in "brotherly concord."[39] When Gardener concluded, the boys rose and marched back to the school and played sports and music. Meanwhile, those who had attended the festivities could sleep easy, knowing that Wamumu was hard at work defeating Mau Mau.

Gardener's speech echoed a recommendation made by John C. Carothers, the psychiatrist hired to review and support Askwith's policy of rehabilitation. Carothers argued that in order to shake young Africans from their allegiance to Mau Mau, they had to "see themselves as part of a vast human organization," an alternative community with tentacles stretching out in all directions.[40] The empire supplied just such an alternative to Mau Mau, kinship, and tribe, and Empire Day put this "vast human organization" on full display, with all the pomp and circumstance a scantily funded youth camp could afford. The performance offered the boys a new vision of themselves as fortunate members of the British Empire, dutiful subjects of the queen, and humble children of God. Having taken this new oath-of-sorts, the boys were tasked with perpetuating the empire and maintaining the welfare of its multiracial brotherhood. Yet as events like Empire Day painted a rosy picture for public consumption, away from the cameras, detainees pushed camp officials to find more concrete ways of making rehabilitation matter.

Its final steps of education, skills training, and, above all, a state-sponsored form of initiation, ultimately set Wamumu apart from adult detention and approved schools. Camp staff initiated the boys into manhood, indelibly linking their coming-of-age to the patronage of the state. Facing the knife became one of the most significant moments for many of the boys held at Wamumu. Circumcising detainees as part of rehabilitation marked a radical intervention in the physical and emotional development as well as the ritual life of young male Gikuyu. In the first few months at Wamumu, a boy could visit the dispensary at any time and request circumcision from Gikubu Karanja, the Gikuyu camp dresser.[41] Gardener noted in his annual reports that about a dozen boys faced Karanja's knife each month. Later, staff regularized circumcisions around school holidays in April, August, and December to avoid detainees' missing classes and to better reflect common practice in the reserves. By then, the former Wamumu detainees with whom I spoke recall, about thirty boys underwent the procedure each season, about one hundred each year.

Not all boys volunteered for circumcision at Wamumu. Some were too young for the procedure, others had already been initiated prior to detention, and still others wanted to wait until they were home with their families. But enough boys had their circumcisions at Wamumu for the camp to gain a reputation throughout the colony. Boys at the Friends Africa Mission at Kaimosi asked a rehabilitation officer during her inspection of the school whether rumors of others being circumcised in detention were true.[42] The rumors were indeed true. Wamumu boys knew the time for circumcision had come when they heard the camp loudspeaker crackle to life, and Roger Owles speaking in Gikuyu challenged them, saying, "Urenda gûikara ta thoguo kana ta nyukwa?" / "Do you want to remain like your mother or your father?" Hearing this, those boys who felt ready to volunteer let camp staff and their fellow detainees know by shouting, "Ta baba!" / "Like our father!"[43] At the heart of this call-and-response between initiator and initiates lay an inescapable challenge: Remain uncut with a foreskin that symbolized a feminized body. Remain like the mother who nurtured you in your carefree infancy. Or bravely face the knife like your forefathers. Become men.

While young Meru girls took charge of their own initiations, circumcising themselves in the forests of Mount Kenya in defiance of efforts to ban the practice, the boys at Wamumu arranged for the colonial state to do it for them. Simon Kariuki answered Owles's call to be like his father;

so, too, did Gabriel Kahugu and Samuel Uiru.[44] Before the procedure, the Gikuyu medical dresser inspected each boy to determine if the volunteers were old enough. If the medical dresser thought a detainee too young, he turned the boy away. For those older boys whose initiation was getting late, circumcision became especially important.[45] After earning the dresser's approval, Simon, Gabriel, and Samuel received a local anesthetic, had their foreskins removed, and stayed in a special room of the dispensary to heal. In a week, the boys returned to their dormitories. If the aim of Wamumu was to make disciplined men out of misguided boys, then its graduates could not leave without carrying the physical scars of their transition. Postponing the circumcision of younger inmates suggests that their rehabilitation remained incomplete and required more time. Getting cut became a marker of maturity for detainees, a way perhaps to represent the age they had earned as Mau Mau and then as detainees.

It should come as little surprise that Wamumu detainees volunteered for circumcision. Initiation rites had always been, especially during the colonial period, a flexible institution. Many boys responded "Ta baba!" simply because they did not know whether they would ever be released. Simon connected his circumcision at Wamumu with his life sentence. "How did I know," he explained, "if I was ever going home?"[46] Word had also spread that initiation rites in the Gikuyu reserves had come under strict administrative supervision. In 1955, provincial administrators and chiefs in Kiambu and Fort Hall limited circumcision to a single week in December so they could more effectively monitor and limit the movement of Gikuyu.[47] A Wamumu boy released in late December might have to wait another year before becoming a man. Furthermore, the uncertainties about what had happened to families during the counterinsurgency compelled many to accept the medical dresser's knife. Who would circumcise them if their fathers sat in detention, battled British forces in the forest, or died victims in the cross fire? The only certainty Wamumu boys knew was the message that Gardener, Griffin, and Owles broadcast each day: Enter the camp a youth; exit a man.

Becoming a man at Wamumu was not just a personal achievement. Circumcision defined age-relations within the camp, and detainees used it to create a moral, masculine code to govern their relationships with one another. Circumcision established age-defined roles for and hierarchies among seniors and juniors. Circumcision brought detainees promotion and new privileges. Gikuyu camp staff, as well as Griffin and Owles, took care to handle circumcised young men differently. They allowed only the circumcised to serve as captains and house prefects.[48] Circumcised detainees no longer showered, played games, or joked around with younger boys. They also enjoyed newfound camaraderie with older housemates, as well as the respect and admiration of their juniors.[49] Older circumcised detainees encouraged and sponsored their younger housemates to volunteer for the procedure. Joseph Gikubu recalls that these age-defined relationships, operated by the boys themselves and encouraged by camp officials, ensured harmony at Wamumu. One might expect such an answer, though, from Wamumu's former school captain.[50] Despite their detention far from home, and in spite of their unconventional surroundings, boys adapted the relationships and meanings associated with initiation and age-relations to camp life, and camp officials eagerly participated.

Circumcision might have initiated Wamumu boys into manhood, but their rehabilitation remained incomplete until they could test that manhood with hard work. After all, that was what so many had taken up arms for in the first place. In the final act of rehabilitation, the young men earned an education, vocational training, job placement, and a steady wage. Gardener and his staff had one final ritual in store, assembling a literate, skilled laboring class employable in colonial industries. In return for entering the colonial economy, these young men could earn the right to marry, own property, and one day become elders in their own right. Both camp officials and Wamumu young men hoped this final process would resolve the uncertainties of age and generational mobility that had driven so many to take the Mau Mau oath and take up arms against the colonial state.

The Wamumu curriculum included three types of training programs: agricultural, vocational, and academic. All detainees were given training in agriculture and animal husbandry. The camp maintained a farm alongside the dormitories so detainees could learn to grow and harvest their own food. The camp also received seventeen cattle from the Kabete Approved School. The detainees took their agricultural work seriously and showed "considerable interest" in the process of land consolidation taking place in the reserves. The young men undoubtedly raised questions about the fate of their families' plots and whether they might get their own property. Unable to answer their questions, Gardener had to send for an agricultural officer to visit the camp.[51]

Not surprisingly, vocational and academic training were more popular than farming and herding. Vocational training had long been an essential component of education and punishment in Kenya. In the earliest years of colonial rule, the government funded technical training programs at mission schools like Tumutumu, hoping to create a semiliterate, semiskilled African workforce. The department of public works opened the Native Industrial Training Depot at Kabete (later known as the Kabete Technical

Training School) to train their own artisans.[52] Approved schools at Kabete and Dagoretti relied heavily on vocational training as a prescription for delinquency. Postwar Kenya witnessed a revival in government-sponsored vocational training, especially for African veterans. The departments of education, prisons, and public works also focused on the value of creating an African working class capable of keeping pace with the demands of postwar colonial development and pressing metropolitan economic needs.[53]

This long history of and renewed enthusiasm for technical training influenced rehabilitation at Wamumu. Older detainees received six weeks of training and three weeks of in-shop experience as carpenters, blacksmiths, tailors, mechanics, and sign-writers. Young men who excelled in these areas continued their vocational training. The rest focused on academic classes up to standard eight, the last level of primary education before secondary school.[54] To run the carpentry workshop, Gardener hired Mr. Dennis, an old colonial hand who had worked as a technical instructor at the Kenya and Uganda Railways and the Tumutumu mission school. The addition of Mr. Dennis's expertise assured that Wamumu detainees would receive some of the best instruction in the colony. Former detainees praise the high quality of instruction at Wamumu. Peter Mwarangu remembers Mr. Dennis as an excellent instructor and strong advocate for the boys in his class. Gabriel Kahugu, who took tailoring classes, prides himself on the level of craftsmanship he honed. Shortly after his release from Wamumu, he took the trade assessment test and placed second of three hundred tailors—bested by only a Goan girl with years of prior apprenticeship.[55]

Had Wamumu detainees been treated like the young offenders at the Kabete Approved School, they would have received years of less intensive education and technical training and been released with little or no aftercare. Instead, hundreds of Wamumu graduates received job placement through the department of community development. The most skilled ex-detainees found high-paying work. Gabriel Kahugu's exceptional tailoring skills landed him a job in Nairobi working for a Goan tailor. Samuel Uiru's writing skills and excellent English got him a job as a clerk at Naku Freight.[56] Both Gabriel and Samuel had spent their childhoods picking through garbage bins on the streets of Nairobi. They had been arrested as suspected Mau Mau and detained at Wamumu, only to return to Nairobi as men with good work and high wages. Wamumu graduates did not need Gabriel's and Samuel's extraordinary skills to obtain good jobs. In 1956, seventy-nine detainees with vocational training were sent to the Rift Valley to fill vacancies on farms owned by settlers and multinational corporations. The following year, the Kenya Sisal Growers Association hired two hundred Wamumu young men. The list of settlers and companies who took Wamumu ex-detainees went on and on: African Breweries, Allsopps, Queens Dryers and Cleaners, Woodlands Hotel, and East African Bag and Cordage, among many others. Most incredible of all, half of the forty places for a five-year railway apprenticeship, a competitive and coveted position, went to young men from Wamumu.[57]

Some Wamumu graduates struck out on their own, following their dreams. Peter Mwarangu's carpentry work with Mr. Dennis got him work doing construction, but his love for the boxing that Gardener had encouraged won the day. He went on to train several generations of Olympic boxers. Others found work with the state as police, special branch officers, and civil servants. Community development hired Wamumu's school captain, Joseph Gikubu, to run a program for street boys in Nairobi, while Simon Kariuki left Wamumu to run the department's youth clubs in Nyeri.[58] Today, Simon lives in the basement of the three-story business complex he owns on the outskirts of Nairobi, a building named Gakono House. He still wears the same prosthetic arm crafted in Mr. Dennis's workshop some fifty years ago. When he speaks, he gesticulates with it proudly, the metal hook spinning wildly at the end of the wooden stump. When asked how he felt about his time at Wamumu, he declared: "I eat because of Wamumu; the education I have is from Wamumu."[59] His wooden prosthesis remains an enduring reminder of the war he fought and the manhood he earned on two battlefields, one as Mau Mau and the other as a Wamumu boy. Many of his fellow ex–Wamumu detainees agree. Joseph Gikubu insists that Wamumu provided direction and discipline at a moment when the violence and socioeconomic upheaval of the counter-insurgency might have thrust him further into poverty, delinquency, and despair. Gabriel Kahugu believes that while "there were problems in the world," Wamumu became a place of refuge to weather the storm, and, for a time, a place to call "home."[60] They all argue that the strange alchemy of Mau Mau and Wamumu made them men. Yet they admit that not all their age-mates were given such an opportunity. Thousands of their age-mates languished in detention or amid the unparalleled violence rocking Central Kenya with no prospects for education, decent wages, or means to become men.

THE LIMITS OF REHABILITATION

Of course, camp and community development officials were convinced of their success. Thomas Askwith noted that among Wamumu detainees, "Mau Mau was not only discarded, it was almost forgotten."[61] He later recalled,

"So it was that after a year or two, the thousand young men . . . found themselves back in the world from which they had been outcast. Although they had mostly been taught the rudiments of trade, it was not this that made them so sought after, but their character and trustworthiness. No one had expected that former Mau Mau thugs would compete with the normal school leaver for the best jobs."[62] Officials believed they had achieved something extraordinary: a prescription for Mau Mau without the hangman's noose or atrocities of detention. Despite Askwith's self-congratulations, the perceived success of rehabilitation remained the exception rather than the rule. In adult camps, detainees endured dehumanizing violence and a whiff of rehabilitation. Detainees like Josiah Kariuki and Gakaara wa Wanjau did more to rehabilitate one another with education and moral direction than community development officers.[63] Only young male detainees experienced the kind of rehabilitative work carried out at Wamumu, and, even then, only some of those under the age of eighteen held by the colonial state went to the youth camp. Wamumu boys were indeed a class of their own. To ensure their success, colonial officials imbued Wamumu graduates with an aura of incorruptibility. They prevented incidents of Wamumu boys' failure from being recorded. When police investigated crimes involving Wamumu alumni, the young men needed only to flash their leaving certificates to absolve themselves of accusation.[64]

Simply being held at Wamumu did not ensure success. Peter Mwarangu believes his time at Wamumu was a pivotal moment of his life, but he also acknowledges that was not the case for some of his fellow graduates. "Some are now dead," he admits, "[and] others came out and became hard-core criminals."[65] By way of illustration, he recounted his first day as a guard at the Naivasha prison. As he walked alongside the cells inspecting the prisoners, outstretched hands burst through the bars and the familiar voices of former Wamumu boys rang out: "Hey! Mwarangu! Huwezi kunikumbuka? [Don't you remember me?]." A Wamumu reunion held in a prison brought Peter face-to-face with the limits of rehabilitation. After these detainees left the camp, they resumed their lives of criminality out of desperation or perhaps inclination. As colonial officials and some former detainees heralded Wamumu's success, others murmured of its malfunction from dark prison cells.

Wamumu's limits might be measured by the lives of its fallen alumni, but the hundreds of young detainees denied access to the youth camp were just as revealing. Most boys under the age of eighteen remained in camps like Manyani and Mwea long after Wamumu had opened its gates. In January 1956, the department of prisons estimated that 1,048 detainees under the age of eighteen still remained scattered throughout the network of camps.[66] By then, most major military operations against Mau Mau had wound down. General Erskine, commander of British military forces in Kenya, and his successor, General Lathbury, began withdrawing their troops, leaving behind smaller "pseudo-gangs" to battle scattered, dwindling bands of forest fighters.[67] For their part, colonial officials accelerated the release of Gikuyu from detention, especially children and young people whose presence in the camps proved unappetizing to the British public. Many boys and young men who might have gone to Wamumu were shuttled from camp to camp and eventually dumped outside their homes. One day at the Kirigiti camp, James Karanja, the streetwise son of a loyalist headman, remembers being ordered to line up by a British official. The official chose James and a few other boys to remain behind, while others, including Samuel Uiru, boarded a lorry for Wamumu. James's memories of Kirigiti differed dramatically from the experiences of other detainees, perhaps because of his father's connections to the government. "I loved that place. It was good in terms of porridge in the morning, *irio* and milk at lunch, and *ugali* and meat for supper. I became really fat."[68] Besides putting on weight, James also studied Gikuyu, played football, and danced with other boys. A short time after, he headed home. By May 1956, the department of prisons reported that the number of young detainees like James who had not gone to Wamumu had fallen steadily.[69]

The state also denied rehabilitation to many young Mau Mau suspects because officials could not manage the complications of the myriad emergency regulations passed during the counterinsurgency. Some young detainees had been under the age of eighteen when convicted of Mau Mau–related crimes, but then sat in detention for so long that they had turned eighteen and could no longer be sent to Wamumu.[70] Other detainees, like Simon "Gakono" Kariuki, were convicted of capital crimes; however, they were spared the death penalty because of their age and given life sentences. What good was rehabilitation at Wamumu, officials asked one another, if boys like Simon were to spend the rest of their lives in prison? The secretary of defense wanted young Mau Mau lifers sent to Wamumu regardless. The deputy governor believed they should be kept "in a separate prison . . . until they are old enough to go onto an ordinary prison."[71] In the end, the secretary of defense and the governor's office compromised. They ordered community development officers to interview each young "lifer" held at Langata. Nineteen of the sixty-six inmates, including Simon, were designated as cooperative and sent on to Wamumu.[72] In a way, the government had stacked the deck in Wamumu's favor, giving Gardener and his staff an excellent hand of seemingly acquiescent detainees, leaving the rest to rot behind bars.

The most egregious shortcoming of rehabilitation, as Luise White has shown, was its gendered bias. Wamumu was not for girls.[73] The youth camp reimagined coming-of-age and articulated an alternative transition to manhood. Meanwhile, the state denied rehabilitation and the Wamumu curriculum to thousands of girls and young women suspected of Mau Mau activity. Most young women were either repatriated back to the Gikuyu reserves, where they were expected to engage in terracing and other communal labor, or incarcerated at the Kamiti women's prison. A few efforts to rehabilitate girls and young women took place at the Kalimoni Catholic Mission and the Salvation Army facility at Quarry Road.[74] And for the briefest moment, the district commissioner of Meru built a youth camp for girls at Igoji. When he heard of the work at Wamumu, he reached out to community development and the treasury for funds to expand his camp for girls. A response came quickly and forcefully: the treasury refused funding, and community development demanded he close the Igoji camp as there was simply no need for it.[75]

At Kamiti, the camp for adult female rehabilitation, staff denied detainees the possibilities offered boys at Wamumu.[76] Eileen Fletcher, a rehabilitation officer at Kamiti, encountered several girls whom she believed to be under the age of fourteen. Some of the girls had received tough sentences. An eleven-year-old was sentenced to seven years of hard labor for taking two oaths. Other girls were sentenced to "indeterminate" periods of time for carrying supplies and "consorting" with Mau Mau. Kamiti girls labored hard—breaking stones, cutting grass, and cultivating crops—a far cry from Wamumu's vocational training, parades, and football matches. Shocked by the girls' mistreatment, Fletcher exposed abuses at Kamiti and elsewhere in Kenya's detention camp system to the British press. Images of imprisoned eleven-year-old girls doing hard labor ignited outrage in Britain. Fumbling for a response, the Colonial Office claimed that the Kamiti girls engaged only in stone chipping, not stone breaking, as well as other forms of work they would be expected to perform at home for their parents or husbands. Officials in Kenya also denied that the girls were underage. Fletcher, they argued, had gotten it all wrong. Governor Baring ordered a Kamiti medical officer and a panel of three senior Gikuyu women to examine the girls in question. Not surprisingly, the panel discovered that each girl was circumcised and of marriageable age. No mention was made as to whether the girls had been circumcised during their detention at Kamiti. For young women, the colonial state used circumcision to snuff out a scandal, rather than as an instrument of rehabilitation.[77]

"THERE IS SOMETHING WRONG WITH YOUTH"

As certain as men like Askwith were that Wamumu had helped defeat Mau Mau, worries did not wane in the later years of the emergency. Small pockets of Mau Mau fighters and new groups like the Kenya Land and Freedom Army continued to harass the state. The costs of counterinsurgency threatened the colony's financial security, and its brutality forced the British to make political concessions to the African community, giving them more seats on the Legislative Council.[78] In the districts, though, provincial administrators and community development officers were exhilarated by the new possibilities of the late emergency. "The whole of Central Province had so many professional government officers working in it," recalled Don Diment, a community development officer in Nyeri. "It was quite extraordinary the amount of money and people the government put into that place."[79] They planned bold initiatives under the banner of development, from Boy Scout troops and women's associations to land reforms and construction projects.[80]

One of the hallmarks of emergency development schemes was the consolidation of Gikuyu landholdings and villages. Under the 1954 Swynnerton Plan, land was swapped among farmers so their property lay contiguous or more closely together. District officials and chiefs claimed that the plan would improve agricultural production, reduce land claims, and increase household incomes; yet consolidation was also a countermeasure to combat Mau Mau. Government evicted landholders and tenants suspected of Mau Mau and rewarded loyal Gikuyu and Home Guard officers with confiscated property or the opportunity to grow coffee and tea.[81] District officials also moved Gikuyu families into 804 fortified villages, relocating over a million Gikuyu into 230,000 homes by late 1955.[82]

In the shadow of Home Guard watchtowers, villagers lived in atrocious conditions. Gikuyu women bore the brunt of life in the new villages, enduring backbreaking communal labor and sexual abuse.[83] The young also suffered. In June 1955, Reverend Macpherson of the Church of Scotland Mission summed up the situation in Kiambu: "gross unemployment rising from restrictions on movement; villagization; repatriation of unattached Nairobi children; break up of families arising from of emergency; and a lack of food."[84] An estimated five thousand Kiambu children lived without one or both parents. The Church Missionary Society believed that one in four children under ten were malnourished or starving.[85] Escaping the violence, disease, and poverty of the reserves, thousands of underage refugees poured into Nairobi. These waves of young migrants inevitably crashed into district and municipal officials, who braced themselves behind extraordinary emergency powers. Never before had officials encountered so many, "against whose weight of numbers" they felt "rather like Canute stopping the tide coming in."[86] In 1954, Operation Anvil had inundated the juvenile court with 2,706 cases. Two years later, municipal authorities had rounded up more than sixty-five hundred young people in Nairobi. In the reserves, district authorities turned to corporal punishment. In 1952, only 127 young men had felt the crack of the cane in the reserves. Three years later the number had risen to nearly two thousand.[87] Compared to its East African neighbors, Kenya's criminalization of the young was staggering. The number of young people convicted of crimes during the emergency exceeded those in Tanganyika, Uganda, Somaliland, and Zanzibar—combined.[88]

At first, no one, from the war council to community development, knew how to interpret the thousands of young refugees circulating the province. Were they bereaved heirs to Mau Mau, another generation bent on violence against the state? Or were they mere victims of the twin traumas of counterinsurgency and rural reconstruction? No one had an answer, Don Diment, a community development officer in Nyeri, recalls:

> When they were picked up from the streets . . . you never knew whom they were. I mean, a little chap siphoning off petrol from a motorcar and inhaling it . . . when brought in by either the police or social services and questioned might turn out to be an orphan from a nearby Central Province district. Or, he could turn out after questioning him . . . that for the last three years he had been a boy in the forest of the Aberdares. It could be an awful mix of vagrancy, of homelessness, or of a former Mau Mau adherent.[89]

A Nyeri district officer working with Diment agreed. Villagization had unleashed "Dick Whittingtons who go off to adventure in the big cities . . . orphans or Oliver Twists who are driven to steal food or run off to Nairobi because they just cannot get enough to fill their tummies with at home [as well as] spivs and Teddy Boys."[90] Just as they had done in the early 1950s with Mau Mau, British officials set out to name the problem they faced, and the word *youth* became a fashionable late-emergency discursive device to make sense of the counterinsurgencies' aftershocks.

In April 1956, officials from dozens of African colonies arrived in Kampala, Uganda, to attend a conference of the Commission for Technical Cooperation in Africa on the issue of juvenile delinquency. Kenya's delegate, Colin Owen, was an obvious choice to attend. He had run Kenya's probation service since its inception and consulted with Askwith on the rehabilitation going on at Wamumu. Owen's audience might have been surprised to learn that Mau Mau was no longer Kenya's most pressing issue. Mau Mau had sounded the alarm to a much "bigger problem," Owen argued, "a problem which is common to the whole world." "One only has to look at the newspapers," he went on, " to realize that there is something wrong with youth."[91] In Kenya as in Britain, a crisis of youth had emerged out of devastating wars, shifting economies, and disintegrating families. Mau Mau merely provided officials in Kenya with a wake-up call to the profound changes in African family and generational life.[92] Owen did not define what he meant by the word *youth*, but he joined a growing chorus in Kenya, and elsewhere around the world, that began to use the term in the late 1950s. Owen found value in the word because it embraced shifting meanings and ambiguities as well as captured young offenders, school-leavers, job seekers, refugees, and orphans of varying ages, from different regions, and with diverse family backgrounds. The word *youth* was a simple, sweeping technological innovation for complicated, poorly understood sets of problems.

As part of the life cycle, youth had only recently emerged in Western scholarship and popular culture. In the postwar years, British social scientists began to use age to think about the rapid, dramatic changes brought on by two world wars as well as demographic and cultural shifts. Age also helped them make sense of their unraveling empires.[93] Decades before, social scientists had focused on the psychological and environmental factors influencing young people's behavior. In part, the disorderliness of the young could be explained by their struggle with emotional turmoil and rapid physical development.[94] Unsettling external stimuli like migration, urbanization, industrialization, poverty, or, worse, catastrophic global war only compounded their internal conflict. In the wake of World War II, European scholars, reformers, and governments feared that the war had further destabilized the minds of young people, leading them to embrace delinquency and countercultures as never before.[95]

These ideas easily translated to colonies like Kenya, where officials had already spent considerable intellectual energy explaining events in terms of age. Having yoked Mau Mau to age and indiscipline, it was easy to reappropriate similar language to the aftermath of the counterinsurgency. What Askwith once described in the late 1940s as organized criminal gangs had slipped into immature Mau Mau gangs in the early 1950s, which in turn became "gangs of hunting children, petty thieves and hen fishers" during decolonization.[96] Yet appropriating an age-defined vocabulary did not mean that the same words carried the same meanings. Provincial administrators and community development officers understood that "hunting children, petty thieves and hen fishers" were not Mau Mau. They feared that their efforts to crush one generation's violent protest had embittered a second, younger generation. In the aching bellies and troubled hearts of orphans, refugees, street kids, and thieves lay the germ of future rebellion.

The solution Owen put forward in his speech at the Kampala conference resembled the emboldened ideas of his colleagues who were consolidating farms and building villages in the districts of Central Province. Owen called for not so much the rehabilitation of youth, but "construction and the building of character [in youth] upon the accepted principles of a conventional world."[97] In the early colonial period, that "conventional world" would have been a neat and tidy household nestled away on a rural farm governed by the strict rule of a patriarch and tribal custom. But that household had been burned, its village consolidated, its chief murdered by Mau Mau, and its tribal custom disintegrated. One way to reclaim it, according to men like Askwith and Owen, was to give Africans their youth back. Colonial rule had stripped boys of their right to be young, to be warriors, to take their time learning to become mature men. "In bygone days," Askwith argued in June 1956, a young man "moved beyond the range of parental authority when he was circumcised, and was expected to exercise himself in warlike arts in company with boys of his own age until he settled down as a husband and householder. Provision for this stage, which corresponds most nearly to our National Service, does not now exist."[98] Unless a boy could afford continued education or hold steady employment, he had no means to express his youthful energy. He had lost the luxury of warriorhood afforded to his forefathers. A colonial youth service, officials believed, could replace that lost youth, re-create seclusion huts, and reinstate a warrior spirit.[99] This was the final act of the colonial elder state: to craft a youth service and make one last generation in a bid to salvage its authority.

Here, too, officials in Kenya echoed efforts undertaken in Europe. The postwar also offered limitless opportunities to remake what had been broken. In Europe, the United States, and the Soviet Union, governments became fascinated with the symbolic power of youth, its potential for mobilization, and its possibilities toward national rejuvenation. In Britain and France, the number of youth organizations increased from the end of the nineteenth century into the twentieth as a response to national insecurities.[100] These organizations also seemed to effectively discipline and mobilize youths in the workplace and schoolhouse as well as prevent delinquency. In Britain, John Springhall argues, "youth movements ensured the continuity of certain broadly conservative, conformist attitudes . . . that were actively resisting change in British society."[101] They encouraged class stability, loyalty in times of national crisis, and deference to the social order.[102] Youth movements made young Britons strong and in turn served as "bricks in the wall of that great edifice—the British Empire."[103]

The empire became a laboratory to test new models of British youth and citizenship. The founders of the Voluntary Service Overseas (VSO) program, Alec and Mora Dickson, saw an emerging prolonged, uncertain age in Britain and conceptualized youth as a global problem—just as Owen had done. Mora wrote of the inaugural VSO class, "They were boys who had thought of themselves as young men before they left England: now, when they were in truth young men, this world brought out in them the humble recognition that they were still boys."[104] By embracing the developmentalist spirit of the postwar era, young Britons could earn their age. And so to forge better Britons, the VSO sent the young abroad to make their colonized peers servile subjects. Programming in Nigeria, Iraq, and Sarawak leaned on intense physical training and respect for labor—just as so many pre–World War II programs in Kenya had done. The aim was to slow the rapid pace of youthful development in the empire and subdue the impatient, "adolescent" political ambitions of African nationalists.[105] Decolonization was cast as a crisis of coming-of-age not unlike Mau Mau and the aftermath of Kenya's dirty war.

Back in Kenya, moves to build a colonial youth service began in the department of community development and provincial administration. In July 1957, Geoffrey Griffin, having completed his work at Wamumu, toured the districts of Central Province, seeking figures of adolescent youths not receiving any form of education or training. His approximations were wholly unscientific and staggering. He believed that 204,000 young Gikuyu lived idly in the province without schooling or employment. In his report, he luridly described the fate of these boys and girls if the colonial state did nothing: "The descent from innocence to hardened criminality is made with terrifying swiftness." At first just a waif and stray, a boy quickly descended into theft, drug addiction, and worst of all a desperate failure "prostituting himself to sexual perverts."[106] To arrest this process, the state created hundreds of youth clubs and a fledgling youth service to mobilize youths, occupy their time, and distract them from their mounting grievances.

In 1957, rehabilitation at Wamumu unraveled. As community development heralded Wamumu's success, those within earshot began sending all manner of boys they had rounded up to the camp. District officers brought war orphans. Probation officers dropped off street kids.[107] Approved school superintendents transferred offenders to ease overcrowding.[108] A few fathers and chiefs even showed up with troublesome sons in tow.[109] Soon Wamumu teemed with "waifs, strays and orphans" too young to have taken an oath or taken up arms against the colonial state.[110] By August, they outnumbered the remaining Mau Mau detainees. Wamumu had not been designed to rehabilitate Nairobi house burglars, Thika market pickpockets, or Nyeri orphans. George Gardener insisted that the new arrivals undergo the same rehabilitation as Mau Mau detainees. Geoffrey Griffin and Roger Owles disagreed. "Roger and I were convinced," recalled Griffin, "that the new boys needed a different form of rehabilitation because they were not hardened in crime."[111] Work at Wamumu reached an impasse. Thomas Askwith arrived with a solution: he broke up the Wamumu team. George Gardener remained at Wamumu, rehabilitating the last Mau Mau detainees and any other boys sent to him. Griffin and Owles were tasked with addressing the "crisis of youth" by developing the plan Colin Owen had laid out the year earlier in Kampala. Owles moved to Othaya in Nyeri, where he established a smaller youth camp for very young boys and orphans. Geoffrey Griffin took up the new post of colony youth organizer and oversaw the organization of hundreds of youth clubs across Kenya.

The idea of youth clubs had been circulating through the halls of the Colonial Office for years. In 1942, the subcommittee on juvenile delinquency, chaired by Alexander Paterson, the architect of British approved schools, recommended that rural youth clubs be established throughout the empire. The clubs, the committee argued, would make village life more attractive and root young people to the countryside without costly investments in rural education, social services, or repatriation. The clubs would be most useful for managing those who had just left or never attended school, trapped without work "during adolescence and early adult life." The committee also envisioned the clubs as a kind of youth movement. In Africa, the committee reported, "the traditional social system [that] organized boys and girls into regular age-grades, of which members were responsible for special duties to the tribe," made the possibility of youth clubs and a wider movement very promising.[112] The clubs "commanded the allegiance of adolescent boys and girls," occupied their time,

Figure 7.4. Kenya's Youth Clubs. Scene at a youth club in the Nyeri district of Kenya, n.d. Photo courtesy of the National Archives, Kew.

minds, and bodies, and provided "initial training in citizenship."[113] After the war, these ideas found a few receptive ears in Kenya. Two settlers, Patrick Williams and Olga Watkins, believed that the creation of a youth movement would ease unemployment, correct delinquency, and instill in the young a sense of personal attachment to colonial rule. Williams envisioned camps in every district where eighteen-year-old African males spent five months working on local development projects. Little came of the efforts of Williams and Watkins. Colonial officials feared the costs. African leaders such as Eliud Mathu called it forced labor. Yet postwar ideas of this type, which had withered on the vine after a drought of support, sprang back to life in the late 1950s.[114]

Griffin's youth clubs blended the aims outlined by Paterson's committee and Williams's proposal with the immediate concerns of the late colonial state. First, community development believed the clubs would distract anxious, discontented school-leavers between the ages of thirteen and twenty, who could neither afford tuition fees nor find employment.[115] Second, by entertaining young people with club programming, Griffin hoped to slow their migration out of the reserves and ease the pressure on provincial and municipal officials, who continued to arrest them by the thousands. Finally, community development saw the clubs as a kind of youth service that might encourage young Africans to legitimate colonial authority and prevent another generation from becoming "ripe fuel for undesirable political agitation."[116]

In late 1957, the provincial administration approved community development plans to open youth clubs first in Central Province, and later throughout the colony. In search of a template for the youth clubs, Griffin visited several independent schemes that had sprung up during the state of emergency. In Nyeri, two enterprising young community development officers, Peter Moll and Don Diment, had begun clubs in Mathira and Othaya divisions.[117] The Mathira club had been one of Moll's pet projects. To get chiefs and local elders on board, Moll offered them coveted movement passes so they and their clients could travel about the province without fear of arrest. When land consolidation began, those same African leaders then offered Moll several acres on which to build a youth club and its sporting facilities. Over time, Moll and Diment expanded the size and number of the clubs in Nyeri. In Mathira, Moll received £2,900 and 209 acres of land, on which he built sixteen more clubs.[118] Inspired by these programs, Griffin planned clubs in Kiambu, Fort Hall, Nakuru, and Kisumu.

Funding proved Griffin's first hurdle. The treasury offered start-up costs for a few of the clubs, but the clubs remained a largely self-help enterprise with chiefs and local communities providing most of the financial assistance. By 1958, African district councils in Central Province had set aside funds in their annual budgets to hire youth leaders to run the clubs. The clubs also relied heavily on membership fees of one to five shillings.[119] Griffin also turned to donations from charitable organizations, securing £10,000 from groups like the Dulverton and Sheikh Charitable Trusts. He scavenged through the decomposing detention camp system, too, for equipment and building materials. For two youth clubs in the Nairobi neighborhoods of Starehe and Kariokor, Griffin got creative. At Starehe, he convinced the department of information to give him a piece of land adjacent to its main radio tower, the prisons department to donate corrugated iron for the roof, and the United States information service to send a 16mm film projector and screen to entertain clubgoers

FIGURE 7.5. Community development, n.d. Community development officer Peter Moll speaks with members of one of the Nyeri youth clubs he organized. Photo courtesy of the National Archives, Kew.

with government propaganda.[120] With money from the Shell Corporation, Griffin hired six full-time employees for the Nairobi clubs.

Griffin wanted community development officers to oversee the club with the help of youth leaders, particularly young men who modeled mature manliness. To find these leaders, Griffin looked no further than Wamumu. For his club in Othaya, Don Diment requested a "real man in the forest" who could demonstrate that it "was all behind him," and he was sent Simon "Gakono" Kariuki.[121] Simon's missing arm and homemade wooden prosthetic attracted the awe of young club members, but he did not enjoy being paraded around as a colonial trophy.[122] He quit a few years later. Other Wamumu graduates enjoyed the work. Joseph Gikubu and another Wamumu detainee ran the Starehe and Kariokor clubs. Each day, as the tower transmitted anti–Mau Mau propaganda over the airwaves, Gikubu tried to entice street kids to join. A few boys checked out the place, but after listening to some of Gikubu's lectures, they stopped coming. He persevered, membership gradually picked up, and the Starehe club became a safe space where the young could come for help or find something to do.[123]

In each club, youth leaders formed miniature Wamumus of their own.[124] During an inspection, Askwith noticed that the youth leaders wore their Wamumu-issued ties and jackets and acted like headmasters in a classroom. Askwith told them to take off their ties and jackets, roll up their sleeves, and get down to serious rehabilitative business. He complained to Griffin about the mentality of the club leaders. Griffin defended his former detainees, noting that they had simply worn their "Sunday best in his honor."[125] But Askwith had seen ex-Wamumu boys drunk with authority, acting as school-masters over their fellow age-mates. Club leaders had intentionally set themselves apart from their peers, a testament to how they felt Mau Mau and Wamumu had changed them. As mature men, they were now expected to display the advanced age they had won for themselves.

Regardless of their dictatorial manner, youth leaders and community development officers did get down to applying some variation of rehabilitation. Many of Askwith's rehabilitative measures, tested at Wamumu, formed part of club curricula.[126] One of the most important changes to this form of rehabilitation was the inclusion of girls. The clubs were one of the first government-run emergency schemes specifically designed for both boys and girls. Although they both participated in full-time occupational and recreational programs, club members were often separated into gender-specific streams. For girls, classes in cooking, sewing, tanning leather, and hygiene kept their skills firmly fixed within an idealized patriarchal household. Griffin did not allow ex-Wamumu club leaders to train girls. Instead, he turned to Maendeleo ya Wanawake (Women's Progress) to run many of the girls' courses. But the boys' work was no less connected to their future households and family life. They trained to become breadwinners out in the wage labor market, learning carpentry, agriculture, and mechanics. At some clubs, boys earned £10 per month selling furniture they had built at the local market. In Othaya, a blind Gikuyu tanner was brought up from Machakos to establish a club workshop that made briefcases. Sports were also a centerpiece of community development efforts. Each youth club was tasked with building facilities to accommodate track and field, football, boxing, and other physical activities. On Saturday afternoons, officers hosted interlocation and interdivision football competitions. According to Diment and Moll, sports allowed both boys and girls to release their kinetic energy, display their prowess and skill, and create among themselves heroes and heroines to admire.[127]

FIGURE 7.6. Gikuyu girls during a needlework lesson at one of the Nyeri youth clubs, n.d. Photo courtesy of the National Archives, Kew.

Club programming neatly assigned specific gender roles for boys and girls, but it also established its members as an age set. Regardless of the diverse range in ages—whether an uncircumcised boy or a circumcised yet unmarried young woman—the clubs swept away any ambiguities over age and constructed a category to classify everyone as "youth." Community development officers took their ideas one step further: the clubs did not simply create youths; the clubs provided them with a controlled environment to learn what it meant to be young. In an article promoting the clubs in the *East African Standard*, Peter Moll described his clubs as a colonial effort to resurrect the seclusion hut, "adapted to meet modern requirements."[128] In the past, the seclusion hut, where recently circumcised Gikuyu recovered, served as a classroom of sorts where sponsors and elders imparted knowledge essential to coming of age. During their time in seclusion, initiates learned community codes of conduct as well as gendered and generational roles.[129] In that in-between space, Gikuyu moved beyond childhood and set out on the path toward manhood or womanhood.

FIGURE 7.7. Kenya's youth clubs, n.d. Peter Mwarangu, a former Wamumu Youth Camp detainee, offers a boxing lesson at one of the Nyeri youth clubs. Photo courtesy of the National Archives, Kew.

Community development officials like Peter Moll explicitly tapped into the language and power of age-relations. Seclusion huts offered the state a way to conceptualize the clubs as a period of organized waiting. They distracted members from their lack of education, employment, security, and freedom in the reserves. The clubs also seized the opportunity to socialize members of diverse backgrounds and ages into "youths" and, "in due course, good citizens of Kenya."[130] Connecting clubs and seclusion represented a bold step for the elder state, which came full circle on the issue of initiation. In 1919, provincial administrators had allowed missionaries to kidnap still-healing schoolboys from seclusion. In the 1920s, they had deliberately shortened the period of initiation and seclusion to push young men into the labor market. Nearly forty years later, the colonial state built its own seclusion huts, where they and their intermediaries, not elders or missionaries, constructed ideas about age and age-appropriate behavior.

Clubs sprang up across the colony. Drawn by education courses, skills training, and athletic activities, the young flocked to the clubs. Poor parents hungry for even a meager helping of education for their children raised the membership fees for enrollment. In Nakuru, community development built a massive club featuring four classrooms, four workshops, a kitchen, a block of showers, and accommodations for up to two hundred students. In its first year, 230 young people applied for membership, of whom seventy were girls.[131] By 1960, ninety-five clubs operated in the colony with more than eleven thousand young members.[132] The Ministry of African Affairs lauded the youth clubs as "an integral part of its social services . . . providing occupation and recreation for youths and young persons in the towns and reserves, and so prevent them drifting into delinquency or actual crime."[133] The clubs spread so quickly that the Boy Scouts Association of Kenya complained to Askwith that the state-run clubs competed with their troops. Askwith reassured the association that the clubs were an altogether different institution: one for the undereducated, poor and wayward—not educated, wealthy, Christian boys.[134]

Throughout the state of emergency, the elder state built an extraordinary collection of institutions for the young. In addition to the Wamumu Youth Camp and its smaller sister camps, as well as hundreds of youth clubs, the prisons department built several remand homes to accommodate young people awaiting trial or repatriation. The department also expanded the number of approved schools from the two at Kabete and Dagoretti to seven. In 1958, Wamumu and Othaya became approved schools, and two years later, the state built two more approved schools, including one for girls at Kirigiti. In Colin Owen's hands, approved schools incorporated Wamumu rehabilitation. Vocational and academic training improved, and circumcisions became a routine, essential part of incarceration.[135] An interlocking network of youth clubs, approved schools, remand homes, and charities formed a nascent youth service just as formal colonial rule came to an end.

CONCLUSION

In the twilight of empire, Griffin daydreamed. He hoped to serve 250,000 young men and women in 2,000 youth clubs dotting the colony. He fantasized about a headquarters for youth training, a youth employment service connecting clubgoers with employers, and a hostel in Nairobi for those just starting out. Kenya was, by Griffin's estimation, at the forefront of youth services on the African continent. After attending the World Youth Assembly in Dar es Salaam in 1960, he returned boasting that he had learned nothing new from his colleagues in other colonies, but they had been eager to hear of Kenya's success.[136] Theatricality aside, Griffin might not have been completely wrong.

Although called a youth camp, Wamumu had been an experiment in rehabilitating young Mau Mau fighters. The use of the word *youth* distinguished it from detention, no doubt to win a few hearts and minds back home. Yet naming Wamumu a youth camp did make sense to a few officials like Askwith and Owen, and to some extent Leakey and Carothers, who imagined Mau Mau as a crisis of youthful rebellion and elder ineptitude. Wamumu gave the state all the trappings of an alternative elder, offering direction and discipline and moral and vocational instruction, as well as initiation into manhood. Many detainees viewed rehabilitation, just as they had Mau Mau, as another arena to enjoy their age, test their manly mettle, and acquire the tools for successful adulthood. The word *youth*, and this more intense relationship between the young and the elder state, also took on descriptive, prescriptive power to comprehend and repair the wreckage of the counterinsurgency. Refugees and orphans, vagrants and thieves, all became youths, a global problem, not just a Kenyan problem, requiring the state's immediate attention. To confront this second crisis of youth, the elder state built dozens of youth clubs, expanded its approved schools, and distributed a diluted version of Wamumu rehabilitation throughout the colony. As they drifted toward decolonization, officials of the elder state were very busy in the late state of emergency.

Not everyone shared Griffin's enthusiasm for the achievements of the elder state. The realization that Kenya was set on the unavoidable path to independence demoralized many officials. In 1960, Kabete inmates jubilantly protested their sentences, aware that the British were preparing to hand the colony over. "Due to the political situation," the superintendent wrote, "it would appear that boys feel that they will all be released upon a given day and there is thus no point in behaving themselves properly."[137] Officials found it difficult to let go of the institutions they had run for so long. As they hired and promoted Africans to replace them, they lamented how these men failed to live up to their expectations and wondered how long their programs would fare without them.[138] Unbeknownst to them, Kenya's future leadership, especially newly elected prime minister Jomo Kenyatta, saw opportunity in these institutions. Kenyatta understood the value of mobilizing the energies of the young for political purposes and using age to augur the authority of the state. Free from the yoke of foreign rulers, young Kenyans found themselves put to work in the very same sorts of institutions, serving their new nation at the mercy of their *Mzee*, the father of the newly independent elder state.

8 ~ "An Army without Guns"

The National Youth Service and Age in Kenyatta's Kenya

THIRTY-SIX DAYS AFTER KENYANS gained their independence, youth wing members of the Kenya African National Union (KANU), the political party of the newly elected prime minister Jomo Kenyatta, wrote to their new leader expressing disappointment. Feeling responsible for Kenyatta's election, they were eager to see the benefits of having their man in power. Within days of independence, their sense of euphoria turned to betrayal. "The Youth," they wrote, "and others who suffered and sacrificed for freedom, are neglected and even denied the opportunity to serve the Nation." Instead, "the old enemies of African Nationalism are entrenched and assured of their old privileged positions." Kenyatta had not, they argued, overturned the colonial socioeconomic order. The youth saw worrying "trends, which tend to destitution and wretchedness among the masses of the common people amid the pomp and affluence of the rich and the privileged few." Kenyatta's inaction "rendered the hard won 'Uhuru' [freedom] meaningless."[1]

But it was not too late. Kenyatta could still count on their loyalty if he created a "dynamic plan . . . which would have an immediate, visible, beneficial effect" on their lives. Although the youth offered no specific details as to what this plan should look like, their letter revealed much about the interplay between age and politics in the days following independence. The letter was a prop in a generational morality play, a form of ritualized rebellion, whereby the young reminded Kenya's newest political elder of his reciprocal

226

obligations to them. The youth identified themselves as a unique actor on Kenya's political stage, mobilized around collective senses of age, economic impoverishment, and political disenfranchisement. Their youthfulness set them apart, as did their concerns over access to education, employment, and land. Taking these grievances directly to Kenyatta, they reinforced his political legitimacy as the only senior statesman who could alleviate their suffering. As Kenyatta assumed the role of paramount elder in Kenya, he was now responsible for the coming-of-age of his followers. The letter was a brilliant piece of stagecraft performed to underscore Kenyatta's benevolence and authority.

Two weeks later, he announced the formation of the National Youth Service (NYS), the "dynamic plan" for which the youth had asked. Announcing the service allowed Kenyatta to display his power to address his citizens' economic and political concerns. And in doing so, the NYS imbued the postcolonial state and its politicians with the authority that supposedly came with elderhood and the promise that it could transition the youth out of their socioeconomic immaturity. Like his political compatriots across the continent, Kenyatta saw political order in terms of age. The state had to teach the young self-discipline and hard work; and if the young obeyed, they received the patronage of elder politicians. Part of statecraft was reimagining precolonial African age-relations as a fantasy in which the obedient young had always served at the pleasure of elders. The NYS became part of Jomo Kenyatta's personal project of rethinking age-relations, authenticating his cultural knowledge and legitimizing his claim on seniority. Yet, unlike Kwame Nkrumah or Julius Nyerere, Kenyatta did not simply look to an idealized precolonial past; he borrowed from the ideas and institutions left in the colonial rubble.

During his fifteen years in power, Kenyatta excavated the colonial past for the logics and instruments of rule. He preserved the power of the provincial administration, providing himself with a powerful, centralized bureaucracy—a "no party state."[2] Servicemen, and later women, of the NYS became part of this bureaucracy, chosen by administrators loyal to Kenyatta and trained to bring his development projects to the countryside. Despite resettlement schemes to address the economic grievances of the landless poor, the Kenyatta regime "grafted an African political and administrative elite onto existing European and Asian economic elites."[3] Economic inequality and financial relationships with the West remained unquestioned. Acceptance into the NYS meant steady work and a wage building the nation's infrastructure as well as the promise of government work down the road. Kenyatta also used the NYS to manipulate Cold War antagonisms to get both the United States and the Soviet Union to provide financial assistance for the NYS and its efforts to harness the energies of the young. Kenyatta fostered a political culture wary of radicalism, paranoid of challengers, and obsessed with stability. This hunger for order gave birth to a state brutally protective of its interests and its longevity.[4] In his search, Kenyatta found the elder state and the NYS. Ultimately, he refashioned his regime as a gerontocracy by which mobility depended upon individuals' willingness to define themselves as juniors and submit to elders, paramount among these, Kenyatta himself. Kenyatta became more than simply the president, but *Mzee*, a "wise elder," and *Baba wa Taifa*, "father of the nation." Meanwhile, servicemen became *Maskini wa Kenyatta*, or "Kenyatta's poor men"; poor youth in the service of the nation and Kenyatta.

"YOU HAVE POLITICIZED THESE CHILDREN"

Kenyatta and the youth were not the only politicians and citizens arguing about age in postcolonial Africa. As colonies transitioned to nation-states across the continent, first-generation leaders viewed the mobilization of the young, especially men, as an essential part of seeking "first the political kingdom." In the 1960s, youth had become a "political phenomenon" and, like ethnicity, an axis on which political conflict turned in decades to come.[5] To Africa's nationalists, though, neither youth nor age was a new variable in their political calculus, but a familiar constant. They had been young men themselves once, often when they founded nationalist organizations that agitated for change under colonialism. They were among the first who attended schools or organized trade unions. They then used these attributes—their youthfulness, literacy, urban networks, and proximity to the agents of empire—to justify their role as the only generation ready for the struggle against colonialism. Some of these young nationalists, like those in Zanzibar, saw themselves "as a vanguard generation, endowed by history to perform, in their island's revolution, the role of agents of progress."[6] Others worked to reconcile their emerging power with that of their elders back home in the countryside. In Kenya, some of the earliest young activists involved in the Kikuyu Central Association sought to bridge the gap between local Gikuyu politics and their nationalist aspirations.[7]

Yet, as the first generation of nationalists grew older, they encountered a rising generation who had their own particular grievances, ideologies, and demands. After World War II, this earlier generation of nationalists found themselves sharing the same anxieties over the young as had late colonial officials. Demographically, there were more young people than ever before, many with a smattering of education but without steady employment and a livable wage.[8] In record numbers these "raw youths" abandoned their fathers' homesteads in search of work, often in towns, where both the colonial state and African nationalists feared they might become a threat to law and order.[9] A creeping conservatism infiltrated the attitudes of early African nationalists as they tried to prevent young women from working in towns and scolded young men for slipping into delinquency.

As multiple generations of nationalists argued over the future and struggled to seize the political initiative, anticolonial movements fractured. In Ghana, the United Gold Coast Convention (UGCC) had become one of the strongest political voices for Africans. By the late 1940s, the party's Committee of Youth Organization (CYO), founded by Hannah Kudjoe and Kwame Nkrumah, among others, criticized its political elders, arguing that the UGCC had become too conservative and elitist. In 1949, the CYO split from the UGCC in an effort to appeal to the working poor and unemployed.[10] The CYO ultimately became the Convention People's Party (CPP), Nkrumah's vehicle to national office in 1957. Yet even Nkrumah was subject to critique from an even younger generation of Ghanaians below him. In the early 1950s, the Asante "youngmen," who had helped launch Nkrumah to power, broke from the CPP, frustrated that the party relied on their support but ignored their demands.[11] In Kenya, too, a rising radicalism among young men in Nairobi, especially among the undereducated and underemployed, led to cracks within established associations like the Kikuyu Central Association and the Kenya African Union after World War II.

In the 1950s and early 1960s, as nationalist leaders made their bid to run the affairs of newly independent nations, they positioned the young at the center of their programs for economic development, cultural renovation, and political consolidation. The young were seen, Mamadou Diouf argues, as "the hope of African nations under construction."[12] Hope, yes, but also fear. The poverty and grievances that had made youths "raw" in the waning years of colonial rule did not disappear on the eve of independence. Nationalists-turned-parliamentarians had to take up these pressing issues before the euphoria of freedom soured. Restless young subjects-turned-citizens gave them precious little time. Postcolonial officials understood the "intrinsic bipolarity" of the young.[13] They had been the vanguard of decolonization, but vandals at the gates of empire. What would stop the young from turning on the aging nationalists whom they had brought to power?

First-generation leaders sought out ways to discipline and mobilize young people.[14] One of their first steps was the formation of youth wings. The youth wings of political parties organized the energies of supporters, mobilized voters, and intimidated opponents. In some regimes, youth wings eventually became paramilitary units used to kidnap, torture, and murder political rivals. In Guinea, Sékou Touré created La Jeunesse Rassemblement Démocratique Africain to communicate his authority throughout the countryside. In Touré's Guinea, young people performed in the theater of revolution, popularizing his policies and promoting the patronage of his regime.[15] In other countries, parties had to rein in their youth wings, fearful of the challenge they might pose. In 1958, the Malian Union Soudanaise created a youth wing, only to eliminate it four years later when party leaders struggled to control its members. The Parti Démocratique de la Côte D'Ivoire also dismantled its youth wing following a failed coup.[16]

Youth wings agitated for more formal organizations to offer the unemployed and uneducated vocational training and work in exchange for their assistance with party business. The Ghanaian Builders Brigade, begun in 1957, was one of the earliest independent youth organizations. By the end of the year, more than twenty-one thousand men and women had applied for membership, hoping for training, work, wages, and a sense of citizenship.[17] Over time the Brigade, and its sibling organization, the Young Pioneers, developed a reputation for being a tool of state repression. Fears arose that Nkrumah's state attracted youths with the lure of uniforms, training, and housing away from their families, turning them into "disrespectful party stooges."[18]

In Tanzania, Julius Nyerere and his party, the Tanzania African National Union (TANU), put young people to work crafting a national culture and crystallizing their authority. In 1963, TANU created the Youth League to mobilize party members in return for "miniscule [sic] wages, enhanced social status, and potential for promotions to higher officers within the party, as well as the possibility (albeit remote) of salaried state employment."[19] Almost immediately the league began disrupting opposition party meetings and stopping people to demand their voter registration certificates.[20] A year later, after the shock of a coup attempt against Nyerere, TANU introduced the National Service, or Jeshila Kujenga Taifa, which explicitly militarized young party members. The Youth League and the National Service fashioned a national culture and state with the "age structures perceived by many as inherent to the natural order of things."[21]

One of the league's most infamous campaigns was Operation Vijana (Operation Youth). Beginning in October 1968, TANU banned the young from wearing miniskirts, wigs, and tight male trousers, all in an effort to defend Tanzanian culture from foreign, immoral influences. Leaguers patrolled the streets of Dar es Salaam searching for salaciously dressed women, and when they found them, they stripped and beat them.[22] Not all youth were captured by the state. Many young, especially urban Tanzanians, found ways to resist TANU and the league. During Operation Vijana, young urban residents reappropriated the word *vijana*, using it to describe themselves and then recasting leaguers as "old-youths" trying desperately to be young. When TANU tried to make the National Service compulsory, university students took to the streets in protest.[23] These youthful dissidents and their counter-national cultures exposed a rift between the state and a rising generation of elites as well as the failure of TANU's efforts to homogenize and yoke youth to the state.

Whether Ghana or Guinea, Mali or Malawi, Tanzania or Zanzibar, nationalists did not look back to the colonial encounter to inspire their elder states—or at least that is the story most historians tell. Nationalist leaders looked to a precolonial fantasy when the young served their wizened elders with respect and discipline. They also looked ahead to an ideologically riven future where funds and institutional ideas could be drawn from Cold War adversaries. Many of the Young Pioneer schemes were inspired, and in many cases set up, by those developed in the Soviet Union and Israel. By contrast, Jomo Kenyatta and his fellow political elders' efforts to harness the energies of Kenyan young were directly related, sometimes explicitly, to the programs and ideas of the colonial elder state. Jomo Kenyatta and his KANU party certainly faced many of the same challenges as their counterparts elsewhere on the continent. The young made up the majority of Kenya's citizenry. Most were poor, underemployed, undereducated, and hungry for improvements in their daily lives. Kenyatta and his party faced a robust opposition in Oginga Odinga's Kenya African Democratic Union (KADU) and Kenya People's Union (KPU) parties, a coup attempt in 1964, and Cold War rivalries. To chart a complicated route through these troubled waters, Kenyatta stayed and steadied the course; and to do that, he needed the elder state.

"NOW WHAT ARE YOU GOING TO DO WITH THEM?"

Weeks before the youth submitted their letter to him, Kenyatta had already set the wheels in motion for their "dynamic plan." At the end of January 1964, Kenyatta requested a meeting at his home in Gatundu with a Kenya-born, former colonial official by the name of Geoffrey Griffin. In their meeting, Kenyatta asked Griffin to organize an "army without guns."[24] As Griffin recalled, the prime minister called the service "one of the most urgent steps toward developing the new state." It had to resolve young people's growing radicalization with training, pay, and activities to occupy their time.

The service also needed to ease the ethnic tensions that had arisen during the election, mobilizing each party's youth wings under one organization. Finally, once disciplined and trained, Griffin must put service members to work on development projects for the benefit of the nation.[25] In short, Kenyatta wanted Griffin to construct a disciplinary regimen to fashion uneducated, unemployed youths into instruments of nation building as well as to subdue the KANU and KADU youth wings.

To craft Kenya's youth service, Kenyatta had not simply turned to a reimagined, precolonial primordium or a program borrowed from Kwame Nkrumah or Leonid Brezhnev. Rather, he looked to the not-so-distant colonial past, where he found the elder state and its experts in waiting. Calling on Geoffrey Griffin had been a shrewd move. As a former colonial official and political outsider, he had no allegiance to KANU or KADU. More importantly, beginning in 1955, Griffin had worked in the department of community development organizing programs for the young. He possessed the institutional memory of the colonial administration and had previously encountered politicized young men willing to employ violence to end their poverty. During the state of emergency in the 1950s, Griffin had been instrumental in running the Wamumu Youth Camp to "rehabilitate" nearly two thousand young Mau Mau under the age of eighteen. He had used hard labor, education, and propaganda to wring the rebellion out of them. In 1957, Griffin left Wamumu to create a network of youth clubs to broadcast a variant of the Wamumu curriculum to boys and girls across the colony. After independence, Griffin hoped to settle into a quiet retirement transforming his Nairobi youth club into a school, the now famous Starehe Boys' Centre and School. In Griffin, Kenyatta had one of the most experienced youth workers in Africa.

Griffin declined the offer. He worried that the job would take away from his work at Starehe. The proposition of a national youth service also "terrified" him.[26] He understood the pitfalls of the kind of program Kenyatta proposed. Similar youth schemes had become instruments of repression and paramilitary organization elsewhere in Africa. Kenyatta refused to take no for an answer. He asked Griffin: "Do you consider yourself a Kenyan or a Briton?" Griffin responded that he was indeed a Kenyan, to which Kenyatta simply replied: "Then do your duty." Kenyatta knew that Griffin had been born and spent most of his life in Kenya. Manipulating Griffin's conflicted sense of citizenship, Kenyatta sealed the deal. It was "very hard to turn down a presidential request," Griffin recalled, "especially under such circumstances."[27]

Griffin went straight to work designing an administrative structure, curriculum, and distinctive red-and-green uniforms. Between 1964 and 1965,

Griffin and his staff recruited more than sixty-eight hundred young men from the ranks of the KANU and KADU youth wings. At first only young men were allowed in the service, though a few women joined in the late 1960s. Most of the servicemen were between eighteen and thirty years of age — a broad swath of ages that has become synonymous with youth. This range of ages is still used to legally define youth in Kenya today. The inaugural class embodied the prolonged, uncertain age that had emerged in the late colonial period. These young men represented multiple age-groups with very different experiences of decolonization whom Kenyatta hoped to merge into a single, identifiable generation. In fact, two generations made up the service. A former NYS employee recalls that servicemen included not only the KANU and KADU youth wings but also "the children who had been left by the Mau Maus; the orphans."[28]

Some of these older youths, in their late twenties and early thirties, might have joined any one of the many militant movements among the different peoples of Kenya who had harried the colonial state in the 1950s, such as the Bukusu and Pokot Dini ya Msambwa religious movement or the Luo guerrillas known as Onegos.[29] Many of the first Gikuyu servicemen had fought for Mau Mau and suffered during the state of emergency. As they returned home from years in detention, they discovered that in their absence the British had provided loyalists with land and positions in government. Politics became a refuge for many former detainees, seeking ways to shape the trajectory of decolonization and outmaneuver colonial efforts to privilege loyalists.[30] The younger generation, those under the age of twenty, had experienced the 1950s differently. Young Gikuyu would have suffered the brutality of life in the reserves, the closure of schools, as well as the agonies of villagization and land consolidation. Other young Kenyans would have struggled to find work, to use the skills they had learned in school, and to afford the rising costs of living. Politicized by late colonial violence and mobilized by African politicians, these two generations rushed to join the political fray.

The violence of the state of emergency compelled the British to make political concessions more swiftly than they would ever have imagined. At the height of the war with Mau Mau, the British opened up a limited number of positions in the provincial administration and elected seats on the Legislative Council to Africans. Many of the jobs in the districts of Central Province went to loyalist Gikuyu who had sided with the state during the war.[31] Those few Africans elected to the Council in 1957 were well educated and well to do. They would play powerful roles in Kenya's first years of independence: men like Oginga Odinga of Central Nyanza, Tom Mboya of Nairobi, Daniel arap Moi of Rift Valley, and Ronald Ngala of the Coast.[32]

Once elected to the Council, they pressed the colonial state, demanding more political freedoms, an end to the state of emergency, and the release of Jomo Kenyatta from detention. In January 1960, at the Lancaster House Constitutional Conference, these men adopted a united front and pushed the British to expand the number of Africans on the Council and affirm that Kenya's African majority would rule its own affairs. On the heels of Lancaster House, the African representatives in the Legislative Council cobbled together two major political parties: KANU, led by Mboya and Oginga; and KADU, run by Ngala and Moi. In 1961, the first African majority was elected to the Council. While the electoral victory went to KANU, the party refused to form a government until Kenyatta was released from detention. In August, the British relented. They realized that Jomo Kenyatta was their best hope for a moderate regime that would orchestrate an orderly political and economic transition.[33] A near decade in detention made Kenyatta a national hero. He had not supported Mau Mau, but the British mistook him for Mau Mau's chief protagonist.[34] Kenyatta's release in late 1961 was met by jubilant crowds. He joined KANU, and the party met with KADU at Lancaster House yet again to hammer out a new constitution. After seven weeks of negotiation, the two parties emerged with a new constitution and elections scheduled for May 1963.

As they prepared for the election, KANU and KADU mobilized their youth wings. Yet, as they did elsewhere in Africa, the youth wings quickly assumed a more coercive character. In Central Province, chiefs complained that youth wing members were seen carrying guns and ammunition and singing "Mau Mau" songs at all hours. Throughout the country, in the run-up to the 1963 election, the youth wings terrorized opposing politicians in their home districts, disrupting their rallies and harrying their voters. The election was "marred by widespread thuggery, bribery, and intimidation."[35] That same summer, some politicians complained to the *East Africa Standard* newspaper that the KANU youth wing "virtually ruled the place."[36] Beginning in 1963, and continuing throughout Kenyatta's rule, the KANU youth wing violently harassed the opposition until Kenyatta's critics no longer existed.[37]

The 1963 election swept Jomo Kenyatta and KANU into power and KADU into the opposition. One of the first pressing questions for politicians newly ensconced in Parliament was, "You have politicized these children, now what are you going to do with them?"[38] There were fears among some Kenyan elites that the youth wings had been given too much power. Harry Thuku, one of Kenya's first and most famous nationalists, reportedly told Richard Cox that "the mistake Kenyatta made was in letting the Youth Wing have its own Treasury." Thuku worried that once the young had their own finances, they would simply break from KANU and try to usurp government control. For his part, Cox feared that the youth wings were overly militarized and pandered to by Kenya's leaders. Odinga had called the youth wingers in Nyanza "Uhuru chiefs," who eventually had to be "disabused of the idea that they were going to be real chiefs."[39]

Tom Mboya understood that government had to do something about its youth wings. After 1963, Mboya joined Kenyatta's cabinet as the minister of justice and constitutional affairs and became a powerful player in the regime. For Mboya, the youth wings had been "the vanguard in the struggle for independence." Once they are organized, Mboya wrote, "they have to be disciplined and—what is even more important—they have to be kept occupied, for otherwise discipline disappears." Mboya warned that the young were already being hired out to do work for politicians that were not always in KANU's best interests.[40] The solution was state control of the young. "We cannot leave them entirely on their own to find jobs," he concluded.[41] The NYS became Kenyatta's and Mboya's plan to insert the state in the disciplining and development of the young—to offer them training and job placement in return for their obedience.

When crafting the NYS curriculum, Griffin applied ideas about the state's role in the lives of young men that he himself had tested throughout the state of emergency. The curricula Griffin developed at the Wamumu Youth Camp and the NYS bore remarkable similarities. Griffin designed the NYS around a two-year curriculum that provided thousands of young men vocational training, rudimentary academic education, and, above all, discipline. In the very first two months of the program, the servicemen performed military-style basic training. During the state of emergency and the war on Mau Mau, Griffin had served in the King's African Rifles, and he found military drill a useful way of maintaining discipline. Yet Griffin fancied himself an educator, not a military man, so he hired African ex-military personnel who had fought alongside the British during World War II to handle drills and discipline. Several of these military instructors had been Mau Mau fighters, and "so there was a rapport between these youths coming into the national youth service and the military officers."[42] The young men saw their instructors as fellow freedom fighters.

The most famous veteran and former Mau Mau working at the NYS was a political appointee of Jomo Kenyatta: Waruhiu Itote, more commonly known by his Mau Mau moniker of General China. After the Mau Mau war, at Kenyatta's insistence, Itote joined the Kenya Army. During his training he endured ridicule and persecution from both British and African officers whom he had fought. Upon completion of his training, he was given the rank of lieutenant in the Kenya Army Reserve, a blow to a man who had once given himself the rank of general. In search of a higher rank, Itote joined the NYS, where he would be a captain.[43] Itote quickly discovered the higher rank meant little in the NYS, yet he persevered and came to enjoy his work with Griffin, so much so that his photo on the back of his memoir pictures him dressed in his NYS uniform.

Itote served as Griffin's deputy of operations at the NYS. To Itote, the NYS was a crucial piece of nation building. One of its greatest advantages, he wrote in his memoir, was pushing young men from different ethnic groups to work together. It also provided continued education and skills training to those who failed their exams. Some of the servicemen learned "to wear shoes for the first time; others put on trousers as a new experience." But above all, the service provided "self-discipline which is so necessary at our present state of national development."[44] Itote had certainly fallen in lock-step with Kenyatta's goals. His position in the service and appointment as ceremonial national youth leader also allowed Kenyatta to pay lip service to former Mau Mau fighters without actually giving them political influence. In reality, few Mau Mau found a place in Kenyatta's government, and many were locked out of politics after independence.[45] Yet the political appointment of Itote signaled to the youth that both Kenyatta and the NYS might resolve their struggles for civic and economic maturity after all.

Together, Geoffrey Griffin and Waruhiu Itote, two men who had fought on opposite sides during the state of emergency, two men intimately acquainted with the tensions between age and authority, set out to craft Kenyatta's "army without guns." During drills, the servicemen carried spades, signifying the work that that they would do later for the program and the nation. After the first two months of military drill, servicemen began several months of grueling manual labor. They traveled the country building roads as well as clearing bush to push back the spread of malaria and sleeping sickness. The young men who persevered through these rigors earned an entire year of academic and vocational training. Servicemen received coursework in carpentry, masonry, mechanics, plumbing, and electrical training. In later years, as Kenya's economy expanded its service industries, the NYS offered courses in catering, hotel management, and tourism.

The vocational and academic training were rudimentary. It took Griffin several years to accumulate enough instructors and equipment to provide the kind of education young men received at other institutions like the Kabete Technical Institute (the former Native Industrial Training Depot) or the Kabete Approved School. And many of the new recruits found the military drill and hard work unbearable. Former KANU and KADU youth wingers fled the NYS barracks in Nairobi to the offices of their ministers of Parliament. They complained of being punished for their political affiliation. Others lamented the inadequate training.[46] When they signed up, none had anticipated spending months performing monotonous drills. Instructors also had a difficult time getting the young men interested in agricultural work because many believed the job was beneath them—women's work, they grumbled.[47] Ten percent dropped out of the program.

The ultimate aim of the training was to get students to pass grade-three trade tests—the highest qualification an artisan could earn—by any means necessary. Vocational instructors at the NYS questioned whether a year was sufficient time to prepare young men with no prior experience for a grade-three test. At Kenya's premier vocational school, the Kabete Technical Institute, young apprentices took several years to achieve a third-grade result. Surprisingly, NYS members passed their tests with flying colors in spite of their inexperience, indicating that the necessity of job placement for the servicemen outweighed the impartiality of their testing. In 1965, the government announced that twenty-six hundred servicemen had been promoted to salaried posts, some having gone from earning twenty shillings per month to over eight hundred.[48] By 1969, one-third of the servicemen had found employment directly out of the NYS. The rest returned to their rural areas with practical grade-tested training in carpentry, masonry, and a host of other vocations.[49] Even a rudimentary background in trades gave servicemen an advantage over school-leavers back home.[50] When their two years came up, these NYS members could return home as semicompetent tradesmen and set up businesses in their local communities. To the servicemen who received job placement, the youth's desire for a "dynamic plan" had come to fruition. To others, especially skeptical ministers of Parliament, these jobs smacked of government patronage and corruption.

The vocabulary of youth mobilization, first articulated throughout the 1950s as a means of strengthening colonial authority, easily slipped into the language of postcolonial nation building and statecraft. In 1965, while promoting the NYS at a conference of newly independent African nations, Griffin remarked: "Custom, tradition, and culture, which gave cohesion to tribal association, no longer fit the pattern of the nation state."[51] Griffin had modified his rhetoric only slightly. The "traditions" he had once viewed as a hindrance to the colonial order were now in the way of forging a Kenyan nation. Likewise, just as the colonial state had used labor, ideas about youth mobilization, and state-sponsored patronage to discipline rebellious young men, those same ideas could be used to subdue the youth wings of KANU and KADU.

Jomo Kenyatta faced several pressing issues when he took office. He had to protect the interests of European and Asian economic elites, yet satiate the appetite of land-starved citizens. He had to tame ethnic animosities, yet rely on his coethnic Gikuyu to shore up his authority. He had to mediate the bitter rivalry between KANU and KADU, yet seek ways to exercise control outside party politics. And he had to negotiate Kenya's Cold War alignment, yet extract aid from both the West and the East. Kenyatta handled these challenges often by staying the course, making changes only when necessary. Much of his success in these early years depended on his mastery of the colonial past and ideas about age. But long before he could master the levers of power, Kenyatta had to learn self-mastery.

Like many of the young men in this book, Kenyatta had a troubled coming-of-age story and complicated history with age-relations. He, too, had been a "wayward youth."[52] Born shortly before the turn of the century, Kenyatta lost both parents before the age of ten, leaving him under the care of a stepfather with whom he did not get along. His stepfather recalled that "Jomo was lonely at home. He was a clever boy, playful, and ambitious. Sometimes he stole food from the stores, but it was difficult for the mothers to discover it. He even used to spend whole nights in the bush if he was angry or slighted. At the age of about ten Jomo ran away. He went off to school."[53] Around the age of ten, Kenyatta joined the Church of Scotland Mission at Thogoto, where he converted to Christianity and learned to read and write.[54] As a convert, Kenyatta's initiation differed from his age-mates', and his circumcision was "exceptional," according to Jeremy Murray-Brown. In 1913, a mission teacher took Kenyatta and a small group of fellow catechists down to the river where they met with Samson Njoroge, one of the first Gikuyu trained as a hospital assistant. Samson had brought a surgical knife with him from the hospital and began to cut the boys one by one.[55] Kenyatta underwent a "purified" Presbyterian initiation ceremony, one that allowed the faithful to become men but without the dancing, singing, and seclusion they would have had back home.[56]

After his initiation, Kenyatta left Thogoto to work on a sisal farm in Thika and then as a clerk in Nairobi. Kenyatta traveled to many of the new spaces opened up by colonial rule. His experiences certainly set him apart from his peers and set him against his elders for defying the cultural norms of the Gikuyu community. Yet, as colonial rule wore on, more and more young men followed Kenyatta's path: conversion, migration, urbanization, and even circumscribed circumcision. Kenyatta's life became—as many others' would—a quest to reconcile his Western embrace and Gikuyu roots.[57] Among his elders, Kenyatta's coming-of-age would have smacked of cultural delinquency. To his age-mates, he had a reputation for being a bit of a "dandy," a ladies' man who wore the latest fashions his literacy, urban life, and wage labor afforded him. Yet Kenyatta did not return home just to flaunt his access to money and foreign commodities, he also came to make peace with his elders. His stepfather recalled that after his schooling, Kenyatta "brought me 190 shillings, a blanket and a piece of linen, and we became reconciled."[58] The "wayward youth" had translated his education at Thogoto and employment in Thika and Nairobi to make something of himself, and he returned home to show his family that he had become a successful man. He was the prodigal son returned, and a political one at that.

Kenyatta had come of age in the midst of intense Gikuyu political activity. In the early 1920s, Gikuyu chiefs had formed the Kikuyu Association with the help of missionaries as a mouthpiece of their conservative brand of politics. In Nairobi, Harry Thuku, a mission-educated clerk, began the East Africa Association to demand an end to the dreaded kipande work pass and harsh taxation as well as the return of land stolen for white settlement. Anxious over Thuku's radical politics, the British arrested him in 1922. His arrest outraged his supporters, who crowded 7,000 to 8,000 strong outside the police station where he was held. Police fired into the crowd, killing as many as fifty-six. In the wake of the massacre, Thuku was exiled, and the East African Association was banned. Undeterred, his former supporters began a new political association in 1924, the Kikuyu Central Association (KCA).[59]

Kenyatta joined the KCA and became its secretary and editor of the association's journal, called *Mwigwithania*, or "one who makes people listen (and agree) together" or "the reconciler."[60] The journal published the news of the day, translated passages from the Bible, and gave lessons in Gikuyu history. Through *Mwigwithania*, KCA members like Kenyatta reminded young men and women of the obligations waiting for them back home. KCA members knew all too well how hard it could be to remember one's connection to elder kin and the past. They had been the first generation in their families to leave home, study at missions, convert to Christianity, and live in towns. *Mwigwithania* became a way to reconcile these two worlds.[61] Readers positioned themselves as "mediators between the new ways and the old [and] used the technology of print to concretize and standardize the oral wisdom of their fathers," which "guarded Gikuyu virtues against social death, against the amnesia induced by wage labor."[62] *Mwigwithania* offered KCA readers a sense of resolution or perhaps redemption. Through the journal and their activities in the KCA, they confessed the cultural sins they had made while embracing new colonial possibilities, reconciled with elders by preserving and respecting their wisdom, and laid claim to the mantle of elderhood themselves. The KCA members were archivists of Gikuyu custom, or at least their own politically minded retelling of it. Indeed, the KCA readers' "repentance proved to be only a preamble to claiming a greater wisdom than their fathers."[63] In short, they had grown up, gotten married, raised children. Their houses were in order. Their education, labor, and town life had made them skilled in new ways—ways essential to the Gikuyu if they were to reclaim their lands and freedom from the British.[64]

In the 1930s, Kenyatta traveled to Great Britain and the Soviet Union to attend school and sharpen his vision of Gikuyu history, custom, and age. In London, he began a master's degree program in anthropology at the London School of Economics under the supervision of Bronislaw Malinowski. Kenyatta's research, an ethnographic study of the culture and politics of the Gikuyu, became famous for being an "authentic" account of Gikuyu life written by a Gikuyu. Like *Mwigwithania*, his dissertation, and the book it would become, *Facing Mount Kenya*, was a political project through which Kenyatta transformed himself from a youth to an elder. In *Facing Mount Kenya*, he idealized the Gikuyu past and its customs by "shaming a corrupted present [to] justify control over the future."[65] *Facing Mount Kenya* was an "elderly" text that espoused a resurrection of romanticized cultural forms to create an authentically African future.

In *Facing Mount Kenya*, Kenyatta emphasized age-relations. He focused on the leadership of elders and a rigidly hierarchical order based on age. Kenyatta argued that the Gikuyu were a well-organized, ethnically cohesive nation led by well-to-do old men. Past paths to material and moral achievement lay in younger generations' willingness to respect and serve the interests of elders.[66] As Bruce Berman argues, "Glorifying a social order based on the authority of responsible age and wealth of [land-owning] elders over the young and the poor, Kenyatta . . . limited the space available for both generational change and the educated young for whom he once spoke."[67] For Kenyatta, his future in politics and the future of the Gikuyu lay in the authority of elders chosen from the generation that had once written for *Mwigwithania*. When he returned to Kenya from abroad, "Kenyatta became, very deliberately, a senior elder."[68] He bought land and began a household of his own, marrying into the family of Chief Koinange, one of the most powerful Gikuyu dynasties.

Kenyatta's thinking about age and its political potential had clearly begun long before his election and the birth of the National Youth Service. Immediately after coming to power in 1963, he consolidated his authority, a process in which the NYS played a crucial role. Declaring the petty squabbles of his fellow politicians in KANU and KADU a threat to nationhood, he strengthened his position at the expense of Parliament.[69] Rather than turn to KANU and party politics, he instead harnessed the power of the provincial administration as former colonial governors had done.[70] Although he championed nationalism as a means to overcome regional ethnic tensions, Kenyatta was keenly aware of the localized authority imbued in the provincial administration. British district officials and commissioners had run the colony; it had been they who liaised with local elders, collected taxes, maintained law and order, and meted out justice. Preserving the provincial administration, Kenyatta wielded a powerful bureaucratic instrument that operated outside the purview of Parliament and answered directly to him.[71] Provincial and district commissioners became the medium through which Kenyatta channeled the wealth of government down to the local level, creating a web of clientage with him at its center.

However, Kenyatta's political position meant little if Kenya teetered on the edge of financial ruin. His custodianship of the former settler colony was just as essential as his consolidation of political power. From 1962 until 1970, the British and then the Kenyatta regime oversaw the resettlement of Kenyans on hundreds of thousands of acres of land mostly taken from European settlers along the edges of the White Highlands. Known as the Million-Acres Scheme, the first resettlements began in 1962. The program purchased 1.5 million acres from settlers and subdivided the land into high-density plots, which were then made available for purchase by Africans, many of them landless. Brokering a deal with European settlers, Kenyatta siphoned off enough land for African farms to create the illusion of a return to African property ownership without disrupting large-scale European-controlled agricultural production.[72] The schemes represented only 20 percent of the White Highlands.[73] African resettlement programs like the Million-Acres Scheme muffled the outcry of Kenya's most poor, at least temporarily. Kenyatta worked hard to suppress debate about further resettlements, and he came under increasing fire from ministers of Parliament such as Josiah M. Kariuki for handing out parcels of land to clients rather than the poor and landless. Accusations of corruption within the Kenyatta family continued to haunt the president until the late 1970s. Meanwhile,

Kenyatta's fiercest accusers went to their deaths. Kariuki was assassinated in 1975, just as Tom Mboya had been in 1969 and Pio Pinto before him in 1965.

The NYS aligned with Kenyatta's efforts both to consolidate his political position and to address, at least superficially, the economic inequalities confronting the young. The NYS also provided Kenyatta the manpower to directly bring development projects to various parts of the country, a legion of traveling semiskilled artisans building roads and airfields as well as laying fencing around national parks. As Kenyatta himself wrote in an October 1964 NYS recruitment pamphlet, "May the National Youth Service be the living demonstration of . . . Harambee!"[74] Part of the president's platform on development, known as Harambee, was that local communities had to take development into their own hands. If a village wanted to build a school or a water reservoir, they worked with their provincial administrators to organize, collect fees, and hire local artisans.[75]

While Harambee became a critical form of development for local communities, it became a tool of political patronage for Kenyatta and local politicians. In exchange for loyalty, local provincial administrators received government funding, personal visits from the president, and donations from other wealthy Kenyans for Harambee projects. Throughout the country, schools, wells, and roads became a tangible symbol of Kenyatta's benevolence.[76] By 1974, Kenyatta could boast that the NYS had cleared 18,286 acres of land, built 1,100 miles of road, planted 100,000 trees, and built 7 airfields.[77] The total value of the projects totaled over eleven million Kenyan shillings. However, when many fresh servicemen experienced the backbreaking work at the NYS and fled to the offices of their MPs complaining that they were being "tortured" for their political affiliation, the MPs quickly washed their hands of participating in the nomination of new NYS members, fearful that dropouts would organize against them. Seizing the opportunity, Kenyatta directed Griffin to alter the recruitment policy. In 1965, at the same time Kenyatta expanded his executive powers under a new constitution and dissolved the opposition party KADU, the recruitment of NYS servicemen came under the purview of the provincial administration, the very bureaucrats who answered to Kenyatta.[78] When chosen for the service, a young man now owed his good fortune to Kenyatta's local man on the spot.

None of Kenyatta's and Griffin's plans for the NYS could have come to fruition without the financial and logistical support of the United States and Great Britain. Early on, Kenyatta manipulated Cold War antagonisms to not only secure funding for the NYS but also augment his own political legitimacy. Kenyan politicians had charted a relatively amiable and gradual course toward independence with the British. In return, the British tried to stabilize Kenyatta's regime in the early years of his rule. After a coup attempt in January 1964, the British deployed the Special Air Service in Nairobi to protect Kenyatta and prevent any further "counterrevolutionary" activity.[79] But the revolutionaries the British and Americans worried most about were the Soviet Union, China, and several KADU politicians like Oginga Odinga, who had become a fierce critic of Kenyatta. Odinga's ties to the Soviet Union and China drew the watchful eye of the United States. After the coup attempt, the US sought to strengthen Kenyatta's political hand. William Attwood, US ambassador to Kenya, recalls that one of the programs Kenyatta wanted help funding was the NYS. He had read reports that the Soviets and Chinese were thinking of supporting the scheme, modeling it after their own brigades, "complete with indoctrination by hand-picked instructors." When Attwood next met Kenyatta, who stressed to him the need for a youth service, Attwood asked him to write a letter to President Johnson. USAID had estimated the cost of the scheme for the US would be about $4 million. While USAID officials worried that the equipment gifted to Kenyatta might fall into the hands of communists, Secretary of State Dean Rusk and Attorney General Robert Kennedy agreed with Attwood, and so did the president.[80] In 1964, USAID provided Kenya with $991,000 for the NYS. The money purchased uniforms, beds and bedding, and trucks and tractors, as well as road-building equipment. The following year, USAID support for the service increased to $1,052,000, with an additional $900,000 to purchase foodstuffs.[81] Without American and British financial assistance, Griffin could not have purchased the food and supplies necessary to shelter the thousands of servicemen living in NYS barracks across the country.

While the American government was willing to provide financial assistance, the US State Department remained wary of taking any credit. The NYS had to remain a symbol of Kenyan nation building, the political benefits of which must be enjoyed by Kenyatta. American financial support of the service was intended to shore up Kenyatta's precarious position and ward off communist meddling. "Our support of the NYS," Department of State officials argued, "should continue but as unobtrusively as possible, as this is a source of Kenyan pride. We must let them reap the harvest of credit. Kenya, and especially Kenyatta, are in a position to exert real leadership; this must be encouraged."[82] The State Department was also unwilling to show "American faces in the camps." Rather than direct USAID and the Peace Corps to send American volunteers to aid Griffin and Itote at the camp, pressure was put on international organizations to provide vocational instructors. Most of the instructors came from the International Secretariat of Volunteer Services and the Organization for Rehabilitation and Training. Griffin hosted carpenters and masons from France, Canada, and Switzerland, as well as mechanics from Germany and Japan.[83]

The millions of dollars drained into the NYS was not simply the result of beneficent American patronage, but also a shrewd game of brinkmanship played by Kenyatta himself. In 1964, he pitted the Soviet Union and the United States against each other, using their thirst for influence in East Africa to provide him with additional economic and political support. In the spring of 1964, after taking money from the United States for the NYS, Kenyatta also accepted an offer from the Soviet Union and China for financial assistance. He indicated that the NYS would be one of those programs that should benefit from communist support. While nothing ever came from the deal between Kenyatta, the Soviet Union, and China, it forced the Americans to increase their efforts. As the State Department noted after Kenyatta's deal with the Soviet Union and Chinese: "It is thus important that every effort be made to carry out our commitments promptly and efficiently."[84] Kenyatta had not only harnessed former colonial officials and programs but also the financial aid of the United States to create a program to alleviate the social and economic grievances of young Kenyan men and strengthen his own influence over Kenya.

CONCLUSION

In the end, the youth who wrote to Jomo Kenyatta in 1964 never received their "dynamic plan." Through the NYS, Kenyatta had harnessed the elder state, negotiated financial aid from the West, and twisted local ideas about the gerontocratic nature of Kenyan communities, all in an effort to bring order and stability to his regime. The service aimed to alleviate the social and economic grievances of two generations of radicalized, politicized young men as well as socialize and discipline them. Kenyatta viewed young people as naturally rebellious, in need of constant discipline and management. They could succeed only if they mastered themselves and worked hard and obediently under their elders' tutelage. This was a warped sense of Africa age-relations, but one deeply infused with colonial ideas. The NYS and Kenyatta also demarcated who was young and old, weak and powerful, in Kenyan postcolonial politics. The service institutionalized maturity as an essential component of African statecraft and nation building. And above all, it granted Kenyatta generational authority, which he wielded to authenticate his position as paramount elder.

On 22 August 1978, the Mzee died, ending his fifteen-year rule and beginning the twenty-four-year presidency of his successor, Daniel arap Moi.

Rather than operate outside party politics as Kenyatta had done, Moi ruled through a one-party state commanded by KANU.[85] Moi redistributed political and economic patronage to his ethnic community, the Kalenjin, at the expense of the Gikuyu. The results were economically disastrous. In the midst of stagnant growth and rising underemployment, Moi freely used extrajudicial violence to rein in the opposition. In the 1990s, under intense local and international pressure, Moi announced the return of multiparty democracy to Kenya. Confronted with a reemerging opposition, his tactics grew more violent and desperate. Throughout the 1990s, he leaned heavily on a resurgent KANU youth wing to perpetrate a reign of "terror and extortion on commuter buses, taxis and kiosk businesses."[86] In July 1990, the KANU youth wing was called in to assist the police during a rally of anti-Moi protesters at the Kamukunyi Grounds. The brutality of the youth wingers sparked four days of rioting across the country, leading to the deaths of twenty people and arrests of over a thousand. The NYS became more akin to the KANU youth wing, traveling the country to intimidate Moi's critics, break up opposition rallies, and incite ethnic violence. In 1996, for the first time in its thirty-year history, servicemen and servicewomen trained with guns, not spades.[87]

The Moi elder state also co-opted and funded gangs and militias of young men known as *majeshi ya wazee*, or "armies of elders." These gangs for hire shrouded themselves in "traditional" ideas about the role of young men in fighting for or defending their communities. Groups like Jeshi la Mzee in Nairobi, Baghdad Boys in Kisumu, Kuzacha Boys in Mombasa, and Chinkororo in Kisii worked for elder political patrons, used violence to displace other ethnic groups in their areas, and terrified opposition politicians.[88] Between 1991 and 2001, these groups killed an estimated 4,000 people and displaced 600,000.[89] The Moi regime refused to admit its support for these groups, but KANU politicians relied heavily on these forms of extrastate violence to outflank their opponents.[90] In response, Moi's opponents struck back with their own personal paramilitary groups of underemployed young men, vigilante groups that sprang up to defend and prey on local communities.

In 2002, as Moi planned his public exit from national politics, he continued to play the politics of age by boldly declaring the death of the elder state. He moved a younger generation of politicians into positions of leadership, men like Uhuru Kenyatta and Raila Odinga, the sons of rival patriarchs of Kenya's decolonization, Jomo Kenyatta and Oginga Odinga, respectively. In choosing Uhuru as his successor, Moi signaled the end of gerontocratic rule. If the peoples of Kenya voted for KANU yet again, they would ensure a transfer of generational power.[91] The idea of a generational transition broadcast by Moi and Uhuru deeply affected disenfranchised young people. Perhaps the most infamous youth movement, Mungiki, came to prominence during the election by endorsing Moi's call for a new, younger generation of leadership. Mungiki was and remains a quasi-religious, exclusively Gikuyu organization that emerged in part to defend Gikuyu from the political attacks orchestrated by politicians under the Moi regime. Over the course of the 1990s, Mungiki moved to Nairobi and became a criminal organization with deep roots in the transportation business and various extortion schemes. Its activities against the state also became increasingly violent and more clandestine.[92] But in 2002, Mungiki joined the KANU campaign, articulating the election as a Gikuyu *ituīka*, or "breaking," and the campaign as a generational struggle. They reimagined themselves as warriors seeking to liberate the Gikuyu from the corruption, greed, and misrule of a generation of elder politicians who had not relinquished control since independence. Their political malfeasance had destroyed Kenya, which needed new, more youthful leadership to restore the moral order. In return, KANU allowed Mungiki to claim profitable transportation routes and turned a blind eye as they expanded their criminal enterprises.[93]

When Uhuru and KANU lost the election to Mwai Kibaki, yet another aged politician of the old guard, and his multiethnic coalition, Mungiki and other youth gangs and militias turned to acts of terror. From 2003 onward, the Kibaki government responded with escalating force to subdue Mungiki. Hundreds of its members were murdered in extrajudicial killings and thousands more were arrested or exiled. Today, the state continues to mobilize young men to battle their age-mates. Elder politicians perpetuate an arms race of youths, including storied institutions like the NYS and criminal gangs for hire, pitting them against one another in proxy wars fought to sustain a gerontocracy forged decades ago by Jomo Kenyatta. The elder state lives on—brought to terrible maturity by Kenya's postcolonial leaders with the broken pieces of British colonial rule.

Conclusion
#Gocutmyhusband

"THERE WAS NO DENYING THE EXCITEMENT." A raucous crowd had gathered at Chwele market in Bungoma, Western Kenya, early in the morning to witness the forced circumcision of James Asega, a thirty-nine-year-old Bukusu man. According to Edith Kimani, a correspondent for the Kenya Television Network (KTN), James awoke "to the shock of thousands of strangers outside his home waiting to circumcise him."[1] Footage from the KTN story, which aired in mid-January 2015, showed a stone-faced James, smeared in mud, led to the market center, facing public humiliation for being so old and still uncircumcised. Amid the throng, he faced the knife. How had the community discovered James's secret? It began, KTN reported, after a recent quarrel between James and his wife, Asha Nalongo. Asha decided his foreskin finally had to go and exposed him to local community leaders.

Asha's revelation and James's forced circumcision were a sensation in Kenya. The Twitter handle "#gocutmyhusband" trended. Hundreds posted about it on Facebook. A week later, KTN reporter Najma Ismail returned to the Asega household for a follow-up story.[2] Eyes lowered, voice soft, Asha told Najma, "I always knew he had not been circumcised."[3] She had pushed him to have the procedure in secret at hospital so no one would know. She would say to him: "You know you never keep your own money. I am going to work . . . and when they pay me, we'll secretly run and go to the hospital."

But James refused. "In our house," James said, "we fought a lot. We fought like two men."

People who knew James were stunned. He had not just humiliated himself and his wife, but he had defied the cultural norms of the Bukusu. Speaking forcefully and directly into the camera, the elder who circumcised James told Najma that "if someone removes their clothes and he still has that piece of skin from their mother . . . then I must circumcise him . . . my people will search everyone to ensure that everyone is clean." "This cleanliness," he added, "helps one not get the virus." The circumciser legitimized his assault on James, conflating James's circumcision and maturity with preserving Bukusu cultural traditions and protecting the community from HIV/AIDS.[4]

Forced circumcisions make news in Kenya.[5] In 2009, the *East African Standard* ran the story of Tom, a middle-aged Gikuyu living near Nakuru, who was forcibly circumcised after his wife informed the village. Married ten years, the father of two, Tom had begged his wife to keep his secret. And she had, in exchange for trips to Mombasa and "leisure needs." Crippled by the stress of his wife's demands, Tom resorted to borrowing money, and then to alcohol, and eventually to violence. Fearful for her life, the wife revealed his secret. A gang of youths broke into his home, stripped him naked in public, and demanded his initiation right then and there. At the last moment, local elders dramatically stepped in and instructed the youths to take Thomas to hospital instead.[6] Duncan, another middle-aged Gikuyu, made news a few years later when he, too, was unable to shoulder the burden of his foreskin. After he began to abuse his wife, his age-mates frog-marched him through Lari to the local hospital. As they passed by the police station, they convinced the officers to give them some money to cover the surgery rather than arrest them for kidnapping Duncan. Disrupting a church service on their way, parishioners poured out to see the spectacle, giving it their blessing with donations.[7]

AGING DISSIDENTS

Fit for an African telenovela, the news stories of James, Tom, and Duncan—these *abasinde*, îhîî, uncircumcised "boys"—have it all: financially and psychologically broken husbands hounded by bitter, outspoken wives; age-mates and elders insistent that maturity long postponed by cowardice must finally be earned with bravery; and a Kenyan audience riveted yet riven over the entangled issues of circumcision, masculinity, and human rights. The media packaged each forced circumcision as a way to discipline past cowardice, reassert gender and marital norms, reinforce dominant ideas about and institutions of masculinity and ethnicity, and reassert the authority of seniors over junior bodies. Yet forced circumcisions are by no means accepted practice. On social media, Kenyans argue back and forth about whether this is a time-honored tradition to be respected, a form of male genital mutilation to be prosecuted, or a Westernized medical practice to be mandated in the age of AIDS.

The politics of foreskin extends well beyond Bukusu and Gikuyu bedrooms. Anxieties about Kenyan men's maturity and masculinity and whether or not they have been circumcised have long histories. Throughout the twentieth century, as spaces for boys outside the surveillance of fathers' households opened to them, so, too, did the possibilities to avoid the painful prospects of initiation. "Boys who were scared," recalled Kimani Maruge, "who were mischievous or took booze, they refused to be circumcised following tradition and would forgo circumcision." If they were ever discovered, they would be "arrested by the community and initiated by force with the blessing of the government."[8] Not even death spared an uncut man from a postmortem circumcision. In 2012, as elders in Gatundu dressed the body of one of their age-mates, they discovered to their horror that he had not been cut. The eighty-year-old man had managed to avoid his initiation since the 1940s. In secret, his age-mates met and decided to circumcise the corpse. No Gikuyu, they argued, could be buried uncircumcised.[9] As abominable as Gatundu elders might have found their age-mate's negligence, it should come as no surprise that some boys who came of age during colonial rule failed in their responsibility to become men. The Gatundu man might have been dragooned into military service and shipped off to Burma on the eve of his initiation. Or he might have left home to work in the sisal mills, earning a wage and enjoying new ways to exhibit his manliness instead of returning home to do so as his forefathers had done. He might simply have been afraid of the pain or bravely hostile to conformity. Whatever his reasoning, the Gatundu man was not alone; many young men took unusual paths to manhood during colonialism.

Many of the stories told in this book were of men whose initiations had been postponed or uncertain. Interpreters for anthropologists like the Routledges and Peristiany had delayed their initiations to assist with the foreigners' research. Harry Kimanji, who had escaped his uncle's brutality and spent his childhood pilfering on the streets of Nairobi, only faced a makeshift blade inside a British detention camp. Simon Kariuki, orphaned and scarred by the Mau Mau war, volunteered for circumcision inside the Wamumu Youth Camp, arguing that his fight in the forest and rehabilitation in the camp had made him a man. Peter Njoroge, incarcerated at the Kabete Approved School, asked that staff circumcise him at the end of his sentence so that he might return home a man. For all these men, the circumstances of and the choices they made during the colonial encounter complicated their coming-of-age. Had their communities or the colonial state not intervened, they might have suffered the same indignities as James, Thomas, and Duncan.

Fascination with foreskin in Kenya today is a consequence of these changes. Rather than being imposed by reckless colonial violence or driven by unimpeded African agency, these changes emerged from the messy yet powerful arguments about age and gender between Africans, young and old, as well as non-African newcomers like government officials, missionaries, and employers. Colonialism introduced a host of new adult actors who claimed authority over young Africans and interjected their own ideas of how one's youth should be spent. One of their first arguments was over male initiation. In the first two decades of the twentieth century, missionaries and colonial officials interfered and tampered with African initiation practices. Provincial administrators, along with local elders, initiated boys at earlier ages, shortened the length of ceremonies, and reduced the time spent in seclusion. They did so to ensure a regular supply of labor, certify African ages that did not neatly map onto a Christian calendar, and ward off the potential scandal of child labor. Such meddling diluted markers of manhood like seclusion and warriorhood and made circumcision the last remaining ritual certainty that a boy had become a man. There were other avenues too. Young men found new paths along which they enjoyed their youth, remade masculinity, and earned maturity: Christianity, education, wage labor, town life, crime, and politics.

Throughout this book, we have explored several of these possibilities. We traced the journeys of young men who left home and migrated to settler farms to work for wages herding cattle, tending tea, and stripping sisal from the 1920s until the end of World War II. Sons struck out for distant colonial industries in search of adventure, distance from elder authority, and financial independence. They poured their savings into flashy clothing, alcohol, and dance parties and invested in setting youthful trends, attracting lovers, besting age-mates, and pressuring fathers to accept their new expressions of masculinity. Some leveraged their newfound success to demand that their fathers' initiate them into manhood. And a few stayed away, resisting their responsibility to return home and undergo initiation.

Their travels also took the young to towns. We have explored the possibilities of street life, from the humble beginnings of towns at the turn of the century until the rapid urbanization of the 1940s. Street boys came to towns looking for something unlike their fathers' herds and grazing fields. They also came fleeing family crises, destitution, and violence. Living on their wits in the back alleys of Nairobi, they patched together lives for themselves woven from the fabric of age and gender. They formed gangs among age-mates and battled older and young rival gangs for territory and respect. They coordinated their strategies for finding food, spending money, and sharing cigarettes, alcohol, and drugs. From the joys and agonies of town life, and the bravado and bravery it required, these young men found new ways to articulate what it meant to be masculine and mature without the ritual certainty of initiation. None of the many former street boys I interviewed had faced the knife at home.

Migrant labor and town life ignited impassioned conversations among seniors and juniors. They quarreled over the value of earning an age in such ways and asserted their dominant or emergent masculinities. Some fathers rejected their sons' decisions to leave home and labor or travel to town. Their flesh and blood had abandoned their herds, wasted their energies on frivolous, foreign things. Worse still, they sometimes postponed their initiations or marriages. Their cultural deviance was unacceptable. Other fathers were more permissive. They understood, especially if they had left home in their youth, how these new possibilities translated into both their sons' and their own maturity and masculinity.

From the 1930s onward, a growing number of young men came to realize that their unconventional efforts did not always guarantee success. Our focus narrowed briefly to postwar Central Kenya, where young Gikuyu men found it harder to get work, pay tuition, and earn a livable wage. They articulated their frustrations as a prolonged and ambiguous age between childhood and adulthood. To escape they turned to militant politics and violence—what the British called Mau Mau. For many, regardless of their biological age, the war became a way to resolve their uncertain age. If their first initiations had not placed them on the road to adulthood, then perhaps their initiation into Mau Mau would. They used the language and symbols of initiation, warriorhood, and age-relations to oath new members, fortify their courage, and maintain chains of command. The Mau Mau generation's struggle ran aground on a brutal British counterinsurgency campaign. The British and loyal Gikuyu killed thousands and detained tens of thousands more, giving rise to a second generation of young refugees orphaned and impoverished. Some had no one left to initiate them, or their ritual transition into manhood went unnoticed in the confines of detention and the drift toward independence. Two generations' entangled crises troubled Kenyan politicians as they assumed leadership of a newly independent Kenya in 1963. Even before the celebrations had subsided, the young—those who had fought for freedom, endured detention, or campaigned for politicians—clamored for education, jobs, and a quality of life befitting their newfound citizenship.

The stories in this book of Christian initiates, migrant tea pruners, street boys, house burglars, Mau Mau fighters, and orphans show how age and gender were and remain the axis along which the everyday lives of Kenyans turn. These young men push historians to reconsider framing Kenya's history solely in terms of ethnicity, class, race, and gender—and show that, together, age and gender are powerful cultural forces and units of historical analysis. Their lives also encourage scholars to move beyond the study of ethnic peculiarities, and to explore the cultural forces that Kenyans shared. But above all, these coming-of-age stories show just how transformative young men's engagement with colonialism was and how that legacy haunts the forced circumcisions of men like James, Thomas, and Duncan and the still-raucous debates about what makes a mature man today.

Age matters now more than ever. Since independence, the population of Kenya has quintupled. The 1962 census estimated that Kenya was home to about nine million citizens. By 2009, the census recorded nearly thirty-nine million. In 2015, Kenya boasted a population of just over forty-six million.[10] The country's citizens are disproportionately young. In 1962, roughly 70 percent of the population was below the age of thirty, a figure that has remained consistent for the past fifty years.[11] This demographic explosion has generated intense competition among young Kenyans, who remain by and large undereducated, underemployed, landless, and angry. Some young people have desperately turned to the informal economy, to criminality, and to violence to survive.[12] Others have creatively used social media and activism to amplify their voices in debates about age, gender, and enfranchisement. Young people today still wrestle with a sense of prolonged, uncertain age that drove so many young Mau Mau into the forests of Central Kenya in the 1950s. And as today's youths seek solutions to resolve this age, they turn to that past for inspiration. Mungiki, a political, quasi-religious, and criminal organization made up of self-identified Gikuyu "youths," uses age in just such a way. They take tobacco at their meetings to evoke a privilege once reserved for elders and speak of Mau Mau and *ituīka*, the late nineteenth-century practice of formalized generational transition in leadership, as ways of reforming contemporary politics. Mungiki members reach back for and then reimagine traditional Gikuyu values to critique the postcolonial state.[13]

Behind the backdrop of these demographic pressures, the now centuries-old elder state thrives. Kenya's leaders speak the language of age to augment authority, obliterate opponents, and cultivate networks of patronage.[14] Meanwhile, Kenya's citizens respond by performing the role of "youth" to access or protest the patronage of their elder statesmen. This gerontocratic stranglehold on wealth and power, this tyranny of elders, is the legacy of the elder state built atop half a century of British colonial rule and brought to terrible fruition by Kenya's political elite in the last half century. Colonial rule entangled age-relations and statecraft, elevating arguments that had once occurred within households and among generations to the broader field of politics. To authenticate and augur their power, the British joined the arguments between juniors and seniors—a process that resulted in what I call the elder state. Like the relationships between fathers and sons, the elder state emerged from sometimes tense and messy negotiations: between British officials and Africans, between different officials posted to disparate parts of the Kenya administration, as well as between those same officials and their superiors in the Colonial Office back in London and a host of other non-African actors, including missionaries, employers, and activists. Age became central to the colonial encounter in Kenya precisely because it mattered so much to this diverse cast of characters. These arguments made the elder state a kind of marketplace of ideas where government officials tinkered with and then traded in local, African, and Western concepts about age and masculinity.

The elder state was one of many tools the British used to navigate the contradictions of nurturing a violent, exploitative settler economy, while also pursuing the moral uplift of the civilizing mission. Conquest depended on the warrior spirit of young soldiers and porters. Governance required literate and semiskilled subjects to serve as interpreters, clerks, carpenters, and masons. The settler economy desperately needed laborers to make an expensive imperial enterprise profitable. And so the colonial state encouraged young men to undergo initiation earlier, migrate and work for wages, and even live in the shantytowns of Nairobi and Mombasa as long as they had jobs and a place to stay. The elder state also fretted over the cultural delinquency it helped foster. These young men, who strayed too far from the authority of their elders and the strict norms of kinship and countryside, risked detribalization and unraveled indirect rule. From the very start, the elder state intervened with growing vigor in the discipline of young men. Beginning in 1902, it cast out dozens then thousands of street boys from towns to protect against and prevent their criminality. Five years later, it built one of the continent's first government-run reformatories to turn the colony's most serious offenders into mature, masculine subjects. Prior to and during World War II, the elder state inspected workplaces for young laborers, fined a few recruiters, and returned wayward sons to their homes. The young were also a touchstone of the civilizing mission and an image of benevolent imperialism projected by the British back at home. Kenya became a site of remarkable experimentation, testing welfare-oriented programs on the young long before the heyday of the post–World War II developmentalist state. Enthusiastic, idealistic officials did inspire these initiatives; but more often than not, they were compelled to consider the well-being of the young, fearful of the scandal that might erupt if the plight of emaciated migrants made the British newspapers.

As the colonial state matured and grew confident in its abilities, it expanded its role in the lives of young African men. Throughout the interwar years, the British ushered in new legislation to define age and regulate the labor and behavior of the young. It also broadened its powers to arrest, repatriate, and institutionalize young men in one of the most expansive juvenile justice systems in colonial Africa. In the midst of the Mau Mau war, when colonial rule seemed its most uncertain, brought to the brink by frustrated young men, the state offered itself up as an alternative elder. At the Wamumu Youth Camp, the elder state tried to rehabilitate thousands of young Mau Mau fighters into disciplined, mature, manly subjects. Then, in the thousands of youth clubs that dotted the colony, they created a short-lived youth movement to prevent a younger undereducated, underemployed generation from turning to violence.

As the British Empire slowly disintegrated, officials in Kenya lamented the failure of the elder state, citing continued migration, growing crime, and bubbling political agency among the young. After independence in 1963, age remained a primary interface between the state and Kenyan citizens. The first president of Kenya, Jomo Kenyatta, and other politicians expertly and explicitly used the rhetoric of age to reshape postcolonial politics as age-relations between "elder" statesmen and "young" constituents. They used the National Youth Service to discipline politicized youths and shackle their citizenship to clientage. The result was a gerontocratic form of politics perpetuating the power of a single generation for five decades.

And in that half century, the postcolonial elder state has used male circumcision as a violent, blunt instrument to whip up the frenzied support of their constituents and marginalize their opponents. They have equated a man's foreskin with immaturity and translated male circumcision into a potent symbol of civic worth. There is incredible political power in the words for uncircumcised boys: *abasinde*, *îhîî*, and *yaa*. The frustrated wives of James, Tom, and Duncan used these words to shock their communities into seizing their husbands and forcing them to correct their cultural deviance. Meanwhile, politicians have weaponized these words to battle and belittle opponents and inspire ethnic, sexual violence. Grace Wangechi, executive director of the Gender Violence Recovery Center in Nairobi, and part Gikuyu herself, argues that "if you call a [G]ikuyu man that, you're dead—literally." "No one looks at your age," she adds, "they look at whether you've gone through the rite of passage. It's that significant." So when politicians use the word to describe their opponents, "crowds will respond to that." "Just that word alone is more than enough to cause chaos in the country."[15]

The words for uncircumcised boys have indeed caused chaos. Since independence in 1963, Kenyan politicians have used the vocabulary of age and the violence of circumcision as weapons of state making and ethnic blood sport. In the late 1950s and early 1960s, as Jomo Kenyatta positioned himself as Kenya's paramount political elder, he and his supporters claimed that their chief political rival, a Luo named Oginga Odinga, was uncircumcised. Luo men do not traditionally undergo circumcision to mark their entrance into manhood. The differences in Luo male initiation were used to emasculate and infantilize Odinga, signal that he lacked the maturity to rule Kenya, and weaken his popularity among other Kenyan ethnic communities.[16]

Today Gikuyu politicians continue to utter the word *îhîî* to marginalize Luo politicians and voters. In the postelection violence of 2007–2008, gangs of machete-wielding Gikuyu youths, many of them Mungiki, shouted "*îhîî*" as they forcibly circumcised their Luo neighbors. The 2007 election pit President Mwai Kibaki and his coalition Party of National Unity (PNU), made up largely of Gikuyu politicians, against Raila Odinga and the Orange Democratic Movement (ODM), which drew much of its support from Luo, Luhya, and Kalenjin supporters.[17] Throughout the campaign, members of Kibaki's PNU party dismissed Raila's ability to rule, questioning whether uncircumcised Kenyans had the maturity and manliness to govern. In a speech, the PNU assistant minister of Public Works, Mwangi Kiunjuri, trotted out a Gikuyu proverb to explain Luo political unpreparedness. "Let me tell you," he said, "uncircumcised boys are not invited to dowry negotiations because, as you know, boys will always take time to sing their play songs. An uncircumcised boy's goings is only ended when he faces the knife."[18] Kiunjuri compared Raila and the Luo to boys playing at politics.

As he campaigned throughout Kenya, Raila often preemptively addressed the circumcision issue. During a rally in Marakwet District, Raila boldly told the crowd that what mattered most was being "circumcised upstairs." His foreskin was especially troublesome in Marakwet, a region that has maintained its tradition of male and female circumcision despite intense pressure from nongovernmental organizations. Moreover, the people of Marakwet "frequently refer to outsiders who are uncircumcised," Henrietta Moore argues, "as lacking the capacity to speak, to conduct themselves appropriately, to demonstrate leadership through judgment."[19] After his speech, Raila's supporters in the district repeated the phrase, emphasizing that being "circumcised upstairs" meant Raila was educated and clever enough to rule the country.

In the days before Kenyans lined up to vote, it looked as though after years in the political wilderness, Raila and ODM might win. Yet, as the results came in, they dramatically turned Kibaki's way. In some parts of the country, the vote had been deliberately rigged.[20] Kenya descended into violence. In Kibera, the largest slum in Africa and home to Nairobi's largest Luo population, gangs of Luo youths killed around fifty Gikuyu. Women and girls were raped. Businesses were reduced to rubble. And in the aftermath rumors swirled via text message that the Gikuyu would retaliate, that Mungiki gangs would descend on Kibera to exterminate the Luo.[21] Gikuyu retaliation was indeed swift. According to the investigation by the International Criminal Court, politicians like Uhuru Kenyatta funded and unleashed criminal Gikuyu gangs like Mungiki to terrorize and murder ODM supporters and politicians.[22] In a handful of widely publicized instances, Luo men were forcibly circumcised or castrated.[23] After the election, Kevin Omollo, a twenty-two-year-old Kibera resident, attended a rally to show his support for Raila and ODM. Police broke up the protest, and as he fled, he ran into a mob of Gikuyu. They grabbed him, beat him, stripped him naked, and cut his foreskin with a six-inch kitchen knife. Through the searing pain he could hear them shouting: "How can a *kîhîi* rule the country? How can we have a president who is not circumcised?"[24] Sixteen-year-old Walter Odoni shared a similar story. He was stripped and his genitals tortured. "It was the greatest pain I have ever felt in my life," Walter said. "It was like a million little pins pricking my manhood."[25]

As violence consumed Nairobi and the Kenyan countryside, the international community pressured Kibaki and Odinga to meet at the negotiating table.[26] By the end of February, both parties had worked out a power-sharing arrangement, one that kept the presidency in Kibaki's hands but offered Odinga the role of prime minister. Calm slowly returned to Kenya, but not before leaving thousands dead and six hundred thousand people internally displaced. In the midst of the postelection violence, the entangled politics of age and ethnicity produced terrifying acts of sexual violence. As Wanjiru Kamau-Rutenberg argues, forced circumcisions became a way for Gikuyu to "wield a masculine power over the feminized Luo men whose flesh they mutilated."[27] Yet this was more than simply a gendered form of violence. As gangs of youths circumcised Luos, they claimed for themselves the privilege of elders and infantilized their victims. They also endeavored to erase Luo cultural and ethnic distinctiveness, removing a cultural marker that the Luo had reappropriated and rallied around to consolidate their political identity.

The wounds of the mutilated had hardly healed when Kibaki's administration began a broader effort, perceived by many Luo as an effort to wipe away their cultural distinctiveness. The Kenyan government announced its participation in a growing international effort to encourage young African men to volunteer for medical circumcision. As most Kenyans already practiced male circumcision, the government's decision was seen as squarely aimed at the Luo.

The World Health Organization had only recently recommended voluntary medical male circumcision (VMCC) to prevent HIV transmission in Africa. VMCC has quickly become a popular supplemental HIV prevention strategy based on emerging evidence that male circumcision lowers the risk of sexual transmission. Several studies conducted in Uganda and Kenya showed that male circumcision reduced the risk of HIV transmission by 60 percent.[28] Following the World Health Organization's recommendation, international aid organizations like the President's Emergency Plan for AIDS Relief (PEPFAR) and the Bill and Melinda Gates Foundation poured resources into VMCC in Eastern and Southern Africa, where more than nine million men were circumcised between 2008 and 2014.[29] In Kenya, the politics of VMCC are all too local. The focus of Kenya's VMCC campaign has been in Nyanza, home to most Luo. Raila Odinga has urged young Luos to undergo the surgery. Throughout 2008, several Luo politicians came forward to announce that they had undergone VMCC. Others promised to follow suit. Raila himself remained vague as to whether he had faced the knife. Between March and September of 2008, over a thousand Luo men were cut at the Lumumba Health Center in Kisumu.[30] The push to circumcise Luo men initially outraged local elders. They argued that Raila, ensconced in the Kibaki regime as part of the power-sharing coalition, wanted to make the Luo culturally, and thereby politically, acceptable to the rest of the country.[31] But by 2012, on the eve of yet another election, Luo elders fell in line alongside Raila. In August, Barrack Tunya, a member of the Luo Council of Elders, admitted that he and five others had undergone VMCC—as did five thousand other Luo men.[32]

When researchers ask young Luo men why they breach their cultural norms to face the knife, they admit how much they struggle with the politics of sexual difference. As they move to multiethnic towns and attend multiethnic schools, they confront the reality that their neighbors and classmates are circumcised. They feel like outcasts, their genitals objects of ridicule. Circumcision becomes a swift way to render themselves acceptable and accessible to other ethnic communities. Joseph Gikubu, who works at the Starehe Boys' Centre and School, told me that after their first encounter with their classmates in the locker room, many of his Luo pupils underwent circumcision to avoid being teased or bullied. Young Luo men also undergo circumcision to improve their sex lives. Rumors swirl among them that circumcision improves their prowess in bed, makes them last longer, and increases their pleasure.[33] Circumcision also makes them more attractive to lovers from other ethnicities. As one young man pointed out, "You know like with condoms, if a woman says no condom no sex, then men would look for it anywhere. . . . So if they insist on circumcision, then it could work. . . . She first asks if I am sharpened [circumcised]. . . . That is the first qualification for sex."[34] Many argue that after the cut, they earned women's trust that they were disease-free.[35] VMCC might make Luo men more trustworthy lovers, but it also tests their manly mettle.[36] All young Luo men know that circumcising communities view initiation as a crucible that makes men of boys. VMCC gives Luo men the opportunity to prove themselves on the same battlefield of age and gender as Gikuyu or Luhya. They face the knife just as bravely, they take Gikuyu and Luhya women home, and they rob politicians of the one cultural artifact used to infantilize and mutilate them. VMCC might very well be a quiet effort by male Luo to discard ethnic difference, access national politics, and certify their maturity and masculinity to the rest of the country.

In March 2013, Kenyans went to the polls with the still-aching scars of the 2007 election violence. Kenyan voters had a truly remarkable choice in the contest for president, the sons of Kenya's most revered nationalists: Uhuru Kenyatta, the son of Jomo Kenyatta; and Raila Odinga, the son of Kenyatta's chief rival, Oginga Odinga.[37] The media cast the candidates as heirs darkly obscured by the long shadows of Kenya's past patriarchs. Raila and Uhuru were powerful senior politicians and wealthy businessmen in their own right; regardless, they were but the "crowing sons" of once "roaring lions."[38] They were not young men, either. Raila was sixty-eight, and Uhuru was fifty-one. Yet they represented a "young" generation of politicians who had yet to hold the office of president, an office that had been held by a single generation of elder politicians since independence. Whatever the outcome, the presidential election of 2013 marked a generational transition. The man chosen by 50.51 percent of Kenyan voters was Uhuru Kenyatta, despite an International Criminal Court investigation into his role in the 2007 violence. In the days that followed, voting irregularities emerged, but Kenya did not descend into violence. Tighter security, ever-present antiviolence propaganda, international pressure, and major political reforms all led to a relatively peaceful transition. The total cost: an estimated twenty-four million shillings, threefold that of the previous election.[39]

The 2013 election had as much to do with the vocabulary of age as it did with ethnicity. In his acceptance speech, written by Juliet Wang'ombe, a twenty-two-year-old spoken-word artist, Uhuru Kenyatta celebrated with his supporters and warned his opponents:[40]

> My fellow Kenyans today, we celebrate the triumph of democracy; the triumph of peace; the triumph of nationhood. Despite the misgivings of many in the world—we demonstrated a level of *political maturity* that surpassed expectations. We dutifully turned out; we voted in peace; we upheld order and respect for the rule of law and we maintained the fabric of our society. That is the real victory today. A victory for our nation. A victory that demonstrates to all that Kenya *has finally come of age.* That this, indeed, is Kenya's moment.[41]

Electing Kenyatta through peaceful elections, Kenyans had exhibited real "political maturity" and shown the world that they had "finally come of age." More than powerful words, the speech was a palimpsest of sorts, one this book has tried to peel back layer by layer.

Kenyatta praised his supporters for exhibiting maturity, for making the right decision. He rather prematurely applauded his opponents for not resorting to violent youthful immaturity. All Kenyans had transitioned out of electoral childishness by "dutifully" voting, "respecting" law and order, and "maintaining" Kenyan society. Kenyans had been obedient, respectful, and conservative. In his own way, Kenyatta had come of age too. He had finally emerged from the political shadow of his father and represented a generational transition at the highest level of Kenyan politics. Fifty years after independence, he had been the man to break through the generational glass ceiling. And now, as Kenya's president, its paramount political elder, he signaled the nation's successful, if not prolonged, initiation.

Age infuses the Kenyan state with tremendous cultural power—a curse, or a gift, of the colonial past. The demagoguery of male circumcision incites ethnic passions and sexual violence to mutilate and murder political opponents. It manipulates the global health industry to press all Kenyan men to conform to a dominant, politicized traditional practice. It ensnares the young in the webs of patrimony spun by elder politicians. Yet age—as uncertain as it might be—ignites a sense of adventure and exploration for new possibilities. It burns with an intense, creative energy to challenge authority and imagine new ways to grow up and grow old.

Notes

INTRODUCTION

1. KNA PC/COAST/1/10/181, Chief Secretary, Circular No. 34, The Rights of Missions to Keep Minors without the Consent of the Guardians, 16 April 1914.

2. KNA PC/COAST/1/10/181, DC Mombasa, 21 April 1914; DC Rabai, 27 April 1914; DC Malindi, 29 April 1914; DC Njale, 11 May 1914; and DC Shimoni, 19 May 1914.

3. KNA PC/COAST/1/10/181, C. W. Hobley, PC Coast, to Chief Secretary, Nairobi, 31 May 1914.

4. John M. Lonsdale, "The Conquest State of Kenya, 1895–1905," in *Unhappy Valley: Conflict in Kenya and Africa*, vol. 1, *State and Class*, ed. Bruce J. Berman and John M. Lonsdale (Athens: Ohio University Press, 1992), 16–18, 22–25.

5. Jonathon Glassman, *Feasts and Riot: Revelry, Rebellion, and Popular Consciousness on the Swahili Coast, 1856–1888* (Portsmouth, NH: Heinemann, 1995), 59.

6. Elsewhere in the discipline, age has been recognized as a useful category of analysis. Steven Mintz, "Reflections on Age as a Category of Historical Analysis," *Journal of the History of Childhood and Youth* 1, no. 1 (2008): 92.

7. Luise White, "Separating the Men from the Boys: Constructions of Gender, Sexuality, and Terrorism in Central Kenya, 1939–1959," *International Journal of African Historical Studies* 23, no. 1 (1990): 1–25.

8. A fine, rare exception is Tabitha M. Kanogo, *African Womanhood in Colonial Kenya, 1900–50* (Athens: Ohio University Press, 2005).

9. Charles H. Ambler, *Kenyan Communities in the Age of Imperialism: The Central Region in the Late Nineteenth Century* (New Haven, CT: Yale University Press, 1988), 23–24, 33–34; and Robert L. Tignor, *Colonial Transformation of Kenya: The Kamba, Kikuyu, and Maasai from 1900–1939* (Princeton, NJ: Princeton University Press, 1976), 11–12.

10. See chapter 1 for a comprehensive but by no means exhaustive list of these ethnographies.

11. Mario I. Aguilar, "Gerontocratic, Aesthetic and Political Models of Age," in *The*

Politics of Age and Gerontocracy in Africa, ed. Mario I. Aguilar (Trenton, NJ: Africa World Press, 1998), 9. See also Paul T. W. Baxter and Uri Almagor, eds., *Age, Generation and Time: Some Features of East African Age Organisations* (New York: St. Martin's, 1978), 1–36; and Bernardo Bernardi, *Age Class Systems: Social Institutions and Polities Based on Age* (Cambridge: Cambridge University Press, 1985), 1–9, 24–37.

12. Monica Wilson, *For Men and Elders: Change in the Relations of Generations and of Men and Women among the Nyakyusa-Ngonde People, 1875–1971* (New York: Africana Publishing, 1977); and Claude Meillassoux, *Maidens, Meal and Money: Capitalism and the Domestic Community* (Cambridge: Cambridge University Press, 1981), 80–81.

13. Paul Spencer, *The Maasai of Matapato: A Study of Rituals of Rebellion* (Bloomington: Indiana University Press, 1988), 63; and Elias C. Mandala, *Work and Control in a Peasant Economy: A History of the Lower Tchiri Valley in Malawi, 1859–1960* (Madison: University of Wisconsin Press, 1990), 25–32.

14. Richard D. Waller, "Age and Ethnography," *Azania* 34, no. 1 (1999): 138–40.

15. Meredith McKittrick, *To Dwell Secure: Generation, Christianity, and Colonialism in Ovamboland* (Portsmouth, NH: Heinemann, 2002), 7.

16. Derek R. Peterson, *Creative Writing: Translation, Bookkeeping, and the Work of Imagination* (Portsmouth, NH: Heinemann, 2004), 13.

17. John M. Lonsdale, "The Moral Economy of Mau Mau: Wealth, Poverty and Civic Virtue," in Berman and Lonsdale, *Unhappy Valley*, vol. 2, *Violence and Ethnicity*, 334–37.

18. Spencer, *Maasai of Matapato*, 79–99.

19. Peterson, *Creative Writing*, 15–16. See also Lonsdale, "Moral Economy of Mau Mau," 344–46, 373–76; and Adriaan H. J. Prins, *East African Age-Class Systems: An Inquiry into the Social Order of Galla, Kipsigis, and Kikuyu* (Westport, CT: Negro Universities Press, 1953), 432–57.

20. Deborah L. Durham, "Youth and the Social Imagination in Africa," *Anthropological Quarterly* 73, no. 3 (2000): 114–16.

21. Nicolas Argenti, *The Intestines of the State: Youth, Violence, and Belated Histories in the Cameroon Grassfields* (Chicago: University of Chicago Press, 2007), 7.

22. McKittrick, *To Dwell Secure*, 6–11; J. D. Y. Peel, *Religious Encounter and the Making of the Yoruba* (Bloomington: Indiana University Press, 2000), 233–40; Kanogo, *African Womanhood*, 197–238; Kenda Mutongi, *Worries of the Heart: Widows, Family, and Community in Kenya* (Chicago: University of Chicago Press, 2007), 23–33, 56–68; and most recently Derek R. Peterson, *Ethnic Patriotism and the East African Revival: A History of Dissent, c. 1935–1972* (Cambridge: Cambridge University Press, 2012).

23. On cultures of soldiering: Timothy H. Parsons, *The African Rank-and-File: Social Implications of Colonial Military Service in the King's African Rifles, 1902–1964* (Portsmouth, NH: Heinemann, 1999); and Myles Osborne, *Ethnicity and Empire in Kenya: Loyalty and Martial Race among the Kamba, c. 1800 to the Present* (Cambridge: Cambridge University Press, 2014). For the effects on age among migrant laborers: Keletso E. Atkins, *The Moon Is Dead! Give Us Our Money! The Cultural Origins of an African Work Ethic, Natal, South Africa, 1843–1900* (Portsmouth, NH: Heinemann, 1993); T. Dunbar Moodie, *Going for Gold: Men, Mines, and Migration* (Berkeley: University of California Press, 1994), 76–179; Benedict Carton, *Blood from Your Children: The Colonial Origins of Generational Conflict in South Africa* (Charlottesville: University of Virginia Press, 2000); and Patrick Harries, *Work, Culture, and Identity:*

Migrant Laborers in Mozambique and South Africa, c. 1860–1910 (Portsmouth, NH: Heinemann, 2004).

24. Richard D. Waller, "Rebellious Youth in Colonial Africa," *Journal of African History* 47, no. 1 (2006): 84–91. For East Africa: Andrew Hake, *African Metropolis: Nairobi's Self-Help City* (London: St. Martin's, 1977), 189–213; Chloe Campbell, "Juvenile Delinquency in Colonial Kenya, 1900–39," *Historical Journal* 45, no. 1 (2002): 129–51; and Andrew Burton, "Urchins, Loafers and the Cult of the Cowboy: Urbanization and Delinquency in Dar es Salaam, 1919–61," *Journal of African History* 42, no. 2 (2001): 199–216. For West Africa: Laurent Fourchard, "Lagos and the Invention of Juvenile Delinquency in Nigeria, 1920–60," *Journal of African History* 47, no. 1 (2006): 115–37; and Simon Heap, "'Their Days Are Spent in Gambling and Loafing, Pimping for Prostitutes, and Picking Pockets': Male Juvenile Delinquents on Lagos Island, 1920s–1960s," *Journal of Family History* 35, no. 1 (2009): 48–70. The literature on Southern Africa is much more extensive, and I include only a few selections here: Paul La Hausse, "'The Cows of Nongoloza': Youth, Crime and Amalaita Gangs in Durban, 1900–1936," *Journal of Southern African Studies* 16, no. 1 (1990): 79–111; Katie Mooney, "'Ducktails, Flick-Knives and Pugnacity': Subcultural and Hegemonic Masculinities in South Africa, 1948–1960," *Journal of Southern African Studies* 24, no. 4 (1998): 753–74; and Clive L. Glaser, *Bo-Tsotsi: The Youth Gangs of Soweto, 1935–1976* (Portsmouth, NH: Heinemann, 2000).

25. Luise White, *The Comforts of Home: Prostitution in Colonial Nairobi* (Chicago: University of Chicago Press, 1990); Jean M. Allman, "Rounding up Spinsters: Gender Chaos and Unmarried Women in Colonial Asante," *Journal of African History* 37, no. 2 (1996): 195–214; Lynn M. Thomas, *Politics of the Womb: Women, Reproduction, and the State in Kenya* (Berkeley: University of California Press, 2003); and Abosede A. George, *Making Modern Girls: A History of Girlhood, Labor, and Social Development in Colonial Lagos* (Athens: Ohio University Press, 2014).

26. Jean Comaroff and John L. Comaroff, "Occult Economies and the Violence of Abstraction: Notes from the South African Postcolony," *American Ethnologist* 26, no. 2 (1999): 284; and Eisei Kurimoto and Simon Simonse, eds., *Conflict, Age, and Power in North East Africa: Age Systems in Transition* (Athens: Ohio University Press, 1998).

27. G. Thomas Burgess, "Introduction to Youth and Citizenship in East Africa," *Africa Today* 51, no. 3 (2005): xii.

28. Carton, *Blood from Your Children*, 2–3, 91–92, 100–112.

29. McKittrick, *To Dwell Secure*, 4.

30. Meredith McKittrick, "Forsaking Their Fathers? Colonialism, Christianity, and Coming of Age in Ovamboland, Northern Namibia," in *Men and Masculinities in Modern Africa*, ed. Lisa A. Lindsay and Stephan F. Miescher (Portsmouth, NH: Heinemann, 2003), 40–41, 44–45.

31. Thomas, *Politics of the Womb*, 79–102; and Kanogo, *African Womanhood*, 73–103.

32. Brett L. Shadle, *"Girl Cases": Marriage and Colonialism in Gusiiland, Kenya, 1890–1970* (Portsmouth, NH: Heinemann, 2006), xxviii–xxix; and Kanogo, *African Womanhood*, 104–28.

33. Corrie Decker, "Fathers, Daughters, and Institutions: Coming of Age in Mombasa's Colonial Schools," in *Girlhood: A Global History*, ed. Jennifer Helgren and Colleen A. Vasconcellos (New Brunswick, NJ: Rutgers University Press, 2010), 274–78; and Mutongi, *Worries of the Heart*, 119–21, 137–38.

34. Tabitha M. Kanogo, *Squatters and the Roots of Mau Mau, 1905–63* (Athens: Ohio University Press, 1987), 96–105; David W. Throup, *Economic and Social Origins of Mau Mau, 1945–53* (Athens: Ohio University Press, 1987), chap. 7 and 8; and Sharon Stichter, *Migrant Labour in Kenya: Capitalism and African Response, 1895–1975* (London: Longman, 1982), 128–33.

35. Waller, "Rebellious Youth," 84–87; John M. Lonsdale, "Town Life in Colonial Kenya," in *The Urban Experience in Eastern Africa, c. 1750–2000*, ed. Andrew Burton (Nairobi: British Institute in Eastern Africa, 2002), 219–20; Michael Tamarkin, "Mau Mau in Nakuru," *Journal of African History* 17, no. 1 (1976): 122–27; and Frank Furedi, "The African Crowd in Nairobi: Popular Movements and Elite Politics," *Journal of African History* 14, no. 2 (1973): 282–87.

36. White, "Separating the Men from the Boys"; and Lonsdale, "Moral Economy of Mau Mau," 265–314. See also G. Thomas Burgess and Andrew Burton, introduction to *Generations Past: Youth in East African History*, ed. Andrew Burton and Hélène Charton-Bigot (Athens: Ohio University Press, 2010), 12; and Carton, *Blood from Your Children*, 140.

37. The scholarship on Tanzania has been exhaustive. See G. Thomas Burgess, "The Young Pioneers and the Rituals of Citizenship in Revolutionary Zanzibar," *Africa Today* 51, no. 3 (2005): 3–29; James R. Brennan, "Youth, the TANU Youth League, and Managed Vigilantism in Dar es Salaam, Tanzania, 1925–1973," *Africa* 76, no. 2 (2006): 221–46; and Andrew Ivaska, *Cultured States: Youth, Gender, and Modern Style in 1960s Dar es Salaam* (Durham, NC: Duke University Press, 2011). For West Africa, see Jean M. Allman, *The Quills of the Porcupine: Asante Nationalism in an Emergent Ghana* (Madison: University of Wisconsin Press, 1993), 28–36; Jay Straker, *Youth, Nationalism, and the Guinean Revolution* (Bloomington: Indiana University Press, 2009); and Jeffrey S. Ahlman, "A New Type of Citizen: Youth, Gender, and Generation in the Ghanaian Builders Brigade," *Journal of African History* 53, no. 1 (2012): 87–105.

38. Alcinda M. Honwana, *The Time of Youth: Work, Social Change, and Politics in Africa* (Boulder, CO: Kumarian, 2012), 4. See also Marc Sommers, *Stuck: Rwandan Youth and the Struggle for Adulthood* (Athens: University of Georgia Press, 2012); and Craig Jeffrey, *Timepass: Youth, Class, and the Politics of Waiting in India* (Stanford, CA: Stanford University Press, 2010). Like gender, youth is described as socially constructed, emerging out of relationships of power that change depending on who takes part and where. See Jon Abbink, "Being Young in Africa: The Politics of Despair and Renewal," in *Vanguard or Vandals: Youth, Politics, and Conflict in Africa*, ed. Jon Abbink and Ineke van Kessel (Leiden: Brill, 2005), 5–6; and Filip de Boeck and Alcinda M. Honwana, "Introduction: Children and Youth in Africa," in *Makers and Breakers: Children and Youth in Postcolonial Africa*, ed. Alcinda M. Honwana and Filip de Boeck (Trenton, NJ: Africa World Press, 2005).

39. Jean Comaroff and John L. Comaroff, "Reflections on Youth: From the Past to the Postcolony," in Honwana and Boeck, *Makers and Breakers*, 20; and Honwana, *Time of Youth*, 4–5.

40. Donal B. Cruise O'Brien, "A Lost Generation? Youth Identity and State Decay in West Africa," in *Postcolonial Identities in Africa*, ed. Richard P. Werbner and Terence O. Ranger (London: Zed Books, 1996), 58; Paul Richards, *Fighting for the Rain Forest: War, Youth, and Resources in Sierra Leone* (Portsmouth, NH: Heinemann, 1996); and Danny Hoffman, *The War Machines: Young Men and Violence in Sierra Leone and Liberia* (Durham, NC: Duke University Press, 2011).

41. For the role of young people in ending apartheid, see Colin Bundy, "Street Sociology and Pavement Politics: Aspects of Youth and Student Resistance in Cape Town, 1985," *Journal of Southern African Studies* 13, no. 3 (1987): 303–30; Jeremy Seekings and David Everatt, *Heroes or Villains? Youth Politics in the 1980s* (Johannesburg: Ravan Press, 1993); and Pamela Reynolds, *War in Worcester: Youth and the Apartheid State* (New York: Fordham University Press, 2012). For work on the roles of youth in creative political participation and cultural production, see Lesley A. Sharp, *The Sacrificed Generation: Youth, History, and the Colonized Mind in Madgascar* (Berkeley: University of California Press, 2002); Mamadou Diouf, "Engaging Postcolonial Cultures: African Youth and Public Space," *African Studies Review* 46, no. 2 (2003): 1–12; Deborah L. Durham, "Apathy and Agency: The Romance of Agency and Youth in Botswana," in *Figuring the Future: Globalization and the Temporalities of Children and Youth*, ed. Jennifer Cole and Deborah L. Durham (Santa Fe, NM: School for Advanced Research Press, 2008), 151–78; and Brad Weiss, *Street Dreams and Hip Hop Barbershops: Global Fantasy in Urban Tanzania* (Bloomington: Indiana University Press, 2009).

42. Abbink, "Being Young in Africa," 7.

43. Durham, "Youth and the Social Imagination in Africa," 114–16.

44. Ibid., 118.

45. Lisa A. Lindsay and Stephan F. Miescher, "Introduction: Men and Masculinities in Modern African History," in Lindsay and Miescher, *Men and Masculinities in Modern Africa*, 10.

46. Claire C. Robertson and Iris Berger, "Introduction: Analyzing Class and Gender—African Perspectives," in *Women and Class in Africa*, ed. Claire C. Robertson and Iris Berger (New York: Africana Publishing, 1986), 7–10, 21–23. See also Margaret Strobel, *Muslim Women in Mombasa, 1890–1975* (New Haven, CT: Yale University Press, 1979); Margaret Jean Hay, "Queens, Prostitutes and Peasants: Historical Perspectives on African Women, 1971–1986," *Canadian Journal of African Studies* 22, no. 3 (1988): 431–47; Jean Davison, *Voices from Mutira: Lives of Rural Gikuyu Women* (Boulder, CO: Rienner, 1989), 199–219; White, *Comforts of Home*; Cora Ann Presley, *Kikuyu Women, the Mau Mau Rebellion, and Social Change in Kenya* (Boulder, CO: Westview Press, 1992); and Claire C. Robertson, *Trouble Showed the Way: Women, Men, and Trade in the Nairobi Area, 1890–1990* (Bloomington: Indiana University Press, 1997), 3–9.

47. Joan W. Scott, "Gender: A Useful Category of Historical Analysis," *American Historical Review* 91, no. 5 (1986): 1067; and Nancy Rose Hunt, "Placing African Women's History and Locating Gender," *Social History* 14, no. 3 (1989): 371–72.

48. Kristin Mann, *Marrying Well: Marriage, Status, and Social Change among the Educated Elite in Colonial Lagos* (Cambridge: Cambridge University Press, 1985); and Jean M. Allman and Victoria B. Tashjian, *"I Will Not Eat Stone": A Women's History of Colonial Asante* (Portsmouth, NH: Heinemann, 2000).

49. Belinda Bozzoli, "Marxism, Feminism and South African Studies," *Journal of Southern African Studies* 9, no. 2 (1983): 149.

50. Dorothy L. Hodgson and Sheryl A. McCurdy, "Introduction: 'Wicked' Women and the Reconfiguration of Gender," in *"Wicked Women" and the Reconfiguration of Gender in Africa*, ed. Dorothy L. Hodgson and Sheryl McCurdy (Portsmouth, NH: Heinemann, 2001), 10–14. See also Margot Lovett, "Gender Relations, Class Formation, and the Colonial State in Africa," in *Women and the State in Africa*, ed. Jane L. Parpart and Kathleen A. Staudt (Boulder, CO: Rienner, 1989), 23–25; and Elizabeth

Schmidt, *Peasants, Traders, and Wives: Shona Women in the History of Zimbabwe, 1870–1939* (Portsmouth, NH: Heinemann, 1992).

51. White, "Separating the Men from the Boys," 1. John Tosh also posed the same challenge to historians of Britain and its empire. Tosh, "What Should Historians Do with Masculinity? Reflections on Nineteenth-Century Britain," *History Workshop* 38, no. 1 (1994): 179–202.

52. Lindsay and Miescher, "Introduction: Men and Masculinities," 4.

53. R. W. Connell, *Masculinities* (Cambridge: Polity Press, 1995), 68, 76.

54. Robert Morrell, "Of Boys and Men: Masculinity and Gender in Southern African Studies," *Journal of Southern African Studies* 24, no. 4 (1998): 608.

55. Connell, *Masculinities*, 79–80.

56. Lindsay and Miescher, "Introduction: Men and Masculinities," 6; Morrell, "Of Boys and Men," 615–16; and Andrea Cornwall and Nancy Lindisfarne, introduction to *Dislocating Masculinity: Comparative Ethnographies* (New York: Routledge, 1994), 5.

57. Cornwall and Lindisfarne, "Dislocating Masculinity: Gender, Power and Anthropology," in Cornwall and Lindisfarne, *Dislocating Masculinity*, 20.

58. Robert Morrell and Lahoucine Ouzgane, "African Masculinities: An Introduction," in *African Masculinities: Men in Africa from the Late Nineteenth Century to the Present*, ed. Lahoucine Ouzgane and Robert Morrell (New York: Palgrave Macmillan, 2005), 8. In India, historians have explored how the British Raj concocted the myth of the effeminate Indian. Nothing masculine could come, the British believed, from such heat and humidity, spicy meatless cuisine, and indulgent princely indiscipline. Yet to devour Sunday roast after hunting tigers beneath an oppressive tropical sun made Britons manly in the face of their subjects. See Mrinalini Sinha, *Colonial Masculinity: The "Manly Englishman" and the "Effeminate Bengali" in the Late Nineteenth Century* (Manchester: Manchester University Press, 1995). See also Joseph Sramek, "'Face Him Like a Briton': Tiger Hunting, Imperialism, and British Masculinity in Colonial India, 1800–1875," *Victorian Studies* 48, no. 4 (2006): 659–80; Jayanta Sengupta, "Nation on a Platter: The Culture and Politics of Food and Cuisine in Colonial Bengal, *Modern Asian Studies* 44, no. 1 (2010): 81–98; and Shruti Kapila, "Masculinity and Madness: Princely Personhood and Colonial Sciences of the Mind in Western India, 1871–1940," *Past and Present* 187, no. 1 (2005): 121–56.

59. Lindsay and Miescher, "Introduction: Men and Masculinities," 2–3; and Stephan F. Miescher, *Making Men in Ghana* (Bloomington: Indiana University Press, 2005).

60. McKittrick, "Forsaking Their Fathers?" 35–36, 40–41, 44–45.

61. Lisa A. Lindsay, "Money, Marriage, and Masculinity on the Colonial Nigerian Railway," in Lindsay and Miescher, *Men and Masculinities in Modern Africa*, 143–49; and Carolyn A. Brown, "A 'Man' in the Village Is a 'Boy' in the Workplace: Colonial Racism, Worker Militance, and Igbo Notions of Masculinity in the Nigerian Coal Industry, 1930–1945," in Lindsay and Miescher, *Men and Masculinities in Modern Africa*, 163–65.

62. Robert Morrell, "The Times of Change: Men and Masculinity in South Africa," in *Changing Men in Southern Africa*, ed. Robert Morrell (New York: Zed Books, 2001), 14. See also Harries, *Work, Culture, and Identity*, 200–281; Moodie, *Going for Gold*, 119–58; and Keith Shear, "'Taken as Boys': The Politics of Black Police Employment and Experience in Early Twentieth-Century South Africa," in Lindsay and Miescher, *Men and Masculinities in Modern Africa*, 109–27.

63. Lindsay and Miescher, "Introduction: Men and Masculinities," 12.

64. Molly McCullers's work on the Herero Otruppa illustrates how young men appropriated a militant masculinity from German soldiers to cope with the aftermath of the war and capitalize on elder weakness. McCullers, "'We Do It So That We Will Be Men': Masculinity Politics in Colonial Namibia, 1915–49," *Journal of African History* 52, no. 1 (2011): 45–48, 62.

65. Lindsay and Miescher explicitly argue that this is their guiding purpose in "Introduction: Men and Masculinities," 3.

66. Jane L. Parpart and Kathleen A. Staudt, "Women and the State in Africa," in Parpart and Staudt, *Women and the State in Africa* (Boulder, CO: Rienner, 1989), 6.

67. Connell, *Masculinities*, 73.

68. Emily Lynn Osborn, *Our New Husbands Are Here: Households, Gender, and Politics in a West African State from the Slave Trade to Colonial Rule* (Athens: Ohio University Press, 2011), 10–11.

69. Thomas, *Politics of the Womb*, 4–6. See also Kanogo, *African Womanhood*, 15–72, 129–96; and White, "Separating the Men from the Boys," 7–9.

70. Crawford Young, *The African Colonial State in Comparative Perspective* (New Haven, CT: Yale University Press, 1994), 95–140; and Mahmood Mamdani, *Citizen and Subject: Contemporary Africa and the Legacy of Late Colonialism* (Princeton, NJ: Princeton University Press, 1996), 18, 48–61.

71. Frederick Cooper, "Conflict and Connection: Rethinking Colonial African History," *American Historical Review* 99, no. 5 (1994): 1533; and Jeffrey Herbst, *States and Power in Africa: Comparative Lessons in Authority and Control* (Princeton, NJ: Princeton University Press, 2000).

72. Ann Laura Stoler and Frederick Cooper, "Between Metropole and Colony: Rethinking a Research Agenda," in *Tensions of Empire: Colonial Cultures in a Bourgeois World*, ed. Frederick Cooper and Ann Laura Stoler (Berkeley: University of California Press, 1997), 6.

73. Bruce J. Berman and John M. Lonsdale, "Coping with the Contradictions: The Development of the Colonial State in Kenya, 1895–1914," in Berman and Lonsdale, *Unhappy Valley*, vol. 1, *State and Class*, 77, 94–95.

74. Stoler and Cooper, "Between Metropole and Colony," 19–20.

75. Marshall S. Clough, *Fighting Two Sides: Kenyan Chiefs and Politicians, 1918–1940* (Boulder: University Press of Colorado, 1990), 4–7, 11–19.

76. Karen E. Fields, *Revival and Rebellion in Colonial Central Africa* (Princeton, NJ: Princeton University Press, 1985), 32–41, 50–60.

77. Thomas, *Politics of the Womb*, 5, 13.

78. Thomas Spear, "Neo-Traditionalism and the Limits of Invention in British Colonial Africa," *Journal of African History* 44, no. 1 (2003): 3–27.

79. Hodgson and McCurdy, "Introduction: 'Wicked' Women and the Reconfiguration of Gender," 11–14. For the colonial state's involvement in Kenyan marriage and divorce practices, see Brett Shadle's "*Girl Cases*." For West Africa, see Kristin Mann's *Marrying Well*; also Barbara Cooper, *Marriage in Maradi: Gender and Culture in a Hausa Society in Niger, 1900–1989* (Portsmouth, NH: Heinemann, 1997), 21–22, 34–39; Sean Hawkins, "'The Woman in Question': Marriage and Identity in the Colonial Courts of Northern Ghana, 1907–1954," in *Women in African Colonial Histories*, ed. Jean Allman, Susan Geiger, and Nakanyike Musisi (Bloomington: Indiana University Press, 2002), 116–43; and Emily S. Burrill, *States*

of Marriage: Gender, Justice, and Rights in Colonial Mali (Athens: Ohio University Press, 2015).

80. John M. Lonsdale, "When Did the Gusii (or Any Other Group) Become a 'Tribe'?" *Kenya Historical Review* 5, no. 1 (1977): 123–33; Peterson, *Creative Writing*, 139–58; Gabrielle Lynch, *I Say to You: Ethnic Politics and the Kalenjin in Kenya* (Chicago: University of Chicago Press, 2011); Julie MacArthur, "When Did the Luyia (or Any Other Group) Become a Tribe?" *Canadian Journal of African Studies* 47, no. 3 (2013): 351–63; and Justin Willis and George Gona, "Tradition, Tribe, and State in Kenya: The Mijikenda Union, 1945–1980," *Comparative Studies in Society and History* 55, no. 2 (2013): 448–73.

81. Katherine Luongo, *Witchcraft and Colonial Rule in Kenya, 1900–1955* (Cambridge: Cambridge University Press, 2011), 11.

82. Berman and Lonsdale, *Unhappy Valley*, vol. 1, *State and Class*, 94.

83. Tabitha Kanogo, Kenda Mutongi, Brett Shadle, and Lynn Thomas all focus primarily on the roles of chiefs, local native councils, and provincial administrators. Frank Furedi and Tabitha Kanogo, among many others, examine the interplay between the department of labor and the provincial administration. Kate Luongo explores the nexus between provincial administrators and the judiciary. For the work of the departments of African affairs and community development, see Joanna Lewis, *Empire State-Building: War and Welfare in Kenya, 1925–52* (Athens: Ohio University Press, 2001). Yet several historians, including Derek Peterson and David Throup, incorporate a much wider range of administrative personnel.

84. Bruce J. Berman, *Control and Crisis in Colonial Kenya: The Dialectic of Domination* (Athens: Ohio University Press, 1990), 80–82.

85. Ibid., 79.

86. Opolot Okia, *Communal Labor in Colonial Kenya: The Legitimization of Coercion, 1912–1930* (New York: Palgrave Macmillan, 2012), 93–113.

87. Jocelyn Murray, "The Kikuyu Female Circumcision Controversy, with Special Reference to the Church Missionary Society's 'Sphere of Influence'" (PhD diss., University of California at Los Angeles, 1974); Susan Pedersen, "National Bodies, Unspeakable Acts: The Sexual Politics of Colony Policy-Making," *Journal of Modern History* 63, no. 4 (1991): 659–60; Lynn M. Thomas, "'Ngaitana (I Will Circumcise Myself)': The Gender and Generational Politics of the 1956 Ban on Clitoridectomy in Meru, Kenya," *Gender and History* 8, no. 3 (1996): 338–63; and Penelope Hetherington, "The Politics of Female Circumcision in the Central Province of Colonial Kenya, 1920–30," *Journal of Imperial and Commonwealth History* 26, no. 1 (1998): 98, 100–101.

88. Lawrence Stone, "The Family in the 1980s: Past Achievements and Future Trends," *Journal of Interdisciplinary History* 12, no. 1 (1981): 69; and Hugh Cunningham, *Children and Childhood in Western Society since 1500* (New York: Longman, 1995).

89. John R. Gillis, *Youth and History: Tradition and Change in European Age Relations, 1770–Present* (New York: Academic Press, 1981), 98; and Harry Hendrick, *Images of Youth: Age, Class, and the Male Youth Problem, 1880–1920* (Oxford: Clarendon, 1990), 97.

90. Gillis, *Youth and History*, 156–57. For child labor in Britain, see Jane Humphries, *Childhood and Child Labour in the British Industrial Revolution* (Cambridge: Cambridge University Press, 2011); and Peter Kirby, *Child Workers and Industrial Health in Britain, 1780–1850* (Rochester, NY: Boydell and Brewer, 2013). For juvenile delinquency in Britain, see Heather Shore, *Artful Dodgers: Youth and Crime in Early*

Nineteenth-Century London (Rochester, NY: Boydell, 2002); Pamela Cox, *Bad Girls in Britain: Gender, Justice and Welfare, 1900–1950* (New York: Palgrave Macmillan, 2003); and Heather Ellis, *Juvenile Delinquency and the Limits of Western Influence, 1850–2000* (New York: Palgrave Macmillan, 2014).

91. Hendrick, *Images of Youth,* 102–4.

92. Victor Bailey, *Delinquency and Citizenship: Reclaiming the Young Offender, 1914–1948* (Oxford: Oxford University Press, 1987).

93. John Springhall, *Youth, Empire and Society: British Youth Movements, 1883–1940* (London: Taylor and Francis, 1977), 14–16, 56–58; and Timothy H. Parsons, *Race, Resistance, and the Boy Scout Movement in British Colonial Africa* (Athens: Ohio University Press, 2004), 49–61.

94. Robert Wohl, *The Generation of 1914* (Cambridge, MA: Harvard University Press, 1979), 1–4, and chap. 3.

95. Gillis, *Youth and History,* 98.

96. Jordanna Bailkin, *The Afterlife of Empire* (Berkeley: University of California Press, 2012), 15–18. The literature on the use of age in France is especially rich. See Richard I. Jobs, *Riding the New Wave: Youth and the Rejuvenation of France after the Second World War* (Stanford, CA: Stanford University Press, 2007), 24–28.

97. Timothy J. Coates, *Convicts and Orphans: Forced and State-Sponsored Colonizer in the Portuguese Empire, 1550–1755* (Stanford, CA: Stanford University Press, 2001), 78–79; Barry M. Coldrey. "'. . . A Place to Which Idle Vagrants May Be Sent': The First Phase of Child Migration during the Seventeenth and Eighteenth Centuries," *Children and Society* 13, no. 1 (1999): 32–47; and Robert C. Johnson, "The Transportation of Vagrant Children from London to Virginia, 1618–1622," in *Early Stuart Studies: Essays in Honor of David Harris Wilson,* ed. Howard S. Reinmuth Jr. (Minneapolis: University of Minnesota Press, 1970), 140–47.

98. John Donne, "Sermon CLVI Preached to the Virginia Company," in *Children and Youth in America: A Documentary History,* vol. 1, 1600–1865, ed. Robert H. Bremner (Cambridge, MA: Harvard University Press, 1970), 8.

99. Ellen Boucher, *Empire's Children: Child Emigration, Welfare, and the Decline of the British World, 1869–1967* (Cambridge: Cambridge University Press, 2014), 7–9. See also David M. Pomfret, *Youth and Empire: Trans-Colonial Childhoods in British and French Asia* (Stanford, CA: Stanford University Press, 2015); and Shirleene Robinson and Simon Sleight, *Children, Childhood and Youth in the British World* (New York: Palgrave Macmillan, 2015).

100. Bianca Premo, *Children of the Father King: Youth, Authority, and Legal Minority in Colonial Lima* (Chapel Hill: University of North Carolina Press, 2005); Tobias Hecht, ed., *Minor Omissions: Children in Latin American History and Society* (Madison: University of Wisconsin Press, 2002); and Ondina E. González and Bianca Premo, eds., *Raising an Empire: Children in Early Modern Iberia and Colonial Latin America* (Albuquerque: University of New Mexico Press, 2007).

101. George, *Making Modern Girls,* 71; and Satadru Sen, *Colonial Childhoods: The Juvenile Periphery of India, 1850–1945* (London: Anthem Press, 2005), 1–8. Sarah Duff has recently shown how both the government of Cape Colony and the Dutch Reformed Church pushed poor young Afrikaners into school to prevent racial degeneration and strengthen colonial rule. Sarah E. Duff, *Changing Childhoods in the Cape Colony: Dutch Reformed Church Evangelicalism and Colonial Childhood, 1860–1895* (New York: Palgrave Macmillan, 2015), 519, and especially chap. 4 and 5.

102. Bailkin, *Afterlife of Empire*, 60–89. The Vichy regime was particularly interested in youth mobilization in the 1940s. Eric T. Jennings, *Vichy in the Tropics: Petain's National Revolution in Madagascar, Guadeloupe, and Indochina* (Stanford, CA: Stanford University Press, 2001), 61–62, 110–12; and Anne Raffin, *Youth Mobilization in Vichy Indochina and Its Legacies, 1940–1970* (Lanham, MD: Lexington Books, 2005).

103. For the ways the state leaned on and tried to strengthen elder patriarchs, though not always successfully, see Thomas, *Politics of the Womb*, especially chap. 1 and 3. For the ways the state's meddling resulted in the "diminishing authority of elders and the surging power of youths," see Carton, *Blood from Your Children*, 1.

104. Berman, *Control and Crisis in Colonial Kenya*, 110.

105. Ibid., 110, 113.

106. Fred Morton, "Small Change: Children in the Nineteenth-Century East African Slave Trade," in *Children in Slavery through the Ages*, ed. Gwyn Campbell, Suzanne Miers, and Joseph C. Miller (Athens: Ohio University Press, 2009), 66–67; Morton, "Pawning and Slavery on the Kenya Coast: The Miji Kenda Case," in *Pawnship in Africa: Debt Bondage in Historical Perspective*, ed. Toyin Falola and Paul E. Lovejoy (Boulder, CO: Westview Press, 1994), 34–35; Ambler, *Kenyan Communities in the Age of Imperialism*, 132–33; and Shadle, *Girl Cases*, 44–45.

107. Berman, *Control and Crisis in Colonial Kenya*, 104–13.

108. Robert G. Gregory, *Sidney Webb and East Africa: Labour's Experiment with the Doctrine of Native Paramountcy* (Berkeley: University of California Press, 1962).

109. George, *Making Modern Girls*, 8–11; Fourchard, "Lagos and the Invention of Juvenile Delinquency," 115–37; and Beverley C. Grier, *Invisible Hands: Child Labor and the State in Colonial Zimbabwe* (Portsmouth, NH: Heinemann, 2006), 161–216.

110. Donald A. Low and John M. Lonsdale, "Introduction: Towards the New Order, 1945–1963," in *History of East Africa*, vol. 3, ed. Donald A. Low and Alison Smith (Oxford: Oxford University Press, 1962), 12–16; Berman, *Control and Crisis in Colonial Kenya*, 361–71; and Frederick Cooper, *Decolonization and African Society: The Labor Question in French and British Africa* (Cambridge: Cambridge University Press, 1996), 384–85. Helen Tilley makes a strong case that the move toward development, particularly in science and medicine, had its origins in much earlier ideas and programs. Tilley, *Africa as a Living Laboratory: Empire, Development, and the Problem of Scientific Knowledge, 1870–1950* (Chicago: University of Chicago Press, 2011), 71–113.

111. Lewis, *Empire State-Building*, 2–4, 13–19, and esp. chap. 6; and Berman, *Control and Crisis in Colonial Kenya*, 361–71.

112. Dane K. Kennedy argues that the most potent view of Mau Mau was a liberal and paternalistic one promoted by a small group of influential missionaries, settlers, and government officials. It is within this liberal paternalistic view that the elder state found its voice in the late 1950s. Kennedy, "Constructing the Colonial Myth of Mau Mau," *International Journal of African Historical Studies* 25, no. 2 (1992): 243–44; and John M. Lonsdale, "Mau Maus of the Mind: Making Mau Mau and Remaking Kenya," *Journal of African History* 31, no. 3 (1990): 404.

113. Caroline Elkins, *Imperial Reckoning: The Untold Story of Britain's Gulag in Kenya* (New York: Holt, 2005), 284–90.

114. Caroline Elkins, "The Colonial Papers: FCO Transparency Is a Carefully Cultivated Myth," *Guardian*, 17 April 2012, accessed 20 January 2016, http://www .theguardian.com/politics/2012/apr/18/colonial-papers-fco-transparency-myth; Richard Drayton, "Britain's Secret Archive of Decolonisation," *History Workshop Online*, 12

April 2012, accessed 20 January 2016, http://www.historyworkshop.org.uk/britains-secret-archive-of-decolonisation/; and David M. Anderson, "Guilty Secrets: Deceit, Denial, and the Discovery of Kenya's 'Migrated Archive,'" *History Workshop Journal* 80, no. 1 (2015): 142–60.

115. Sidney H. Fazan, *Colonial Kenya Observed: British Rule, Mau Mau and the Wind of Change*, ed. John Lonsdale (London: Tauris, 2014), esp. John Lonsdale's foreword; and Thomas G. Askwith, *From Mau Mau to Harambee: Memoirs and Memoranda of Colonial Kenya* (Cambridge: African Studies Centre, 1995).

CHAPTER 1: AN "ARBITRARY LINE"

1. This was not the first time the reverend had interfered with the right of elders to initiate the young. In December 1916, he had sent a group of converts to seize two recent initiates. Jeffrey A. Fadiman, *When We Began, There Were Witchmen: An Oral History from Mount Kenya* (Berkeley: University of California Press, 1993), 226.

2. KNA PC/CP/7/1/1, A. E. Chamier, DC Meru, to H. R. Tate, PC Central, Circumcision of Mission Boys and Girls, 26 September 1919.

3. Suzette Heald argues that male circumcision is an anachronism, a ritual once meant to create warriors who had no place after colonial conquest. Yet the ritual persists in part because the colonial state found ways to make it useful beyond merely making warriors. Heald, *Manhood and Morality: Sex, Violence and Ritual in Gisu Society* (London: Routledge, 1999), 8–11, 43.

4. Paul V. Kollman, *The Evangelization of Slaves and Catholic Origins in Eastern Africa* (Maryknoll, NY: Orbis, 2005), 88–89, 94–95.

5. Roland A. Oliver, *The Missionary Factor in East Africa* (London: Longman, 1966), 15–23.

6. Fred Morton, "Small Change: Children in the Nineteenth-Century East African Slave Trade," in *Children in Slavery through the Ages*, ed. Gwyn Campbell, Suzanne Miers, and Joseph C. Miller (Athens: Ohio University Press, 2009), 66–67.

7. Fred Morton, "Pawning and Slavery on the Kenya Coast: The Miji Kenda Case," in *Pawnship in Africa: Debt Bondage in Historical Perspective*, ed. Toyin Falola and Paul E. Lovejoy (Boulder, CO: Westview Press, 1994), 34–35.

8. Charles H. Ambler, *Kenyan Communities in the Age of Imperialism: The Central Region in the Late Nineteenth Century* (New Haven, CT: Yale University Press, 1988), 132–33.

9. KNA PC/COAST/1/12/9, H. B. Johnstone, Assistant Collector Rabai, 2 June 1899; and Morton, "Small Change," 57.

10. KNA PC/COAST/1/17/58, P. L. Deacon, Assistant DC Rabai, to PC Mombasa, 14 November 1912; and KNA DC/KIS/1/5/6, Assistant DC Meru to DC Kismayu, 28 September 1917.

11. Morton, "Pawning and Slavery on the Kenya Coast," 35.

12. KNA PC/COAST/1/10/181, Chief Secretary, Circular No. 34, The Rights of Missions to Keep Minors without the Consent of the Guardians, 16 April 1914.

13. KNA PC/COAST/1/10/181, DC Mombasa, 21 April 1914.

14. KNA PC/COAST/1/10/181, DC Rabai, 27 April 1914; DC Shimoni, 19 May 1914.

15. KNA PC/COAST/1/10/181, DC Malindi, 29 April 1914; DC Njale, 11 May 1914.

16. KNA PC/COAST/1/10/181, C. W. Hobley, PC Coast, to Chief Secretary, Nairobi, 31 May 1914.

17. Ibid.

18. John R. Gillis, *Youth and History: Tradition and Change in European Age Relations, 1770–Present* (New York: Academic Press, 1981), 98–105, 115–28. See also Philippe Aries, *Centuries of Childhood: A Social History of Family Life* (New York: Vintage Books, 1962); David Bakan, "Adolescence in America: From Idea to Social Fact," *Daedalus* 100, no. 4 (1971): 979–95; Hugh Cunningham, *Children and Childhood in Western Society since 1500* (New York: Longman, 1995); and Steven Mintz, *Huck's Raft: A History of American Childhood* (Cambridge, MA: Harvard University Press, 2004).

19. Margaret May, "Innocence and Experience: The Evolution of the Concept of Juvenile Delinquency in the Mid-Nineteenth Century," *Victorian Studies* 17, no. 1 (1973): 16–18, 22; John R. Gillis, "The Evolution of Juvenile Delinquency in England, 1890–1914," *Past and Present* 67, no. 1 (1975): 96–126; Geoffrey Pearson, *Hooligan: A History of Respectable Fears* (London: Macmillan, 1983); Heather Shore, "Introduction: Re-Inventing the Juvenile Delinquent in Britain and Europe, 1650–1950," in *Becoming Delinquent: British and European Youth, 1650–1950*, ed. Pamela Cox and Heather Shore (Aldershot: Ashgate, 2002), 2–3; and Pamela Cox, *Bad Girls in Britain: Gender, Justice and Welfare, 1900–1950* (New York: Palgrave Macmillan, 2003).

20. Harry Hendrick, *Images of Youth: Age, Class, and the Male Youth Problem, 1880–1920* (Oxford: Clarendon, 1990), 4.

21. John Springhall, *Youth, Empire and Society: British Youth Movements, 1883–1940* (London: Taylor and Francis, 1977), 14–15; and Pamela Cox, "Race, Delinquency and Difference in Twentieth Century Britain," in Cox and Shore, *Becoming Delinquent*, 162.

22. Timothy H. Parsons, *Race, Resistance, and the Boy Scout Movement in British Colonial Africa* (Athens: Ohio University Press, 2004), 51–61.

23. Robert S. S. Baden-Powell, *Scouting for Boys: A Handbook for Instruction in Good Citizenship* (London: Horace Cox, 1908), 282.

24. Robert Wohl, *The Generation of 1914* (Cambridge, MA: Harvard University Press, 1979), 88–89, 93–94.

25. Katherine Luongo, *Witchcraft and Colonial Rule in Kenya, 1900–1955* (Cambridge: Cambridge University Press, 2011), 12–13.

26. John Middleton and Greet Kershaw, *The Kikuyu and Kamba of Kenya* (London: International African Institute, 1965), 61.

27. Henrietta L. Moore, "Forms of Knowing and Un-Knowing: Secrets about Society, Sexuality and God in Northern Kenya," in *Secrecy and Silence in the Research Process: Feminist Reflections*, ed. Róisín Ryan-Flood and Rosalind Gill (New York: Routledge, 2010), 32–36. During my own fieldwork, I found some men who were willing to share with me a little of life during seclusion. When I asked them why they would break their oaths of secrecy, they responded that seclusion had begun to disappear altogether, and in its absence, young men became undisciplined and irresponsible. They believed that if seclusion were better understood, if the period after circumcision could be brought back into force, then younger generations would be better behaved and more acquiescent to their elders.

28. Godfrey Muriuki, *A History of the Kikuyu, 1500–1900* (Nairobi: Oxford University Press, 1974), 39.

29. William S. Routledge and Katherine Routledge, *With a Prehistoric People: The Akikuyu of British East Africa* (London: Arnold, 1910), 154–55.

30. Alfred C. Hollis, *The Nandi: Their Language and Folk-Lore* (Oxford: Clarendon, 1909), iv.

31. Gerhard Lindblom, *The Akamba in British East Africa* (Uppsala: Appelbergs Boktryckeri Aktiebolag, 1920), 46.

32. John G. Peristiany, *The Social Institutions of the Kipsigis* (London: Routledge and Sons, 1939), 27–28.

33. G. Barra, *1,000 Kikuyu Proverbs: With Translations and English Equivalents* (London: Macmillan, 1960), 57. Gikuyu men whom I interviewed repeatedly shared the same proverb with me, though without the emphasis on stealing: "Mũici na kĩhĩĩ akaega kĩarua." Beth Maina Ahlberg and Kezia Muthoni Njoroge, "'Not Men Enough to Rule!': Politicization of Ethnicities and Forcible Circumcision of Luo Men during the Postelection Violence in Kenya," *Ethnicity and Health* 18, no. 5 (2013): 458. My thanks to Derek Peterson for providing some very last-minute help with this proverb.

34. Routledge and Routledge, *With a Prehistoric People*, 154; Charles W. Hobley, *Bantu Beliefs and Magic* (London: Cass, 1922, repr. 1967), 77; Jomo Kenyatta, *Facing Mount Kenya: The Tribal Life of the Gikuyu* (London: Vintage Books, 1965), 128; and Louis S. B. Leakey, *The Southern Kikuyu before 1903* (London: Academic Press, 1977), 587.

35. John S. Akama and Solomon Monyenye, "Circumcision Ceremony," in *Ethnography of the Gusii of Western Kenya: A Vanishing Cultural Heritage*, ed. John S. Akama and Robert M. Maxon (Lewiston, NY: Edwin Mellen, 2006), 176; Peristiany, *Social Institutions of the Kipsigis*, 6; and Paul Spencer, *The Maasai of Matapato: A Study of Rituals of Rebellion* (Bloomington: University of Indiana Press, 1988), 82.

36. During the early colonial period, Luo initiates had their bottom front teeth removed as a symbol of bravery and community membership. While initiates were still too young to be considered men, they continued along a path toward maturity, working to build a homestead and then marry. See Paul Mboya, *Paul Mboya's "Luo Kitgi gi Timbegi,"* trans. Jane Achieng (Nairobi: Atai Joint, 2001).

37. Kenyatta, *Facing Mount Kenya*, 110; Peristiany, *Social Institutions of the Kipsigis*, 7–8; Lindblom, *Akamba in British East Africa*, 42–43; Alfred M. M'Imanyara, *The Restatement of Bantu Origin and Meru History* (Nairobi: Longman, 1992), 125; and Daniel Nyaga, *Customs and Traditions of the Meru* (Nairobi: East African Educational Publishers, 1997), 52–53.

38. Interview by author: Wachira Mwaniki, 25 May 2008, Burguret, Laikipia.

39. Charles W. Hobley, *Ethnology of A-Kamba and Other East African Tribes* (Cambridge: Cambridge University Press, 1910), 68; and Lindblom, *Akamba in British East Africa*, 42–43.

40. Interview by author: Wachira Mwaniki, 25 May 2008, Burguret, Laikipia.

41. Interview by author: David Chege Njuguna, 19 May 2008, Kagwe, Kiambu. Meru initiates were treated to a song and dance performed by the generation ahead of them to encourage them and teach them the life lessons they needed once they, too, became young men. M'Imanyara, *Restatement of Bantu Origin and Meru History*, 125–26; and Nyaga, *Customs and Traditions of the Meru*, 56–59.

42. Routledge and Routledge, *With a Prehistoric People*, 162–63; Costanzo Cagnolo, *The Agikuyu, Their Customs, Traditions and Folklore* (Nyeri: Mission Printing School, 1933), 92–95; Hobley, *Bantu Beliefs and Magic*, 82–85; Kenyatta, *Facing Mount Kenya*, 132–37; and Leakey, *Southern Kikuyu before 1903*, 619–20.

43. Akama and Monyenye, "Circumcision Ceremony," 179–80.

44. Peristiany, *Social Institutions of the Kipsigis*, 9–14; and interview by author: John Tumbo Soi, 6 June 2008, Saunet, Sotik.

45. Lindblom, *Akamba in British East Africa*, 50–57; Hobley, *Bantu Beliefs and Magic*, 70–72; and Middleton and Kershaw, *Kikuyu and Kamba of Kenya*, 88–89.

46. Routledge and Routledge, *With a Prehistoric People*, 164; Kenyatta, *Facing Mount Kenya*, 147–48; Leakey, *Southern Kikuyu before 1903*, 624–65; Nyaga, *Customs and Traditions of the Meru*, 56, 59, 77–78, 81.

47. Interview by author: David Chege Njuguna, 19 May 2008, Kagwe, Kiambu.

48. Interview by author: Wachira Mwaniki, 25 May 2008, Burguret, Laikipia. For the Gusii, see John S. Akama, "The Indigenous Education System: The Making of a Gusii Man or Woman," in Akama and Maxon, *Ethnography of the Gusii of Western Kenya*, 115.

49. Peristiany, *Social Institutions of the Kipsigis*, 14–16, 26; and Hollis, *Nandi*, 56–57.

50. Interview by author: Anthony King'etich Rotich, 9 June 2008, Kaplong, Sotik; Peristiany, *Social Institutions of the Kipsigis*, 14–16, 26.

51. Interview by author: Jonah Kiprono Chepkwony, 12 June 2008, Kamarai, Sotik.

52. Interview by author: Thomas Kipsigei Tamutwa, 12 June 2008, Kamirai, Sotik.

53. Interviews by author: Joseph Kibelyon Korir, 8 June 2008, Chepilat, Sotik; Daniel Langat, 13 June 2008, Kabianga, Kericho.

54. Paul T. W. Baxter and Uri Almagor, eds., *Age, Generation and Time: Some Features of East African Age Organisations* (New York: St. Martin's, 1978), 1–36; and Bernardo Bernardi, *Age Class Systems: Social Institutions and Polities Based on Age* (Cambridge: Cambridge University Press, 1985), 1–9, 24–37.

55. RHL Mss Afr. s. 1153, Fazan Kenya Native Affairs, The Circumcision Ages, n.d.; and Hobley, *Bantu Beliefs and Magic*, 88–90.

56. Interview by author: Wachira Mwaniki, 25 May 2008, Burguret, Laikipia.

57. Cagnolo, *Akikuyu*, 96, 104–7; Adriaan H. J. Prins, *East African Age-Class Systems: An Inquiry into the Social Order of Galla, Kipsigis, and Kikuyu* (Westport, CT: Negro Universities Press, 1953), 48–54, 104–5.

58. Leakey, *Southern Kikuyu before 1903*, 589.

59. Akama, "Indigenous Education System," 117–18.

60. Akama and Monyenye, "Circumcision Ceremony," 179–80; Leakey, *Southern Kikuyu before 1903*, 620–21; Lindblom, *Akamba in British East Africa*, 50–57; and M'Imanyara, *Restatement of Bantu Origin and Meru History*, 125–26.

61. These are known as Kipkoymet, Kablelach, Kimnyige, Nyonge (1901–1916); Maina (1917–1931); Chuma (1931–1947); and Sawe (1947–1962).

62. Peristiany, *Social Institutions of the Kipsigis*, 30–33; Paul Spencer, "Becoming Maasai, Being in Time," in *Being Maasai: Ethnicity and Identity in East Africa*, ed. Thomas T. Spear and Richard D. Waller (Athens: Ohio University Press, 1993), 141; and George W. B. Huntingford, *The Nandi of Kenya: Tribal Control in a Pastoral Society* (London: Routledge and Kegan Paul, 1953), 68.

63. Interview by author: Thomas Kisigei Tamutwa, 12 June 2008, Kamarai, Sotik. See also Peristiany, *Social Institutions of the Kipsigis*, 30–31; and Prins, *East African Age-Class Systems*, 35–39.

64. Robert L. Tignor, *Colonial Transformation of Kenya: The Kamba, Kikuyu, and Maasai from 1900–1939* (Princeton, NJ: Princeton University Press, 1976), 74–75.

65. Routledge and Routledge, *With a Prehistoric People*, 166–67; and Leakey, *Southern Kikuyu before 1903*, 589.

66. Justin Willis, *Potent Brews: A Social History of Alcohol in East Africa, 1850–1999* (Athens: Ohio University Press, 2002), 52–53.

67. Lynn M. Thomas, *Politics of the Womb: Women, Reproduction, and the State in Kenya* (Berkeley: University of California Press, 2001), 17.

68. Kenyatta, *Facing Mount Kenya*, 193–96.

69. Spencer, *Maasai of Matapato*, 63.

70. Spencer, "Becoming Maasai," 144.

71. Ibid. For the Nandi, see Huntingford, *Nandi of Kenya*, 70.

72. Nyaga, *Customs and Traditions of the Meru*, 81.

73. John M. Lonsdale, "The Moral Economy of Mau Mau: Wealth, Poverty and Civic Virtue," in *Unhappy Valley: Conflict in Kenya and Africa*, vol. 2, *Violence and Ethnicity*, ed. Bruce J. Berman and John M. Lonsdale (Athens: Ohio University Press, 1992), 334.

74. Brett L. Shadle, *"Girl Cases": Marriage and Colonialism in Gusiiland, Kenya, 1890–1970* (Portsmouth, NH: Heinemann), 7.

75. PTSSL Reel 366, G3A50, Original Papers, 1910, V. V. Verbi, Annual Letter, Wusi Station, December 1909.

76. David P. Sandgren, *Christianity and the Kikuyu: Religious Divisions and Social Conflict* (New York: Lang, 1989), 68–69; and Kenda Mutongi, *Worries of the Heart: Widows, Family, and Community in Kenya* (Chicago: University of Chicago Press, 2007), 67.

77. Fadiman, *When We Began*, 222; J. Forbes Munro, *Colonial Rule and the Kamba: Social Change in the Kenya Highlands, 1889–1939* (Oxford: Clarendon, 1975), 107–8; and Jean Comaroff and John L. Comaroff, *Of Revelation and Revolution: Christianity, Colonialism, and Consciousness in South Africa* (Chicago: University of Chicago Press, 1991), 261.

78. Mutongi, *Worries of the Heart*, 45–68; and Tabitha M. Kanogo, *African Womanhood in Colonial Kenya, 1900–50* (Athens: Ohio University Press, 2005), 202–8, 211–18.

79. KNA PC/CP/7/1/1, Rev. R. T. Worthington, United Methodist Church, Meru, 24 September 1919.

80. Lonsdale, "Moral Economy of Mau Mau," 388.

81. KNA MA/3/1, Elwood L. Davis, Regarding Kikuyu Custom, n.d., likely early 1930s. See also Fadiman, *When We Began*, 222–25; and interview by author: Gideon Gatuthu Nyaga, 8 March 2008, Gilgil.

82. Comaroff and Comaroff, *Of Revelation and Revolution*, 259.

83. Kollman, *Evangelization of Slaves*, 106–7.

84. KNA PC/CP/7/1/1, A. E. Chamier, DC Meru, to H. R. Tate, PC Central, Circumcision of Mission Boys and Girls, 26 September 1919.

85. H. R. Tate, "Further Notes on the Southern Gikuyu of British East Africa," *Journal of the Royal African Society* 10, no. 39 (1911): 285–90.

86. KNA PC/CP/7/1/1, H. R. Tate, PC Central, to DC Meru, Circumcision of Mission Boys and Girls, 28 October 1919. See also Oliver, *Missionary Factor in East Africa*, 178.

87. Bruce J. Berman, *Control and Crisis in Colonial Kenya: The Dialectic of Domination* (Athens: Ohio University Press, 1990), 113–14.

88. Shadle, *"Girl Cases,"* 46.

89. Susan Pedersen, "National Bodies, Unspeakable Acts: The Sexual Politics of Colony Policy-Making," *Journal of Modern History* 63, no. 4 (1991): 659–60. Some missionary groups, such as the Church Missionary Society, took a quieter, accommodating

approach to ending female circumcision among their converts. See Robert W. Strayer, *The Making of Mission Communities in East Africa: Anglicans and Africans in Colonial Kenya, 1875–1935* (London: Heinemann, 1978), 149–50. Also see Jocelyn Murray, "The Kikuyu Female Circumcision Controversy, with Special Reference to the Church Missionary Society's 'Sphere of Influence'" (PhD diss., University of California at Los Angeles, 1974).

90. Penelope Hetherington, "The Politics of Female Circumcision in the Central Province of Colonial Kenya, 1920–30," *Journal of Imperial and Commonwealth History* 26, no. 1 (1998): 98, 100–101.

91. Thomas, *Politics of the Womb*, 27–28.

92. KNA PC/CP/2/1/4, Kiambu LNC Meeting Minutes, 5 March 1928. For the Gikuyu, see Leakey, *Southern Kikuyu before 1903*, 588. For the Gusii, see Akama and Monyenye, "Circumcision Ceremony," 184.

93. Thomas, *Politics of the Womb*, 44–47.

94. Kanogo, *African Womanhood in Colonial Kenya*, 91; and Hetherington, "Politics of Female Circumcision," 109.

95. For the broader political theater of the female circumcision crisis of the 1920s and 1930s, see David M. Anderson, *Histories of the Hanged: The Dirty War in Kenya and the End of Empire* (New York: Norton, 2005), 18–20.

96. Pedersen, "National Bodies, Unspeakable Acts," 670.

97. Ronald Hyam, *Understanding the British Empire* (Cambridge: Cambridge University Press, 2010), 410.

98. Linda Colley, *Captives: Britain, Empire, and the World, 1600–1850* (New York: Pantheon, 2002), 288–89, 305.

99. Hyam, *Understanding the British Empire*, 411.

100. TNA:PRO CO/544/1, Annual Report of the Principal Medical Officer, 1908; and CO/544/4, Annual Report of the Principal Medical Officer, 1910.

101. KNA AP/1/698, Committee of Visitors Meeting Minutes, Kabete Reformatory, 1 November 1916.

102. KNA BY/12/44, S. M. Swann, Superintendent, Approved Schools, to C. S. Owen, PPO, 14 April 1948; and C. S. Owen, PPO and CIAS, to the Director of Medical Service, 24 February 1958.

103. KNA PC/CEN/2/1/10, Nyeri LNC Meeting Minutes, 11–15 August 1947; and KNA PC/CEN/2/1/9, Meru LNC Meeting Minutes, 10 December 1947.

104. KNA PC/CP/6/4/2, D. R. Crampton, Acting PC Central, to CNC, Circumcision, 27 May 1920; and D. R. Crampton, Acting PC Central, to all DCs, 28 May 1920.

105. KNA PC/CP/7/1/2, DC Fort Hall to PC Central, Circumcision, 8 September 1920; DC Nyeri to PC Central, Circumcision, 13 September 1920.

106. KNA PC/CEN/2/1/4, Kiambu LNC Meeting Minutes, 4 April 1927.

107. Tignor, *Colonial Transformation of Kenya*, 47–48, 164–67.

108. Peristiany, *Social Institutions of the Kipsigis*, 30–31.

109. Interview by author: Thomas Kipsigei Tamutwa, 12 June 2008, Kamarai, Sotik.

110. Interview by author: Jonah Kiprono Chepkwony, 12 June 2008, Kamarai, Sotik.

111. Ibid.

112. Interviews by author: Lazarus arap Bor and Samuel Kipkurui Bor, 11 June 2008, Kapkatet, Bomet; and David Bett, 12 June 2008, Kamarai, Sotik.

113. Interviews by author: John Kiptalam Tesot, Daniel Langat, Terer arap Korir, Kimeli Too, and Kiprotich Ngetich, 13 June 2008, Kabianga, Kericho.

114. KNA OP/1/483, P. F. Foster, DC Kapsabet, to PC Rift Valley, Circumcision of Chuma in KAR, 23 April 1942.

115. Timothy H. Parsons, *The African Rank-and-File: Social Implications of Colonial Military Service in the King's African Rifles, 1902–1964* (Portsmouth, NH: Heinemann, 1999), 106–7.

116. Routledge and Routledge, *With a Prehistoric People*, 155; Cagnolo, *Akikuyu*, 89; Kenyatta, *Facing Mount Kenya*, 104; and Prins, *East African Age-Class Systems*, 102.

117. Leakey, *Southern Kikuyu before 1903*, 587.

118. Routledge and Routledge, *With a Prehistoric People*, 156; and Kenyatta, *Facing Mount Kenya*, 104.

119. KNA PC/CP/2/1/5, Fort Hall LNC Meeting Minutes, 25–26 July 1935; and PC/CEN/2/1/12, Embu LNC Meeting Minutes, 22–23 May 1947.

120. Peristiany, *Social Institutions of the Kipsigis*, 30–31.

121. Interviews by author: Lazarus arap Bor and Samuel Kipkurui Bor, 11 June 2008, Kapkatet, Bomet; David Bett and Thomas Kipsigei Tamutwa, 12 June 2008, Kamarai, Sotik; and John Kiptalam Tesot, Daniel Langat, Terer arap Korir, Kimeli Too, and Kiprotich Ngetich, 13 June 2008, Kabianga, Kericho.

122. KNA DC/KER/4/2, H. E. Lambert to Mr. Hosking, Acting CNC, 8 April 1938.

123. Kenyatta, *Facing Mount Kenya*, 203.

124. Richard D. Waller, "Bad Boys in the Bush? Disciplining Murran in Colonial Maasailand," in *Generations Past: Youth in East African History*, ed. Andrew Burton and Hélène Charton-Bigot (Athens: Ohio University Press, 2010), 141–45; and Tignor, *Colonial Transformation of Kenya*, 80–83, 87.

125. George L. Simpson, "Gerontocrats and Colonial Alliances," in *The Politics of Age and Gerontocracy in Africa*, ed. Mario I. Aguilar (Trenton, NJ: Africa World Press, 1998), 65.

126. Peristiany, *Social Institutions of the Kipsigis*, 37–39.

127. Huntingford, *Nandi of Kenya*, 67–68.

128. DC/KER/4/2, H. E. Lambert to Hosking, Acting Chief Native Commissioner, 8 April 1938.

129. Kenyatta, *Facing Mount Kenya*, 203; emphasis mine.

130. Interview by author: Thomas Kipsigei Tamutwa, 12 June 2008, Kamarai, Sotik

131. Interview by author: John Kiptalam Tesot, 13 June 2008, Kabianga, Kericho.

132. Interview by author: Daniel Langat, 13 June 2008, Kabianga, Kericho.

133. Interview by author: Nicholas Soi, 10 June 2008, Kapsinendet, Sotik.

134. As early as the late nineteenth century, Nyamwezi porters saw their work on caravans in the late nineteenth century as part of their initiation into manhood. Jonathon Glassman, *Feasts and Riot: Revelry, Rebellion, and Popular Consciousness on the Swahili Coast, 1856–1888* (Portsmouth, NH: Heinemann, 1995), 59.

135. Interview by author: Anthony King'etich Rotich, 9 June 2008, Kaplong, Sotik. The figures on how many young men had been medically circumcised comes from KNA DC/KER/4/2, E. S. Cooper, Principal of Government African School Kabianga, Memorandum on Circumcision of Schoolboys, 23 October 1945.

136. Mario I. Aguilar, "Gerontocratic, Aesthetic and Political Models of Age," in Aguilar, *Politics of Age*, 17–18.

137. BNA CO/533/716, Edward Deuhaur, Acting Governor, to Leo Amery, SSC, 8 July 1927.

CHAPTER 2: "I WANTED TO MAKE
SOMETHING OF MYSELF"

1. KNA PC/NZA/3/20/17/1, Izaji Mamuji v. Mzee Mzee bin Ali, 297/1917, Resident Magistrate, Mombasa, June 1917.

2. KNA PC/NZA/3/20/17/1, Inspector of Labour Londiani to SC Nyanza, Juveniles Labour, 8 July 1927.

3. Sharon Stichter, *Migrant Labour in Kenya: Capitalism and African Response, 1895–1975* (London: Longman, 1982), 14–15.

4. John M. Lonsdale, "The Conquest State of Kenya, 1895–1905," in *Unhappy Valley: Conflict in Kenya and Africa*, vol. 1, *State and Class*, ed. Bruce Berman and John Lonsdale (Athens: Ohio University Press, 1992), 13–42.

5. Charles H. Ambler, *Kenyan Communities in the Age of Imperialism: The Central Region in the Late Nineteenth Century* (New Haven, CT: Yale University Press, 1977); and Godfrey Muriuki, *A History of the Kikuyu, 1500–1900* (Nairobi: Oxford University Press, 1974).

6. Maurice P. K. Sorrenson, *Origins of European Settlement in Kenya* (Oxford: Oxford University Press, 1968).

7. TNA:PRO CO 544/1, A. C. MacDonald, Director of Agriculture, Department of Agriculture, British East Africa, Annual Report, 1907–1908, 13.

8. TNA:PRO CO 544/1, EAP, Annual Report, 1908–1909, 620.

9. Stichter, *Migrant Labour in Kenya*, 30.

10. Robert L. Tignor, *Colonial Transformation of Kenya: The Kamba, Kikuyu, and Maasai from 1900–1939* (Princeton, NJ: Princeton University Press, 1976), 104–5.

11. Opolot Okia, *Communal Labor in Colonial Kenya: The Legitimization of Coercion, 1912–1930* (New York: Palgrave Macmillan, 2012), 93–113.

12. Anthony Clayton and Donald C. Savage, *Government and Labour in Kenya, 1895–1963* (London: Cass, 1974), 28, 38–39; and Stichter, *Migrant Labour in Kenya*, 35, 42. See also Leigh A. Gardner, *Taxing Colonial Africa: The Political Economy of British Imperialism* (Oxford: Oxford University Press, 2012).

13. KNA PC/CP/2/1/5, Fort Hall LNC Meeting Minutes, 25–26 July 1935; and PC/CEN/2/1/12, Embu LNC Meeting Minutes, 22–23 May 1947.

14. Tabitha M. Kanogo, *Squatters and the Roots of Mau Mau, 1905–63* (Athens: Ohio University Press, 1987); and Frank Furedi, *The Mau Mau War in Perspective* (Athens: Ohio University Press, 1989).

15. Kanogo, *Squatters and the Roots of Mau Mau*, 12–16, 22–23.

16. Stichter, *Migrant Labour in Kenya*, 84–86.

17. Nicholas J. Westcott, "The East African Sisal Industry, 1929–1949: The Marketing of a Colonial Commodity during Depression and War," *Journal of African History* 25, no. 4 (1984): 446; and Michael D. McWilliam, "The Kenya Tea Industry," *East African Economics Review* 6, no. 1 (1959): 32, 40–42.

18. Frederick Cooper, *From Slaves to Squatters: Plantation Labor and Agriculture in Zanzibar and Coastal Kenya, 1890–1925* (New Haven, CT: Yale University Press, 1980), 92–94.

19. TNA:PRO CO 544/3, EAP, Minutes of the Executive Council, 23 December 1908.

20. TNA:PRO CO 544/7, EAP, Annual Report, 1913–1914, 221.

21. Stichter, *Migrant Labour in Kenya*, 38.

22. TNA:PRO CO 544/16, CNC, Native Affairs Department Annual Report, 1923.

23. KNA AG/25/80, John Ainsworth, PC Nyanza, to Principal Medical Officer, 31 March 1914. For patterns in the seasonal migration of African workers, see Stichter, *Migrant Labour in Kenya*, 84–86.

24. KNA PC/NZA/3/20/17/1, Assistant DC Central Kavirondo, to DC Kavirondo, 25 March 1925; P. de V. Allen, Labor Inspector to CNC, Juvenile Labour on Plantations, 28 July 1925; DC Fort Hall to SC Nyanza, Immature Labourers, 11 August 1925; and R. A. W. Proctor, MO Fort Hall, to PMO Nairobi, Toto Labour, 3 September 1925.

25. William Beinart, "Transkeian Migrant Workers and Youth Labour in the Natal Sugar Estates, 1918–1948," *Journal of African History* 32, no. 1 (1991): 41–42.

26. KNA PC/NZA/3/20/17/1, Labour Inspector to SC, Nyanza, 17 April 1926; Assistant DC, South Kavirondo, to SC, Nyanza, 29 April 1926; F. E. Yates to SC, Nyanza; and F. R. Mackey to Senior Commissioner, Nyanza, 26 May 1926.

27. KNA PC/NZA/3/20/17/1, C. E. Campbell Clause, Manager of Thika Sisal Co., to CNC, 24 April 1925.

28. KNA PC/NZA/3/20/17/1, Acting PC Nyanza to Ismali Imamdin, 21 September 1928; and LO Kisumu to Principal Labour Inspector Nairobi, Juvenile Labour, 29 January 1930.

29. KNA PC/NZA/3/20/17/1, DC S. Kavirondo to SC Nyanza, Re: Juvenile Labour, 26 August 1925.

30. KNA PC/NZA/3/20/2/1, DC S. Kavirondo to SC Nyanza, Labour Agents, 12 November 1925.

31. KNA PC/NZA/3/20/17/1, SC Nyanza to DC South Kavirondo, 12 January 1927.

32. KNA PC/NZA/3/20/2/1, DC Kisii to SC Nyanza, 11 March 1926.

33. Interview by author: Raphael Abisalom Ndai, 31 March 2008, Bondo.

34. KNA PC/NZA/3/20/17/1, SC Nyanza to Labor Inspector, Native Affairs Department, 2 September 1925; J. L. Riddoch, Notes in Connection with the Medical Examination of Juveniles, 14 July 1926; and PC/NZA/3/20/2/1, SC Nyanza to CNC, Labour Agents, 28 March 1926.

35. J. M. Osoro, "Unity and Disunity in Labour Recruitment and Welfare: The Tea Estates versus Other Employers of Labour, 1925–1938" (paper presented at the annual conference of the Historical Association of Kenya, 1977), 4–5.

36. Interview by author: Edward Arthur Adera Osawa, 30 March 2008, Kisumu.

37. Interviews by author: Lazaro Ochieng Weke, 26 March 2008, Awendo; and Abiathar Omondi Opudo, 28 March 2008, Homa Bay.

38. J. M. Osoro, "'A Lull before the Storm': A Study of the African Labourers in the Kericho Tea Estates, 1939–1958" (paper presented to the Department of History, University of Nairobi, 1977–1978), 9–11.

39. Osoro, "Unity and Disunity," 15.

40. KNA PC/NZA/3/20/2/1, SC Nyanza to CNC, Labour Agents, 28 March 1926.

41. Interview by author: Andrew Albert Ater Odundo, 30 March 2008, Kisumu.

42. Interview by author: Christopher Onduru Achar, 26 March 2008, Awendo.

43. KNA AG/12/208, Official Gazette, Government Notice No. 89, 14 February 1933.

44. KNA ABK/14/140, G. V. Maxwell, CNC, to Chief Secretary, Native Juvenile Employment, 6 June 1937; and Acting Chief Registrar of Natives to CNC, Identification of Juveniles, 19 October 1937. British officials had become very animated when they read the Southern Rhodesia Native Juvenile Employment Act of 1926. The act required all young laborers to be registered with the government and obtain parental consent before leaving home. Their reading of the Rhodesian law inspired them to

promote similar legislation in Kenya. Beverly C. Grier, *Invisble Hands: Child Labor and the State in Colonial Zimbabwe* (Portsmouth, NH: Heinemann, 2006), 111–60.

45. Okia, *Communal Labor in Colonial Kenya*, 93–113.

46. Archdeacon W. E. Owen, "Child Labour in Kenya: Contracts at Early Age," *Manchester Guardian*, 12 May 1938, 20.

47. TNA:PRO CO 533/497/1, D. M. Jordan Coleman to MP Louis W. Smith, 16 May 1938; and "Native Labour in Kenya, 'Penal Sanctions,'" *Manchester Guardian*, 7 June 1938; and "Child Labour in Kenya, Not a Local Matter," *Manchester Guardian*, 23 June 1938.

48. "Child Labour in Kenya: Position Contrasted with Portuguese, French, and Spanish Colonies," *Manchester Guardian*, 3 June 1938; and "Child Labour in Kenya: Age Not Lowered," *Manchester Guardian*, 23 June 1938.

49. TNA:PRO CO 847/12/14, J. J. Paskin to Mr. Creasy, 13 October 1938.

50. Charles Chenevix Trench, *Men Who Ruled Kenya: The Kenya Administration, 1892–1963* (London: Radcliffe Press, 1993), 111.

51. Colony and Protectorate of Kenya (CPK), Report of the Employment of Juveniles Committee, 1938, 5.

52. Ibid., 9.

53. KNA AG/37/130, R. Brooke-Popham, Governor, 18 July 1939.

54. Cap. 109, No. 2 of 1938, Employment of Servants Ordinance, 1937, sections 2, 32–39.

55. TNA:PRO CO 847/12/14, R. Brooke-Popham, Governor, to SSC Malcolm MacDonald, 16 December 1938.

56. KNA ABK/14/140, A. E. T. Imbert, Chief Registrar of Natives, to E. C. McInnes, Labour Superintendent, 21 February 1940.

57. KNA ABK/14/140, Acting Crown Counsel for Attorney General to Chief Secretary, 8 March 1940; and C. M. Johnston, Chief Secretary, to A. E. T. Imbert, Chief Registrar of Natives, Employment of Servants Ordinance—Identification of Juveniles, 22 April 1940.

58. KNA ABK/14/140, Secretariat, The Employment of Servants Ordinance and the Native Registration Ordinance—Identification of Juveniles, 17 July 1940.

59. TNA:PRO CO 533/497/3, A. J. Dawe to Henry Moore, 19 January 1942; and J. G. Hibbert to Mr. Seel. 2 December 1942.

60. KNA ABK/14/140, G. Wedderburn, Registrar of Natives, to CNC, Juvenile Registration, 20 April 1942.

61. KNA ABK/14/140, A. H. Kneller, Acting LC, to Chief Secretary of the Secretariat, 8 May 1942; and P. Wyn Labour, Juveniles Registration, 21 November 1944.

62. KNA ABK/12/68, H. Borman, Secretary of the Kenya Tea Growers' Association, to LC P. de. V. Allen, 27 January 1943.

63. KNA ABK/12/68, Labour Superintendent, Tea Estates Labour Department, Memorandum, 31 January 1943.

64. Ibid.

65. KNA DC/KSM/1/17/27, F. D. Hislop, District Commissioner, to Provincial Commissioner Nyanza, Employment of Juveniles, 13 February 1943.

66. TNA:PRO CO 533/527/20, Telegram from Sir H. Moore, Governor of Kenya, to Secretary of State for the Colonies, 24 February 1943.

67. KNA PC/CEN/2/1/4, Kiambu LNC Meeting, 1 October 1925; and KNA PC/NZA/3/20/2/1, SC Nyanza to CNC, Labour Agents, 28 March 1926.

68. Interviews by author: Thomas Kipsigei Tamutwa, 12 June 2008, Kamarai, Sotik; and Siamba Maina, 8 June 2008, Chepilat, Sotik.

69. Claude Meillassoux, *Maidens, Meal and Money: Capitalism and the Domestic Community* (Cambridge: Cambridge University Press, 1981); Simon Ottenberg, *Boyhood Rituals in an African Society* (Seattle: University of Washington Press, 1989); and Pamela Reynolds, *Dance, Civet Cat: Child Labour in the Zambezi Valley* (Athens: Ohio University Press, 1991).

70. Interviews by author: Christopher Onduru Achar, 26 March 2008, Awendo; John Opyio Osawa, 27 March 2008, Awendo; Abiathar Omondi Opudo, 28 March 2008, Homa Bay; Jaramongi Joseph Wanga Sidho, 31 March 2008, Bondo; Wachira Mwaniki, 25 May 2008, Burguret, Laikipi; Nicholas Kinyua Mwai, 28 May 2008, Kiamwathi, Nyeri; and Thomas Kipsigei Tamutwa, 12 June 2008, Kamarai, Sotik; among many others.

71. Interview by author: Thomas Kipsigei Tamutwa, 12 June 2008, Kamarai, Sotik.

72. Ibid.

73. Ibid.

74. Interviews by author: Christopher Onduru Achar, 26 March 2008, Awendo; Yason Omwenyo, 26 March 2008, Awendo; David Bett, 12 June 2008, Kamarai, Sotik; Daniel Langat, 13 June 2008, Kabianga, Kericho; Terer arap Korir, 13 June 2008, Kabianga, Kericho; among many others. See also Stichter, *Migrant Labour in Kenya*, 32.

75. Interview by author: Yason Omwenyo, 26 March 2008, Awendo.

76. Interview by author: Thomas Kipsigei Tamutwa, 12 June 2008, Kamarai, Sotik.

77. Interview by author: Christopher Onduru Achar, 26 March 2008, Awendo.

78. Interview by author: Thomas Kipsigei Tamutwa, 12 June 2008, Kamarai, Sotik.

79. Interview by author: Kimeli Too, 13 June 2008, Kabianga, Kericho.

80. Ibid.

81. Ibid.

82. Derek R. Peterson, *Creative Writing: Translation, Bookkeeping, and the Work of Imagination in Colonial Kenya* (Portsmouth, NH: Heinemann, 2004), 97; and Lonsdale, "Conquest State of Kenya," 17.

83. KNA DC/MKS/10B/13/1. I would like to thank Derek Peterson for providing me with access to the journal.

84. KNA ABK/14/26, Notes for the Purpose of Giving Evidence at the Commission of Enquiry Re: Employment of Juveniles, Kericho, 29 March 1951.

85. See Jane Humphries, *Childhood and Child Labour in the British Industrial Revolution* (Cambridge: Cambridge University Press, 2011); Carolyn Tuttle, *Hard at Work in Factories and Mines: The Economics of Child Labor during the British Industrial Revolution* (Boulder, CO: Westview Press, 1999); and Clark Nardinelli, *Child Labor and the Industrial Revolution* (Bloomington: Indiana University Press, 1990).

86. KNA ABK/14/142, H. A. Nisbet, Acting PLO, to LO, Kisumu, Juvenile Labour, 3 November 1936; and H. A. Nisbet, PLO, to AG, 30 November 1936.

87. Interviews by author: Thomas Kipsigei Tamutwa, 12 June 2008, Kamarai, Sotik; Daniel Langat, 13 June 2008, Kabianga, Kericho; and Dominic Obondo Gaga, 27 March 2008, Awendo.

88. Interview by author: Thomas Kipsigei Tamutwa, 12 June 2008, Kamarai, Sotik.

89. Interviews by author: Thomas Kipsigei Tamutwa, 12 June 2008, Kamarai, Sotik; Daniel Langat, 13 June 2008, Kabianga, Kericho; and Dominic Obondo Gaga, 27 March 2008, Awendo.

90. KNA DC/KSM/1/17/27, F. D. Hislop, DC, to PC Nyanza, Employment of Juveniles, 13 February 1943.

91. Interviews by author: Dominic Obondo Gaga, 27 March 2008, Awendo; Daniel Langat, 13 June 2008, Kabianga, Kericho; and Kimeli Too, 13 June 2008, Kabianga, Kericho.

92. KNA ABK/14/26, Young Persons and Children Committee, Notes of Evidence, Sub-Committee at Kakamega, 28–29 March 1951.

93. Interviews by author: Thomas Kipsigei Tamutwa, 12 June 2008, Kamarai, Sotik; and Kimeli Too, 13 June 2008, Kabianga, Kericho.

94. Interviews by author: Lazaro Ochieng Weke, 26 March 2008, Awendo; and Christopher Onduru Achar, 26 March 2008, Awendo.

95. KNA ABK/11/21, J. H. B. Murphy, LO, Labour Inspection Report No. 153/42, 7 July 1942.

96. KNA ABK/11/21, P. de V. Allen, LC, Labour Inspection Report No. 269/43, 12 August 1943.

97. KNA ABK/14/140, A. E. T. Imbert, Chief Registrar of Natives, to PLO Nairobi, Employment and Registration of Natives, 21 July 1938; and Kanogo, *Squatters and the Roots of Mau Mau*, 82.

98. TNA:PRO CO 544/10, CNC, Report on Native Affairs, 1918–1919, 285.

99. Interview by author: Abiathar Omondi Opudo, 28 March 2008, Homa Bay.

100. Interview by author: Wachira Mwaniki, 25 May 2008, Burguret, Laikipia.

101. Interviews by author: Christopher Onduru Achar, 26 March 2008, Awendo; Yason Omwenyo, 26 March 2008, Awendo; Joseph Kibelyon Korir, 8 June 2008, Chepilat, Sotik; David Bett, 12 June 2008, Kamarai, Sotik; Daniel Langat, 13 June 2008, Kabianga, Kericho; and Terer arap Korir, 13 June 2008, Kabianga, Kericho; among many others.

102. Interview by author: Thomas Kipsigei Tamutwa, 12 June 2008, Kamarai, Sotik.

103. Interviews by author: Terer arap Korir, 13 June 2008, Kabianga, Kericho; and. Daniel Langat, 13 June 2008, Kabianga, Kericho.

104. Interview by author: David Bett, 12 June 2008, Kamarai, Sotik.

105. Interview by author: Dominic Obondo Gaga, 27 March 2008, Awendo.

106. Interview by authro: Wachira Mwaniki, 25 May 2008, Burguret, Laikipia.

107. Interview by author: Dominic Obondo Gaga, 27 March 2008, Awendo.

108. Interview by author: Wachira Mwaniki, 25 May 2008, Burguret, Laikipia.

109. Charles H. Ambler, "Drunks, Brewers, and Chiefs: Alcohol Regulation in Colonial Kenya, 1900–1939," in *Drinking: Behavior and Belief in Modern History*, ed. Susanna Barrows and Robin Room (Berkeley: University of California Press, 1991), 169.

110. Justin Willis, *Potent Brews: A Social History of Alcohol in East Africa, 1850–1999* (Athens: Ohio University Press, 2002), 123–25, 129–33; and Ambler, "Drunks, Brewers, and Chiefs," 171.

111. KNA PC/CEN/2/1/2, Embu LNC Meeting Minutes, 30 October 1925; and PC/CEN/2/1/4, Kiambu LNC Meeting Minutes, 12 July 1927.

112. Willis, *Potent Brews*, 71; and Ambler, "Drunks, Brewers, and Chiefs," 165.

113. KNA PC/CEN/2/1/6, Nyeri LNC Meeting Minutes, 29 January 1935.

114. KNA PC/CEN/2/1/5, Fort Hall LNC Meeting Minutes, 20–22 November 1926.

115. KNA PC/CEN/2/1/1, Nyeri LNC Meeting Minutes, 14–15 October 1931; PC/CEN/2/1/2, Embu LNC Meeting Minutes, 30 October 1925; Embu LNC Meeting Minutes, 9 February 1931; PC/CEN/2/1/5, Fort Hall LNC Meeting Minutes, 26–27 No-

vember 1929; PC/CEN/2/1/9, Meru LNC Meeting Minutes, 23–26 September 1947; and PC/CEN/2/1/13, Kiambu LNC Meeting Minutes, 25–27 October 1949.

116. Willis, *Potent Brews*, 52–53.

117. KNA ABK/14/138, LC to Member for Labour, Confidential, 13 April 1949.

CHAPTER 3: "I SAW A PARADISE"

1. Ogayo's home village might have been in present-day Karachuonyo, near Kendu Bay on the shores of Lake Victoria.

2. KNA PC/NZA/3/20/17/1, SC Nyanza to DC Central Kavirondo, 4 May 1925.

3. KNA PC/NZA/3/20/17/1, Ernest McInnes, Labour Inspector, 25 April 1925.

4. KNA PC/NZA/3/20/17/1. In a sad twist, there would one day be a neighborhood in Nairobi called Mariakani, located just southeast of the Industrial Area, where Ogayo might have found work. Andrew Hake, *African Metropolis: Nairobi's Self-Help City* (London: St. Martin's, 1977), 88–89.

5. KNA PC/COAST/1/1/81, J. D. Ainsworth to Acting Sub-Commissioner, Mombasa, 18 May 1901.

6. Mary Parker, *Political and Social Aspects of the Development of Municipal Government in Kenya with Special Reference to Nairobi* (London: Colonial Office, 1948), appendix 1.

7. Hake, *African Metropolis*, 22.

8. KNA PC/COAST/1/10/81, Secretariat Circular, 16 April 1914; and Robert L. Tignor, *Colonial Transformation of Kenya: The Kamba, Kikuyu, and Maasai from 1900–1939* (Princeton, NJ: Princeton University Press, 1976), 128–32.

9. TNA:PRO CO/544/10, CNC, Report on Native Affairs, 31 March 1919, 390.

10. KNA ABK/14/140, Acting Chief Registrar of Natives to CNC, Identification of Juveniles, 19 October 1937.

11. CPK, *Crime Committee Report*, 11, 13.

12. For a comprehensive, comparative examination of colonial urban policy in British Africa, see Andrew Burton, *African Underclass: Urbanization, Crime and Colonial Order in Dar es Salaam* (Athens: Ohio University Press, 2005), 17–42.

13. For example, see Henry Mayhew, *London Labor and the London Poor*, 4 vols. (London: Griffin, Bohn, 1851–1861); Charles J. Ribton-Turner, *A History of Vagrants and Vagrancy and Beggars and Begging* (London: Chapman and Hall, 1887); William Booth, *The Vagrant and the Unemployable* (London: Salvation Army, 1904); and William H. Dawson, *The Vagrancy Problem* (London: King and Son, 1910).

14. Charles F. G. Masterman, *The Heart of the Empire: Discussions of Problems of Modern City Life in England* (London: Unwin, 1902), 125.

15. Gareth S. Jones, *Outcast London: A Study in the Relationship between Classes in Victorian Society* (Oxford: Clarendon, 1971), 128.

16. Heather Shore, *Artful Dodgers: Youth and Crime in Early Nineteenth-Century London* (Rochester, NY: Boydell, 2002), 7, 17, 29–34.

17. Alexis de Tocqueville, quoted in Asa Briggs, *Victorian Cities* (London: Odhams Press, 1963), 68.

18. John Shaw, quoted in Andrew Lees, *Cities Perceived: Urban Society in European and American Thought, 1820–1940* (Manchester: Manchester University Press, 1985), 28.

19. CPK, *Crime Committee Report*, 2.

20. Briggs, *Victorian Cities*, 60–62.

21. Dane K. Kennedy, *Islands of White: Settler Society and Culture in Kenya and Southern Rhodesia, 1890–1939* (Chapel Hill: University of North Carolina Press, 1987).

22. TNA:PRO CO/544/1, Annual Report of the East African Protectorate, 1908–1909, 620; and John Iliffe, *The African Poor: A History* (Cambridge: Cambridge University Press, 1987), 172.

23. TNA:PRO CO/544/10, CNC, Report on Native Affairs, 31 March 1919, 390.

24. KNA ABK/14/140, Deputy Registrar of Domestic Servants to DC Nairobi, 2 July 1931.

25. KNA AB/12/208, Government Notice No. 89, Employment of Women, Young Persons, and Children Ordinance, 1933, 14 February 1933.

26. For similar legislation that predates the Kenya case, see Beverley C. Grier, *Invisible Hands: Child Labor and the State in Colonial Zimbabwe* (Portsmouth, NH: Heinemann, 2006), esp. chap. 4.

27. Parker, *Political and Social Aspects*, 2. In Kisumu, the population doubled in the decade following 1938. See Godfrey Anyumba, *Kisumu Town: History of the Built Form, Planning, and Environment, 1890–1990* (Delft: Delft University Press, 1995), 156–57.

28. Parker, *Political and Social Aspects*, 2; and Hake, *African Metropolis*, 67.

29. Luise White, *The Comforts of Home: Prostitution in Colonial Nairobi* (Chicago: University of Chicago Press, 1990), 29–50; and Margaret Strobel, *Muslim Women in Mombasa, 1890–1975* (New Haven, CT: Yale University Press, 1979), 141.

30. Bodil F. Frederiksen, "African Women and Their Colonization of Nairobi: Representations and Realties," in *The Urban Experience in Eastern Africa*, ed. Andrew Burton (Nairobi: British Institute in Eastern Africa, 2002), 226.

31. Interview by author: James Karanja Kariuki, 6 April 2008, Gilgil.

32. Interview by author: Harry Joseph Kimanji, 6 April 2008, Gilgil.

33. Interview by author: Gabriel Kahugu Muchahi, 26 April 2008, Ndenderu, Kiambu.

34. Interview by author: Samuel Uiru Kaguara, 26 April 2008, Ndenderu, Kiambu.

35. Interview by author: Gabriel Kahugu Muchahi, 26 April 2008, Ndenderu, Kiambu.

36. John M. Lonsdale, "Town Life in Colonial Kenya," in Burton, *Urban Experience in Eastern Africa*, 209.

37. Carl A. Dutto, *Nyeri Townsmen, Kenya* (Kampala: East African Literature Bureau, 1975), 60–61; and John G. Blacker, "Population Growth and Urbanization in Kenya," in *United Nations Mission to Kenya on Housing*, ed. Lawrence N. Bloomberg and Charles Abrams (Nairobi: United Nations, 1965), appendix A.

38. Claire C. Robertson, *Trouble Showed the Way: Women, Men, and Trade in the Nairobi Area, 1890–1990* (Bloomington: Indiana University Press, 1997), 83–84, 94. Girls selling goods at market were everywhere in Lagos, Nigeria, too, and attracted the ire of the colonial state after the 1940s. Abosede A. George, *Making Modern Girls: A History of Girlhood, Labor, and Social Development in Colonial Lagos* (Athens: Ohio University Press, 2014), 121.

39. Marc H. Ross, *Grass Roots in an African City: Political Behavior in Nairobi* (Cambridge, MA: MIT Press, 1975), 10.

40. Hake, *African Metropolis*, 36.

41. Alison Hay and Richard Harris, "'Shauri ya Sera Kali': The Colonial Regime of

Urban Housing in Kenya to 1939," *Urban History* 34, no. 3 (2007): 511, 525–27; Richard E. Stren, "The Evolution of Housing Policy in Kenya," in *Urban Challenge in East Africa*, ed. John Hutton (Nairobi: East African Publishing, 1970), 57–68.

42. Kenneth G. McVicar, "Twilight of an East African Slum: Pumwani and the Evolution of African Settlement in Nairobi" (PhD diss., University of California, Los Angeles, 1968).

43. David W. Throup, *Economic and Social Origins of Mau Mau, 1945–53* (Athens: Ohio University Press, 1987), 179.

44. Ibid., 188.

45. Herbert H. Werlin, *Governing an African City: A Study of Nairobi* (New York: Africana Publishing, 1974), 45, 51.

46. Interviews by author: Samuel Uiru Kaguara, 26 April 2008, Ndenderu, Kiambu; and Alan Ale Kanyingi Ngugi, 19 May 2008, Githunguri, Kiambu.

47. KNA ARC(MD) 4/1/2, Return of Juvenile Offenders Brought before the Courts, 1949–50.

48. Ibid.

49. Interview by author: Samuel Uiru Kaguara, 26 April 2008, Ndenderu, Kiambu.

50. Interview by author: Gabriel Kahugu Muchahi, 26 April 2008, Ndenderu, Kiambu.

51. Garth A. Myers, *Verandahs of Power: Colonialism and Space in Urban Africa* (Syracuse, NY: Syracuse University Press, 2003); interviews by author: Harry Joseph Kimanji and James Karanja Kariuki, 6 April 2008, Gilgil; and Samuel Uiru Kaguara, 26 April 2008, Ndenderu, Kiambu.

52. Interview by author: Peter Mwarangu Ngugi, 26 April 2008, Ndenderu, Kiambu.

53. White, *Comforts of Home*, 103–25; and Fredericksen, "African Women and Their Colonization of Nairobi," 227.

54. Fredericksen, "African Women and Their Colonization of Nairobi," 229–30; and interview by author: Peter Mwarangu Ngugi, 26 April 2008, Ndenderu, Kiambu.

55. Parker, *Political and Social Aspects*, 76.

56. Hake, *African Metropolis*, 25.

57. Myers, *Verandahs of Power*, 34.

58. Hake, *African Metropolis*, 26; Myers, *Verandahs of Power*, 36; George K. Kingoriah, "The Causes of Nairobi's City Structure," *Ekistics* 50, no. 301 (1983): 246–54; Dorothy M. Halliman and William T. W. Morton, "The City of Nairobi," in *Nairobi: City and Region*, ed. William T. M. Morton (London: Oxford University Press, 1967): 98–120; and Earl Smith, "The Evolution of Nairobi, Kenya, 1889–1939" (PhD diss., University of Connecticut, 1984).

59. Myers, *Verandahs of Power*, 39–40. Also see L. W. Thornton White, L. Silberman, and P. R. Anderson, *Nairobi: Master Plan for a Colonial Capital: A Report Prepared for the Municipal Council of Nairobi* (London: Her Majesty's Stationery Office, 1948).

60. Deyssi Rodriguez-Torres, "Nairobi: Les gangs de la rue en direct," in *Jeunes, culture de la rue et violence urbanie en Afrique*, ed. George Hérault and Pius Adesanmi (Ibadan: IFRA, 1997), 9–88. The South African historiography has produced the most nuanced research on youth gangs and urban youth subculture. See, especially, Paul La Hausse, "'The Cows of Nongoloza': Youth, Crime and Amalaita Gangs in Durban, 1900–1936," *Journal of Southern African Studies* 16, no. 1 (1990): 79–111; William Beinart, "The Origins of the *Indlavini*: Male Associations and Migrant Labour in the

Transkei," *African Studies* 50, no. 1 (1991): 103–28; and Clive L. Glaser, *Bo-Tsotsi: The Youth Gangs of Soweto, 1935–1976* (Portsmouth, NH: Heinemann, 2000).

61. Interview by author: James Karanja Kariuki, 6 April 2008, Gilgil.

62. Ibid.

63. Kinshasa youths also relied on territoriality. J. S. La Fontaine, "Two Types of Youth Group in Kinshasa (Leéopoldville)," in *Socialization: The Approach from Social Anthropology*, ed. Philip Mayer (London: Tavistock, 1970), 202–4.

64. Interview by author: Gabriel Kahugu Muchahi, 26 April 2008, Ndenderu, Kiambu.

65. Interviews by author: Harry Joseph Kimanji, 6 April 2008, Gilgil; and Gabriel Kahugu Muchahi, 26 April 2008, Ndenderu, Kiambu.

66. Interview by author: James Karanja Kariuki, 6 April 2008, Gilgil.

67. Interview by author: Harry Joseph Kimanji, 6 April 2008, Gilgil.

68. Ibid.

69. Interviews by author: Gabriel Kahugu Muchahi and Samuel Uiru Kaguara, 26 April 2008, Ndenderu, Kiambu.

70. Interview by author: Samuel Uiru Kaguara, 26 April 2008, Ndenderu, Kiambu.

71. Interview by author: Peter Mwarangu Ngugi, 26 April 2008, Ndenderu, Kiambu.

72. Interview by author: James Karanja Kariuki, 6 April 2008, Gilgil.

73. Interview by author: Harry Joseph Kimanji, 6 April 2008, Gilgil.

74. Justin Willis, *Potent Brews: A Social History of Alcohol in East Africa, 1850–1999* (Athens: Ohio University Press, 2002).

75. Interview by author: James Ng'ang'a Kamau, 17 April 2008, Gilgil.

76. Interview by author: Harry Joseph Kimanji, 6 April 2008, Gilgil.

77. Interviews by author: James Karanja Kariuki, 6 April 2008, Gilgil; and Samuel Uiru Kaguara, Gabriel Kahugu Muchahi, and Peter Mwarangu Ngugui, 26 April 2008, Ndenderu, Kiambu.

78. David W. Throup, "Crimes, Politics, and the Police in Colonial Kenya, 1939–63," in *Policing and Decolonisation: Nationalism, Politics and the Police, 1917–65*, ed. David M. Anderson and David Killingray (Manchester: Manchester University Press, 1992), 131.

79. W. Robert Foran, *The Kenya Police, 1887–1960* (London: Hale, 1962), 66.

80. Arnold L. Epstein, "The Network and Urban Social Organization," *Rhodes-Livingstone Journal* 29 (1961): 29–62.

81. EAP, Ordinances and Regulations, vol. 2, 1900, article 1. European vagrants were quickly swept under the colonial carpet: deported, imprisoned, or institutionalized at Mathari Mental Hospital. See Will Jackson, *Madness and Marginality: The Lives of Kenya's White Insane* (Manchester: Manchester University Press, 2013).

82. KNA AP/1/484, Gov. J. H. Sadler to SSC Lord Elgin, No. 512, 27 November 1907.

83. KNA AP/1/484, Minute No. 12, no author or date provided.

84. CPK, No. 9 Vagrancy Ordinance, Ordinances and Regulations, 1920, section 2.

85. CPK, No. 9 Vagrancy Ordinance, Ordinances and Regulations, 1920, sections 14 and 16.

86. CPK, Native Affairs Department, Annual Report, 1928, 74.

87. CPK, Native Affairs Department, Annual Report, 1931, 82.

88. KNA ABK/14/139, J. L. H. Webster, for Chief Secretary to Labour Commissioner, 5 January 1944; and Labour Officer Nairobi to Labour Commissioner Nairobi, 9 April 1943.

89. CPK, *Crime Committee Report,* 39.

90. Justin Willis, "Thieves, Drunkards, and Vagrants: Defining Crime in Colonial Mombasa, 1902–32," in *Policing the Empire: Government, Authority and Control, 1830–1940,* ed. David M. Anderson and David Killingray (Manchester: Manchester University Press, 1991), 228–30.

91. Sharon Stichter, *Migrant Labour in Kenya: Capitalism and African Response, 1895–1975* (London: Longman, 1982), 95.

92. Parker, *Political and Social Aspects,* appendix 1.

93. CPK, Native Affairs Department, Annual Report 1932, 120.

94. KNA ABK/14/140, DC Nairobi to Town Clerk, 31 July 1931.

95. TNA:PRO CO/859/18/8, Return of All Cases of Juvenile Offenders Brought before the Courts, 1938; and KNA AP/1/1699, Return of All Cases of Juvenile Offenders Brought before the Courts, 1939.

96. CPK, Native Affairs Department, Annual Report 1928, 74; and CPK, Native Affairs Department, Annual Report 1929, 71.

97. TNA:PRO CO/859/18/8, Return of All Cases of Juvenile Offenders Brought before the Courts, 1938; KNA AP/1/1699, Return of All Cases of Juvenile Offenders Brought before the Courts, 1939.

98. The colonial state used repatriation, in concert with African men, to periodically cast out women from Nairobi as well. Matthew Carotenuto, "Repatriation in Colonial Kenya: African Institutions and Gendered Violence," *International Journal of African Historical Studies* 45, no. 1 (2012): 9–28.

99. Iliffe, *African Poor,* 186.

100. George, *Making Modern Girls,* 113–16, 145–46, 178–79, and 183–84.

101. Frederiksen, "African Women and Their Colonisation of Nairobi," 225; and Robertson, *Trouble Showed the Way,* 95–96.

102. Carotenuto, "Repatriation in Colonial Kenya," 15–18; Kenda Mutongi, *Worries of the Heart: Widows, Family, and Community in Kenya* (Chicago: University of Chicago Press, 2007), 139–44; and Derek R. Peterson, *Ethnic Patriotism and the East African Revival: A History of Dissent, c. 1935–1972* (Cambridge: Cambridge University Press, 2012), 224–25.

103. Carotenuto, "Repatriation in Colonial Kenya," 13.

104. KNA ABK/14/140, Secretariat, 17 July 1940.

105. Throup, *Economic and Social Origins of Mau Mau,* 183.

106. KNA ABK/12/68, P. de V. Allen, Labour Commissioner, to NAO, 5 June 1941. See also KNA RN/1/58, Municipal Native Affairs Officer, 28 March 1944.

107. TNA:PRO CO/859/18/8, Return of All Cases of Juvenile Offenders Brought before the Courts, 1938; KNA AP/1/1699, Return of All Cases of Juvenile Offenders Brought before the Courts, 1939.

108. Carol W. Dickerman, "Africans in Nairobi during the Emergency: Social and Economic Changes, 1952–1960" (master's thesis, University of Wisconsin-Madison, 1978).

109. KNA MAA/8/22, T. S. Askwith, AAO, to Superintendent, 29 October 1947; and KNA MAA/2/5/223, Crime Committee, 19, 26 June 1946 and 15 August 1947.

110. CPK, No. 22, Removal of Undesirable Natives Ordinance, Ordinances and Regulations, 1946, section 5.

111. CPK, Cap 59, Vagrancy Amendment, The Laws of Kenya, 1948, sections 8–9, 13.

112. ARC/MD/4/1/2, Return of All Cases of Juvenile Offenders Brought before the Courts, 1945–1950; and KNA MAA/2/5/223, T. G. Askwith, AAO, Nairobi African Advisory Council, 1–2 March 1948.

113. Interview by author: Gabriel Kahugu Muchahi, 26 April 2008, Ndenderu, Kiambu.

114. Interview by author: Samuel Uiru Kaguara, 26 April 2008, Ndenderu, Kiambu.

115. KNA AP/1/1700, D. C. Cameron, Super. Approved Schools, to CIAS, 27 October 1945; and T. G. Askwith, AAO, Nairobi African Advisory Council, 1–2 March 1948.

116. KNA PC/CEN/2/1/4, Kiambu Local Native Council Meeting Minutes, 19–20 February 1932.

117. Sidney Webb and Beatrice Webb, *English Local Government from the Revolution to the Municipal Corporations Act: The Parish and the County* (London: Longmans, 1906), 469–84; A. L. Beier, *Masterless Men: The Vagrancy Problem in England, 1560–1640* (New York: Methuen, 1985), 152–58; and John F. Pound, *Poverty and Vagrancy in Tudor England* (London: Longman, 1971), 39–41.

118. KNA PC/CEN/2/1/9, Meru Local Native Council Meeting Minutes, 8–9 August 1939.

119. Frank Furedi, "The African Crowd in Nairobi: Popular Movements and Elite Politics," *Journal of African History* 14, no. 2 (1973), 282–83.

120. Robert J. Gordon, "Vagrancy, Law and 'Shadow Knowledge': Internal Pacification, 1915–1939," in *Namibia under South African Rule: Mobility and Containment, 1915–46*, ed. Patricia Hayes et al. (Athens: Ohio University Press, 1998), 75; and Jeremy Martens, "Polygamy, Sexual Danger, and the Creation of Vagrancy Legislation in Colonial Natal," *Journal of Imperial and Commonwealth History* 31, no. 3 (2003): 24–45.

CHAPTER 4: "THE OLD WAY . . . THE ONLY WAY"

1. RHL MSS Afr. r. 126, EAP Audit Office, "Funny Book." Much thanks to Brett Shadle for finding and letting me use this absolutely brilliant, albeit dark poem.

2. "Child Punishment: A Nairobi Court Case," *Kenya Daily Mail*, 22 March 1931; the specific regulations Amritlal had broken were sections 3, 12/1, and 18/3 of the 1928 Traffic Ordinance.

3. KNA AP/1/484, J. H. Sadler, Governor, East African Protectorate, to Lord Elgin, Secretary of State for the Colonies, 27 November 1907.

4. TNA:PRO CO/533/412/6, F. C. Gamble, Resident Magistrate, to Registrar, Supreme Court, 24 March 1931. Adult offenders could receive no more than twenty-four strokes of the cane.

5. *Kiboko* is the Kiswahili term for "hippopotamus," but it has also referred to whips made of animal hide. Later, *kiboko* became synonymous with tools of corporal punishment generally.

6. David Killingray, "The 'Rod of Empire': The Debate over Corporal Punishment in the British African Colonial Forces, 1888–1946," *Journal of African History* 35, no. 2 (1994): 204–5.

7. David Killingray, "Punishment to Fit the Crime? Penal Policy and Practice in British Colonial Africa," in *A History of Prison and Confinement in Africa*, ed. Florence Bernault (Portsmouth, NH: Heinemann, 2003), 107–8.

8. TNA:PRO CO 323/1399/3, Penal Reform in the Colonies: Corporal Punishment, 1936.

9. Bernard K. Mbenga, "Forced Labour in the Pilanesberg: The Flogging of Chief Kgamanyane by Commandant Paul Kruger, Saulspoort, April 1870," *Journal of Southern African Studies* 23, no. 1 (1997): 127; and Stephen Peté and Annie Devenish, "Flogging, Fear and Food: Punishment and Race in Colonial Natal," *Journal of Southern African Studies* 31, no. 1 (2005): 7, 10–12.

10. Keith Breckenridge, "The Allure of Violence: Men, Race and Masculinity on the South African Goldmines, 1900–1950," *Journal of Southern African Studies* 24, no. 4 (1998): 669–93; and Marie-Bénédicte Dembour, "La chicote comme symbole du colonialisme belge?" *Canadian Journal of African Studies* 26, no. 2 (1992): 205–25.

11. T. Dunbar Moodie, "Maximum Average Violence: Underground Assaults on the South African Gold Mines, 1913–1965," *Journal of Southern African Studies* 31, no. 3 (2005): 549.

12. David Crawford Jones, "Wielding the *Epokolo*: Corporal Punishment and Traditional Authority in Colonial Ovamboland" *Journal of African History* 56, no. 2 (2015): 305–6.

13. Evidence that corporal punishment predated colonial rule in Africa is contradictory. See Murray Last, "Children and the Experience of Violence: Contrasting Cultures of Punishment in Northern Nigeria," *Africa* 70, no. 3 (2000): 383–84, 360–61.

14. Moodie, "Maximum Average Violence," 549.

15. Victor Bailey, *Delinquency and Citizenship: Reclaiming the Young Offender, 1914–1948* (Oxford: Oxford University Press, 1987), 114; George R. Scott, *The History of Corporal Punishment: A Survey of Flagellation in Its Historical, Anthropological and Sociological Aspects* (New York: Columbia University Press, 2005), 94–110.

16. Stephen J. Rockel, *Carriers of Culture: Labor on the Road in Nineteenth-Century East Africa* (Portsmouth, NH: Heinemann, 2006), 170–79.

17. John M. Lonsdale, "The Conquest State of Kenya, 1895–1905," in *Unhappy Valley: Conflict in Kenya and Africa*, vol. 1, *State and Class*, ed. Bruce J. Berman and John M. Lonsdale (Athens: Ohio University Press, 1992), 21–30.

18. Timothy H. Parsons, *The African Rank-and-File: Social Implications of Colonial Military Service in the King's African Rifles, 1902–1964* (Portsmouth, NH: Heinemann, 1999), 186–87; and Killingray, "Rod of Empire," 203, 205–14.

19. David M. Anderson, "Punishment, Race, and 'The Raw Native': Settler Society and Kenya's Flogging Scandals, 1895–1930," *Journal of Southern African Studies* 37, no. 3 (2011): 481.

20. KNA PC/COAST/1/10/70, R. W. Hamilton, Chief Justice, to Chief Secretary, 27 December 1912.

21. Brett L. Shadle, *The Souls of White Folk: White Settlers in Kenya, 1900s–1920s* (Manchester: Manchester University Press, 2015), 123.

22. Ibid., 124–26.

23. Anderson, "Punishment, Race, and 'The Raw Native,'" 481.

24. KNA ARC/MD/4/1/3, A. Creech Jones to Government of Kenya, Circular, 15 January 1948.

25. Anderson, "Punishment, Race, and 'The Raw Native,'" 482–89.

26. KNA PC/COAST/1/10/70, R. W. Hamilton, Chief Justice, to Chief Secretary, 27 December 1912; and Brett L. Shadle, "'Changing Traditions to Meet Current Altering Conditions': Customary Law, African Courts and the Rejection of Codification in Kenya, 1930–60," *Journal of African History* 40, no. 3 (1999): 411–31.

27. Jones, "Wielding the *Epokolo*," 303–4.

28. KNA AP/1/863, H. C. Belfield, Governor, EAP, No. 409, 28 May 1913.

29. KNA AP/1/863, T. A. Gray, Inspector of Prisons, to PC Mombasa, 30 May 1913.

30. In Ovamboland, Namibians differentiate between the *sjambok*, typically an animal-hide whip, introduced by colonial authorities, and the *epokolo*, or palm branch, used by traditional authorities. Jones, "Wielding the *Epokolo*," 308–9.

31. KNA AP/1/843, Chief Justice R. W. Hamilton to Chief Secretary, 30 August 1915.

32. Brett Shadle, "Settlers, Africans, and Inter-Personal Violence in Kenya, ca. 1900–1920s," *International Journal of African Historical Studies* 45, no. 1 (2012): 61.

33. KNA AG/7/2, Colony and Protectorate of Kenya (CPK), Native Punishment Commission Report, 1923, 2.

34. Ibid., 5.

35. Ibid., 2.

36. KNA AG/7/2, R. W. Lyall-Grant, Attorney General, to Colonial Secretary, Report of the Native Punishment Commission, 20 June 1924.

37. KNA AP/1/863, C. E. Spencer, Comm. Prisons, to Colonial Secretary, 17 April 1926.

38. Anderson, "Punishment, Race, and 'The Raw Native,'" 479–80; and Shadle, "Settlers, Africans, and Inter-Personal Violence," 63–65.

39. Killingray, "Rod of Empire," 203.

40. Scott, *History of Corporal Punishment*, 94–110.

41. Bailey, *Delinquency and Citizenship*, 114.

42. Michel Foucault, *Discipline and Punish: The Birth of the Prison* (New York: Vintage Books, 1979), 3–31.

43. Mark Gould, "Sparing the Rod," *Guardian*, 9 January 2007.

44. CPK, Prisons Department Annual Reports, 1932–1935; CPK, Kenya Police Department Annual Reports, 1932–1948; TNA:PRO CO/533/483/14, CO/533/496/8, CO/859/18/8; and KNA ARC/MD/4/1/2.

45. KNA DC/KSM/1/15/225, Member for Legal Affairs to Registrar Supreme Court, Corporal Punishment Returns for 1952, 4 June 1953.

46. The court registers I have compiled are incomplete. I was unable to find the files issued for 1934, 1935, and 1948, as well as those submitted during the war years, 1940–1944. It is possible that no registers were submitted during the war. In addition, these registers include only the cases compiled for Colonial Office perusal and do not necessarily contain every single case that ended in the caning of a young person.

47. TNA:PRO CO/533/381/12 for 1928, CO/533/399/2 for 1929, CO/533/416/17 for 1931, CO/533/434/12 for 1932–1933, CO/533/483/14 for 1936, CO/533/496/8 for 1937, CO/859/18/8 for 1938; KNA AP/1/1699 for 1939, ARC/MD/4/1/2 for 1945–1947, ARC/MD/4/1/3 for 1949, AP/1/1840 for 1950–1951, AH/6/16 for 1952–1953, and AP/1/1876 for 1954–1955.

48. KNA PC/COAST/1/10/70, R. W. Hamilton, Chief Justice, to Chief Secretary, 27 December 1912.

49. Steven Pierce, "Punishment and the Political Body: Flogging and Colonialism in Northern Nigeria," in *Discipline and the Other Body: Correction, Corporeality, Colonialism*, ed. Steven Pierce and Anupama Rao (Durham, NC: Duke University Press, 2006), 186.

50. Greg T. Smith, "Civilized People Don't Want to See That Sort of Thing: The Decline of Physical Punishment in London, 1760–1840," in *Qualities of Mercy: Justice, Punishment, and Discretion*, ed. Carolyn Strange (Vancouver: University of British Columbia Press, 1996), 21–51.

51. TNA:PRO CO/859/18/8 for 1938; KNA AP/1/1699 for 1939; and ARC/MD/4/1/2 for 1945–1947 and 1949–1950.

52. Laurent Fourchard, "Lagos and the Invention of Juvenile Delinquency in Nigeria, 1920–60," *Journal of African History* 47, no. 1 (2006): 133–34.

53. Lynn M. Thomas, *Politics of the Womb: Women, Reproduction, and the State in Kenya* (Berkeley: University of California Press, 2003), 3–17.

54. Luise White, *The Comforts of Home: Prostitution in Colonial Nairobi* (Chicago: University of Chicago Press, 1990), 97–98; Tabitha M. Kanogo, *African Womanhood in Colonial Kenya, 1900–50* (Athens: Ohio University Press, 2005), 33–34; Brett L. Shadle, *"Girl Cases": Marriage and Colonialism in Gusiiland, Kenya, 1890–1970* (Portsmouth, NH: Heinemann, 2006), 152–78.

55. TNA:PRO CO 533/412/6, F. C. Gamble, Resident Magistrate, to Registrar, Supreme Court, 24 March 1931.

56. Geoffrey W. Griffin and Yusuf M. King'ala, *The Autobiography of Dr. G. W. Griffin: Kenya's Champion Beggar* (Nairobi: Falcon Crest, 2005), 14–16.

57. Interview by author: John Tumbo Soi, 6 June 2008, Saunet, Sotik; and KNA BY/52/1, M. M. Bali et al., Age Determination of Male Africans, 31 July 1954.

58. KNA DC/KAPT/1/17/20, throughout, files illustrate that medical officers noted circumcision in court cases; and KNA AP/1/1699, D. Edwards, Resident Magistrate, Nairobi, to Registrar Supreme Court, 1 November 1934.

59. Muga Gicaru, *Land of Sunshine: Scenes of Life in Kenya before Mau Mau* (London: Lawrence and Wishart, 1958), 97, 100–101.

60. David M. Anderson, "Master and Servant in Colonial Kenya, 1895–1939," *Journal of African History* 41, no. 3 (2000): 474.

61. TNA:PRO CO/533/381/12, CO/533/399/2, CO/533/416/17, CO/533/434/12, CO/533/483/14, CO/533/496/8, CO/859/18/8; and KNA AP/1/1699, KNA ARC(MD)/4/12, ARC(MD)/4/1/3, AH/6/16, and AP/1/1840.

62. Chloe Campbell, "Juvenile Delinquency in Colonial Kenya, 1900–39," *Historical Journal* 45, no. 1 (2002): 129–51; and Paul Ocobock, "'Joy Rides for Juveniles': Vagrant Youth and Colonial Control in Nairobi, Kenya, 1901–52," *Social History* 31, no. 1 (2006): 39–59.

63. KNA AP/1/865, J. Sheridan, Chief Justice, Memorandum on Corporal Punishment, 19 June 1939.

64. Satadru Sen, "A Separate Punishment: Juvenile Offenders in Colonial India," *Journal of Asian Studies* 63, no. 1 (2004): 100–101.

65. Justin Willis, "Thieves, Drunkards, and Vagrants," in *Policing the Empire: Government, Authority and Control, 1830–1940*, ed. David M. Anderson and David Killingray (Manchester: Manchester University Press, 1991), 227–28.

66. David Anderson, "Policing, Prosecution, and the Law in Colonial Kenya, c. 1905–39," in Anderson and Killingray, *Policing the Empire*, 194–96.

67. W. Robert Foran, *The Kenya Police, 1887–1960* (London: Hale, 1962), 67–68, 80, 153.

68. David W. Throup, "Crimes, Politics, and the Police in Colonial Kenya, 1939–63," in *Policing and Decolonisation: Nationalism, Politics and the Police, 1917–65*, ed. David M. Anderson and David Killingray (Manchester: Manchester University Press, 1991), 130–31.

69. TNA:PRO CO/533/381/12, Annual Register of Juvenile Corporal Punishment, 1928, CO/533/399/2 for 1929, CO/533/416/17 for 1931, and CO/533/434/12 for 1932–1933.

70. KNA ARC/MD/4/1/2, Annual Registers of Juvenile Corporal Punishment, 1945–1947, ARC/MD/4/1/3 for 1949, AP/1/1840 for 1950–1951, AH/6/16 for 1952–1953, and AP/1/1876 for 1954–1955.

71. Yash P. Ghai and J. Patrick McAuslan, *Public Law and Political Change in Kenya: A Study of the Legal Framework of Government from Colonial Times to the Present* (Nairobi: Oxford University Press, 1970), 134–35; and David M. Anderson, "Policing the Settler State: Colonial Hegemony in Kenya, 1900–1952," in *Contesting Colonial Hegemony: State and Society in Africa and India*, ed. Dagmar Engels and Shula Marks (London: British Academic Press, 1994), 256. Juvenile caning ordered by second- and third-class courts represented only a fraction of the total sentences in the registers.

72. TNA:PRO CO/533/412/6, F. L. R. Miller, Medical Officer, Nairobi Prison, to Director of Medical and Sanitary Services, 24 March 1931.

73. "Child Punishment: A Nairobi Court Case," *Kenya Daily Mail*, 22 March 1931; and TNA:PRO CO 533/412/6, C. E. Spencer, Comm. Prisons, to Colonial Secretary, 25 March 1931.

74. Interview by author: Harry Joseph Kimanji, 6 April 2008, Gilgil.

75. Interviews by author: Gabriel Kahugu Muchahi and Peter Mwarangu Ngugi, 26 April 2008, Ndenderu, Kiambu.

76. Interview by author: James Ng'ang'a Kamau, 17 April 2008, Gilgil.

77. Interview by author: Harry Joseph Kimanji, 6 April 2008, Gilgil.

78. Interview by author: Moses Mwanja Mutahi Nyatia, 26 May 2008, Gilgil.

79. Stacey Hynd, "Killing the Condemned: The Practice and Process of Capital Punishment in British Africa, 1900–1950s," *Journal of African History* 49, no. 3 (2008): 409–12.

80. Thomas W. Laqueur, "Crowds, Carnival and the State in English Executions, 1604–1868," in *The First Modern Society: Essays in English History in Honour of Lawrence Stone*, ed. A. L. Beier, David Cannadine, and James M. Rosenheim (Oxford: Oxford University Press, 1989): 305–55; and V. A. C. Gatrell, *The Hanging Tree: Execution and the English People, 1770–1868* (Oxford: Oxford University Press, 1994).

81. Pierce, "Punishment and the Political Body," 189–90.

82. Henry Seaton, *Lion in the Morning* (London: Murray, 1963), 41.

83. Ibid.

84. KNA AH/14/3, G. H. Heaton, Comm. Prisons, to Chief Secretary, Re: Corporal Punishment, 13 November 1946.

85. KNA AH/14/3, Colonial Office Circular to Government of Kenya, Corporal Punishment, 1 August 1950.

86. KNA JZ/6/18, Report of Committee on Corporal Punishment, 1951; emphasis mine.

87. Interview by author: Gabriel Kahugu Muchahi, 26 April 2008, Ndenderu, Kiambu.

88. Pierce, "Punishment and the Political Body," 199.

89. KNA AP/1/864, U. K. Oza, Secretary Indian Association of Nairobi, to Colonial Secretary, 19 March 1931.

90. "Child Punishment: A Nairobi Court Case," *Kenya Daily Mail*, 22 March 1931.

91. TNA:PRO CO 533/412/6, F. C. Gamble, Resident Magistrate, to Registrar, Supreme Court, 24 March 1931.

92. TNA:PRO CO 533/412/6, L. R. Miller, Medical Officer, Nairobi Prison, to Director of Medical and Sanitary Services, 24 March 1931; C. E. Spencer, Comm. Prisons, to Colonial Secretary, 25 March 1931.

93. KNA AP/1/864, Lord Passfield, SSC, to J. A. Byrne, Governor, 26 May 1931.

94. Pierce, "Punishment and the Political Body," 194–96.

95. KNA JZ/6/18, Report of Committee on Corporal Punishment, 1951.

96. Killingray, "Rod of Empire," 202.

97. Caroline Archambault, "Pain with Punishment and the Negotiation of Childhood: An Ethnographic Analysis of Children's Rights Processes in Maasailand," *Africa* 79, no. 2 (2002): 289–91.

98. Interview by author: Augustine Ruto, 9 June 2008, Kaplong, Sotik.

99. Interviews by author: Abiathar Omondi Opudo, 28 March 2008, Homa Bay; Jaramongi Joseph Wanga Sidho, 31 March 2008, Bondo; and Joseph Mutai Kiprop, 7 June 2008, Kapsinendet, Sopik.

100. Interview by author: Erick Kipkwai Bargetet, 10 June 2008, Tenwek, Bomet.

101. Interview by author: Veronica Mwihaki, 8 March 2008, Gilgil.

102. Richard D. Waller, "Bad Boys in the Bush? Disciplining Murran in Colonial Maasailand," in *Generations Past: Youth in East African History*, ed. Andrew Burton and Hélène Charton-Bigot (Athens: Ohio University Press, 2010), 151–52.

103. Interviews by author: Joseph arap Soi, 6 June 2008, Saunet, Sotik; and Jonah Kiprono Chepkwony, 12 June 2008, Kamarai, Sotik.

104. Interview by author: Gabriel Kahugu Muchahi, 26 April 2008, Ndenderu, Kiambu.

105. Interview by author: Philip Oduok Ayoo, 27 March 2008, Awendo; and Archambault, "Pain with Punishment," 292.

106. Interview by author: Erick Kipkwai Bargetet, 10 June 2008, Tenwek, Bomet.

107. KNA PC/CP/6/4/2, D. R. Crampton, Acting PC Central, to all DCs, 28 May 1920; PC/CP/7/1/2, DC Fort Hall to PC Central, Circumcision, 8 September 1920; and DC Nyeri to PC Central, Circumcision 13 September 1920; and PC/CEN/2/1/4, Kiambu LNC Meeting Minutes, 4 April 1927. See also Robert L. Tignor, *Colonial Transformation of Kenya: The Kamba, Kikuyu, and Maasai from 1900–1939* (Princeton, NJ: Princeton University Press, 1976), 47–48, 164–67; and John S. Peristiany, *The Social Institutions of the Kipsigis* (London: Routledge and Sons, 1939), 30–31.

108. Interview by author: John Opyio Osawa, 27 March 2008, Awendo; and Gicaru, *Land of Sunshine*, 82–85.

109. Interview by author: Moses Mwanja Mutahi Nyatia, 26 May 2008, Nyeri.

110. Anderson, "Policing the Settler State," 258–59.

111. Interview by author: Joseph Chepkwony, 6 June 2008, Saunet, Sotik.

112. Interview by author: Siamba Maina, 8 June 2008, Chepilat, Sotik.

113. Interview by author: Joseph Kibelyon Korir, 8 June 2008, Chepilat, Sotik.

114. Interview by author: Christopher Onduru Achar, 26 March 2008, Awendo.

115. KNA PC/CEN/2/1/12, Embu Local Native Council Meeting Minutes, 11–12 March 1948.

116. Interview by author: Willis Opiyo Otondi, 30 March 2008, Nyahera.

117. Interview by author: James Ng'ang'a Kamau, 17 April 2008, Gilgil.

118. Interview by author: Alan Ale Kanyingi Ngugi, 19 May 2008, Githunguri, Kiambu.

119. Interviews by author: Anthony King'etich Rotich, 9 June 2008, Kaplong, Sotik; and Kimani Ng'ang'a Maruge, 23 June 2008, Kariobangi, Nairobi.

120. KNA JZ/6/18, Report of Committee on Corporal Punishment, 1951.

1. Interview by author: Alan Ale Kanyingi Ngugi, 19 May 2008, Githunguri, Kiambu.

2. Ibid.

3. KNA AB/14/32, APO Kiambu, Probation Officer's Report, 10 April 1954.

4. Ibid.

5. Abosede A. George, *Making Modern Girls: A History of Girlhood, Labor, and Social Development in Colonial Lagos* (Athens: Ohio University Press, 2014), 7–8. See also Frederick Cooper, *Decolonization and African Society: The Labor Question in French and British Africa* (Cambridge: Cambridge University Press, 1996), 110–24; and Frederick Cooper, *Africa since 1940: The Past of the Present* (Cambridge: Cambridge University Press, 2002), 4.

6. Much of this chapter is informed by interviews I conducted with former inmates of Kabete, Dagoretti, and Wamumu approved schools in the 1940s and 1950s. These men were willing to share stories of life behind bars with me.

7. KNA AP/1/484, J. H. Sadler, Governor EAP, to V. A. Bruce, SSC, 27 November 1907.

8. Andrew Lees, *Cities Perceived: Urban Society in European and American Thought, 1820–1940* (Manchester: Manchester University Press, 1985), 116–17.

9. In Senegal, the first reformatory for young offenders was built by the government in 1916 and was also housed beside the experimental farm. Ibrahima Thioub, "Juvenile Delinquency and the First Penitentiary Schools in Senegal, 1888–1927," in *A History of Prison and Confinement in Africa*, ed. Florence Bernault (Portsmouth, NH: Heinemann, 2003), 87.

10. Robert L. Tignor, *Colonial Transformation of Kenya: The Kamba, Kikuyu, and Maasai from 1900–1939* (Princeton, NJ: Princeton University Press, 1976), 216.

11. Ibid., 217. See also Donald G. Schilling, "British Policy for African Education in Kenya, 1895–1939" (PhD diss., University of Wisconsin-Madison, 1972).

12. For a history of Alliance High School, see Benjamin E. Kipkorir, "The Alliance High School and the Origins of the Kenya African Elite, 1926–1962" (PhD diss., University of Cambridge, 1969); and Hélène Charton-Bigot, "Colonial Youth at the Crossroads: Fifteen Alliance 'Boys,'" in *Generations Past: Youth in East African History*, ed. Andrew Burton and Hélène Charton-Bigot (Athens: Ohio University Press, 2010), 86–87.

13. John A. Stack, "Reformatory and Industrial Schools and the Decline of Child Imprisonment in Mid-Victorian England and Wales," *History of Education* 23, no. 1 (1994): 62–64.

14. John Stewart, "Children, Parents and the State: The Children Act, 1908," *Children and Society* 9, no. 1 (1995): 92.

15. Victor Bailey, *Delinquency and Citizenship: Reclaiming the Young Offender, 1914–1948* (Oxford: Oxford University Press, 1987), 1–4.

16. Satadru Sen, *Colonial Childhoods: The Juvenile Periphery of India, 1850–1945* (London: Anthem Press, 2005); Linda Chisholm, "The Pedagogy of Porter: The Origins of the Reformatory in the Cape Colony, 1882–1910," *Journal of African History* 27, no. 3 (1986): 481–95; and Mine Ener, *Managing Egypt's Poor and the Politics of Benevolence, 1800–1952* (Princeton, NJ: Princeton University Press, 2003), 114–15.

17. George, *Making Modern Girls*, 74–79; Laurent Fourchard, "Lagos and the In-

vention of Juvenile Delinquency in Nigeria, 1920–60," *Journal of African History* 47, no. 1 (2006): 127–28; and Robert B. Seidman and J. D. Abaka Eyison, "Ghana," in *African Penal Systems*, ed. Alan Milner (New York: Praeger, 1969), 79–80.

18. KNA AP/1/484, R. N. Combs, Crown Advocate, to Principal Judge, 28 January 1909, and Principal Judge, Circular to Magistrates 1 of 1909.

19. KNA AP/1/698, J. Johnson, Superintendent, to Director of Agriculture, 17 November 1912.

20. TNA:PRO CO/544/5, Annual Report of the EAP for 1912–1913, 400; and TNA:PRO CO/544/7, Annual Report for the EAP for 1913–1914, 198.

21. Annual Reports of Kabete Reformatory can be found in KNA AP/1/698; KNA AP/1/699; and KNA AP/1/701.

22. KNA AP/1/484, R. W. Hamilton, Principal Judge, Memorandum on the Government Reformatory, 6 August 1910.

23. KNA AP/1/484, Committee of Visitors, Kabete Reformatory, to Chief Justice, 23 May 1922.

24. KNA AP/1/698, J. W. Barth, Chief Justice, to Colonial Secretary, 7 January 1925.

25. Bailey, *Delinquency and Citizenship*, 47–48.

26. Heather Shore, "Introduction: Re-Inventing the Juvenile Delinquent in Britain and Europe, 1650–1950," in *Becoming Delinquent: British and European Youth, 1650–1950*, ed. Pamela Cox and Heather Shore (Aldershot: Ashgate, 2002), 3.

27. George, *Making Modern Girls*, 74–76; Chisholm, "Pedagogy of Porter," 487.

28. Chloe Campbell, "Juvenile Delinquency in Colonial Kenya, 1900–39," *Historical Journal* 45, no. 1 (2002): 133.

29. KNA AP/1/700, Mr. Ayub Abda to Colonial Secretary, 20 October 1936; and Pritam Kaur to J. A. Byrne, Governor, Petition, 28 October 1936.

30. KNA AP/1/698, J. Finch, Acting Super. Kabete Reformatory, Annual Report, 6 January 1927; KNA AP/1/700, W. H. Wood, Super. Kabete Reformatory, Annual Report, 9 January 1929; and W. H. Wood, Super. Kabete Reformatory, Annual Report, 25 February 1930; and KNA AP/1/699, W. H. Wood, Super. Kabete Reformatory, Annual Report, 16 January 1931.

31. KNA AP/1/698, J. Johnson, Super. Kabete Reformatory, to Dir. of Agriculture, 17 November 1912; and Committee of Visitors Meeting Minutes, Kabete Reformatory, 27 May 1914.

32. KNA AP/1/698, R. W. Hamilton to Chief Secretary, 13 June 1916.

33. KNA AP/1/698, F. S. F. Traill, Acting PC, Ukamba, to Chief Secretary, 24 June 1916.

34. KNA AP/1/698, J. Finch, Acting Super. Kabete, Annual Report 1926, 6 January 1927; and KNA AP/1/701, W. H. Wood, Super. Kabete Reformatory, Annual Report 1928, 9 January 1929.

35. KNA AP/1/698, J. Finch, Acting Super. Kabete, Annual Report 1926, 6 January 1927.

36. KNA PC/COAST/1/14/148, W. H. Tanner, Acting Director of Public Works, to PC Coast, P. W. D. Training Depot, 10 January 1916; and KNA AV/12/77, H. L. Sikes, Director of Public Works, to Acting Colonial Secretary, 7 June 1925.

37. Kenneth J. King, "Africa and the Southern States of the U.S.A.: Notes on J. H. Oldham and American Negro Education for Africans," *Journal of African History* 10, no. 4 (1969): 659–77.

38. Schilling, "British Policy for African Education," 245; and Andrew Zimmerman,

Alabama in Africa: Booker T. Washington, the German Empire, and the Globalization of the New South (Princeton, NJ: Princeton University Press, 2012), 40–60, 139–61.

39. Thomas J. Jones, *Education in East Africa: A Study of East, Central and South* (New York: Phelps-Stokes Fund, 1925), 134.

40. KNA AP/1/701, W. H. Wood, Super. Kabete, Annual Report of 1928, 9 January 1929.

41. Shore, "Introduction: Re-Inventing the Juvenile Delinquent," 12.

42. George, *Making Modern Girls*, 78–79.

43. KNA AP/1/701, Agricultural Officer, Scott's Agricultural Laboratory, to Registrar Supreme Court, 12 February 1930.

44. KNA AP/1/699, W. H. Wood, Super. Kabete, to Committee of Visitors, 14 August 1930; G. R. Sandford, Treasurer, to Colonial Secretary, 31 October 1930; Board of Visitors to DC Nairobi, 5 August 1931; and Committee Enquiry: Kabete Reformatory, Charges for Labour, 31 August to 10 September 1931.

45. KNA AP/1/700, H. M. Moore, Colonial Secretary, to Committee of Visitors, 14 May 1930.

46. W. Robert Foran, *The Kenya Police, 1887–1960* (London: Hale, 1962), 66–68; David M. Anderson, "Policing, Prosecution and the Law in Colonial Kenya, c. 1905–39," in *Policing the Empire: Government, Authority and Control, 1830–1940*, ed. David M. Anderson and David Killingray (Manchester: Manchester University Press, 1991), 192–93.

47. Colony and Protectorate of Kenya (CPK), *Crime Committee Report* (Nairobi: Government Printer, 1932), 4.

48. Ibid., 19.

49. TNA:PRO CO 533/426/17, S. H. La Fontaine, Report on Borstal and Other Reformatory Institutions in England, 1933.

50. Ibid., 30.

51. Phyllida Parsloe, *Juvenile Justice in Britain and the United States: The Balance of Needs and Rights* (London: Routledge and Kegan Paul, 1978), 139; and Steven Schlossman, "Delinquent Children: The Juvenile Reform School," in *The Oxford History of the Prison: The Practice of Punishment in Western Society*, ed. Norval Morris and David J. Rothman (Oxford: Oxford University Press, 1995), 343.

52. KNA AG/12/197, Lord Passfield, Secretary of State for the Colonies, 11 September 1930.

53. George, *Making Modern Girls*, 68–70.

54. CPK, Report of the Committee on Juvenile Crime and Kabete Reformatory, 1934.

55. CPK, Ordinance 32 of 1934, Juveniles Ordinance, Sec. 10.

56. Ibid., Sec. 12 and 16.

57. Ibid., Sec. 27–33.

58. Ibid., Sec. 11.

59. KNA AP/1/701, M. M. Jack, Registrar Supreme Court, Circular to Magistrates, No. 2 of 1935, Juvenile Offenders Ordinance, 1934.

60. KNA ARC(MD)/4/1/13, J. L. Willcocks, Comm. Prisons and CIAS, Visit of Sir. M. Hailey, Juvenile Crime in Kenya, 22 November 1935.

61. Alexander Paterson, *Across the Bridges; or, Life by the South London River-Side* (London: Arnold, 1911).

62. John R. Gillis, "The Evolution of Juvenile Delinquency in England, 1890–1914," *Past and Present* 67, no. 1 (1975): 97; and Harry Hendrick, *Images of Youth: Age, Class, and the Male Youth Problem, 1880–1920* (Oxford: Clarendon, 1990), 102–4.

63. KNA ARC(MD)/4/1/13, J. L. Willcocks, Comm. Prisons and CIAS, Visit of Sir. M. Hailey, Juvenile Crime in Kenya, 22 November 1935.

64. CPK, Prisons Department Annual Report, 1934, 22.

65. Schilling, "British Policy for African Education," 355–58.

66. Sharon Stichter, *Migrant Labour in Kenya: Capitalism and African Response, 1895–1975* (Harlow: Longman, 1982), 95.

67. KNA AB/14/44, Approved School, Dagoretti, 13 September 1944; and Paterson, *Across the Bridges*, 204.

68. Willcocks lifted these quotes directly from Miriam van Waters's book *Youth in Conflict*. Van Waters, a contemporary of Alexander Paterson, developed several juvenile reform facilities in California in the 1920s and the Massachusetts Reformatory for Women in the 1930s. Van Waters, *Youth in Conflict* (New York: Republic, 1925), 200.

69. Bailey, *Delinquency and Citizenship*, 198–99.

70. CPK, Prisons Department Annual Report, 1935 and 1945.

71. TNA:PRO FCO/141/6393, AG to CS, "Mr. R. Kennison," 11 March 1957.

72. TNA:PRO FCO/141/6393, Colin S. Owen, PPO, to SCD, "Mr. R. Kennison," 2 April 1957.

73. CPK, Prisons Department Annual Report, 1945 and 1946.

74. For a similar dynamic in all-male boarding schools, see Stephen O. Murray, "'A Feeling within Me': Kamau, a Twenty-Five-Year-Old Kikuyu," in *Boy-Wives and Female Husbands: Studies in African Homosexualities*, ed. Stephen O. Murray and Will Roscoe (New York: St. Martin's, 1998), 41–65.

75. Interviews by author: Rev. Patrick Mugwe Njoroge, 27 May 2008, Mukurweini, Nyeri; and Joseph Mutai Kiprop, 7 June 2008, Kapsinendet, Sotik.

76. Interview by author: Moses Mwanja Mutahi Nyatia, 26 May 2008, Nyeri.

77. Joram Wamweya, *Freedom Fighter* (Nairobi: East African Publishing, 1971), 11. A few of the men I spoke to mentioned sexual games played out on the grazing fields, such as masturbating in front of one another. However, evidence from other scholars suggests that this sort of behavior was unheard of. See Robert A. LeVine and Donald T. Campbell, *Gusii of Kenya*, 2 vols. (New Haven, CT: Human Relations Area Files, 1972), 471. Yet the grazing fields were one of the few places boys could play, fight, and enjoy their days largely free of adult supervision—as long as they minded the livestock. It seems more than likely that boys got up to a little sexual mischief there.

78. Interview by author: Alan Ale Kanyingi Ngugi, 19 May 2008, Githunguri, Kiambu.

79. Interview by author: Joseph Mutai Kiprop, 7 June 2008, Kapsinendet, Sotik.

80. KNA AG/12/204, J. Harland Frank, Comm. Prisons, to AG, 16 November 1937.

81. KNA AP/1/698, R. W. Hamilton, Chief Justice, Kabete Reformatory, 26 November 1913.

82. KNA BY/12/44, Medical Officer, Infectious Disease Hospital, to Acting Director of Medical Services, 6 June 1938.

83. TNA:PRO FCO/141/6393, Director of Establishments to Chief Secretary, 4 April 1957; T. M. Skinner for Chief Secretary to Attorney General, Secret, 7 April 1957; and D. W. Conroy, Solicitor General, "Mr. R. Kennison," 15 April 1957.

84. KNA AHL/2/2, Letter to G. H. Heaton, 21 December 1940.

85. KNA AB/14/32, Probation Report, Mary Kenny, APO, 24 November 1953.

86. KNA AB/14/32, Probation Report, 29 December 1953.

87. CPK, Prisons Department Annual Report, 1938, 27.

88. CPK, Prisons Department Annual Report, 1945, 1 and 17.

89. KNA AP/1/1700, D. C. Cameron, Super. Approved Schools, to CIAS, 27 October 1945; and KNA AHL/2/2, Archdeacon G. Burns, Report on Visit to Approved School, Dagoretti, 18 March 1941.

90. CPK, Prisons Department Annual Report 1944, 3.

91. CPK, Prisons Department Annual Report 1951, 24–25.

92. KNA AB/1/137, C. S. Owen, PPO/CIAS, Daily Programme, Kabete Approved School, 7 November 1955; and CPK, Report on Treatment of Offenders, 1954–1956.

93. Interview by author: Alan Ale Kanyingi Ngugi, 19 May 2008, Githunguri, Kiambu.

94. Ibid.

95. CPK, Prisons Department Annual Reports, 1946–1951; and KNA DC/FH/3/12/14, Mary D. Kenny, PPO, to DC Fort Hall, 7 January 1954.

96. KNA AB/14/31, Mary Kenny, PO, Probation Officer's Report for Peter John Uzice, 9 September 1952.

97. KNA AB/14/32, APO, Probation Officer's Report for Wahuria Gitwaria, 10 November 1953.

98. Only twenty-five boys among the 381 cases had lost both parents, about 6 percent of the total.

99. KNA AB/14/28, S. J. Moore, PO, Probation Officer's Report for Ngungu Mbogo, 14 January 1952.

100. Abosede George notes as well that by the 1940s, Nigerian families also began to imagine the Enugu Approved School as part of an accepted disciplinary regime. George, *Making Modern Girls*, 81–84.

101. KNA AB/14/28, E. S. Oluseno, APO, Probation Officer's Report for Michael Bwile, 9 May 1951.

102. KNA AB/14/31, APO, Probation Officer's Report for Toho Kareithi, 15 January 1952.

103. KNA AB/14/28, C. S. Owen, PO, Probation Officer's Report for Kihio Kibanjwa, 22 October 1947.

104. KNA AB/14/31, S. J. Moore, PO, Probation Officer's Report for Mathenge Kamau, 30 April 1952.

105. KNA AB/14/31, S. J. Moore, PO, Probation Officer's Report for Guta Isoe, 29 November 1952.

106. KNA AB/14/31, H. J. Wanguche, APO, "Re: Report on Guta s/o Isoe, 20 November 1952.

107. KNA AB/14/31, S. J. Moore, PO, Probation Office's Report for Ngige Kimani, 22 April 1952.

108. Ibid.

109. Interview by author: Rev. Patrick Mugwe Njoroge, 27 May 2008, Mukurweini, Nyeri; and CPK, Prisons Department Annual Report, 1953.

CHAPTER 6: "IN THE PAST, THE COUNTRY BELONGED TO THE YOUNG MEN"

1. Tabitha M. Kanogo, *Squatters and the Roots of Mau Mau, 1905–63* (Athens: Ohio University Press, 1987), 97; and David W. Throup, *Economic and Social Origins of Mau Mau, 1945–53* (Athens: Ohio University Press, 1989), 92–95.

2. Michael Tamarkin, "Mau Mau in Nakuru," *Journal of African History* 17, no. 1 (1976): 115, 125–28; Kanogo, *Squatters and the Roots of Mau Mau*, 115–20, 125–29; and Throup, *Economic and Social Origins of Mau Mau*, 110–15.

3. David M. Anderson, *Histories of the Hanged: The Dirty War in Kenya and the End of Empire* (New York: Norton, 2005), 26.

4. Throup, *Economic and Social Origins of Mau Mau*, 139–48, 157.

5. Robert L. Tignor, *Colonial Transformation of Kenya: The Kamba, Kikuyu, and Maasai from 1900–1939* (Princeton, NJ: Princeton University Press, 1976), 267–72; and John E. Anderson, *The Struggle for the School: The Interaction of Missionary, Colonial Government and Nationalist Enterprise in the Development of Formal Education in Kenya* (London: Longman, 1970).

6. Colony and Protectorate of Kenya (CPK), *African Education in Kenya* (Nairobi, 1949); Derek R. Peterson, *Creative Writing: Translation, Bookkeeping, and the Work of Imagination in Colonial Kenya* (Portsmouth, NH: Heinemann, 2004), 193–95; and Joanna Lewis, *Empire State-Building: War and Welfare in Kenya, 1925–52* (Athens: Ohio University Press, 2000), 307–8.

7. KNA MAA/8/22, T. G. Askwith, African Affairs Officer, Lawlessness in Nairobi, 29 October 1947; Anderson, *Histories of the Hanged*, 37–38, 190; John Spencer, "KAU and 'Mau Mau': Some Connections," *Kenya Historical Review* 5, no. 2 (1977): 211–12; and Frank Furedi, "The African Crowd in Nairobi: Popular Movements and Elite Politics," *Journal of African History* 14, no. 2 (1973): 282–83.

8. Greet Kershaw, *Mau Mau from Below* (Athens: Ohio University Press, 1997), 220.

9. For a complete literature review of Mau Mau, see John M. Lonsdale, "The Moral Economy of Mau Mau: Wealth, Poverty and Civic Virtue," in *Unhappy Valley: Conflict in Kenya and Africa*, vol. 2, *Violence and Ethnicity*, ed. Bruce J. Berman and John M. Lonsdale (Athens: Ohio University Press, 1992), 282–302. For Mau Mau as a nationalist movement, see Carl G. Rosberg and John C. Nottingham, *The Myth of "Mau Mau": Nationalism in Kenya* (Stanford, CA: Hoover Institute, 1966); and Donald L. Barnett and Karai Njama, *Mau Mau from Within: Autobiography and Analysis of Kenya's Peasant Revolt* (London: MacGibbon and Kee, 1966). For class analyses, see Kanogo, *Squatters and the Roots of Mau Mau*; and Frank Furedi, *The Mau Mau War in Perspective* (Athens: Ohio University Press, 1989). For women's histories, see Cora A. Presly, *Kikuyu Women, the Mau Mau Rebellion, and Social Change in Kenya* (Boulder, CO: Westview Press, 1992).

10. Luise White, "Separating the Men from the Boys: Constructions of Gender, Sexuality, and Terrorism in Central Kenya, 1939–1959," *International Journal of African Historical Studies* 23, no. 1 (1990): 10–15, 19–25; and Lonsdale, "Moral Economy of Mau Mau," 316–17.

11. Benedict Carton, *Blood from Your Children: The Colonial Origins of Generational Conflict in South Africa* (Charlottesville: University of Virginia Press, 2000), 140.

12. Kershaw, *Mau Mau from Below*, 323; and KNA AB/2/60, E. D. Emley, First Class Magistrate, NEPD, Memorandum on Juveniles, 18 November 1955.

13. Lonsdale, "Moral Economy of Mau Mau," 360–68.

14. Anderson, *Histories of the Hanged*, 5.

15. John M. Lonsdale, "Mau Maus of the Mind: Making Mau Mau and Remaking Kenya," *Journal of African History* 31, no. 3 (1990): 393–421; and Dane K. Kennedy, "Constructing the Colonial Myth of Mau Mau," *International Journal of African Historical Studies* 25, no. 2 (1992): 241–60.

16. Waruhiu Itote, *"Mau Mau" General* (Nairobi: East African Publishing, 1967), 31–32; emphasis mine.

17. Ibid., 35–40.

18. Kiboi Muriithi with Peter Ndoria, *War in the Forest* (Nairobi: East African Publishing, 1971), 9.

19. Lonsdale, "Moral Economy of Mau Mau," 360–68.

20. Barnett and Njama, *Mau Mau from Within*, 43.

21. A few Mau Mau memoirists explicitly described oathing as initiation. Ngugi Kabiro, *The Man in the Middle: The Story of Ngugi Kabiro*, ed. Don Barnett (Richmond, BC: Liberation Support Movement Information Centre, 1971), 33–34, 40, 55; Mohamed Mathu, *The Urban Guerrilla: The Story of Mohamed Mathu*, ed. Donald Barnett (Richmond, BC: Liberation Support Movement Information Centre, 1974), 10–11; and Josiah Mwangi Kariuki, *"Mau Mau" Detainee: The Account by a Kenya African of His Experiences in Detention Camps, 1953–1960* (Baltimore: Penguin, 1963), 55.

22. Muriithi, *War in the Forest*, 2.

23. Renison M. Githige, "The Religious Factor in Mau Mau with Particular Reference to Mau Mau Oaths" (master's thesis, University of Nairobi, 1978), 47. My thanks to Daniel Branch for this quote.

24. Gucu G. Gikoyo, *We Fought for Freedom: Tulipigania Uhuru* (Nairobi: East African Publishing, 1979), 37.

25. Joram Wamweya, *Freedom Fighter* (Nairobi: East African Publishing, 1971), 63.

26. Karigo Muchai, *The Hardcore: The Story of Karigo Muchai*, ed. Donald Barnett (Richmond, BC: Liberation Support Movement Information Centre, 1973), 14.

27. Ibid., 27–29, 31–32.

28. Timothy H. Parsons, *The African Rank-and-File: Social Implications of Colonial Military Service in the King's African Rifles, 1902–1964* (Portsmouth, NH: Heinemann, 1999), 186–89; and David Killingray, "The 'Rod of Empire': The Debate over Corporal Punishment in the British African Colonial Forces, 1888–1946," *Journal of African History* 35, no. 2 (1994): 212–13.

29. Muchai, *Hardcore*, 19; and Mathu, *Urban Guerrilla*, 22.

30. Kabiro, *Man in the Middle*, 34.

31. Ibid., 61; and Mathu, *Urban Guerrilla*, 14.

32. Wamweya, *Freedom Fighter*, 63.

33. Anderson, *Histories of the Hanged*, 4.

34. Maina wa Kinyatii, ed., *Kenya's Freedom Struggle: The Dedan Kimathi Papers* (London: Zed Books, 1986), 28–29.

35. David Anderson, "The Battle of Dandora Swamp: Reconstructing the Mau Mau Land Freedom Army, October 1954," in *Mau Mau and Nationhood: Arms, Authority and Narration*, ed. E. S. Atieno Odhiambo and John M. Lonsdale (Athens: Ohio University Press, 2003), 172.

36. Kershaw, *Mau Mau from Below*, 248; and David A. Percox, *Britain, Kenya and the Cold War: Imperial Defence, Colonial Security and Decolonization* (New York: Palgrave Macmillan, 2012), 48–76.

37. Interview by author: Joseph Gikubu, 24 August 2005, Starehe, Nairobi.

38. Interview by author: Nicholas Kinyua Mwai, 28 May 2008, Kiamwathi, Nyeri. Other scholars of Mau Mau have argued that children did not receive the oath. See Kanogo, *Squatters and the Roots of Mau Mau*, 147; and Cora A. Presley, "The Mau

Mau Rebellion, Kikuyu Women, and Social Change," *Canadian Journal of African Studies* 22, no. 3 (1988): 510.

39. Interview by author: Nicholas Kinyua Mwai, 28 May 2008, Kiamwathi, Nyeri; G. Barra, *1,000 Kikuyu Proverbs: With Translations and English Equivalents* (London: Macmillan, 1960), 57; and Beth Maina Ahlberg and Kezia Muthoni Njoroge, "'Not Men Enough to Rule!': Politicization of Ethnicities and Forcible Circumcision of Luo Men during the Postelection Violence in Kenya," *Ethnicity and Health* 18, no. 5 (2013): 458. My thanks to Derek Peterson for providing some very last-minute help with this proverb.

40. Interview by author: Simon Kariuki Kuriaa, 22 May 2008, Ongata-Rongai.

41. Ibid.

42. Wamweya, *Freedom Fighter*, 55–62.

43. Rosberg and Nottingham, *Myth of "Mau Mau,"* 276.

44. Anderson, *Histories of the Hanged*, 125.

45. Daniel Branch, "The Enemy Within: Loyalists and the War against Mau Mau in Kenya," *Journal of African History* 48, no. 2 (2007): 294–96.

46. Ibid., 309.

47. Kennedy, "Constructing the Colonial Myth of Mau Mau," 243–47; and Lonsdale, "Mau Maus of the Mind," 395–96, 407–8.

48. Lonsdale, "Mau Maus of the Mind," 410.

49. White, "Separating the Men from the Boys," 7; Thomas G. Askwith, *From Mau Mau to Harambee: Memoirs and Memoranda of Colonial Kenya* (Cambridge: African Studies Centre, 1995), 62–63; and Louis S. B. Leakey, *Mau Mau and the Kikuyu* (London: Methuen, 1952), 105.

50. A. S. Cleary, "The Myth of Mau Mau in Its International Context," *African Affairs* 89, no. 355 (1990): 233–34; and Kennedy, "Constructing the Colonial Myth of Mau Mau," 250.

51. John C. Carothers, *The Psychology of Mau Mau* (Nairobi: Government Printer, 1954), 15.

52. Ibid., 5.

53. Ibid,. 10.

54. Ibid., 17–18.

55. Bruce J. Berman and John M. Lonsdale, "Louis Leakey's Mau Mau: A Study in the Politics of Knowledge," *History and Anthropology* 5, no. 2 (1991): 145–50.

56. Louis S. B. Leakey, *Defeating Mau Mau* (London: Methuen, 1954), 132.

57. Ibid., 133.

58. Ibid., 78–81.

59. Caroline Elkins, "The Struggle for Mau Mau Rehabilitation in Late Colonial Kenya," *International Journal of African Historical Studies* 33, no. 1 (2000): 32–33.

60. RHL MSS. Afr. s. 2100, T. G. Askwith Papers, File 1: Rehabilitation, Talk Given to the African Affairs Sub-Committee of the Electors' Union, 16 November 1953.

61. White, "Separating the Men from the Boys," 19–20.

62. Audrey Wipper, "The Maendeleo ya Wanawake Organization: The Co-Optation of Leadership," *African Studies Review* 18, no. 3 (1975): 99–102.

63. KNA AB/2/31, T. G. Askwith, Rehabilitation, 12 April 1954; and Elkins, "Struggle for Mau Mau Rehabilitation," 38–39.

64. Caroline Elkins, *Imperial Reckoning: The Untold Story of Britain's Gulag in Kenya* (New York: Holt, 2005), 110–15.

65. KNA BZ/16/1, C. M. Johnston, PC Rift Valley, to CNC, Juvenile Mau Mau Oath-Takers, 19 November 1952; S. J. Moore, PO, to PC Rift Valley, Juvenile Mau Mau Oath-Takers, 2 January 1953; and C. S. Owen, PPO, to PC Rift Valley, Juvenile Mau Mau Cases, 21 April 1953.

66. KNA BZ/16/1, O. E. B. Hughes, DC Nyeri, Mau Mau Juveniles, 13 August 1953; and S. H. La Fontaine, Assistant Comm. Prisons, Mau Mau Young Offenders, 20 August 1953.

67. KNA AH/6/15 and AP/1/1876, see corporal punishment figures for 1953–1955 located in the file.

68. Elkins, *Imperial Reckoning*, 53.

69. Anderson, *Histories of the Hanged*, 234–35.

70. John M. Lonsdale, "Town Life in Colonial Kenya," in *The Urban Experience in Eastern Africa, c. 1750–2000*, ed. Andrew Burton (Nairobi: British Institute in Eastern Africa, 2002): 219–20; and Frank Furedi, "African Crowd in Nairobi," 282–85.

71. Spencer, "KAU and 'Mau Mau,'" 205.

72. Interview by author: Alan Ale Kanyingi Ngugi, 19 May 2008, Githunguri, Kiambu.

73. Interview by author: Gabriel Kahugu Muchahi, 26 April 2008, Ndenderu, Kiambu.

74. Anderson, *Histories of the Hanged*, 201.

75. Eileen Fletcher, *Truth about Kenya: An Eye-Witness Account* (London: Movement for Colonial Freedom, 1956).

76. Anderson, *Histories of the Hanged*, 201–4.

77. Compared to Nigeria, Kenya was late in establishing a juvenile court. In Lagos, the court opened in 1946. It became known as "the Welfare" and was feared by young town dwellers. Abosede A. George, *Making Modern Girls: A History of Girlhood, Labor, and Social Development in Colonial Lagos* (Athens: Ohio University Press, 2014), 174–75.

78. KNA AB/8/13, C. S. Owen, PPO, Remedial Treatment of Offenders and Kindred Social Work of the Courts, 10 March 1954; D. Dewar, Acting PPO, to CCD, 4 August 1954; and RN/13/28, City Council of Nairobi, Annual Report, 1954; and KNA AH/14/25, E. W. Moylan, EO, NEPD, to War Council, Juveniles in Nairobi, 16 May 1955 and 14 June 1955.

79. Interview by author: James Karanja Kariuki, 6 April 2008, Gilgil.

80. KNA AH/14/25, Secretariat, Establishment of Homes for Parentless Children and Unattached Females in Nairobi, 15 July 1954.

81. CPK, Government Notice No. 16, Emergency (Welfare of Children) Regulations, 1954, sec. 2(1), 2(3), 3(1), 8.

82. KNA AB/17/65, T. G. Askwith, SCD to IUCW, 28 June 1954; and SSC to Governor Kenya, 13 June 1954.

83. My thanks to Matthew Hilton for his insights on this background of the Save the Children Fund. Hilton, "Ken Loach and the Save the Children Film: Humanitarianism, Imperialism, and the Changing Role of Charity in Postwar Britain," *Journal of Modern History* 87, no. 2 (2015): 357–94; and Emily Baughan, "'Every Citizen of Empire Implored to Save the Children!' Empire, Internationalism and the Save the Children Fund in Inter-War Britain," *Historical Research* 86, no. 231 (2013): 116–37.

84. KNA AB/17/65, T. G. Askwith, SCD to IUCW, 28 June 1954; and SSC to Governor Kenya, 13 June 1954.

85. Interview by author: Gabriel Kahugu Muchahi,26 April 2008, Ndenderu, Kiambu.

86. Other religious and charitable organizations assisted the state with welfare programming designed for the young during the counterinsurgency. The Christian Council of Kenya established the Dagoretti Children's Center in 1955 for orphans of the war. Over two years, the center handled more than six hundred cases. The Consolata Catholic Mission and the Salvation Army school at Quarry Road also opened their doors to hundreds of children whose parents had been detained or killed in the violence. KNA AB/16/67, "Welfare Centre for Kikuyu Children," *East African Standard*, 27 August 1955; SOAS CBMS A/T/2/6 Box 279, File 1, Kenya Rehabilitation, Miss Haig, 1955, R. G. M. Calderwood, Chairmen, CCK, Rehabilitation Committee, February 1957; and KNA AB/17/68; J. J. de G. Delmege to J. Miller, Assistant SCD, 12 February 1958.

87. KNA AB/17/66, "Langata 'Boys' Town' for Kikuyu Children," *Sunday Post*, 6 November 1955.

88. Interview by author: Gabriel Kahugu Muchahi, April 2008, Ndenderu, Kiambu.

89. Kariuki, "*Mau Mau*" *Detainee*, 61; and Elkins, *Imperial Reckoning*, 95–96, 131, 149.

90. Elkins, *Imperial Reckoning*, 124, 131.

91. Anderson, *Histories of the Hanged*, 5.

92. Kariuki, "*Mau Mau*" *Detainee*, 60–61; and interview by author: Alan Ale Kanyingi Ngugi, 19 May 2008, Githunguri, Kiambu.

93. Kariuki, "*Mau Mau*" *Detainee*, 79–80; and Elkins, *Imperial Reckoning*, 109, 135–36.

94. Interview by author: James Karanja Kariuki, 6 April 2008, Gilgil.

95. Interview by author: Joseph Gikubu, 24 August 2005, Starehe, Nairobi.

96. LSHTM PNHU 113, Kenya Medical and Health Surveys, Dr. H. Stott, Medical Advisor, Labour Department, "Report on Health and Hygiene in Emergency Camps," 6 November 1954; and G. R. Wadsworth, Pellagra in Kenya, 23 January to 6 April 1956.

97. Interview by author: Joseph Gikubu, 24 August 2005, Starehe, Nairobi.

98. Elkins, *Imperial Reckoning*, 190.

99. Interview by author: Joseph Gikubu, 24 August 2005, Starehe, Nairobi.

100. Wamweya, *Freedom Fighter*, 178–87.

101. Kariuki, "*Mau Mau*" *Detainee*, 65–77.

102. Derek R. Peterson, "The Intellectual Lives of Mau Mau Detainees," *Journal of African History* 49, no. 1 (2008): 75.

103. Interview by author: Harry Joseph Kimanji, 6 April 2008, Gilgil.

104. Ibid.

105. TNA:PRO CO 859/575, Outward Telegram from SSC to Governor of Kenya, 3 December 1954; and KNA AH/14/25, Emergency Joint Staff, Measures to Control Juvenile Vagrants, 29 January 1955.

106. KNA BZ/16/3, G. M. Kimani, APO, Langata: Ending Report, 31 March 1955; and KNA AB/1/116, W. F. B. Pollock-Morris, Sec. Defense to Comm. Prisons, Transfer of Juvenile Detainees from Manyani, 15 June 1955.

107. KNA BZ/16/3, G. M. Kimani, APO to PPO, 4 February 1955 and 31 March 1955.

108. Interview by author: Joseph Gikubu, 24 August 2005, Starehe, Nairobi.

109. Anderson, *Histories of the Hanged*, 7.

110. KNA BY/52/1, W. G. S. Hopkirk, Adviser in Radiology, European Hospital, Kariuki Karuma v. Regina, 24 August 1954.

111. I believe it is possible that through a corruption of Gikuyu or misspelling, Kariuki Karuma was in fact Simon Kariuki Kuriaa. The timing of their cases also suggests they might be the same person.

112. Interview by author: Simon Kariuki Kuriaa, 22 May 2008, Ongata-Rongai.

113. Interview by author: John Nottingham, 17 August 2005, Nairobi.

114. KNA ARC/MAA/7/821, PC Central to MAA, Youth Camps: Kangema, Kandara, and Kigumo, 6 December 1954.

115. Ibid.

116. KNA VB/2/21, T. G. Askwith, CCDR, Rehabilitation, 6 January 1954; and Askwith, *From Mau Mau to Harambee*, 148.

CHAPTER 7: "WE'RE THE WAMUMU BOYS"

1. Interview by author: Joseph Gikubu, 24 August 2005, Starehe, Nairobi; Geoffrey W. Griffin and Yusuf M. King'ala, *The Autobiography of Dr. G. W. Griffin: Kenya's Champion Beggar* (Nairobi: Falcon Crest, 2005), 45–46.

2. Griffin, *Autobiography of Dr. G. W. Griffin*, 49. On Wamumu, see also Erin Bell, "'A Most Horrifying Maturity in Crime': Age, Gender and Juvenile Delinquency in Colonial Kenya during the Mau Mau Uprising," *Atlantic Studies* 11, no. 4 (2014): 480–81.

3. Interview by author: Simon Kariuki Kuriaa, 22 May 2008, Ongata-Rongai.

4. KNA AB/1/116 W. F. B. Pollock-Morris, Sec. Defense, to Com. Prisons, Transfer of Juvenile Detainees from Manyani, 15 June 1955; and G. Gardener, OC Wamumu to PPO, Monthly Report, 6 June 1956.

5. Caroline Elkins, *Imperial Reckoning: The Untold Story of Britain's Gulag in Kenya* (New York: Holt, 2005), 190.

6. KNA AB/2/31, T. G. Askwith, Rehabilitation, 12 April 1954.

7. Caroline Elkins, "Alchemy of Evidence: Mau Mau, the British Empire, and the High Court of Justice," *Journal of Imperial and Commonwealth History* 39, no. 5 (2011): 731–48.

8. TNA:PRO FCO/141/6331, Thomas Askwith, Comm. Community Development and Rehabilitation, to Secretary of the Official Committee on Resettlement, Juvenile Detainees, 2 May 1955.

9. Linda Chisholm, "Education, Punishment and the Contradictions of Penal Reform: Alan Paton and Diepkloof Reformatory, 1934–1948," *Journal of Southern African Studies* 17, no. 1 (1991): 23–42.

10. KNA AB/1/116, W. F. B. Pollock-Morris, Sec. Defense, to Com. Prisons, Transfer of Juvenile Detainees from Manyani, 15 June 1955.

11. TNA:PRO FCO/141/6331, R. F. F. Owles, CDO, Report on Juvenile Mau Mau Detainees (Under 16 Years) at Manyani Special Camp, Appendix 1 to R.C. (55)33, no date, and R. F. F. Owles, CDO, to Comm. of Community Development, Juveniles/Manynai, 11 May 1955.

12. KNA AB/1/116, W. F. B. Pollock-Morris, Secretary of Defense, to Commissioner of Prisons, "Transfer of Juvenile Detainees from Manyani," 15 June 1955; and Griffin, *Autobiography of Dr. G. W. Griffin*, 46–47.

13. KNA AB/1/116, DC Fort Hall to Secretary of Defense, "Transfer of Juvenile Detainees," 2 August 1955.

14. Interviews by author: James Karanja Kariuki, 6 April 2008, Gilgil; and Samuel Uiru Kaguara, 26 April 2008, Ndenderu, Kiambu.

15. KNA VB/2/21, Rehabilitation Progress Report, 1955, 3 January 1956; and KNA AB/1/116, CCD to Sec. Defense, Juveniles, 19 August 1955, Press Handout: New Rehabilitation Camp for African Youths, 8 September 1955; and *East African Standard*, 14 September 1955.

16. Ngugi Kabiro, *The Man in the Middle: The Story of Ngugi Kabiro* (Richmond, BC: Liberation Support Movement Information Centre, 1973), 70–71; and KNA VQ/21/3, Wamumu Approved School and Youth Camp Annual Report, 1956.

17. Interview by author: Simon Kariuki Kuriaa, 22 May 2008, Ongata-Rongai.

18. Griffin, *Autobiography of Dr. G. W. Griffin*, 51–52.

19. Interview by author: Joseph Gikubu, 24 August 2005, Starehe, Nairobi; Griffin, *Autobiography of Dr. G. W. Griffin*, 51–52; and KNA AB/1/116, G. Gardener, OC Wamumu, to CCD, Escape from Wamumu, 28 September 1955; G. Gardener, OC Wamumu to CCD, Exile of Detainees, 28 September 1955. It should be noted that George Gardener referred to the escapee as Edward Maina Kamau in his correspondences with the department of community development. Yet Joseph Gikubu and Geoffrey Griffin each separately confirmed that it had been Simon Kariuki. Simon himself also recounted the story to me.

20. KNA VQ/21/3, G. Gardener, OC Wamumu, Approved School and Youth Camp Annual Report, 1956.

21. Griffin, *Autobiography of Dr. G. W. Griffin*, 51; and KNA VQ/21/3, Rehabilitation of Youth, 1956.

22. Colony and Protectorate of Kenya (CPK), Annual Report of the Ministry of Community Development, 1956, 39–40.

23. SOAS CBMS A/T/2/6 Box 279, Rev. H. D. Hooper, "We're the Wamumu Boys," December 1956; emphasis mine.

24. KNA VQ/21/3, G. Gardener, OC Wamumu, Approved School and Youth Camp Annual Report, 1956.

25. KNA BZ/16/1, S. J. Moore, Probation to PPO, "Re: Surrendered Terrorists," 14 June 1954; AB/1/116, G. Gardener, OC Wamumu, Policy: Approved School and Youth Camp, Wamumu, 24 November 1955; Thomas G. Askwith, *From Mau Mau to Harambee: Memoirs and Memoranda of Colonial Kenya* (Cambridge: African Studies Centre, 1995); and Louis S. B. Leakey, *Defeating Mau Mau* (London: Methuen, 1954), 85–86.

26. TNA:PRO FCO/141/6331, Thomas Askwith, Comm. of Community Development and Rehabilitation, to Secretary of the Official Committee on Resettlement, Juvenile Detainees, 2 May 1955.

27. Derek R. Peterson, *Ethnic Patriotism and the East African Revival: A History of Dissent, c. 1935–1972* (Cambridge: Cambridge University Press, 2012), 240.

28. Interviews by author: Gabriel Kahugu Muchahi, Samuel Uiru Kaguara, and Peter Mwarangu Ngugi, 26 April 2008, Ndenderu, Kiambu. Later, a fifth dormitory called Junior was built for Wamumu's youngest members. Junior house members' uniforms were white.

29. KNA AH/9/23, "Re-Shaping Minds Warped by Mau Mau," *East African Standard*, 19 January 1956.

30. Interview by author: Peter Mwarangu Ngugi, 26 April 2008, Ndenderu, Kiambu.

31. KNA VQ/21/3, Wamumu Approved School and Youth Camp Annual Report, 1956; and CPK, Annual Report of the Ministry of Community Development, 1956,

40–41. Scouting was also an integral part of daily life at Wamumu. Timothy H. Parsons, *Race, Resistance, and the Boy Scout Movement in British Colonial Africa* (Athens: Ohio University Press, 2004), 171–74.

32. Interview by author: Peter Mwarangu Ngugi, 26 April 2008, Ndenderu, Kiambu.

33. Ibid.

34. Interviews by author: Peter Mwarangu Ngugi, 26 April 2008, Ndenderu, Kiambu; Simon Kariuki Kuriaa, 22 May 2008, Ongata-Rongai; and interview by John Gitau Kariuki: John Mwangi Chege, 8 June 2008, Gilgil.

35. Interviews by author: Joseph Gikubu, 24 August 2005, Starehe, Nairobi; Peter Mwarangu Ngugi, Gabriel Kahugu Muchahi, and Samuel Uiru Kaguara, 26 April 2008, Ndenderu, Kiambu; Joseph Kingara Kimani, 7 May 2008, Kagwe, Kiambu; Simon Kariuki Kuriaa, 22 May 2008, Ongata-Rongai; and Patrick Michael Gichengu Njoroge, 27 May 2008, Mukurweini, Nyeri.

36. Kabiro, *Man in the Middle*, 70; and interview by author: Simon Kariuki Kuriaa, 22 May 2008, Ongata-Rongai.

37. KNA AB/1/116, Officer-in-Charge, Monthly Report, 4 April 1956.

38. KNA AB/1/116, Empire Day Parade, Wamumu Approved School, n.d..

39. Ibid.

40. John C. Carothers, *The Psychology of Mau Mau* (Nairobi: Government Printer, 1954), 25.

41. Interview by author: Joseph Gikubu, 14 May 2008, Starehe, Nairobi.

42. Eileen Fletcher, *Truth about Kenya: An Eye-Witness Account* (London: Movement for Colonial Freedom, 1956).

43. Interview by author: Joseph Kingara Kimani, 7 May 2008, Kagwe, Kiambu. Several Gikuyu men, who had never set foot in the youth camp and had been initiated in their villages, insisted that this was a common phrase spoken during initiation to motivate those about to face the knife. I would like to thank Chege Njuguna, John Gitau Kairuki, and Kingara Kimani for stressing this point.

44. Interviews by author: Simon Kariuki Kuriaa, 22 May 2008, Ongata-Rongai; Gabriel Kahugu Muchahi and Samuel Uiru Kaguara, 26 April 2008, Ndenderu, Kiambu.

45. Interview by author: Joseph Gikubu, 14 May 2008, Starehe, Nairobi.

46. Interview by author: Simon Kariuki Kuriaa, 22 May 2008, Ongata-Rongai.

47. KNA MA/1/3, DC Limuru to DC Kiambu, 22 November 1955.

48. KNA VQ/21/3, G. Gardener, OC Wamumu, Wamumu Approved School and Youth Camp Annual Report, 1956.

49. Interview by John Gitau Kariuki: John Mwangi Chege, 8 June 2008, Gilgil.

50. Interview by author: Joseph Gikubu, 14 May 2008, Starehe, Nairobi.

51. KNA AB/1/116, G. Gardener, OC Wamumu, Monthly Report, 4 April 1956; and VQ/21/3, C. M. Johnston to PAO Nyeri, Wamumu Approved School, 15 June 1956.

52. Donald G. Schilling, "British Policy for African Education in Kenya, 1895–1939" (PhD diss., University of Wisconsin-Madison, 1972), 245; and Kenneth J. King, "Africa and the Southern States of the U.S.A.: Notes on J. H. Oldham and American Negro Education for Africans," *Journal of African History* 10, no. 4 (1969): 659–77.

53. RHL MSS Afr. s. 424 ff. 158–68, F. J. Harlow, Assistant Educational Advisor for Technical Education, "Memorandum on the Problem of Training Skilled Craftsmen in East Africa," n.d.. See also Kenneth J. King, *Jua Kali Kenya: Change and Development in an Informal Economy, 1970–95* (Athens: Ohio University Press, 1995).

54. Interview by John Gitau Kariuki: John Mwangi Chege, 8 June 2008, Gilgil;

KNA AB/1/116, G. Gardener, OC Wamumu, Monthly Report, 5 December 1955; and CPK, Annual Report of the Ministry of Community Development, 1956, 40.

55. Interviews by author: Peter Mwarangu Ngugi and Gabriel Kahugu Muchahi, 26 April 2008, Ndenderu, Kiambu.

56. Interviews by author: Gabriel Kahugu Muchahi and Samuel Uiru Kaguara, 26 April 2008, Ndenderu, Kiambu.

57. KNA AB/1/117, Wamumu Approved School to Civic Nairobi, Kenya Prisons Signal, 26 October 1957, and G. Gardener, OC Wamumu, to Sec. Kenya Sisal Growers Association, 15 September 1957; and KNA VQ/21/3, Letter from C. R. Tofte to G. Gardener, OC Wamumu, 26 October 1956; Riverglade Manager to G. Gardener, OC Wamumu, 28 January 1957, among many other citations in the file.

58. KNA VQ/21/3, Special Assistant to Special Commissioner, Ref. 67 and 74, 1956; and interviews by author: Joseph Gikubu, 24 August 2005, Starehe, Nairobi; and Simon Kariuki Kuriaa, 22 May 2008, Ongat-Rongai.

59. Interview by author: Simon Kariuki Kuriaa, 22 May 2008, Ongat-Rongai.

60. Interview by author: Gabriel Kahugu Muchahi, 26 April 2008, Ndenderu, Kiambu.

61. KNA VQ/21/3, Rehabilitation of Youth, 1956.

62. Askwith, *From Mau Mau to Harambee*, 152.

63. Derek R. Peterson, "The Intellectual Lives of Mau Mau Detainees," *Journal of African History* 49, no. 1 (2008): 76–79, 81–86.

64. CPK, Annual Report of the Ministry of Community Development, 1956, 39, 42.

65. Interview by author: Peter Mwarangu Ngugi, 26 April 2008, Ndenderu, Kiambu.

66. KNA AB/2/45, Comm. Prisons to Sec. Defence, Juveniles in E.R. Camps, 21 January 1956.

67. Anthony Clayton, *Counter-Insurgency in Kenya* (Manhattan, KS: Sunflower Press, 1984), 30–31.

68. Interview by author: James Karanja Kariuki, 6 April 2008, Gilgil.

69. KNA AB/2/45, Comm. Prisons to Sec. Community Development, Juveniles in Camps (E.R.), 17 May 1956.

70. KNA BZ/16/3, SCD to PPO, 7 January 1957.

71. KNA AB/2/45, Sec. Defence to SCD, 23 September 1955.

72. KNA AB/2/45, J. Cusack, Defence, to B. A. Ohanga, Community Development, Disposal of Juvenile Convicts, 4 February 1957.

73. Luise White, "Separating the Men from the Boys: Constructions of Gender, Sexuality, and Terrorism in Central Kenya, 1939–1959," *International Journal of African Historical Studies* 23, no. 1 (1990): 20; Cora A. Presley, *Kikuyu Women, the Mau Mau Rebellion, and Social Change in Kenya* (Boulder, CO: Westview Press, 1992), 165–67; and Elkins, *Imperial Reckoning*, 261–62.

74. KNA AB/2/67, B. A. Ohanga, Community Development, Declaration of Approved School, 2 November 1956.

75. KNA AB/1/115, P. Mulcahy-Morgan, SCD, to DC Meru, Mau Mau Camp: Igoji, 9 March 1956; E. M. Usher, Sec. Treasury, to SCD, 21 May 1956; D. G. Hughes, DC Meru, to R. Tatton-Brown, CCD, 16 June 1956; and D. G. Hughes, DC Meru, to Sec. Defence, 16 June 1956.

76. Elkins, *Imperial Reckoning*, 220–29, 287–90.

77. Tabitha M. Kanogo, *Squatters and the Roots of Mau Mau, 1905–63* (Athens: Ohio University Press, 1987), 137–48; Presley, *Kikuyu Women*, 140–44; and SOAS

CBMS Papers, A/T/2/5 Box 278 and TNA:PRO CO 822/1239, Kenya Further Memorandum on Allegations Published by Miss Eileen Fletcher on Conditions in Prisons and Camps.

78. Bethwell A. Ogot, "The Decisive Years: 1956–63," in *Decolonization and Independence in Kenya, 1940–93,* ed. Bethwell A. Ogot and William R. Ochieng' (Athens: Ohio University Press, 1995), 61; and Robert L. Tignor, *Capitalism and Nationalism at the End of Empire: State and Business in Decolonizing Egypt, Nigeria, and Kenya, 1945–1963* (Princeton, NJ: Princeton University Press, 1998), 335–38.

79. Interview by author: Don Diment, 15 June 2004, Farnham; and Bruce J. Berman, *Control and Crisis in Colonial Kenya: The Dialectic of Domination* (Athens: Ohio University Press, 1990), 364.

80. Berman, *Control and Crisis in Colonial Kenya,* 361.

81. Maurice P. K. Sorrenson, *Land Reform in the Gikuyu Country: A Study in Government Policy* (Nairobi: Oxford University Press, 1967), 110; Berman, *Control and Crisis in Colonial Kenya,* 367–78; and Daniel Branch, "The Enemy Within: Loyalists and the War against Mau Mau in Kenya," *Journal of African History* 48, no. 2 (2007): 303–6.

82. Elkins, *Imperial Reckoning,* 235.

83. KNA AB/2/62, P. Crichton for Secretary of Health to Chief Inspector of Children, Nairobi, 25 August 1956.

84. KNA MA/5/12, Rev. Macpherson, Orphans and Other Necessitous Children in the Peri-Urban Areas of Kiambu, 29 June 1955.

85. KNA BY/12/30, CSM Gikuyu, Children in Kiambu District, 29 July 1955; and SOAS CBMS A/T/2/6 Box 279, Christian Council of Kenya, Committee on Rehabilitation, 6 September 1955.

86. KNA DC/EMB/2/1/1, J. C. Nottingham, DO North Tetu, Juvenile Reception Centres, 26 February 1959. See also KNA MA/5/12, Minutes of the Sociological Committee, 14 February 1956; and BZ/9/20, Scorrer Report, 1957.

87. KNA AH/14/25, E. W. Moylan, EO, NEPD to War Council, Juveniles in Nairobi, 16 May 1955 and 14 June 1955; and AB/2/66, Mrs. E. E. Jackson, DO NEPD, Nairobi, 4 May 1956. For corporal punishment records, see KNA AH/6/16 and KNA AP/1/1876.

88. TNA:PRO CO 859/573, SSA. 63/6/01, SSC to the Officers Administrating the Governments of Kenya, Uganda, Tanganyika, Somaliland Protectorate, and the British Resident, Zanzibar, 28 June 1956. Adding Mau Mau and emergency-related offenses to the figure, the rate of convictions totaled six times the number of young people convicted in the rest of East Africa.

89. Interview by author: Don Diment, 15 June 2004, Farnham.

90. KNA DC/EMB/2/1/1, J. C. Nottingham, DO North Tetu, Juvenile Reception Centres, 26 February 1959.

91. KNA BZ/8/13, C. S. Owen, Rehabilitation of Youth, 23 April 1956.

92. KNA BZ/8/6, C. S. Owen, Working Paper, Commission for Technical Cooperation in Africa South of the Sahara (CCTA), Second Meeting of the Conference on the Treatment of Offenders (Juvenile Delinquents), Kampala, 1956.

93. Jordanna Bailkin, *The Afterlife of Empire* (Berkeley: University of California Press, 2012), 15–18; and David Bakan, "Adolescence in America: From Idea to Social Fact," *Daedalus* 100, no. 4 (1971): 979–95.

94. Harry Hendrick, *Images of Youth: Age, Class, and the Male Youth Problem, 1880–1920* (Oxford: Clarendon, 1990), 86–88, 104; Victor Bailey, *Delinquency and Citi-*

zenship: Reclaiming the Young Offender, 1914–1948 (Oxford: Oxford University Press, 1987), 11–14. See also Geoffrey Pearson, Hooligan: A History of Respectable Fears (London: Macmillan, 1983).

95. John Springhall, Youth, Popular Culture and Moral Panics: Penny Gaffs to Gangsta-Rap, 1830–1996 (New York: Palgrave Macmillan, 1999); David Fowler, Youth Culture in Modern Britain, c.1920–1970 (New York: Palgrave Macmillan, 2008); Sarah Fishman, The Battle for Children: World War II, Youth Crime, and Juvenile Justice in Twentieth-Century France (Cambridge, MA: Harvard University Press, 2002); and Richard I. Jobs, Riding the New Wave: Youth and the Rejuvenation of France after the Second World War (Stanford, CA: Stanford University Press, 2007).

96. KNA DC/EMB/2/1/1, John C. Nottingham, District Officer, North Tetu Division. "Juvenile Reception Centres."

97. KNA BZ/8/13, C. S. Owen, Rehabilitation of Youth, 23 April 1956.

98. KNA JZ/6/26, P. Mulcahy-Morgan for Acting SCD, The Juvenile Problem: The Character Training of Juveniles, 29 June 1956.

99. Hendrick, Images of Youth, 96.

100. Joanna Lewis, Empire State-Building: War and Welfare in Kenya, 1925–52 (Athens: Ohio University Press, 2001); Eric T. Jennings, Vichy in the Tropics: Petain's National Revolution in Madagascar, Guadeloupe, and Indochina (Stanford, CA: Stanford University Press, 2001), 66–68; and Anne Raffin, Youth Mobilization in Vichy Indochina and Its Legacies, 1940–1970 (Lanham, MD: Lexington Books, 2005).

101. John Springhall, Youth, Empire and Society: British Youth Movements, 1883–1940 (London: Taylor and Francis, 1977), 18.

102. Springhall, Youth, Empire and Society, 125–26; Hendrick, Images of Youth, 158–80.

103. Robert S. S. Baden-Powell, Scouting for Boys: A Handbook for Instruction in Good Citizenship (London: Horace Cox, 1908), 282.

104. Bailkin, Afterlife of Empire, 73.

105. Ibid., 60–61, 74.

106. KNA AB/16/11, G. W. Griffin, CYO, to Ministry of Community Development, A Study of the Youth Problem among the Gikuyu, Embu, and Meru Tribes, 17 November 1957.

107. Interview by author: Joseph Kingara Kimani, 7 May 2008, Kagwe, Kiambu.

108. KNA BZ/1/23, C. S. Owen, PPO and CIAS, to All Probation Stations, Approved School Admissions, 7 June 1957.

109. KNA VQ/21/3, J. Miller, SCD, to PC Central, Emergency Welfare of Children Regulations, 9 April 1958.

110. KNA AB/4/44, W. E. Moseley, OC Mukurweini, Annual Report, 13 February 1958.

111. Griffin, Autobiography of Dr. G. W. Griffin, 55–56.

112. TNA:PRO CO 885/103, Juvenile Welfare in the Colonies, 8 October 1942, 11.

113. Ibid., 10.

114. Lewis, Empire State-Building, 174–77; and interview by author: June Knowles, 8 June 2004, Watlington, Oxford. With permission from June Knowles, I also consulted the personal papers of Olga Watkins: E. Carey Francis, Alliance High School, to Olga Watkins, Whispers Farm, 4 May 1946; and Letter from Pat Williams to Olga Watkins, 6 May 1946. The Scorrer Report of 1957 also resuscitated the idea of rural youth clubs.

TNA:PRO CO 822/1240, W. H. Chinn, Colonial Officer, from Commissioner of Prisons, 28 February 1957; and BZ/9/20, Scorrer Report, 1957.

115. KNA BY/12/33, G. W. Griffin, Chief Executive Officer, Kenya Association of Youth Clubs, "Youth Organization: Kenya Colony, Progress Report," January 1960.

116. KNA AB/16/139, G. W. Griffin, CYO, "Youth Organization—Kenya Colony: Interim Report to the Council of the Kenya Association of Youth Clubs," 8 June 1958.

117. KNA AB/16/11, T. G. Askwith, SCD, to G. W. Griffin, CYO, 2 September 1957; and T. G. Askwith, SCD, Youth Scheme, 12 November 1957.

118. Interviews by author: Don Diment, 15 June 2004, Farnham; and Peter Moll, 14 May 2008, Westlands, Nairobi.

119. KNA AB/16/139, J. Miller for SCD to all PCs, Kenya Association of Youth Clubs, 8 July 1958; and G. Griffin, Colony Youth Organizer, Youth Organization—Kenya Colony: Interim Report to the Council of the Kenya Association of Youth Clubs, Together with Recommendations for Future Policy, 8 June 1958, 7.

120. TNA:PRO CO 822/1671, Press Office, Department of Information, Handout No. 842, Minister for African Affairs Opens Starehe Youth Club, 14 November 1959.

121. Interview by author: Don Diment, 15 June 2004, Farnham.

122. Interview by author: Simon Kariuki Kuriaa, 22 May 2008, Ongata-Rongai.

123. Interview by author: Joseph Gikubu, 24 August 2005, Starehe, Nairobi.

124. Griffin held his youth leadership training courses at Wamumu, offering detainees a chance to transition out of the camp. As the number of Mau Mau detainees dwindled and the pool of youth leaders dried up, Griffin moved the training program to Jeane's School. KNA BY/12/33, G. W. Griffin, Chief Executive Officer, Kenya Association of Youth Clubs, Youth Organization: Kenya Colony, Progress Report, January 1960.

125. KNA AB/16/20, G. W. Griffin, CYO, to T. G. Askwith CCD, 12 April 1958.

126. TNA:PRO CO 822/1672, "Chain of Youth Clubs Cuts Juvenile Crime in Gikuyuland," East African Standard, 19 September 1958.

127. Interviews by author: Don Diment, 15 June 2004, Farnham; and Peter Moll, 21 August 2005, Westlands, Nairobi.

128. KNA AB/16/18, "Old Gikuyu Custom Helps Solve A Problem for Modern Youth," East African Standard, 23 August 1957.

129. William S. Routledge and Katherine Routledge, With a Prehistoric People: The Akikuyu of British East Africa (London: Arnold, 1910), 164; Jomo Kenyatta, Facing Mount Kenya: The Tribal Life of the Gikuyu (New York: Vintage Books, 1965), 147–48; Leakey, Defeating Mau Mau, 624–65; and interviews by author: David Chege Njuguna, 19 May 2008, Kagwe, Kiambu; and Wachira Mwaniki, 25 May 2008, Burguret, Laikipia.

130. KNA AB/16/18, "Old Gikuyu Custom Helps Solve A Problem for Modern Youth," East African Standard, 23 August 1957.

131. TNA:PRO CO 822/1671, Office of Information, Handout No. 471, 14 July 1959, and Handout No. 701, 9 October 1959.

132. KNA BY/12/33, G. W. Griffin, Chief Executive Officer, Kenya Association of Youth Clubs, Youth Organization: Kenya Colony, Progress Report, January 1960.

133. KNA DC/GRSSA/7/22, Ministry of African Affairs, Directive by the Minister for African Affairs, 26 January 1960.

134. KNA AB/16/13, T. G. Askwith, CCD, to CYO, Youth Club: Boys Scouts, 3 April 1958.

135. Interviews by author: Alan Ale Kanyingi Ngugi, 19 May 2008, Githunguri, Kiambu; and Rev. Patrick Mugwe Njoroge, 27 May 2008, Mukurweini, Nyeri. In fact, today the institutions are known as "rehabilitation schools."

136. KNA AB/16/139, G. W. Griffin, CYO, Youth Organization—Kenya Colony: Interim Report to the Council of the Kenya Association of Youth Clubs, 8 June 1958.

137. CPK, Report on the Treatment of Offenders for the Year 1960.

138. KNA AHL/2/9, R. G. Strong, CIAS, Inspection Report of Nairobi Juvenile Remand Home, 21 August 1961; and AHL/2/7, R. G. Strong, CIAS, Report to Minister No. 1, 11 July 1963.

CHAPTER 8: "AN ARMY WITHOUT GUNS"

1. *Kenya Weekly News*, 21 February 1964.

2. Daniel Branch and Nicholas Cheeseman, "Introduction: Our Turn to Eat," in *Our Turn to Eat: Politics in Kenya since 1950*, ed. Daniel Branch, Nicholas Cheeseman, and Leigh Gardner (New Brunswick, NJ: Transaction Publishers, 2010), 11–12; and Jennifer A. Widner, *The Rise of a Party-State in Kenya: From "Harambee!" to "Nyayo!"* (Berkeley: University of California Press, 1992).

3. Daniel Branch and Nicholas Cheeseman, "The Politics of Control in Kenya: Understanding the Bureaucratic-Executive State, 1952–78," *Review of African Political Economy* 33, no. 107 (2006): 21.

4. Branch and Cheeseman, "Introduction: Our Turn to Eat," 13.

5. Aristide R. Zolberg, "Youth as a Political Phenomenon in Tropical Africa," *Youth and Society* 1, no. 2 (1969): 199–200.

6. G. Thomas Burgess and Andrew Burton, introduction to *Generations Past: Youth in East African History*, ed. Andrew Burton and Hélène Charton-Bigot (Athens: Ohio University Press, 2010), 11–12.

7. Bruce J. Berman and John M. Lonsdale, "The Labors of *Muigwithania*: Jomo Kenyatta as Author, 1928–45," *Research in African Literatures* 29, no. 1 (1998): 16–42.

8. Andrew Burton, "Raw Youth, School-Leavers, and the Emergence of Structural Unemployment in Late-Colonial Urban Tanganyika," *Journal of African History* 47, no. 3 (2006): 365.

9. John M. Lonsdale, "KAU's Cultures: Imaginations of Community and Constructions of Leadership in Kenya after the Second World War," *Journal of African Cultural Studies* 13, no. 1 (2000): 117.

10. Dennis Austin, "The Working Committee of the United Gold Coast Convention," *Journal of African History* 2, no. 2 (1961): 273–97; and Jean M. Allman, "The Disappearing of Hannah Kudjoe: Nationalism, Feminism, and the Tyrannies of History," *Journal of Women's History* 21, no. 3 (2009): 19–23.

11. Jean M. Allman, *The Quills of the Porcupine: Asante Nationalism in an Emergent Ghana* (Madison: University of Wisconsin Press, 1993), 33–36.

12. Mamadou Diouf, "Engaging Postcolonial Cultures: African Youth and Public Space," *African Studies Review* 46, no. 2 (2003): 3–4.

13. Jean Comaroff and John L. Comaroff, "Reflections on Youth: From the Past to the Postcolony," in *Makers and Breakers: Children and Youth in Postcolonial Africa*, ed. Alcinda M. Honwana and Filip de Boeck (Trenton, NJ: Africa World Press, 2005), 29.

14. Andrew Ivaska, *Cultured States: Youth, Gender, and Modern Style in 1960s Dar es Salaam* (Durham, NC: Duke University Press, 2011), 41.

15. Jay Straker, *Youth, Nationalism, and the Guinean Revolution* (Bloomington: Indiana University Press, 2009), 89, 102–4.

16. Zolberg, "Youth as a Political Phenomenon," 208, 212.

17. Jeffrey S. Ahlman, "A New Type of Citizen: Youth, Gender, and Generation in the Ghanaian Builders Brigade," *Journal of African History* 53, no. 1 (2012): 92, 96–98.

18. Ibid., 102. See also Jeremy J. Pool, "Now Is the Time of Youth: Youth, Nationalism and Cultural Change in Ghana, 1940–1966" (PhD diss., Emory University, 2009), 187–232; Catie Coe, *Dilemmas of Culture in African Schools: Youth, Nationalism, and the Transformation of Knowledge* (Chicago: University of Chicago Press, 2005), 65–70; and Peter Hodge, "The Ghana Workers Brigade: A Project for Unemployed Youth," *British Journal of Sociology* 15, no. 2 (1964): 113–28. Eager to assist his newly elected colleagues, Nkrumah sent his Young Pioneers to Malawi, where they assisted the Israeli National Service Brigade with establishing a similar organization for Hastings Banda. Banda used the Young Pioneers and his party's youth wing to violently tighten his grip on power. Kings M. Phiri, "A Case of Revolutionary Change in Contemporary Malawi: The Malawi Army and the Disarming of the Malawi Young Pioneers," *Journal of Peace, Conflict and Military Studies* 1, no. 1 (2000), http://malawi.freehosting.net /article3.html.

19. James R. Brennan, "Youth, the TANU Youth League and Managed Vigilantism in Dar es Salaam, Tanzania, 1925–73," *Africa* 76, no. 2 (2006): 229. For the most recent treatment of the TANU Youth League, see Priya Lal, *African Socialism in Postcolonial Tanzania: Between the Village and the World* (Cambridge: Cambridge University Press, 2015), 79–101.

20. In revolutionary Zanzibar, too, the language of age permeated calls for nation building and development in the 1960s and 1970s. Like Nyerere, Zanzibari politicians linked youth with obedience to elder authority and a spirit of volunteerism. The Afro-Shirazi Party Youth League, and later its own version of the Young Pioneers, was crucial in bringing Abeid Karume to power in 1964, and then sustaining his regime and that of his predecessor, Aboud Jumbe. G. Thomas Burgess, "Remembering Youth: Generation in Revolutionary Zanzibar," *Africa Today* 46, no. 2 (1999): 39–43; and Burgess, "The Young Pioneers and the Rituals of Citizenship in Revolutionary Zanzibar," *Africa Today* 51, no. 3 (2005): 11.

21. Paul Bjerk, *Building a Peaceful Nation: Julius Nyerere and the Establishment of Sovereignty in Tanzania, 1960–1964* (Rochester, NY: University of Rochester Press, 2015), 178.

22. Ivaska, *Cultured States*, 60–68.

23. Brennan, "Youth, the TANU Youth League and Managed Vigilantism," 233.

24. Geoffrey W. Griffin and Yusuf M. King'ala, *The Autobiography of Dr. G. W. Griffin: Kenya's Champion Beggar* (Nairobi: Falcon Crest, 2005), 77.

25. Richard L. Coe, *The Kenya National Youth Service: A Governmental Response to Young Political Activists* (Athens: Ohio University Press, 1973), 11–13; and Kenya National Youth Service, *National Youth Service* (Nairobi: Government of Kenya, October 1964).

26. Griffin, *Autobiography of Dr. G. W. Griffin*, 77.

27. Ibid., 78.

28. Interview by author: Michael Muthee, 9 March 2008, Gilgil. Note that Michael Muthee is not the interviewee's real name. While willing to talk with me about his employment at the National Youth Service, Michael expressed some concern that the

issues we discussed were sensitive, political. He did not request his name be changed, but I have done so out of precaution and respect for what I believed were some of his anxieties.

29. E. S. Atieno-Odhiambo, "The Formative Years, 1945–55," in *Decolonization and Independence in Kenya, 1940–93,* ed. Bethwell A. Ogot and William R. Ochieng' (Athens: Ohio University Press, 1995), 40.

30. Daniel Branch, *Defeating Mau Mau, Creating Kenya: Counterinsurgency, Civil War, and Decolonization* (Cambridge: Cambridge University Press, 2009), 185–91.

31. Ibid., 155–77.

32. Bethwell A. Ogot, "The Decisive Years: 1956–63," in Ogot and Ochieng', *Decolonization and Independence in Kenya,* 51–61. For more on the various constitutions and meetings between African nationalists and the British during decolonization, see Robert M. Maxon, *Britain and Kenya's Constitutions, 1950–1960* (Amherst, NY: Cambria Press, 2011).

33. Charles Hornsby, *Kenya: A History since Independence* (New York: Taurus, 2012), 67–68.

34. Branch, *Defeating Mau Mau,* 179–82; and Jeremy Murray-Brown, *Kenyatta* (New York: Duncan, 1973), 366–71.

35. Ogot, "Decisive Years," 75.

36. *East African Standard,* 14 August 1963.

37. Cherry J. Gertzel, *The Politics of Independent Kenya* (Evanston, IL: Northwestern University Press, 1970), 82; and David W. Throup and Charles Hornsby, *Multi-Party Politics in Kenya: The Kenyatta and Moi States and the Triumph of the System in the 1992 Election* (Athens: Ohio University Press, 1998), 14.

38. Interview by author: Michael Muthee, 9 March 2008, Gilgil.

39. Richard H. F. Cox, *Kenyatta's Country* (New York: Praeger, 1965), 197–98.

40. Tom Mboya, *Freedom and After* (Boston: Little, Brown, 1963), 88–89.

41. Ibid., 90.

42. Interview by author: Michael Muthee, 9 March 2008, Gilgil.

43. Waruhiu Itote, *"Mau Mau" General* (Nairobi: East African Publishing, 1967), 261–68.

44. Ibid., 269–70.

45. Daniel Branch, "The Enemy Within: Loyalists and the War against Mau Mau in Kenya," *Journal of African History* 48, no. 2 (2007): 314–15.

46. Griffin, *Autobiography of Dr. G. W. Griffin,* 78–79; and Coe, *Kenya National Youth Service,* 27.

47. Diana Quarmby and Andrew Quarmby, *The Kenya National Youth Service* (Washington, DC: International Secretariat of Volunteer Services, 1969), 9, 14.

48. CPK, *National Assembly, Official Report,* 12 May 1965, 2131.

49. Kenneth J. King, *Jua Kali Kenya: Change and Development in an Informal Economy, 1970–95* (Athens: Ohio University Press, 1996).

50. Quarmby and Quarmby, *Kenya National Youth Service,* 5.

51. KNA AAL/14/1, CCTA, Second Symposium on Unemployed Youth, 1965.

52. Berman and Lonsdale, "Labors of *Muigwithania,*" 19.

53. George Delf, *Jomo Kenyatta: Towards Truth about "The Light of Kenya"* (Garden City, NY: Doubleday, 1961), 26.

54. Ibid., 43–45.

55. Murray-Brown, *Kenyatta,* 62. I suspect we will know much, much more about

Kenyatta's initiation with the arrival of John Lonsdale and Bruce Berman's forthcoming study of his life and times, especially what Murray-Brown meant by "exceptional."

56. Lynn M. Thomas, *Politics of the Womb: Women, Reproduction, and the State in Kenya* (Berkeley: University of California Press, 2000), 22–23.

57. Berman and Lonsdale, "Labors of *Muigwithania*," 19.

58. Delf, *Towards Truth about "The Light of Kenya*," 26.

59. David M. Anderson, *Histories of the Hanged: The Dirty War in Kenya and the End of Empire* (New York: Norton, 2005), 15–17; and Carl G. Rosberg and John C. Nottingham, *The Myth of "Mau Mau": Nationalism in Kenya* (Stanford, CA: Hoover Institute, 1966), 35–70.

60. Derek R. Peterson, *Creative Writing: Translation, Bookkeeping, and the Work of Imagination in Colonial Kenya* (Portsmouth, NH: Heinemann, 2004), 97; and Berman and Lonsdale, "Labors of *Muigwithania*," 17.

61. KNA DC/MKS/10B/13/1. I would like to thank Derek Peterson for providing me with access to the journal; and John M. Lonsdale, "'Listen While I Read': Patriotic Christianity among the Young Gikuyu," in *Christianity and Social Change in Africa: Essays in Honor of J. D. Y. Peel*, ed. Toyin Falola (Durham, NC: Carolina Academic Press, 2005), 572–73.

62. Peterson, *Creative Writing*, 97.

63. Berman and Lonsdale, "Labors of *Muigwithania*," 21.

64. Lonsdale, "Listen While I Read," 569.

65. Berman and Lonsdale, "Labors of *Muigwithania*," 20–22, 31–32.

66. Jomo Kenyatta, *Facing Mount Kenya: The Tribal Life of the Gikuyu* (New York: Vintage Books, 1965), 193–96.

67. Bruce J. Berman, "Ethnography as Politics, Politics as Ethnography: Kenyatta, Malinowski, and the Making of *Facing Mount Kenya*," *Canadian Journal of African Studies* 30, no. 3 (1996): 337.

68. Lonsdale, "KAU's Cultures," 114.

69. Throup and Hornsby, *Multi-Party Politics in Kenya*, 10–12; and Peter Anyang' Nyong'o, "State and Society in Kenya: The Disintegration of the Nationalist Coalitions and the Rise of Presidential Authoritarianism, 1963–78," *African Affairs* 88, no. 351 (1989): 229–51.

70. Gertzel, *Politics of Independent Kenya*, 170.

71. Ibid., 36–37; and Branch and Cheeseman, "Politics of Control in Kenya," 21–22.

72. Gary Wasserman, *Politics of Decolonization: Kenya Europeans and the Land Issue, 1960–1965* (Cambridge: Cambridge University Press, 1976).

73. Colin Leys, *Underdevelopment in Kenya: The Political Economy of Neo-Colonialism, 1964–1971* (Berkeley: University of California Press, 1975), 73–85; and Hornsby, *Kenya*, 74–77, 88, 116–21.

74. Kenya National Youth Service, *National Youth Service* (Nairobi: Government of Kenya, October 1964).

75. Library of Congress, Africa and Middle Easter Reading Room, Pamphlet Archive, Box Kenya Economics and Agriculture, Pamphlet 30 East African Literature Bureau, *Community Development: This Is Community Development in Kenya* (Nairobi, 1964); Pamphlet 8, Ministry of Cooperatives and Social Services, Youth Development Division, *How to Start a Work Group at Your Village Polytechnic* (Nairobi, 1972).

76. Widner, *Rise of a Party-State in Kenya*, 62–63.

77. Commonwealth Youth Programme, *Youth for Development: An African Per-

spective: *Report of a Workshop on National Youth Programmers and National Service,* Accra, Ghana, March 1975, 123–24.

78. Coe, *Kenya National Youth Service,* 14, 29–31.

79. David A. Percox, *Britain, Kenya and the Cold War: Imperial Defense, Colonial Security and Decolonization* (New York: Palgrave Macmillan, 2012), 170–71.

80. William Attwood, *The Reds and the Blacks: A Personal Adventure* (New York: Harper and Row, 1967), 160–64.

81. National Archives at College Park (NACP), Department of State, RG 59, Kenya, Political Affairs, Josiah Kariuki, Edward Mulcahy to Governor Williams, 8 June 1965. I would like to thank Daniel Branch for pointing me in the direction of these documents.

82. NACP Department of State, RG 59, Kenya, Political Affairs and Relations, China-Kenya Relations, Nalle, Department of State, Bureau of African Affairs, East Africa desk, "Countering Chicom Intrusion: Kenya," 18 May 1965.

83. NACP Department of State, RG 59, Kenya, Political Affairs & Relations, National Youth Service, MacKnight to Williams, 7 April 1965.

84. Ibid.

85. Widner, *Rise of a Party-State in Kenya,* 130–46.

86. Peter Mwangi Kagwanja, "'Power to Uhuru': Youth Identity and Generational Politics in Kenya's 2002 Elections," *African Affairs* 105, no. 418 (2005): 55–56.

87. Interview by author: Michael Muthee, 9 March 2008, Gilgil.

88. David M. Anderson, "Vigilantes, Violence and the Politics of Public Order in Kenya," *African Affairs* 101, no. 405 (2002): 547–53.

89. Peter Mwangi Kagwanja, "Facing Mount Kenya or Facing Mecca? The Mungiki, Ethnic Violence and the Politics of the Moi Succession in Kenya, 1987–2002," *African Affairs* 102, no. 406 (2002): 35.

90. Susanne D. Mueller, "The Resilience of the Past: Government and Opposition in Kenya," *Canadian Journal of African Studies* 48, no. 2 (2014): 339–41.

91. Peter Mwangi Kagwanja, "The Clash of Generations? Youth Identity, Ethnic Violence and the Politics of Moi Succession, 1991–2002," in *Vanguard or Vandals: Youth, Politics, and Conflict in Africa,* ed. Jon Abbink and Ineke van Kessel (Leiden: Brill, 2005), 81–109.

92. Kagwanja, "Facing Mount Kenya or Facing Mecca?" 36–41. For other perspectives on Mungiki, see Grace Nyatugah Wamue, "Revisiting Our Indigenous Shrines through Mungiki," *African Affairs* 100, no. 400 (2001): 453–67; and Terisae E. Turner and Leigh S. Brownhill, "African Jubliee: Mau Mau Resurgence and the Fight for Fertility in Kenya, 1986–2002," *Canadian Journal of Development Studies* 22, no. 4 (2001): 1037–88.

93. Kagwanja, "Power to Uhuru," 62–65.

CONCLUSION: #GOCUTMYHUSBAND

1. Edith Kimani, "39 Year Old Man Forcibly Circumcised in Bungoma County," KTN, 16 January 2015, accessed 27 July 2015, http://www.standardmedia.co.ke/ktnhome/video/watch/2000087928/39-year-old-man-forcefully-circumcised-in-bungoma-county.

2. Facebook, Inc., "KTN Kenya's Facebook page," last modified 18 January 2015, accessed 27 July 2015, https://www.facebook.com/hashtag/gocutmyhusband; and Twitter,

Inc., "#GoCutMyHusband twitter post," last modified 10 December 2015, accessed 27 July 2015, https://twitter.com/hashtag/gocutmyhusband.

3. Najma Ismail, "#GoCutMyHusband: Bungoma Woman Reveals Why She Ordered the Circumcision of Her Husband," *KTN*, 27 January 2015, accessed 25 July 2015, http://standardmedia.co.ke/ktnnews/video/watch/2000087966/-gocutmyhusband bungoma-woman-reveals-why-she-ordered-the-circumcision-of-her-husband. My thanks to Brian Mukhaya for his assistance with this translation.

4. Omar Egesah, *Male Circumcision in Africa: Ethnographic Evidence from the Bukusu, Kenya* (Saarbrücken: VDM, 2008); and Jan Jacob de Wolf, "Circumcision and Initiation in Western Kenya and Eastern Uganda: Historical Reconstructions and Ethnographic Evidence," *Anthropos* 78, nos. 3–4 (1983): 369–410.

5. The forced circumcision of older men who refused initiation in their youth also occurs in Uganda. Suzette Heald has discussed forced circumcision among the Gisu in Uganda. Heald, *Manhood and Morality: Sex, Violence and Ritual in Gisu Society* (London: Routledge, 1999), 13.

6. James Kuria, "Man Faces Knife after Wife's Betrayal," *East African Standard*, 27 April 2009, accessed 13 January 2016, http://www.standardmedia.co.ke/article /1144012605/man-faces-the-knife-after-wife-s-betrayal.

7. George Mugo, "Wife Sets Up Husband for Circumcision," *Star*, 21 July 2014, accessed 13 January 2016, http://allafrica.com/stories/201407212409.html.

8. Interview by author: Kimani Ng'ang'a Maruge, 23 June 2008, Kariobangi, Nairobi.

9. Mary Kamande, "Uncircumcised Elder Reckons with Peers in Death," *East African Standard*, 20 April 2012, accessed 13 January 2016, http://www.standardmedia.co.ke/article /2000057266/uncircumcised-elder-reckons-with-peers-in-death.

10. United Nations, *World Population Prospects, 2015 Revision* (New York: United Nations, 2015).

11. In 2006, the Kenyan government defined "youth" as those between the ages of fifteen and thirty. I therefore used the age of twenty-nine as the cutoff when calculating the proportion of Kenya's population defined as children and youth when using the United Nations population database. See the Ministry of Youth Affairs, *Kenya National Youth Policy, 2006* (Nairobi: Government of Kenya, 2006).

12. Daniel Branch, *Kenya: Between Hope and Despair, 1963–2011* (New Haven, CT: Yale University Press, 2011), 17–18.

13. Jacob Rasmussen, "Mungiki as Youth Movement: Revolution, Gender and Generational Politics in Nairobi, Kenya," *Young* 18, no. 3 (2010): 307–8, 311.

14. Peter Mwangi Kagwanja, "Facing Mount Kenya or Facing Mecca? The Mungiki, Ethnic Violence and the Politics of the Moi Succession in Kenya, 1987–2002," *African Affairs* 102, no. 406 (2003): 25–49; and Nicholas Cheeseman, "The Kenyan Elections of 2007: An Introduction," *Journal of Eastern African Studies* 2, no. 2 (2008): 168.

15. Robbie Corey-Boulet, "In Kenya, Forced Male Circumcision and a Struggle for Justice," *Atlantic*, 1 August 2011, accessed 13 January 2016, http://www.theatlantic.com /international/archive/2011/08/in-kenya-forced-male-circumcision-and-a-struggle-for-justice/242757.

16. Koigi wa Wamwere, *Towards Genocide in Kenya: The Curse of Negative Ethnicity* (Nairobi: Mvule Africa, 2008), 189.

17. Peter Mwangi Kagwanja and Roger Southall, eds., *Kenya's Uncertain Democracy: The Electoral Crisis of 2008* (London: Routledge, 2010), 57.

18. Integrated Regional Information Networks (IRIN), "Kenya: Plea to ICC over Forced Male Circumcision," 25 April 2011, accessed 13 January 2016, http://www.irinnews.org /report/92564/kenya-plea-to-icc-over-forced-male-circumcision.

19. Henrietta L. Moore, "Forms of Knowing and Un-Knowing: Secrets about Society, Sexuality and God in Northern Kenya," in *Secrecy and Silence in the Research Process: Feminist Reflections*, ed. Róisín Ryan-Flood and Rosalind Gill (New York: Routledge, 2010), 34–35.

20. David W. Throup, "The Count," *Journal of Eastern African Studies* 2, no. 2 (2008): 290–304.

21. Michelle Osborn, "Fuelling the Flames: Rumour and Politics in Kibera," *Journal of Eastern African Studies* 2, no. 2 (2008): 322–24.

22. International Criminal Court, "Situation in The Republic of Kenya, The Prosecutor v. Uhuru Muigai Kenyatta, Case No. ICC-01/09-02/11," 4 February 2014. See the following WikiLeaks cables: 07NAIROBI2215, "Mungiki: Kenya's Largest Criminal Organization," 24 May 2007; 09NAIROBI1296, "Uhuru Kenyatta: President Ambitions and the . . . ," 26 June 2009; and 10NAIROBI11, "Kenya: Inadequate Witness Protection Poses Painful Dilemma," 5 January 2010.

23. United Nations, High Commissioner for Human Rights, *Report from OHCHR Fact-Finding Mission to Kenya*, 6–28 February 2008, 14; and Waki Commission, "The Report of the Commission of Inquiry on Post Election Violence" (Nairobi: Government Printer, 2008), 258.

24. IRIN, "Kenya: Plea to ICC Over Forced Male Circumcision," 25 April 2011; and Beth Maina Ahlberg and Kezia Muthoni Njoroge, "'Not Men Enough to Rule!': Politicization of Ethnicities and Forcible Circumcision of Luo Men during the Post-election Violence in Kenya," *Ethnicity and Health* 18, no. 5 (2013): 461–62.

25. Corey-Boulet, "In Kenya, Forced Male Circumcision and a Struggle for Justice."

26. In the Rift Valley, Gikuyu had also been beaten, murdered, and expelled from their homes. And as they did in Nairobi, gangs of young Gikuyu men hunted down Luos and mutilated their genitals. Twenty-two men and thirty-seven boys were treated for sexual violence at Rift Valley hospitals. In Eldoret, local leaders described the violence that engulfed the smoldering town as nothing more sinister than "a normal circumcision ceremony." Waki Commission, 68–69, 107, 197, 251, 258–59, 336; Vitalis Kimutai, "Kenyan Outlawed Sect Members Raped, Amputated Victims' Genitals— ICC," *East African Standard*, 23 September 2011, accessed 19 April 2016, http://www .standardmedia.co.ke/business/article/2000043340/mungiki-raped-forcibly -circumcised-and-amputated-victims-genitals; and David M. Anderson and Emma Lochery, "Violence and Exodus in Kenya's Rift Valley, 2008: Predictable and Preventable?" *Journal of Eastern African Studies* 2, no. 2 (2008): 330–33.

27. Wanjiru Kamau-Rutenberg, "Watu Wazima: A Gender Analysis of Forced Male Circumcisions during Kenya's Post-Election Violence" (working paper, Oxford Transitional Justice Research, 17 July 2009); and Ahlberg and Njoroge, "Not Men Enough to Rule!" 455.

28. World Health Organization and Joint United Nations Program on HIV/AIDS, *Male Circumcision: Global Trends and Determinants in Prevalence, Safety, and Acceptability* (Geneva: WHO Press, 2007). For a review of the scientific literature, see Nelli Westercamp and Robert C. Bailey, "Acceptability of Male Circumcision for Prevention of HIV/AIDS in Sub-Saharan Africa: A Review," *AIDS and Behavior* 11, no. 3 (2007): 341–55. Some doubts have been raised that male circumcision is an effective

prevention strategy, especially if it encourages men to have unprotected sex. Ahlberg and Njoroge, "Not Men Enough to Rule!" 456–57.

29. World Health Organization, *WHO Progress Brief: Voluntary Medical Male Circumcision for HIV Prevention in 14 Priority Counties in East and Southern Africa* (Geneva: WHO Press, 2015).

30. Daily Nation, "Raila Intent on Making Male Cut More Popular," 13 September 2008, accessed 13 January 2016, http://www.nation.co.ke/news/regional/-/1070/470230 /k1d6c8/-/ index.html; Muliro Telewa, "Kenyan MPs Admit to Circumcision," *BBC News*, 23 September 2008, accessed 13 January 2016, http://news.bbc.co.uk/2/hi/africa /7584269.stm.

31. "Raila, Circumcision, and the Luo," *Nairobi Chronicle*, 7 October 2008, accessed 13 January 2016, https://nairobichronicle.wordpress.com/2008/10/07/raila-circumcision -and-the-luo.

32. Henry Wanyama, "Luo Elders Take Part in Voluntary Circumcision," *Weekend Star*, 11–12 August 2012, accessed 13 January 2016, http://allafrica.com/stories /201208110719.html.

33. Salome N. Wawire, "Negotiating Identity: Identity Dynamics in the Context of Male Circumcision and HIV/AIDS among Luo Youth in Kisumu, Kenya" (PhD diss., Brown University, 2010), 149–52.

34. Alfredo F. X. O. Obure, Erick O. Nyambedha, and Boniface O. Oindo, "Interpersonal Influences in the Scale-Up of Male Circumcision Services in a Traditionally Non-Circumcising Community in Rural Western Kenya," *Global Journal of Community Psychology Practice* 1, no. 3 (2011): 4.

35. On the interplay of AIDS, sex, and trust, see Daniel Jordan Smith, *AIDS Doesn't Show Its Face: Inequality, Morality, and Social Change in Nigeria* (Chicago: University of Chicago Press, 2014).

36. Wawire, "Negotiating Identity," 161–66.

37. Gaku Mathenge, "Kenyatta, Odinga Roared, and Their Sons Are Crowing," *Standard*, 21 February 2009, accessed 13 January 2016, http://www.standardmedia.co.ke/mobile /?articleID=1144007170&story_title=Kenyatta,%20Odinga%20roared%20and%20their%20 sons%20are%20crowing; and Emeka Mayaka-Gekara, "Kenyatta-Odinga Rivalry Replayed," *Daily Nation*, 9 April 2011, accessed 13 January 2016, http://www.nation.co.ke/news/politics /Kenyatta-Odinga-rivalry-replayed-/-/1064/1141866/-/view/printVersion/-/u8cye9/-/index .html.

38. Parselelo Kantai, "Kenya: 50 Years On: The Odinga-Kenyatta Rematch," *Africa Report*, 2 March 2013, accessed 13 January 2016, http://www.theafricareport.com/East-Horn-Africa/kenya-50-years-on-the-odinga-kenyatta-rematch.html.

39. Jeffery Gettleman, "Kenya Reaction to Disputed Election Is Far Calmer Than Last Time," *New York Times*, 12 March 2013, accessed 13 January 2016, http://www.nytimes .com/2013/03/12/world/africa/kenyan-reaction-to-disputed-election-is-far-calmer-than-last -time.html?_r=0; and "Costly affair," *Daily Nation*, 3 February 2013, accessed 13 January 2016, http://www.nation.co.ke/lifestyle/lifestyle/Costly-affair/-/1214/1682302/-/5tivfj/-/index .html.

40. "Kenya Election: Meet Uhuru Kenyatta's Victory Speechwriter," BBC News, 12 March 2013, accessed 13 January 2016, http://news.bbc.co.uk/2/hi/africa/7584269.stm.

41. The emphasis is mine. "Kenya's President Elect Uhuru Kenyatta Acceptance Speech," 9 March 2013, accessed 19 April 2016, https://kenyanvoice.com/2013/03/09 /kenyas-president-elect-uhuru-kenyatta-acceptance-speech.

Bibliography

ARCHIVAL SOURCES

Kenya National Archives, Nairobi (KNA)

AAL	Labour
AB	Community Development
ABK	Labour
ACW	Treasury
AF	Labour
AG	Attorney General
AH	Defence
AHL	Home Affairs
AP	Judiciary
ARC/MAA	African Affairs
ARC/MD	Defence
ARC/MLA	Legal Affairs
AV	Education
BN	Land
BY	Medical
BZ	Probation
C	Secretariat
CA	Provincial Commissioner, Coast
CB	District Commissioner, Kilifi
CS	Secretariat
DC/EMB	District Commissioner, Embu
DC/GRSSA	District Commissioner, Garissa
DC/KAJ	District Commissioner, Kajiado
DC/KAP	District Commissioner, Kapsabet
DC/KER	District Commissioner, Kericho
DC/KIS	District Commissioner, Kisamayu

DC/KMG	District Commissioner, Kakamega
DC/KPNRIA	District Commissioner, Kapenguria
DC/KSM	District Commissioner, Kisumu
DC/KTI	District Commissioner, Kitui
DC/MERU	District Commissioner, Meru
DC/MKS	District Commissioner, Machakos
DC/MUR	District Commissioner, Fort Hall
DC/NKU	District Commissioner, Nakuru
GH	Governor General
JZ	Prisons and Police
MA	District Commissioner, Kiambu
MAA	African Affairs
ME	Community Development
MOH	Medical
OP	Office of the President
PC/CEN	Provincial Commissioner, Central
PC/COAST	Provincial Commissioner, Coast
PC/CP	Provincial Commissioner, Central
PC/NZA	Provincial Commissioner, Nyanza
PC/RVP	Provincial Commissioner, Rift Valley
PQ	Labour
RN	Office-in-Charge, Nairobi Extra-Provincial District
VB	Community Development
VQ	Community Development
VT	Community Development

Library of Congress, Africa and Middle East Reading Room, Pamphlet Archive
     LC   Box Kenya and Economics and Agriculture

London School of Hygiene and Tropical Medicine, London (LSHTM)
     PNHU   Public Nutrition and Health Unit

National Archives of Britain, Public Records Office, Kew (TNA:PRO)
     CO   Colonial Office
     FCO   Foreign and Commonwealth Office
     INF   Central Office of Information

National Archives at College Park, Washington DC (NACP)
     RG59   Department of State Archives, Kenya, Political Affairs

National Museum of Kenya, Nairobi (NMK)
     Den/G   Gordon Dennis Photographic Collection

Princeton Theological Seminar Spear Library, Princeton (PTSSL)
     Church Missionary Society Archive

Rhodes House Library, University of Oxford, Oxford (RHL)
     Mss. Afr. s. 424   F. J. Harlow

Mss. Afr. s. 1069 Evan Biss
Mss. Afr. s. 1153 Sidney H. Fazan
Mss. Afr. s. 1154 Major Rosalie Trembeth
Mss. Afr. s. 1318 E. J. L Harris
Mss. Afr. s. 1671 Maboonde Estate
Mss. Afr. s. 1829 J. H. Oldham
Mss. Afr. s 1843 Patrick E. W. Williams
Mss. Afr. s. 2100 Thomas Askwith
Mss. Afr. t. 13   E. R. St. A. Davies

Salvation Army Heritage Center Archive, New Denmark, London (SA)
    Folder A   Africa: East Africa (General)
                 East Africa Territory, Kenya Correspondence

School of Oriental and African Studies, London (SOAS)
    CBMS   Conference of British Missionary Societies Archive
    IMC   International Missionary Council

INTERVIEWS

Achar, Christopher Onduru: 26 March 2008, Awendo
Ayoo, Philip Oduok: 27 March 2008, Awendo
Bargetet, Erick Kipkwai: 10 June 2008, Tenwek, Bomet
Bargetet, Samuel Kipkoech: 10 June 2008, Tenwek, Bomet
Bett, David: 12 June 2008, Kamarai, Sotik
Bor, Lazarus arap: 11 June 2008, Kapkatet, Bomet
Bor, Samuel Kipkurui: 11 June 2008, Kapkatet, Bomet
Chege, John Mwangi: 8 June 2008, Gilgil (interview conducted by John Gitau Kariuki)
Chepkwony, Jonah Kiprono: 12 June 2008, Kamarai, Bureti, Sotik
Chepkwony, Joseph: 6 June 2008, Saunet, Sotik
Chirchir, Wilson: 6 June 2008, Saunet, Sotik
Diment, Don: 15 June 2004, Farnham
Gaga, Dominic Obondo: 27 March 2008, Awendo
Gavaghan, Terence: 19 July 2004, Putney, London
Gikubu, Joseph: 24 August 2005 and 14 May 2008, Starehe, Nairobi
Gikuhi, Joseph Gichigo: 26 May 2008, Othaya, Nyeri
Johnson, John: 19 March 2004, Oxford
Kaguara, Samuel Uiru: 26 April 2008, Ndenderu, Kiambu
Kamau, James Ng'ang'a: 17 April 2008, Gilgil
Kariuki, James Karanja: 6 April 2008, Gilgil
Kenduiywa, Sammy Sauron: 8 June 2008, Chepilat, Sotik
Khaoya, Khaemba: 5 April 2008, Gilgil
Kimani, Joseph Kingara: 7 May 2008, Kagwe, Kiambu
Kimanji, Harry Joseph: 6 April 2008, Gilgil
Kiprop, Joseph Mutai: 7 June 2008, Kapsinendet, Sotik
Kirima, Muthoni: 28 May 2008, Nyeri
Knowles, June: 8 June 2004, Watlington, Oxford

Knowles, Oliver: 8 June 2004, Watlington, Oxford
Korir, Joseph Kibelyon: 8 June 2008, Chepilat, Sotik
Korir, Terer arap: 13 June 2008, Kabianga, Kericho
Kosgei, Paul Kipkorir: 10 June 2008, Kapsinendet, Sotik
Kuriaa, Simon Kariuki "Gakono": 22 May 2008, Ongata-Rongai
Langat, Daniel: 13 June 2008, Kabianga, Kericho
Magolo, Joshua Obuho: 27 March 2008, Awendo
Maina, Kipkemo: 6 June 2008, Saunet, Sotik
Maina, Siamba: 8 June 2008, Chepilat, Sotik
Maruge, Kimani Ng'ang'a: 23 June 2008, Kariobangi, Nairobi
Meting, Musa Chelule: 11 June 2008, Kapkatet, Bomet
Mitei, Francis Koskei: 7 June 2008, Kapsinendet, Sotik
Moll, Peter: 25 August 2005 and 14 May 2008, Westlands, Nairobi
Muchahi, Gabriel Kahugu: 26 April 2008, Ndenderu, Kiambu
Muthee, Michael: 9 March 2008, Gilgil
Mwai, Nicholas Kinyua: 28 May 2008, Kiamwathi, Nyeri
Mwaniki, Wachira: 25 May 2008, Burguret, Laikipia
Mwihaki, Veronica: 8 March 2008, Gilgil
Ndai, Raphael Abisalom: 31 March 2008, Bondo
Ndiang'ui, Daniel Gichangi: 9 March 2008, Gilgil
Ngetich, Kiprotich: 13 June 2008, Kabianga, Kericho
Ngugi, Alan Ale Kanyingi: 19 May 2008, Githunguri, Kiambu
Ngugi, Peter Mwarangu: 26 April 2008, Ndenderu, Kiambu
Nightengale, Clarissa: August 2005, Vipingo
Njoroge, Patrick Kumo: 9 March 2008, Gilgil
Njoroge, Patrick Michael Gichengu: 27 May 2008, Mukurweini, Nyeri
Njoroge, Rev. Patrick Mugwe: 27 May 2008, Mukurweini, Nyeri
Njuguna, David Chege: 19 May 2008, Kagwe, Kiambu
Nottingham, John: 17 August 2005, Nairobi
Nyaga, Gideon Gatuthu: 8 March 2008, Gilgil
Nyatia, Moses Mwanja Mutahi: 26 May 2008, Nyeri
Odundo, Andrew Albert Ater: 30 March 2008, Kisumu
Omwenyo, Yason: 26 March 2008, Awendo
Opudo, Abiathar Omondi: 28 March 2008, Homa Bay
Osawa, Edward Arthur Adera: 30 March 2008, Kisumu
Osawa, John Opyio: 27 March 2008, Awendo
Otondi, Willis Opiyo: 30 March 2008, Nyahera
Rotich, Anthony King'etich: 9 June 2008, Kaplong, Sotik
Ruto, Augustine: 9 June 2008, Kaplong, Sotik
Sidho, Jaramongi Joseph Wanga: 31 March 2008, Bondo
Sitienei, Paul Cheruiyot: 10 June 2008, Kapsinendet, Sotik
Soi, Jacob: 12 June 2008, Kamarai, Sotik
Soi, John Tumbo: 6 June 2008, Saunet, Sotik
Soi, Joseph arap: 6 June 2008, Saunet, Sotik
Soi, Nicholas: 10 June 2008, Kapsinendet, Sotik
Tamutwa, Thomas Kipsigei: 12 June 2008, Kamarai, Sotik
Tegutwa, Cheboss arap: 11 June 2008, Kapkatet, Bomet
Tesot, John Kiptalam: 13 June 2008, Kabianga, Kericho

Ti-Ikere, Njamba: 8 March 2008, Gilgil
Too, Kimeli: 13 June 2008, Kabianga, Kericho
Weere, Lukio Okkoth: 20 March 2008, Nairobi
Weke, Lazaro Ochieng: 26 March 2008, Awendo
Weke, Paul Ambogo: 26 March 2008, Awendo

Print and Online News Sources
  Africa Report
  Atlantic
  BBC News
  Daily Monitor
  Daily Nation
  Guardian
  Facebook, Inc.
  IRIN News
  KTN
  Nairobi Chronicl
  New York Times
  Standard, formerly *East African Standard*
  Star
  Twitter, Inc.
  WikiLeaks.org

BOOKS AND ARTICLES

Abbink, Jon. "Being Young in Africa: The Politics of Despair and Renewal." In Abbink and Van Kessel, *Vanguard or Vandals*, 1–36.

Abbink, Jon, and Ineke van Kessel, eds. *Vanguard or Vandals: Youth, Politics, and Conflict in Africa*. Leiden: Brill, 2005.

Aguilar, Mario I. "Gerontocratic, Aesthetic and Political Models of Age." In Aguilar, *Politics of Age and Gerontocracy in Africa*, 3–30.

———, ed. *The Politics of Age and Gerontocracy in Africa*. Trenton, NJ: Africa World Press, 1998.

Ahlberg, Beth Maina, and Kezia Muthoni Njoroge. "'Not Men Enough to Rule!': Politicization of Ethnicities and Forcible Circumcision of Luo Men during the Postelection Violence in Kenya." *Ethnicity and Health* 18, no. 5 (2013): 454–68.

Ahlman, Jeffrey S. "A New Type of Citizen: Youth, Gender, and Generation in the Ghanaian Builders Brigade." *Journal of African History* 53, no. 1 (2012): 87–105.

Akama, John S. "The Indigenous Education System: The Making of a Gusii Man or Woman." In Akama and Maxon, *Ethnography of the Gusii of Western Kenya*, 105–18.

Akama, John S., and Robert M. Maxon, eds. *Ethnography of the Gusii of Western Kenya: A Vanishing Cultural Heritage*. Lewiston, NY: Edwin Mellen, 2006.

Akama, John S., and Solomon Monyenye. "Circumcision Ceremony." In Akama and Maxon, *Ethnography of the Gusii of Western Kenya*, 175–90.

———. "The Initiates' Seclusion Period." In Akama and Maxon, *Ethnography of the Gusii of Western Kenya*, 191–208.

Allman, Jean M. "The Disappearing of Hannah Kudjoe: Nationalism, Feminism, and the Tyrannies of History." *Journal of Women's History* 21, no. 3 (2009): 13–35.

———. *The Quills of the Porcupine: Asante Nationalism in an Emergent Ghana*. Madison: University of Wisconsin Press, 1993.

———. "Rounding up Spinsters: Gender Chaos and Unmarried Women in Colonial Asante." *Journal of African History* 37, no. 2 (1996): 195–214.

Allman, Jean M., and Victoria B. Tashjian. "*I Will Not Eat Stone*": A Women's History of Colonial Asante. Portsmouth, NH: Heinemann, 2000.

Ambler, Charles H. "Drunks, Brewers, and Chiefs: Alcohol Regulation in Colonial Kenya, 1900–1939." In *Drinking: Behavior and Belief in Modern History*, edited by Susanna Barrows and Robin Room, 165–83. Berkeley: University of California Press, 1991.

———. *Kenyan Communities in the Age of Imperialism: The Central Region in the Late Nineteenth Century*. New Haven, CT: Yale University Press, 1988.

Anderson, David M. "The Battle of Dandora Swamp: Reconstructing the Mau Mau Land Freedom Army, October 1954." In Odhiambo and Lonsdale, *Mau Mau and Nationhood*, 155–75.

———. "Guilty Secrets: Deceit, Denial, and the Discovery of Kenya's 'Migrated Archive.'" *History Workshop Journal* 80, no. 1 (2015): 142–60.

———. *Histories of the Hanged: The Dirty War in Kenya and the End of Empire*. New York: Norton, 2005.

———. "Juveniles on Trial: The Prosecutions of Mau Mau's Child Soldiers." Paper presented at the annual African Studies Association Conference, Washington, DC, 17–20 November 2005.

———. "Master and Servant in Colonial Kenya, 1895–1939." *Journal of African History* 41, no. 3 (2000): 459–85.

———. "Policing, Prosecution and the Law in Colonial Kenya, c. 1905–39." In Anderson and Killingray, *Policing the Empire*, 183–201.

———. "Policing the Settler State: Colonial Hegemony in Kenya, 1900–1952." In *Contesting Colonial Hegemony: State and Society in Africa and India*, edited by Dagmar Engels and Shula Marks, 248–64. London: British Academic Press, 1994.

———. "Punishment, Race and 'The Raw Native': Settler Society and Kenya's Flogging Scandals, 1895–1930." *Journal of Southern African Studies* 37, no. 3 (2011): 479–97.

———. "Vigilantes, Violence and the Politics of Public Order in Kenya." *African Affairs* 101, no. 405 (2002): 531–55.

Anderson, David M., and David Killingray, eds. *Policing the Empire: Government, Authority and Control, 1830–1940*. Manchester: Manchester University Press, 1991.

Anderson, David M., and Emma Lochery. "Violence and Exodus in Kenya's Rift Valley, 2008: Predictable and Preventable?" *Journal of Eastern African Studies* 2, no. 2 (2008): 328–43.

Anderson, John E. *The Struggle for the School: The Interaction of Missionary, Colonial Government and Nationalist Enterprise in the Development of Formal Education in Kenya*. London: Longman, 1970.

Anyang' Nyong'o, Peter. "State and Society in Kenya: The Disintegration of the Nationalist Coalitions and the Rise of Presidential Authoritarianism, 1963–78." *African Affairs* 88, no. 351 (1989): 229–51.

Anyumba, Godfrey. *Kisumu Town: History of the Built Form, Planning and Environment, 1890–1990*. Delft: Delft University Press, 1995.

Archambault, Caroline. "Pain with Punishment and the Negotiation of Childhood: An Ethnographic Analysis of Children's Rights Processes in Maasailand." *Africa* 79, no. 2 (2009): 282–302.

Argenti, Nicolas. *The Intestines of the State: Youth, Violence, and Belated Histories in the Cameroon Grassfields*. Chicago: University of Chicago Press, 2007.

Aries, Philippe. *Centuries of Childhood: A Social History of Family Life*. New York: Vintage Books, 1962.

Askwith, Thomas G. *From Mau Mau to Harambee: Memoirs and Memoranda of Colonial Kenya*. Cambridge: African Studies Centre, 1995.

Atieno-Odhiambo, E. S. "The Formative Years, 1945–55." In Ogot and Ochieng', *Decolonization and Independence in Kenya*, 25–47.

Atkins, Keletso E. *The Moon Is Dead! Give Us Our Money! The Cultural Origins of an African Work Ethic, Natal, South Africa, 1843–1900*. Portsmouth, NH: Heinemann, 1993.

Attwood, William. *The Reds and the Blacks: A Personal Adventure*. New York: Harper and Row, 1967.

Austin, Dennis. "The Working Committee of the United Gold Coast Convention." *Journal of African History* 2, no. 2 (1961): 273–97.

Baden-Powell, Robert S. S. *Scouting for Boys: A Handbook for Instruction in Good Citizenship*. London: Horace Cox, 1908.

Bailey, Victor. *Delinquency and Citizenship: Reclaiming the Young Offender, 1914–1948*. Oxford: Oxford University Press, 1987.

Bailkin, Jordanna. *The Afterlife of Empire*. Berkeley: University of California Press, 2012.

Bakan, David. "Adolescence in America: From Idea to Social Fact." *Daedalus* 100, no. 4 (1971): 979–95.

Barnett, Donald L., and Karari Njama. *Mau Mau from Within: Autobiography and Analysis of Kenya's Peasant Revolt*. London: MacGibbon and Kee, 1966.

Barra, G. *1,000 Kikuyu Proverbs: With Translations and English Equivalents*. London: Macmillan, 1960.

Baughan, Emily. "'Every Citizen of Empire Implored to Save the Children!' Empire, Internationalism and the Save the Children Fund in Inter-War Britain." *Historical Research* 86, no. 231 (2013): 116–37.

Baxter, Paul T. W., and Uri Almagor, eds. *Age, Generation and Time: Some Features of East African Age Organisations*. New York: St. Martin's, 1978.

Beier, A. L. *Masterless Men: The Vagrancy Problem in England, 1560–1640*. London: Methuen, 1985.

Beinart, William. "The Origins of the *Indlavini*: Male Associations and Migrant Labour in the Transkei." *African Studies* 50, no. 1 (1991): 103–28.

———. "Transkeian Migrant Workers and Youth Labour in the Natal Sugar Estates, 1918–1948." *Journal of African History* 32, no. 1 (1991): 41–63.

Bell, Erin. "'A Most Horrifying Maturity in Crime': Age, Gender and Juvenile Delinquency in Colonial Kenya during the Mau Mau Uprising." *Atlantic Studies* 11, no. 4 (2014): 473–90.

Bennet, Huw. *Fighting the Mau Mau: The British Army and Counter-Insurgency in the Kenya Emergency*. Cambridge: Cambridge University Press, 2012.

Berman, Bruce J. *Control and Crisis in Colonial Kenya: The Dialectic of Domination.* Athens: Ohio University Press, 1990.

———. "Ethnography as Politics, Politics as Ethnography: Kenyatta, Malinowski, and the Making of *Facing Mount Kenya.*" *Canadian Journal of African Studies* 30, no. 3 (1996): 313–44.

Berman, Bruce J., and John M. Lonsdale. "Coping with the Contradictions: The Development of the Colonial State, 1895–1914." In Berman and Lonsdale, *Unhappy Valley,* vol. 1, *State and Class,* 77–100.

———. "The Labors of *Muigwithania*: Jomo Kenyatta as Author, 1928–45." *Research in African Literatures* 29, no. 1 (1998): 16–42.

———. "Louis Leakey's Mau Mau: A Study in the Politics of Knowledge." *History and Anthropology* 5, no. 2 (1991): 143–204.

———, eds. *Unhappy Valley: Conflict in Kenya and Africa.* 2 vols. Athens: Ohio University Press, 1992.

Bernardi, Bernardo. *Age Class Systems: Social Institutions and Polities Based on Age.* Cambridge: Cambridge University Press, 1985.

Bernault, Florence, ed. *A History of Prison and Confinement in Africa.* Portsmouth, NH: Heinemann, 2003.

Bjerk, Paul. *Building a Peaceful Nation: Julius Nyerere and the Establishment of Sovereignty in Tanzania, 1960–1964.* Rochester, NY: University of Rochester Press, 2015.

Blacker, John G. "The Demography of Mau Mau: Fertility and Mortality in Kenya in the 1950s; a Demographer's Viewpoint." *African Affairs* 106, no. 423 (2007): 205–27.

———. "Population Growth and Urbanization in Kenya." In Bloomberg and Abrams, *United Nations Mission to Kenya on Housing,* appendix A.

Bloomberg, Lawrence N., and Charles Abrams. *United Nations Mission to Kenya on Housing.* Nairobi: United Nations, 1965.

Blundell, Michael. "The Present Situation in Kenya." *African Affairs* 34, no. 215 (1955): 99–108.

Boeck, Filip de, and Alcinda Honwana. "Introduction: Children and Youth in Africa." In Honwana and de Boeck, *Makers and Breakers,* 1–18.

Bonner, Philip L. "The Russians on the Reef, 1947–1957: Urbanisation, Gang Warfare and Ethnic Mobilisation." In *Apartheid's Genesis, 1935–1962,* edited by Philip L. Bonner, Peter Delius, and Deborah Posel, 160–94. Johannesburg: Ravan, 2001.

Booth, William. *The Vagrant and the Unemployable.* London: Salvation Army, 1904.

Boucher, Ellen. *Empire's Children: Child Emigration, Welfare, and the Decline of the British World, 1869–1967.* Cambridge: Cambridge University Press, 2014.

Bozzoli, Belinda. "Marxism, Feminism and South African Studies." *Journal of Southern African Studies* 9, no. 2 (1983): 139–71.

Branch, Daniel. *Defeating Mau Mau, Creating Kenya: Counterinsurgency, Civil War, and Decolonization.* Cambridge: Cambridge University Press, 2009.

———. "The Enemy Within: Loyalists and the War against Mau Mau in Kenya." *Journal of African History* 48, no. 2 (2007): 291–315.

———. "Imprisonment and Colonialism in Kenya, c. 1930–1952: Escaping the Carceral Archipelago." *International Journal of African Historical Studies* 38, no. 2 (2005): 239–65.

———. "Introduction: Our Turn to Eat." In *Our Turn to Eat: Politics in Kenya since 1950,* edited by Daniel Branch, Nicholas Cheeseman, and Leigh Gardner, 1–22. New Brunswick, NJ: Transaction Publishers, 2010.

————. *Kenya: Between Hope and Despair, 1963–2011*. New Haven, CT: Yale University Press, 2011.

Branch, Daniel, and Nicholas Cheeseman. "The Politics of Control in Kenya: Understanding the Bureaucratic-Executive State, 1952–78." *Review of African Political Economy* 33, no. 107 (2006): 11–31.

Breckenridge, Keith. "The Allure of Violence: Men, Race and Masculinity on the South African Goldmines, 1900–1950." *Journal of Southern African Studies* 24, no. 4 (1998): 669–93.

Bremner, Robert H., ed. *Children and Youth in America: A Documentary History.* Vol. 1, 1600–1865. Cambridge, MA: Harvard University Press, 1970.

Brennan, James R. "Youth, the TANU Youth League and Managed Vigilantism in Dar es Salaam, Tanzania, 1925–73." *Africa* 76, no. 2 (2006): 221–46.

Briggs, Asa. *Victorian Cities*. London: Odhams Press, 1963.

Brown, Carolyn A. "A 'Man' in the Village Is a 'Boy' in the Workplace: Colonial Racism, Worker Militance, and Igbo Notions of Masculinity in the Nigerian Coal Industry, 1930–1945." In Lindsay and Miescher, *Men and Masculinities in Modern Africa*, 157–76.

Buijtenhuijs, Robert. *Le mouvement "Mau-Mau": Une révolte paysanne et anticolonialeen Afrique noire*. Le Hague: Mouton, 1971.

————. *Mau Mau: Twenty Years After; The Myth and the Survivors*. The Hague: Mouton, 1974.

Bundy, Colin. "Street Sociology and Pavement Politics: Aspects of Youth and Student Resistance in Cape Town, 1985." *Journal of Southern African Studies* 13, no. 3 (1987): 303–30.

Burgess, G. Thomas. "Cinema, Bell Bottoms, and Miniskirts: Struggles over Youth and Citizenship in Revolutionary Zanzibar." *International Journal of African Historical Studies* 35, nos. 2–3 (2002): 287–313.

————. "Introduction to Youth and Citizenship in East Africa." *Africa Today* 51, no. 3 (2005): vii–xxiv.

————. "Remembering Youth: Generation in Revolutionary Zanzibar." *Africa Today* 46, no. 2 (1999): 29–50.

————. "The Young Pioneers and the Rituals of Citizenship in Revolutionary Zanzibar." *Africa Today* 51, no. 3 (2005): 3–29.

Burgess, G. Thomas, and Andrew Burton. Introduction to Burton and Charton-Bigot, *Generations Past*, 1–25.

Burrill, Emily S. *States of Marriage: Gender, Justice, and Rights in Colonial Mali*. Athens: Ohio University Press, 2015.

Burton, Andrew. *African Underclass: Urbanization, Crime and Colonial Order in Dar es Salaam*. Athens: Ohio University Press, 2005.

————. "Raw Youth, School-Leavers and the Emergence of Structural Unemployment in Late-Colonial Urban Tanganyika." *Journal of African History* 47, no. 3 (2006): 363–87.

————, ed. *The Urban Experience in Eastern Africa, c. 1750–2000*. Nairobi: British Institute in Eastern Africa, 2002.

————. "Urbanization in Eastern Africa: An Historical Overview, c. 1750–2000." In *Urban Experience in Eastern Africa*, 1–28.

————. "Urchins, Loafers and the Cult of the Cowboy: Urbanization and Delinquency in Dar es Salaam, 1919–61." *Journal of African History* 42, no. 2 (2001): 199–216.

Burton, Andrew, and Hélène Charton-Bigot, eds. *Generations Past: Youth in East African History*. Athens: Ohio University Press, 2010.

Burton, Andrew, and Paul Ocobock. "The 'Travelling Native': Vagrancy and Colonial Control in British East Africa." In *Cast Out: Vagrancy and Homelessness in Global and Historical Perspective*, edited by A. L. Beier and Paul Ocobock, 270–301. Athens: Ohio University Press, 2009.

Cagnolo, Costanzo. *The Akikuyu, Their Customs, Traditions and Folklore*. Nyeri: Mission Printing School, 1933.

Campbell, Chloe. "Juvenile Delinquency in Colonial Kenya, 1900–39." *Historical Journal* 45, no. 1 (2002): 129–51.

———. *Race and Empire: Eugenics in Colonial Kenya*. Manchester: Manchester University Press, 2007.

Carotenuto, Matthew. "Repatriation in Colonial Kenya: African Institutions and Gendered Violence." *International Journal of African Historical Studies* 45, no. 1 (2012): 9–28.

Carothers, John C. *The Psychology of Mau Mau*. Nairobi: Government Printer, 1954.

Carton, Benedict. *Blood from Your Children: The Colonial Origins of Generational Conflict in South Africa*. Charlottesville: University of Virginia Press, 2000.

Chanock, Martin. *Law, Custom, and Social Order: The Colonial Experience in Malawi and Zambia*. Cambridge: Cambridge University Press, 1985.

Charton-Bigot, Hélène. "Colonial Youth at the Crossroads: Fifteen Alliance 'Boys.'" In Burton and Charton-Bigot, *Generations Past*, 84–107.

Cheeseman, Nicholas. "The Kenyan Elections of 2007: An Introduction." *Journal of Eastern African Studies* 2, no. 2 (2008): 166–84.

Chenevix Trench, Charles. *Men Who Ruled Kenya: The Kenya Administration, 1892–1963*. London: Radcliffe Press, 1993.

Chirwa, Wiseman Chijere. "Child and Youth Labour on the Nyasaland Plantations, 1890–1953." *Journal of Southern African Studies* 19, no. 4 (1993): 662–80.

Chisholm, Linda. "Education, Punishment and the Contradictions of Penal Reform: Alan Paton and Diepkloof Reformatory, 1934–1948." *Journal of Southern African Studies* 17, no. 1 (1991): 23–42.

———. "The Pedagogy of Porter: The Origins of the Reformatory in the Cape Colony, 1882–1910." *Journal of African History* 27, no. 3 (1986): 481–95.

Clayton, Anthony. *Counter-Insurgency in Kenya*. Manhattan, KS: Sunflower Press, 1984.

Clayton, Anthony, and Donald C. Savage. *Government and Labour in Kenya, 1895–1963*. London: Cass, 1974.

Cleary, A. S. "The Myth of Mau Mau in Its International Context." *African Affairs* 89, no. 355 (1990): 227–45.

Clough, Marshall S. *Fighting Two Sides: Kenyan Chiefs and Politicians, 1918–1940*. Boulder: University Press of Colorado, 1990.

———. *Mau Mau Memoirs: History, Memory, and Politics*. Boulder, CO: Rienner, 1998.

Coates, Timothy J. *Convicts and Orphans: Forced and State-Sponsored Colonizer in the Portuguese Empire, 1550–1755*. Stanford, CA: Stanford University Press, 2001.

Coe, Cati. *Dilemmas of Culture in African Schools: Youth, Nationalism, and the Transformation of Knowledge*. Chicago: University of Chicago Press, 2005.

Coe, Richard L. *The Kenya National Youth Service: A Governmental Response to Young Political Activists*. Athens: Ohio University Press, 1973.

Coldrey, Barry M. "'. . . A Place to Which Idle Vagrants May Be Sent': The First Phase of Child Migration during the Seventeenth and Eighteenth Centuries." *Children and Society* 13, no. 1 (1999): 32–47.

Colley, Linda. *Captives: Britain, Empire, and the World, 1600–1850.* New York: Pantheon, 2002.

Colony and Protectorate of Kenya (CPK).

———. Annual Reports of the Ministry of Community Development, 1954–1958.

———. *Crime Committee Report.* Nairobi: Government Printer, 1932.

———. National Assembly. *Official Report,* 12 May 1965.

———. Native Affairs Department Annual Reports, 1928–1932.

———. Native Punishment Commission, 1923.

———. Police Department Annual Reports, 1926–1962.

———. Prisons Department Annual Reports, 1925–1962.

———. Report of the Committee on Juvenile Crime and Kabete Reformatory, 1934.

———. Report of the Committee on Young Persons and Children, 1953.

———. Report of the Employment of Juveniles Committee, 1938.

Comaroff, Jean, and John L. Comaroff. "Occult Economies and the Violence of Abstraction: Notes from the South African Postcolony." *American Ethnologist* 26, no. 2 (1999): 279–303.

———. *Of Revelation and Revolution: Christianity, Colonialism, and Consciousness in South Africa.* Chicago: University of Chicago Press, 1991.

———. "Reflections on Youth: From the Past to the Postcolony." In Honwana and Boeck, *Makers and Breakers,* 19–30.

Connell, R. W. *Masculinities.* Cambridge: Polity Press, 1995.

Cooper, Barbara. *Marriage in Maradi: Gender and Culture in a Hausa Society in Niger, 1900–1989.* Portsmouth, NH: Heinemann, 1997.

Cooper, Frederick. *Africa since 1940: The Past of the Present.* Cambridge: Cambridge University Press, 2002.

———. "Conflict and Connection: Rethinking Colonial African History." *American Historical Review* 99, no. 5 (1994): 1516–45.

———. *Decolonization and African Society: The Labor Question in French and British Africa.* Cambridge: Cambridge University Press, 1996.

———. *From Slaves to Squatters: Plantation Labor and Agriculture in Zanzibar and Coastal Kenya, 1890–1925.* New Haven, CT: Yale University Press, 1980.

———. "Industrial Man Goes to Africa." In Lindsay and Miescher, *Men and Masculinities in Modern Africa,* 128–37.

Corfield, Frank D. *The Origins and Growth of Mau Mau: An Historical Survey.* Nairobi: Colony and Protectorate of Kenya, 1960.

Cornwall, Andrea, and Nancy Lindisfarne. "Dislocating Masculinity: Gender, Power and Anthropology." In Cornwall and Lindisfarne, *Dislocating Masculinity,* 11–47.

———. eds. *Dislocating Masculinity: Comparative Ethnographies.* New York: Routledge, 1994.

Cox, Pamela. *Bad Girls in Britain: Gender, Justice and Welfare, 1900–1950.* New York: Palgrave Macmillan, 2003.

———. "Race, Delinquency and Difference in Twentieth Century Britain." In Cox and Shore, *Becoming Delinquent,* 159–78.

Cox, Pamela, and Heather Shore, eds. *Becoming Delinquent: British and European Youth, 1650–1950.* Aldershot: Ashgate, 2002.

Cox, Richard H. F. *Kenyatta's Country*. New York: Praeger, 1965.

Cruise O'Brien, Donal B. "A Lost Generation? Youth Identity and State Decay in West Africa." In *Postcolonial Identities in Africa*, edited by Richard P. Werbner and Terence O. Ranger, 55–74. London: Zed Books, 1996.

Cunningham, Hugh. *Children and Childhood in Western Society since 1500*. New York: Longman, 1995.

Davison, Jean. *Voices from Mutira: Lives of Rural Gikuyu Women*. Boulder, CO: Rienner, 1989.

Dawson, William H. *The Vagrancy Problem*. London: King and Son, 1910.

Decker, Corrie. "The Elusive Power of Colonial Prey: Sexualizing the Schoolgirl in the Zanzibar Protectorate." *Africa Today* 61, no. 4 (2015): 42–60.

———. "Fathers, Daughters, and Institutions: Coming of Age in Mombasa's Colonial Schools." In *Girlhood: A Global History*, edited by Jennifer Helgren and Colleen A. Vasconcellos, 268–88. New Brunswick, NJ: Rutgers University Press, 2010.

———. "Schoolgirls and Women Teachers: Colonial Education and the Shifting Boundaries between Girls and Women in Zanzibar." In *Gendered Lives in the Western Indian Ocean: Islam, Marriage, and Sexuality on the Swahili Coast*, edited by Erin E. Stiles and Katrina Daly Thompson, 33–59. Athens: Ohio University Press, 2015.

Delf, George. *Jomo Kenyatta: Towards Truth about "The Light of Kenya."* Garden City, NY: Doubleday, 1961.

Dembour, Marie-Bénédicte. "La chicote comme symbole du colonialisme belge?" *Canadian Journal of African Studies* 26, no. 2 (1992): 205–25.

Dickerman, Carol W. "Africans in Nairobi during the Emergency: Social and Economic Changes, 1952–1960." Master's thesis, University of Wisconsin-Madison, 1978.

Diouf, Mamadou. "Engaging Postcolonial Cultures: African Youth and Public Space." *African Studies Review* 46, no. 2 (2003): 1–12.

Donne, John. "Sermon CLVI Preached to the Virginia Company." In Bremner, *Children and Youth in America*, 8–9.

Drayton, Richard. "Britain's Secret Archive of Decolonisation." *History Workshop Online*. 12 April 2012. Accessed 20 January 2016. http://www.historyworkshop.org .uk/britains-secret-archive-of-decolonisation/.

Duff, Sarah E. *Changing Childhoods in the Cape Colony: Dutch Reformed Church Evangelicalism and Colonial Childhood, 1860–1895*. New York: Palgrave Macmillan, 2015.

Durham, Deborah L. "Apathy and Agency: The Romance of Agency and Youth in Botswana." In *Figuring the Future: Globalization and the Temporalities of Children and Youth*, edited by Jennifer Cole and Deborah L. Durham, 151–78. Santa Fe, NM: School for Advanced Research Press, 2008.

———. "Youth and the Social Imagination in Africa." *Anthropological Quarterly* 73, no. 3 (2000): 113–20.

Dutto, Carl A. *Nyeri Townsmen, Kenya*. Kampala: East African Literature Bureau, 1975.

Edgerton, Robert B. *Mau Mau: An African Crucible*. New York: Ballantine, 1989.

Egesah, Omar. *Male Circumcision in Africa: Ethnographic Evidence from the Bukusu, Kenya*. Saarbrücken: VDM, 2008.

Elkins, Caroline. "Alchemy of Evidence: Mau Mau, the British Empire, and the High Court of Justice." *Journal of Imperial and Commonwealth History* 39, no. 5 (2011): 731–48.

———. "The Colonial Papers: FCO Transparency Is a Carefully Cultivated Myth." *Guardian.* 17 April 2012. Accessed 20 January 2016. http://www.theguardian.com /politics/2012/apr/18/colonial-papers-fco-transparency-myth.

———. "Detention, Rehabilitation and the Destruction of Kikuyu Society." In Odhiambo and Lonsdale, *Mau Mau and Nationhood,* 191–226.

———. *Imperial Reckoning: The Untold Story of Britain's Gulag in Kenya.* New York: Holt, 2005.

———. "The Struggle for Mau Mau Rehabilitation in Late Colonial Kenya." *International Journal of African Historical Studies* 33, no. 1 (2000): 25–57.

Ellis, Heather. *Juvenile Delinquency and the Limits of Western Influence, 1850–2000.* New York: Palgrave Macmillan, 2014.

Ener, Mine. *Managing Egypt's Poor and the Politics of Benevolence, 1800–1952.* Princeton, NJ: Princeton University Press, 2003.

Epstein, Arnold L. "The Network and Urban Social Organization." *Rhodes-Livingstone Journal* 29 (1961): 29–62.

Fadiman, Jeffrey A. *When We Began, There Were Witchmen: An Oral History from Mount Kenya.* Berkeley: University of California Press, 1993.

Fazan, Sidney H. *Colonial Kenya Observed: British Rule, Mau Mau and the Wind of Change.* Edited by John Lonsdale. London: Tauris, 2014.

Fields, Karen E. *Revival and Rebellion in Colonial Central Africa.* Princeton, NJ: Princeton University Press, 1985.

Fishman, Sarah. *The Battle for Children: World War II, Youth Crime, and Juvenile Justice in Twentieth-Century France.* Cambridge, MA: Harvard University Press, 2002.

Fletcher, Eileen. *Truth about Kenya: An Eye-Witness Account.* London: Movement for Colonial Freedom, 1956.

Foran, W. Robert. *The Kenya Police, 1887–1960.* London: Hale, 1962.

Foucault, Michel. *Discipline and Punish: The Birth of the Prison.* New York: Vintage Books, 1979.

Fourchard, Laurent. "Lagos and the Invention of Juvenile Delinquency in Nigeria, 1920–60." *Journal of African History* 47, no. 1 (2006): 115–37.

Fowler, David. *Youth Culture in Modern Britain, c. 1920–1970.* New York: Palgrave Macmillan, 2008.

Frederiksen, Bodil F. "African Women and Their Colonisation of Nairobi: Representation and Realities." In Burton, *Urban Experience in Eastern Africa,* 223–34.

Furedi, Frank. "The African Crowd in Nairobi: Popular Movements and Elite Politics." *Journal of African History* 14, no. 2 (1973): 275–90.

———. *The Mau Mau War in Perspective.* Athens: Ohio University Press, 1989.

Gardner, Leigh A. *Taxing Colonial Africa: The Political Economy of British Imperialism.* Oxford: Oxford University Press, 2012.

Gatrell, V. A. C. *The Hanging Tree: Execution and the English People, 1770–1868.* Oxford: Oxford University Press, 1994.

George, Abosede A. *Making Modern Girls: A History of Girlhood, Labor, and Social Development in Colonial Lagos.* Athens: Ohio University Press, 2014.

Gertzel, Cherry J. *The Politics of Independent Kenya, 1963–8.* Evanston, IL: Northwestern University Press, 1970.

Ghai, Yash P., and J. Patrick McAuslan. *Public Law and Political Change in Kenya: A Study of the Legal Framework of Government from Colonial Times to the Present.* Nairobi: Oxford University Press, 1970.

Gicaru, Muga. *Land of Sunshine: Scenes of Life in Kenya before Mau Mau*. London: Lawrence and Wishart, 1958.

Gikoyo, Gucu G. *We Fought for Freedom: Tulipigania Uhuru*. Nairobi: East African Publishing, 1979.

Gillis, John R. "The Evolution of Juvenile Delinquency in England, 1890–1914." *Past and Present* 67, no. 1 (1975): 96–126.

————. *Youth and History: Tradition and Change in European Age Relations, 1770–Present*. New York: Academic Press, 1981.

Githige, Renison M. "The Religious Factor in Mau Mau with Particular Reference to Mau Mau Oaths." Master's thesis, University of Nairobi, 1978.

Glaser, Clive L. *Bo-Tsotsi: The Youth Gangs of Soweto, 1935–1976*. Portsmouth, NH: Heinemann, 2000.

Glassman, Jonathon. *Feasts and Riot: Revelry, Rebellion, and Popular Consciousness on the Swahili Coast, 1856–1888*. Portsmouth, NH: Heinemann, 1995.

González, Ondina E., and Bianca Premo, eds. *Raising an Empire: Children in Early Modern Iberia and Colonial Latin America*. Albuquerque: University of New Mexico Press, 2007.

Gordon, David F. *Decolonization and the State in Kenya*. Boulder, CO: Westview Press, 1986.

Gordon, Robert J. "Vagrancy, Law and 'Shadow Knowledge': Internal Pacification, 1915–1939." In *Namibia under South African Rule: Mobility and Containment, 1915–46*, edited by Patricia Hayes, Jeremy Silvester, Marion Wallace, and Wolfram Hartmann, 51–76. Athens: Ohio University Press, 1998.

Green, Maia. "Mau Mau Oathing Rituals and Political Ideology in Kenya: A Re-Analysis.*Africa* 60, no. 1 (1990): 69–87.

Gregory, Robert G. *Sidney Webb and East Africa: Labour's Experiment with the Doctrine of Native Paramountcy*. Berkeley: University of California Press, 1962.

Grier, Beverly C. *Invisible Hands: Child Labor and the State in Colonial Zimbabwe*. Portsmouth, NH: Heinemann, 2006.

Griffin, Geoffrey W., and Yusuf M. King'ala. *The Autobiography of Dr. G. W. Griffin: Kenya's Champion Beggar*. Nairobi: Falcon Crest, 2005.

Hailey, W. M. *An African Survey: A Study of Problems Arising in Africa South of the Sahara*. London: Macmillan, 1938.

Hake, Andrew. *African Metropolis: Nairobi's Self-Help City*. London: St. Martin's, 1977.

Halliman, Dorothy M., and William T. W. Morton. "The City of Nairobi." In *Nairobi: City and Region*, edited by William T. M. Morton, 98–120. London: Oxford University Press, 1967.

Harries, Patrick. *Work, Culture, and Identity: Migrant Laborers in Mozambique and South Africa, c. 1860–1910*. Portsmouth, NH: Heinemann, 2004.

Hawkins, Sean. "'The Woman in Question': Marriage and Identity in the Colonial Courts of Northern Ghana, 1907–1954." In *Women in African Colonial Histories*, edited by Jean Allman, Susan Geiger, and Nakanyike Musisi, 116–43. Bloomington: Indiana University Press, 2002.

Hay, Alison, and Richard Harris. "'Shauri ya Sera Kali': The Colonial Regime of Urban Housing in Kenya to 1939." *Urban History* 34, no. 3 (2007): 504–30.

Hay, Margaret Jean. "Changes in Clothing and Struggles over Identity in Colonial Western Kenya." In *Fashioning Africa: Power and the Politics of Dress*, edited by Jean Allman, 67–83. Bloomington: Indiana University Press, 2004.

————. "Queens, Prostitutes and Peasants: Historical Perspectives on African Women, 1971–1986." *Canadian Journal of African Studies* 22, no. 3 (1988): 431–47.

Heald, Suzette. *Manhood and Morality: Sex, Violence and Ritual in Gisu Society.* London: Routledge, 1999.

Heap, Simon. "'Their Days Are Spent in Gambling and Loafing, Pimping for Prostitutes, and Picking Pockets': Male Juvenile Delinquents on Lagos Island, 1920s–1960s." *Journal of Family History* 35, no. 1 (2009): 48–70.

Hecht, Tobias, ed. *Minor Omissions: Children in Latin American History and Society.* Madison: University of Wisconsin Press, 2002.

Hendrick, Harry. *Images of Youth: Age, Class, and the Male Youth Problem, 1880–1920.* Oxford: Clarendon, 1990.

Herbst, Jeffrey. *States and Power in Africa: Comparative Lessons in Authority and Control.* Princeton, NJ: Princeton University Press, 2000.

Hetherington, Penelope. "The Politics of Female Circumcision in the Central Province of Colonial Kenya, 1920–30." *Journal of Imperial and Commonwealth History* 26, no. 1 (1998): 93–126.

Hilton, Matthew. "Ken Loach and the Save the Children Film: Humanitarianism, Imperialism, and the Changing Role of Charity in Postwar Britain." *Journal of Modern History* 87, no. 2 (2015): 357–94.

Hobley, Charles W. *Bantu Beliefs and Magic.* London: Cass, 1922.

————. *Ethnology of A-Kamba and Other East African Tribes.* Cambridge: Cambridge University Press, 1910.

Hodge, Peter. "The Ghana Workers Brigade: A Project for Unemployed Youth." *British Journal of Sociology* 15, no. 2 (1964): 113–28.

Hodgson, Dorothy L. "Being Maasai Men: Modernity and the Production of Maasai Masculinities." In Lindsay and Miescher, *Men and Masculinities in Modern Africa,* 211–29.

Hodgson, Dorothy L., and Sheryl A. McCurdy. "Introduction: 'Wicked' Women and the Reconfiguration of Gender." In *"Wicked Women" and the Reconfiguration of Gender in Africa,* edited by Dorothy L. Hodgson and Sheryl McCurdy, 1–24. Portsmouth, NH: Heinemann, 2001.

Hoffman, Danny. *The War Machines: Young Men and Violence in Sierra Leone and Liberia.* Durham, NC: Duke University Press, 2011.

Hollis, Alfred C. *The Nandi: Their Language and Folk-Lore.* Oxford: Clarendon, 1909.

Honwana, Alcinda M. *The Time of Youth: Work, Social Change, and Politics in Africa.* Boulder, CO: Kumarian, 2012.

Honwana, Alcinda M., and Filip de Boeck, eds. *Makers and Breakers: Children and Youth in Postcolonial Africa.* Trenton, NJ: Africa World Press, 2005.

Hornsby, Charles. *Kenya: A History since Independence.* New York: Tauris, 2012.

Humphries, Jane. *Childhood and Child Labour in the British Industrial Revolution.* Cambridge: Cambridge University Press, 2011.

Hunt, Nancy Rose. "Placing African Women's History and Locating Gender." *Social History* 14, no. 3 (1989): 359–79.

Huntingford, George W. B. *The Nandi of Kenya: Tribal Control in a Pastoral Society.* London: Routledge and Kegan Paul, 1953.

Hyam, Ronald. *Understanding the British Empire.* Cambridge: Cambridge University Press, 2010.

Hynd, Stacey. "Killing the Condemned: The Practice and Process of Capital Punishment in British Africa, 1900–1950s." *Journal of African History* 49, no. 3 (2008): 403–18.

Iliffe, John. *The African Poor: A History*. Cambridge: Cambridge University Press, 1987.

International Criminal Court. "Situation in the Republic of Kenya. The Prosecutor v. Uhuru Muigai Kenyatta, Case No. ICC-01/09-02/11." Accessed 12 January 2016. https://www.icc-cpi.int/iccdocs/PIDS/publications/KenyattaEng.pdf.

Itote, Waruhiu. *"Mau Mau" General*. Nairobi: East African Publishing, 1967.

Ivaska, Andrew. *Cultured States: Youth, Gender, and Modern Style in 1960s Dar es Salaam*. Durham, NC: Duke University Press, 2011.

Jackson, Will. *Madness and Marginality: The Lives of Kenya's White Insane*. Manchester: Manchester University Press, 2013.

Jeffrey, Craig. *Timepass: Youth, Class, and the Politics of Waiting in India*. Stanford, CA: Stanford University Press, 2010.

Jennings, Eric T. *Vichy in the Tropics: Petain's National Revolution in Madagascar, Guadeloupe, and Indochina*. Stanford, CA: Stanford University Press, 2001.

Jobs, Richard I. *Riding the New Wave: Youth and the Rejuvenation of France after the Second World War*. Stanford, CA: Stanford University Press, 2007.

Johnson, Robert C. "The Transportation of Vagrant Children from London to Virginia, 1618–1622." In *Early Stuart Studies: Essays in Honor of David Harris Wilson*, edited by Howard S. Reinmuth Jr., 137–51. Minneapolis: University of Minnesota Press, 1970.

Jones, David Crawford. "Wielding the *Epokolo*: Corporal Punishment and Traditional Authority in Colonial Ovamboland." *Journal of African History* 56, no. 2 (2015): 301–20.

Jones, Gareth S. *Outcast London: A Study in the Relationship between Classes in Victorian Society*. Oxford: Clarendon, 1971.

Jones, Thomas J. *Education in East Africa: A Study of East, Central and South*. New York: Phelps-Stokes Fund, 1925.

Kabiro, Ngugi. *The Man in the Middle: The Story of Ngugi Kabiro*. Edited by Don Barnett. Richmond, BC: Liberation Support Movement Information Centre, 1973.

Kaggia, Bildad. *Roots of Freedom, 1921–1963: The Autobiography of Bildad Kaggia*. Nairobi: East African Publishing, 1975.

Kagwanja, Peter Mwangi. "The Clash of Generations? Youth Identity, Ethnic Violence and the Politics of Moi Succession, 1991–2002." In Abbink and Van Kessel, *Vanguard or Vandals*, 81–109.

———. "Facing Mount Kenya or Facing Mecca? The Mungiki, Ethnic Violence and the Politics of the Moi Succession in Kenya, 1987–2002." *African Affairs* 102, no. 406 (2003): 25–49.

———. "'Power to Uhuru': Youth Identity and Generational Politics in Kenya's 2002 Elections." *African Affairs* 105, no. 418 (2005): 51–75.

Kagwanja, Peter Mwangi, and Roger Southall, eds. *Kenya's Uncertain Democracy: The Electoral Crisis of 2008*. London: Routledge, 2010.

Kamau-Rutenberg, Wanjiru. "Watu Wazima: A Gender Analysis of Forced Male Circumcisions during Kenya's Post-Election Violence." Working paper, Oxford Transitional Justice Research, 17 July 2009.

Kanogo, Tabitha M. *African Womanhood in Colonial Kenya, 1900–50*. Athens: Ohio University Press, 2005.

———. *Squatters and the Roots of Mau Mau, 1905–63.* Athens: Ohio University Press, 1987.

Kapila, Shruti. "Masculinity and Madness: Princely Personhood and Colonial Sciences of the Mind in Western India, 1871–1940." *Past and Present* 187, no. 1 (2005): 121–56.

Kariuki, Josiah Mwangi. *"Mau Mau" Detainee: The Account by a Kenya African of His Experiences in Detention Camps, 1953–1960.* Baltimore: Penguin, 1963.

Kennedy, Dane K. "Constructing the Colonial Myth of Mau Mau." *International Journal of African Historical Studies* 25, no. 2 (1992): 241–60.

———. *Islands of White: Settler Society and Culture in Kenya and Southern Rhodesia, 1890–1939.* Durham, NC: Duke University Press, 1987.

Kenya National Youth Service. *National Youth Service.* Nairobi: Government of Kenya, October 1964.

Kenyatta, Jomo. *Facing Mount Kenya: The Tribal Life of the Gikuyu.* New York: Vintage Books, 1965.

Kershaw, Greet. *Mau Mau from Below.* Athens: Ohio University Press, 1997.

Killingray, David. "Punishment to Fit the Crime? Penal Policy and Practice in British Colonial Africa." In Bernault, *History of Prison and Confinement in Africa,* 97–118.

———. "The 'Rod of Empire': The Debate over Corporal Punishment in the British African Colonial Forces, 1888–1946." *Journal of African History* 35, no. 2 (1994): 201–16.

King, Kenneth J. "Africa and the Southern States of the U.S.A.: Notes on J. H. Oldham and American Negro Education for Africans." *Journal of African History* 10, no. 4 (1969): 659–77.

———. *Jua Kali Kenya: Change and Development in an Informal Economy, 1970–95.* Athens: Ohio University Press, 1995.

Kingoriah, George K. "The Causes of Nairobi's City Structure." *Ekistics* 50, no. 301 (1983): 246–54.

Kinyatti, Maina wa, ed. *Kenya's Freedom Struggle: The Dedan Kimathi Papers.* London: Zed Books, 1986.

Kipkorir, Benjamin E. "The Alliance High School and the Origins of the Kenya African Elite, 1926–1962." PhD diss., University of Cambridge, 1969.

———. "Mau Mau and the Politics of the Transfer of Power in Kenya, 1957–1960." *Kenya Historical Review* 5, no. 2 (1977): 313–28

Kirby, Peter. *Child Workers and Industrial Health in Britain, 1780–1850.* Rochester, NY: Boydell and Brewer, 2013.

Kollman, Paul V. *The Evangelization of Slaves and Catholic Origins in Eastern Africa.* Maryknoll, NY: Orbis, 2005.

Kurimoto, Eisei, and Simon Simonse, eds. *Conflict, Age, and Power in North East Africa: Age Systems in Transition.* Athens: Ohio University Press, 1998.

La Fontaine, J. S. "Two Types of Youth Group in Kinshasa (Léopoldville)." In *Socialization: The Approach from Social Anthropology,* edited by Philip Mayer, 191–214. London: Tavistock, 1970.

La Hausse, Paul. " 'The Cows of Nongoloza': Youth, Crime and Amalaita Gangs in Durban, 1900–1936." *Journal of Southern African Studies* 16, no. 1 (1990): 79–111.

Lal, Priya. *African Socialism in Postcolonial Tanzania: Between the Village and the World.* Cambridge: Cambridge University Press, 2015.

Lambert, H. E. *Kikuyu Social and Political Institutions.* London: Oxford University Press, 1956.

Laqueur, Thomas W. "Crowds, Carnival and the State in English Executions, 1604–1868." In *The First Modern Society: Essays in English History in Honour of Lawrence Stone*, edited by A. L. Beier, David Cannadine, and James M. Rosenheim, 305–56. Oxford: Oxford University Press, 1989.

Last, Murray. "Children and the Experience of Violence: Contrasting Cultures of Punishment in Northern Nigeria." *Africa* 70, no. 3 (2000): 359–93.

Leakey, Louis S. B. *Defeating Mau Mau*. London: Methuen, 1954.

———. *Mau Mau and the Kikuyu*. London: Methuen, 1952.

———. *The Southern Kikuyu before 1903*. London: Academic Press, 1977.

Lees, Andrew. *Cities Perceived: Urban Society in European and American Thought, 1820–1940*. Manchester: Manchester University Press, 1985.

LeVine, Robert A., and Donald T. Campbell. *Gusii of Kenya*. 2 vols. New Haven, CT: Human Relations Area Files, 1972.

Lewis, Joanna. *Empire State-Building: War and Welfare in Kenya, 1925–52*. Athens: Ohio University Press, 2001.

Leys, Colin. *Underdevelopment in Kenya: The Political Economy of Neo-Colonialism, 1964–1971*. Berkeley: University of California Press, 1975.

Lindblom, Gerhard. *The Akamba in British East Africa*. Uppsala: Appelbergs Boktryckeri Aktiebolag, 1920.

Lindsay, Lisa A. "Money, Marriage, and Masculinity on the Colonial Nigerian Railway." In Lindsay and Miescher, *Men and Masculinities in Modern Africa*, 138–55.

Lindsay, Lisa A., and Stephan F. Miescher. "Introduction: Men and Masculinities in Modern African History." In Lindsay and Miescher, *Men and Masculinities in Modern Africa*, 1–32.

———. eds. *Men and Masculinities in Modern Africa*. Portsmouth, NH: Heinemann, 2003.

Lonsdale, John M. "The Conquest State of Kenya, 1895–1905." In Berman and Lonsdale, *Unhappy Valley*, vol. 1, *State and Class*, 11–44.

———. "KAU's Cultures: Imaginations of Community and Constructions of Leadership in Kenya after the Second World War." *Journal of African Cultural Studies* 13, no. 1 (2000): 107–24.

———. "'Listen While I Read': Patriotic Christianity among the Young Gikuyu." In *Christianity and Social Change in Africa: Essays in Honor of J. D. Y. Peel*, edited by Toyin Falola, 563–93. Durham, NC: Carolina Academic Press, 2005.

———. "Mau Maus of the Mind: Making Mau Mau and Remaking Kenya." *Journal of African History* 31, no. 3 (1990): 393–421.

———. "The Moral Economy of Mau Mau: Wealth, Poverty and Civic Virtue." In Berman and Lonsdale, *Unhappy Valley*, vol. 2, *Violence and Ethnicity*, 315–504.

———. "Town Life in Colonial Kenya." In Burton, *Urban Experience in Eastern Africa*, 207–22.

———. "When Did the Gusii (or Any Other Group) Become a 'Tribe'?" *Kenya Historical Review* 5, no. 1 (1977): 123–33.

Lovett, Margot. "Gender Relations, Class Formation, and the Colonial State in Africa." In Parpart and Staudt, *Women and the State in Africa*, 23–46.

Low, Donald A., and John M. Lonsdale. "Introduction: Towards the New Order, 1945–1963." In *History of East Africa*, vol. 3, edited by Donald A. Low and Alison Smith, 1–64. Oxford: Oxford University Press, 1962.

Luongo, Katherine. *Witchcraft and Colonial Rule in Kenya, 1900–1955.* Cambridge: Cambridge University Press, 2011.

Lynch, Gabrielle. *I Say to You: Ethnic Politics and the Kalenjin in Kenya.* Chicago: University of Chicago Press, 2011.

MacArthur, Julie. "When Did the Luyia (or Any Other Group) Become a Tribe?" *Canadian Journal of African Studies* 47, no. 3 (2013): 351–63.

Maloba, Wunyabari O. *Mau Mau and Kenya: An Analysis of a Peasant Revolt.* Bloomington: Indiana University Press, 1993.

Mamdani, Mahmood. *Citizen and Subject: Contemporary Africa and the Legacy of Late Colonialism.* Princeton, NJ: Princeton University Press, 1996.

Mandala, Elias C. *Work and Control in a Peasant Economy: A History of the Lower Tchiri Valley in Malawi, 1859–1960.* Madison: University of Wisconsin Press, 1990.

Mann, Kristin. *Marrying Well: Marriage, Status, and Social Change among the Educated Elite in Colonial Lagos.* Cambridge: Cambridge University Press, 1985.

Martens, Jeremy. "Polygamy, Sexual Danger, and the Creation of Vagrancy Legislation in Colonial Natal." *Journal of Imperial and Commonwealth History* 31, no. 3 (2003): 24–45.

Masterman, Charles F. G. *The Heart of the Empire: Discussions of Problems of Modern City Life in England.* London: Unwin, 1902.

Mathu, Mohamed. *The Urban Guerrilla: The Story of Mohamed Mathu.* Edited by Donald Barnett. Richmond, BC: Liberation Support Movement Information Centre, 1974.

Maxon, Robert M. *Britain and Kenya's Constitutions, 1950–1960.* Amherst, NY: Cambria Press, 2011.

May, Margaret. "Innocence and Experience: The Evolution of the Concept of Juvenile Delinquency in the Mid-Nineteenth Century." *Victorian Studies* 17, no. 1 (1973): 7–29.

Mayhew, Henry. *London Labor and the London Poor.* 4 vols. London: Griffin, Bohn, 1851–1861.

Mbenga, Bernard K. "Forced Labour in the Pilanesberg: The Flogging of Chief Kgamanyane by Commandant Paul Kruger, Saulspoort, April 1870." *Journal of Southern African Studies* 23, no. 1 (1997): 127–40.

Mboya, Paul. *Paul Mboya's "Luo Kitgi gi Timbegi."* Translated by Jane Achieng. Nairobi: Atai Joint, 2001.

Mboya, Tom. *Freedom and After.* Boston: Little, Brown, 1963.

McClendon, Thomas V. *Genders and Generations Apart: Labor Tenants and Customary Law in Segregation-Era South Africa, 1920s to 1940s.* Portsmouth, NH: Heinemann, 2002.

McCullers, Molly. "'We Do It So That We Will Be Men': Masculinity Politics in Colonial Namibia, 1915–49." *Journal of African History* 52, no. 1 (2011): 43–62.

McKittrick, Meredith. "Forsaking Their Fathers? Colonialism, Christianity, and Coming of Age in Ovamboland, Northern Namibia." In Lindsay and Miescher, *Men and Masculinities in Modern Africa,* 33–51.

———. *To Dwell Secure: Generation, Christianity, and Colonialism in Ovamboland.* Portsmouth, NH: Heinemann, 2002.

McVicar, Kenneth G. "Twilight of an East African Slum: Pumwani and the Evolution of African Settlement in Nairobi." PhD diss., University of California, Los Angeles, 1968.

McWilliam, Michael D. "The Kenya Tea Industry." *East African Economics Review* 6, no. 1 (1959): 32–48.

Meillassoux, Claude. *Maidens, Meal and Money: Capitalism and the Domestic Community*. Cambridge: Cambridge University Press, 1981.

Meiu, George Paul. "'Beach-Boy Elders' and 'Young Big-Men': Subverting the Temporalities of Ageing in Kenya's Ethno-Erotic Economies." *Ethnos* 80, no. 4 (2015): 472–96.

———. "'Mombasa Morans': Embodiment, Sexual Morality, and Samburu Men in Kenya." *Canadian Journal of African Studies* 43, no. 1 (2009): 105–28.

Middleton, John, and Greet Kershaw. *The Central Tribes of the North-Eastern Bantu*. London: International African Institute, 1953.

———. *The Kikuyu and Kamba of Kenya*. London: International African Institute, 1965.

Miescher, Stephan F. *Making Men in Ghana*. Bloomington: Indiana University Press, 2005.

Milner, Alan, ed. *African Penal Systems*. New York: Praeger, 1969.

M'Imanyara, Alfred M. *The Restatement of Bantu Origin and Meru History*. Nairobi: Longman, 1992.

Ministry of Youth Affairs. *Kenya National Youth Policy, 2006*. Nairobi: Government of Kenya, 2006.

Mintz, Steven. *Huck's Raft: A History of American Childhood*. Cambridge, MA: Harvard University Press, 2004.

———. "Reflections on Age as a Category of Historical Analysis." *Journal of the History of Childhood and Youth* 1, no. 1 (2008): 91–94.

Moodie, T. Dunbar. *Going for Gold: Men, Mines, and Migration*. Berkeley: University of California Press, 1994.

———. "Maximum Average Violence: Underground Assaults on the South African Gold Mines, 1913–1965." *Journal of Southern African Studies* 31, no. 3 (2005): 547–67.

Mooney, Katie. "'Ducktails, Flick-Knives and Pugnacity': Subcultural and Hegemonic Masculinities in South Africa, 1948–1960." *Journal of Southern African Studies* 24, no. 4 (1998): 753–74.

Moore, Henrietta L. "Forms of Knowing and Un-Knowing: Secrets about Society, Sexuality and God in Northern Kenya." In *Secrecy and Silence in the Research Process: Feminist Reflections*, edited by Róisín Ryan-Flood and Rosalind Gill, 30–41. New York: Routledge, 2010.

Morrell, Robert. "Of Boys and Men: Masculinity and Gender in Southern African Studies." *Journal of Southern African Studies* 24, no. 4 (1998): 605–30.

———. "The Times of Change: Men and Masculinity in South Africa." In *Changing Men in Southern Africa*, edited by Robert Morrell, 3–40. New York: Zed Books, 2001.

Morrell, Robert, and Lahoucine Ouzgane. "African Masculinities: An Introduction." In *African Masculinities: Men in Africa from the Late Nineteenth Century to the Present*, edited by Lahoucine Ouzgane and Robert Morrell, 1–20. New York: Palgrave Macmillan, 2005.

Morton, Fred. "Pawning and Slavery on the Kenya Coast: The Miji Kenda Case." In *Pawnship in Africa: Debt Bondage in Historical Perspective*, edited by Toyin Falola and Paul E. Lovejoy, 27–42. Boulder, CO: Westview Press, 1994.

————. "Small Change: Children in the Nineteenth-Century East African Slave Trade." In *Children in Slavery through the Ages*, edited by Gwyn Campbell, Suzanne Miers, and Joseph C. Miller, 55–70. Athens: Ohio University Press, 2009.

Muchai, Karigo. *The Hardcore: The Story of Karigo Muchai*. Edited by Donald Barnett. Richmond, BC: Liberation Support Movement Information Centre, 1973.

Mueller, Susanne D. "The Resilience of the Past: Government and Opposition in Kenya." *Canadian Journal of African Studies* 48, no. 2 (2014): 333–52.

Munro, J. Forbes. *Colonial Rule and the Kamba: Social Change in the Kenya Highlands, 1889–1939*. Oxford: Clarendon, 1975.

Muriithi, Kiboi, with Peter Ndoria. *War in the Forest*. Nairobi: East African Publishing, 1971.

Muriuki, Godfrey. *A History of the Kikuyu, 1500–1900*. Nairobi: Oxford University Press, 1974.

Murray, Jocelyn. "The Kikuyu Female Circumcision Controversy, with Special Reference to the Church Missionary Society's 'Sphere of Influence.'" PhD diss., University of California at Los Angeles, 1974.

Murray, Stephen O. "'A Feeling within Me': Kamau, a Twenty-Five-Year-Old Kikuyu." In *Boy-Wives and Female Husbands: Studies in African Homosexualities*, edited by Stephen O. Murray and Will Roscoe, 41–65. New York: St. Martin's, 1998.

Murray-Brown, Jeremy. *Kenyatta*. New York: Duncan, 1973.

Mutongi, Kenda. *Worries of the Heart: Widows, Family, and Community in Kenya*. Chicago: University of Chicago Press, 2007.

Myers, Garth A. *Verandahs of Power: Colonialism and Space in Urban Africa*. Syracuse, NY: Syracuse University Press, 2003.

Nardinelli, Clark. *Child Labor and the Industrial Revolution*. Bloomington: University of Indiana Press, 1990.

Neubauer, Carol E. "One Voice Speaking for Many: The Mau Mau Movement and Kenyan Autobiography." *Journal of Modern African Studies* 21, no. 1 (1983): 113–31.

Nyaga, Daniel. *Customs and Traditions of the Meru*. Nairobi: East African Educational Publishers, 1997.

Obure, Alfredo F. X. O., Erick O. Nyambedha, and Boniface O. Oindo. "Interpersonal Influences in the Scale-Up of Male Circumcision Services in a Traditionally Non-Circumcising Community in Rural Western Kenya." *Global Journal of Community Psychology Practice* 1, no. 3 (2011): 1–11.

Ocobock, Paul. "'Joy Rides for Juveniles': Vagrant Youth and Colonial Control in Nairobi, Kenya, 1901–52." *Social History* 31, no. 1 (2006): 39–59.

————. "Spare the Rod, Spoil the Colony: Corporal Punishment, Colonial Violence, and Generational Authority in Kenya, 1897–1952." *International Journal of African Historical Studies* 45, no. 1 (2012): 29–56.

Odhiambo, E. S. Atieno, and John M. Lonsdale, eds. *Mau Mau and Nationhood: Arms, Authority and Narration*. Athens: Ohio University Press, 2003.

Ogot, Bethwell A. "British Administration in the Central Nyanza District of Kenya, 1900–60." *Journal of African History* 4, no. 2 (1963): 249–73.

————. "The Decisive Years: 1956–63." In Ogot and Ochieng', *Decolonization and Independence in Kenya*, 48–82.

Ogot, Bethwell A., and William R. Ochieng', eds. *Decolonization and Independence in Kenya, 1940–93*. Athens: Ohio University Press, 1995.

Ojiambo, Peter Otiato. "Gift of Education: Joseph Kamiru Gikubu and the Development of Kenyan Youth Education from 1957 to the Present." *Africa Review* 7, no. 1 (2015): 55–66.

———. *Teaching beyond Teaching: Dr. Geoffrey William Griffin and Starehe Boys Centre and School.* Saarbrücken: VDM, 2008.

Okia, Opolot. *Communal Labor in Colonial Kenya: The Legitimization of Coercion, 1912–1930.* New York: Palgrave Macmillan, 2012.

Oliver, Roland A. *The Missionary Factor in East Africa.* London: Longman, 1966.

Osborn, Emily Lynn. *Our New Husbands Are Here: Households, Gender, and Politics in a West African State from the Slave Trade to Colonial Rule.* Athens: Ohio University Press, 2011.

Osborn, Michelle. "Fuelling the Flames: Rumour and Politics in Kibera." *Journal of Eastern African Studies* 2, no. 2 (2008): 315–27.

Osborne, Myles. *Ethnicity and Empire in Kenya: Loyalty and Martial Race among the Kamba, c. 1800 to the Present.* Cambridge: Cambridge University Press, 2014.

Osogo, John. *A History of the Baluyia.* London: Oxford University Press, 1966.

Osoro, J. M. "'A Lull before the Storm': A Study of the African Labourers in the Kericho Tea Estates, 1939–1958." Paper presented to the Department of History, University of Nairobi, 1977–1978.

———. "Unity and Disunity in Labour Recruitment and Welfare: The Tea Estates versus Other Employers of Labour, 1925–1938." Paper presented at the annual conference of the Historical Association of Kenya, 1977.

Ottenberg, Simon. *Boyhood Rituals in an African Society: An Interpretation.* Seattle: University of Washington Press, 1989.

Parker, Mary. *Political and Social Aspects of the Development of Municipal Government in Kenya with Special Reference to Nairobi.* London: Colonial Office, 1948.

Parpart, Jane L., and Kathleen A. Staudt. "Women and the State in Africa." In *Women and the State in Africa*, 1–19.

———, eds. *Women and the State in Africa.* Boulder, CO: Rienner, 1989.

Parsloe, Phyllida. *Juvenile Justice in Britain and the United States: The Balance of Needs and Rights.* London: Routledge and Kegan Paul, 1978.

Parsons, Timothy H. *The African Rank-and-File: Social Implications of Colonial Military Service in the King's African Rifles, 1902–1964.* Portsmouth, NH: Heinemann, 1999.

———. *Race, Resistance, and the Boy Scout Movement in British Colonial Africa.* Athens: Ohio University Press, 2004.

Paterson, Alexander. *Across the Bridges; or, Life by the South London River-Side.* London: Arnold, 1911.

Pearson, Geoffrey. *Hooligan: A History of Respectable Fears.* London: Macmillan, 1983.

Pedersen, Susan. "National Bodies, Unspeakable Acts: The Sexual Politics of Colonial Policy-Making." *Journal of Modern History* 63, no. 4 (1991): 647–80.

Peel, J. D. Y. *Religious Encounter and the Making of the Yoruba.* Bloomington: Indiana University Press, 2000.

Percox, David A. *Britain, Kenya and the Cold War: Imperial Defence, Colonial Security and Decolonization.* New York: Palgrave Macmillan, 2012.

Peristiany, John S. *The Social Institutions of the Kipsigis.* London: Routledge and Sons, 1939.

Peté, Stephen, and Annie Devenish. "Flogging, Fear and Food: Punishment and Race in Colonial Natal." *Journal of Southern African Studies* 31, no. 1 (2005): 3–21.

Peterson, Derek R. *Creative Writing: Translation, Bookkeeping, and the Work of Imagination in Colonial Kenya.* Portsmouth, NH: Heinemann, 2004.

———. *Ethnic Patriotism and the East African Revival: A History of Dissent, c. 1935–1972.* Cambridge: Cambridge University Press, 2012.

———. "The Intellectual Lives of Mau Mau Detainees." *Journal of African History* 49, no. 1 (2008): 73–91.

Phiri, Kings M. "A Case of Revolutionary Change in Contemporary Malawi: The Malawi Army and the Disarming of the Malawi Young Pioneers." *Journal of Peace, Conflict and Military Studies* 1, no. 1 (March 2000). Accessed 21 January 2016. http://malawi.freehosting.net/article3.html.

Pierce, Steven. "Punishment and the Political Body: Flogging and Colonialism in Northern Nigeria." In *Discipline and the Other Body: Correction, Corporeality, Colonialism,* edited by Steven Pierce and Anupama Rao, 186–214. Durham, NC: Duke University Press, 2006.

Pomfret, David M. *Youth and Empire: Trans-Colonial Childhoods in British and French Asia.* Stanford, CA: Stanford University Press, 2015.

Pool, Jeremy J. "Now Is the Time of Youth: Youth, Nationalism and Cultural Change in Ghana, 1940–1966." PhD diss., Emory University, 2009.

Pound, John F. *Poverty and Vagrancy in Tudor England.* London: Longman, 1971.

Premo, Bianca. *Children of the Father King: Youth, Authority, and Legal Minority in Colonial Lima.* Chapel Hill: University of North Carolina Press, 2005.

Presley, Cora A. *Kikuyu Women, the Mau Mau Rebellion, and Social Change in Kenya.* Boulder, CO: Westview Press, 1992.

———. "The Mau Mau Rebellion, Kikuyu Women, and Social Change." *Canadian Journal of African Studies* 22, no. 3 (1988): 502–27.

Prins, Adriaan H. J. *East African Age-Class Systems: An Inquiry into the Social Order of Galla, Kipsigis, and Kikuyu.* Westport, CT: Negro Universities Press, 1953.

Quarmby, Diana, and Andrew Quarmby. *The Kenya National Youth Service.* Washington, DC: International Secretariat of Volunteer Services, 1969.

Raffin, Anne. *Youth Mobilization in Vichy Indochina and Its Legacies, 1940–1970.* Lanham, MD: Lexington Books, 2005.

Rasmussen, Jacob. "Mungiki as Youth Movement: Revolution, Gender and Generational Politics in Nairobi, Kenya." *Young* 18, no. 3 (2010): 301–19.

Read, James S. "Kenya, Tanzania, and Uganda." In Milner, *African Penal Systems,* 89–164.

Republic of Kenya. *National Assembly, Official Report.* 12 May 1965.

Reynolds, Pamela. *Dance, Civet Cat: Child Labour in the Zambezi Valley.* Athens: Ohio University Press, 1991.

———. *War in Worcester: Youth and the Apartheid State.* New York: Fordham University Press, 2012.

Ribton-Turner, Charles J. *A History of Vagrants and Vagrancy and Beggars and Begging.* London: Chapman and Hall, 1887.

Richards, Paul. *Fighting for the Rain Forest: War, Youth, and Resources in Sierra Leone.* Portsmouth, NH: Heinemann, 1996.

Robertson, Claire C. *Trouble Showed the Way: Women, Men, and Trade in the Nairobi Area, 1890–1990.* Bloomington: Indiana University Press, 1997.

Robertson, Claire C., and Iris Berger. "Introduction: Analyzing Class and Gender—African Perspectives." In *Women and Class in Africa,* edited by Claire C. Robertson and Iris Berger, 3–26. New York: Africana Publishing, 1986.

Robinson, Shirleene, and Simon Sleight. *Children, Childhood and Youth in the British World*. New York: Palgrave Macmillan, 2015.

Rockel, Stephen J. *Carriers of Culture: Labor on the Road in Nineteenth-Century East Africa*. Portsmouth, NH: Heinemann, 2006.

Rodriguez-Torres, Deyssi. "Nairobi: Les gangs de la rue en direct." In *Jeunes, culture de la rue et violence urbaine en Afrique*, edited by George Hérault and Pius Adesanmi, 9–88. Ibadan: IFRA, 1997.

Rosberg, Carl G., and John C. Nottingham. *The Myth of "Mau Mau": Nationalism in Kenya*. Stanford, CA: Hoover Institute, 1966.

Ross, Marc H. *Grass Roots in an African City: Political Behavior in Nairobi*. Cambridge, MA: MIT Press, 1975.

Routledge, William S., and Katherine Routledge. *With a Prehistoric People: The Akikuyu of British East Africa*. London: Arnold, 1910.

Saberwall, Satish. *Embu of Kenya*. New Haven, CT: Human Relations Area Files, 1972.

Sandgren, David P. *Christianity and the Kikuyu: Religious Divisions and Social Conflict*. New York: Lang, 1989.

———. *Mau Mau's Children: The Making of Kenya's Postcolonial Elite*. Madison: University of Wisconsin Press, 2012.

Schilling, Donald G. "British Policy for African Education in Kenya, 1895–1939." PhD diss., University of Wisconsin-Madison, 1972.

Schlossman, Steven. "Delinquent Children: The Juvenile Reform School." In *The Oxford History of the Prison: The Practice of Punishment in Western Society*, edited by Norval Morris and David J. Rothman, 325–49. Oxford: Oxford University Press, 1995.

Schmidt, Elizabeth. *Peasants, Traders, and Wives: Shona Women in the History of Zimbabwe, 1870–1939*. Portsmouth, NH: Heinemann, 1992.

Scott, George R. *The History of Corporal Punishment: A Survey of Flagellation in Its Historical, Anthropological and Sociological Aspects*. New York: Columbia University Press, 2005.

Scott, Joan W. "Gender: A Useful Category of Historical Analysis." *American Historical Review* 91, no. 5 (1986): 1053–75.

Seaton, Henry. *Lion in the Morning*. London: Murray, 1963.

Seekings, Jeremy, and David Everatt. *Heroes or Villains? Youth Politics in the 1980s*. Johannesburg: Ravan Press, 1993.

Seidman, Robert B., and J. D. Abaka Eyison. "Ghana." In Milner, *African Penal Systems*, 59–88.

Sen, Satadru. *Colonial Childhoods: The Juvenile Periphery of India, 1850–1945*. London: Anthem Press, 2005.

———. "A Separate Punishment: Juvenile Offenders in Colonial India." *Journal of Asian Studies* 63, no. 1 (2004): 81–104.

Sengupta, Jayanta. "Nation on a Platter: The Culture and Politics of Food and Cuisine in Colonial Bengal." *Modern Asian Studies* 44, no. 1 (2010): 81–98.

Shadle, Brett L. "Bridewealth and Female Consent: Marriage Disputes in African Courts, Gusiiland, Kenya." *Journal of African History* 44, no. 2 (2003): 241–62.

———. "'Changing Traditions to Meet Current Altering Conditions': Customary Law, African Courts and the Rejection of Codification in Kenya, 1930–60." *Journal of African History* 40, no. 3 (1999): 411–31.

———. "Girl Cases": Marriage and Colonialism in Gusiiland, Kenya, 1890–1970. Portsmouth, NH: Heinemann, 2006.

———. "Settlers, Africans, and Inter-Personal Violence in Kenya, ca. 1900–1920s." International Journal of African Historical Studies 45, no. 1 (2012): 57–80.

———. The Souls of White Folk: White Settlers in Kenya, 1900s–1920s. Manchester: Manchester University Press, 2015.

Shannon, Mary I. "Rebuilding the Social Life of the Kikuyu." African Affairs 56, no. 225 (1957): 276–84.

———. "Social Revolution in Kikuyuland." African World (1955): 7–9.

Sharp, Lesley A. The Sacrificed Generation: Youth, History, and the Colonized Mind in Madagascar. Berkeley: University of California Press, 2002.

Shear, Keith. "'Taken as Boys': The Politics of Black Police Employment and Experience in Early Twentieth-Century South Africa." In Lindsay and Miescher, Men and Masculinities in Modern Africa, 109–27.

Shore, Heather. Artful Dodgers: Youth and Crime in Early Nineteenth-Century London. Rochester, NY: Boydell, 2002.

———. "Introduction: Re-Inventing the Juvenile Delinquent in Britain and Europe, 1650–1950." In Cox and Shore, Becoming Delinquent, 1–22.

Simpson, George L. "Gerontocrats and Colonial Alliances." In Aguilar, Politics of Age and Gerontocracy in Africa, 65–99.

Sinha, Mrinalini. Colonial Masculinity: The "Manly Englishman" and the "Effeminate Bengali" in the Late Nineteenth Century. Manchester: Manchester University Press, 1995.

Smith, Daniel Jordan. AIDS Doesn't Show Its Face: Inequality, Morality, and Social Change in Nigeria. Chicago: University of Chicago Press, 2014.

Smith, Earl. "The Evolution of Nairobi, Kenya, 1889–1939." PhD diss., University of Connecticut, 1984.

Smith, Greg T. "Civilized People Don't Want to See That Sort of Thing: The Decline of Physical Punishment in London, 1760–1840." In Qualities of Mercy: Justice, Punishment, and Discretion, edited by Carolyn Strange, 21–51. Vancouver: University of British Columbia Press, 1996.

Sommers, Marc. Stuck: Rwandan Youth and the Struggle for Adulthood. Athens: University of Georgia Press, 2012.

Sorrenson, Maurice P. K. Land Reform in the Kikuyu Country: A Study in Government Policy. Nairobi: Oxford University Press, 1967.

———. Origins of European Settlement in Kenya. Oxford: Oxford University Press, 1968.

Spear, Thomas. "Neo-Traditionalism and the Limits of Invention in British Colonial Africa." Journal of African History 44, no. 1 (2003): 3–27.

Spencer, John. "KAU and 'Mau Mau': Some Connections." Kenya Historical Review 5, no. 2 (1977): 201–24.

Spencer, Paul. "Becoming Maasai, Being in Time." In Being Maasai: Ethnicity and Identity in East Africa, edited by Thomas T. Spear and Richard Waller, 140–56. Athens: Ohio University Press, 1993.

———. The Maasai of Matapato: A Study of Rituals of Rebellion. Bloomington: University of Indiana Press, 1988.

Springhall, John. Coming of Age: Adolescence in Britain, 1860–1960. Dublin: Gill and Macmillan, 1986.

————. *Youth, Empire and Society: British Youth Movements, 1883–1940*. London: Taylor and Francis, 1977.

————. *Youth, Popular Culture and Moral Panics: Penny Gaffs to Gangsta-Rap, 1830–1996*. New York: Palgrave Macmillan, 1999.

Sramek, Joseph. "'Face Him Like a Briton': Tiger Hunting, Imperialism, and British Masculinity in Colonial India, 1800–1875." *Victorian Studies* 48, no. 4 (2006): 659–80.

Stack, John A. "Reformatory and Industrial Schools and the Decline of Child Imprisonment in Mid-Victorian England and Wales." *History of Education* 23, no. 1 (1994): 59–73.

Stewart, John. "Children, Parents and the State: The Children Act, 1908." *Children and Society* 9, no. 1 (1995): 90–99.

Stichter, Sharon. *Migrant Labour in Kenya: Capitalism and African Response, 1895–1975*. London: Longman, 1982.

Stoler, Ann Laura, and Frederick Cooper. "Between Metropole and Colony: Rethinking a Research Agenda." In *Tensions of Empire: Colonial Cultures in a Bourgeois World*, edited by Frederick Cooper and Ann Laura Stoler, 1–58. Berkeley: University of California Press, 1997.

Stone, Lawrence. "The Family in the 1980s: Past Achievements and Future Trends." *Journal of Interdisciplinary History* 12, no. 1 (1981): 51–87.

Straker, Jay. *Youth, Nationalism, and the Guinean Revolution*. Bloomington: Indiana Univeristy Press, 2009.

Strayer, Robert W. *The Making of Mission Communities in East Africa: Anglicans and Africans in Colonial Kenya, 1875–1935*. London: Heinemann, 1978.

Stren, Richard E. "The Evolution of Housing Policy in Kenya." In *Urban Challenge in East Africa*, edited by John Hutton, 57–96. Nairobi: East African Publishing, 1970.

Strobel, Margaret. *Muslim Women in Mombasa, 1890–1975*. New Haven, CT: Yale University Press, 1979.

Sytek, William. *Luo of Kenya*. New Haven, CT: Human Relations Area Files, 1972.

Tamarkin, Michael. "Mau Mau in Nakuru." *Journal of African History* 17, no. 1 (1976): 119–34.

Tate, H. R. "Further Notes on the Southern Gikuyu of British East Africa." *Journal of the Royal African Society* 10, no. 39 (1911): 285–97.

Thioub, Ibrahima. "Juvenile Delinquency and the First Penitentiary Schools in Senegal, 1888–1927." In Bernault, *History of Prison and Confinement in Africa*, 79–96.

Thomas, Lynn M. "'Ngaitana (I Will Circumcise Myself)': The Gender and Generational Politics of the 1956 Ban on Clitoridectomy in Meru, Kenya." *Gender and History* 8, no. 3 (1996): 338–63.

————. *Politics of the Womb: Women, Reproduction, and the State in Kenya*. Berkeley: University of California Press, 2003.

Thornton White, L. W., L. Silberman, and P. R. Anderson. *Nairobi: Master Plan for a Colonial Capital: A Report Prepared for the Municipal Council of Nairobi*. London: Her Majesty's Stationery Office, 1948.

Throup, David W. "The Count." *Journal of Eastern African Studies* 2, no. 2 (2008): 290–304.

————. "Crimes, Politics, and the Police in Colonial Kenya, 1939–63." In *Policing and Decolonisation: Nationalism, Politics and the Police, 1917–65*, edited by David M. Anderson and David Killingray, 127–57. Manchester: Manchester University Press, 1992.

————. *Economic and Social Origins of Mau Mau, 1945–53*. Athens: Ohio University Press, 1987.

Throup, David W., and Charles Hornsby. *Multi-Party Politics in Kenya: The Kenyatta and Moi States and the Triumph of the System in the 1992 Election*. Athens: Ohio University Press, 1998.

Tignor, Robert L. *Capitalism and Nationalism at the End of Empire: State and Business in Decolonizing Egypt, Nigeria, and Kenya, 1945–1963*. Princeton, NJ: Princeton University Press, 1998.

————. *Colonial Transformation of Kenya: The Kamba, Kikuyu, and Maasai from 1900–1939*. Princeton, NJ: Princeton University Press, 1976.

Tilley, Helen. *Africa as a Living Laboratory: Empire, Development, and the Problem of Scientific Knowledge, 1870–1950*. Chicago: University of Chicago Press, 2011.

Tosh, John. "What Should Historians Do with Masculinity? Reflections on Nineteenth-Century Britain." *History Workshop* 38, no. 1 (1994): 179–202.

Trench, Charles Chenevix. *Men Who Ruled Kenya: The Kenya Administration, 1892–1963*. London: Radcliffe Press, 1993.

Turner, Terisa E., and Leigh S. Brownhill. "African Jubilee: Mau Mau Resurgence and the Fight for Fertility in Kenya, 1986–2002." *Canadian Journal of Development Studies* 22, no. 4 (2001): 1037–88.

Tuttle, Carolyn. *Hard at Work in Factories and Mines: The Economics of Child Labor during the British Industrial Revolution*. Boulder, CO: Westview Press, 1999.

United Nations. *Report from OHCHR Fact-Finding Mission to Kenya*. New York: United Nations, 2008.

————. *World Population Prospects, 2015 Revision*. New York: United Nations, 2015.

Van Waters, Miriam. *Youth in Conflict*. New York: Republic, 1925.

Wachanga, H. K. *The Swords of Kirinyaga: The Fight for Land and Freedom*. Nairobi: East African Literature Bureau, 1975.

Waki Commission. *The Report of the Commission of Inquiry on Post Election Violence*. Nairobi: Government Printer, 2008.

Waller, Richard D. "Age and Ethnography." *Azania* 34, no. 1 (1999): 135–44.

————. "Bad Boys in the Bush? Disciplining Murran in Colonial Maasailand." In Burton and Charton-Bigot, *Generations Past*, 135–74.

————. "The Lords of East Africa: The Maasai in the Mid-Nineteenth Century (c. 1840–c. 1855)." PhD diss., University of Cambridge, 1978.

————. "Rebellious Youth in Colonial Africa." *Journal of African History* 47, no. 1 (2006): 77–92.

Wamue, Grace Nyatugah. "Revisiting Our Indigenous Shrines through Mungiki." *African Affairs* 100, no. 400 (2001): 453–67.

Wamwere, Koigi wa. *Towards Genocide in Kenya: The Curse of Negative Ethnicity*. Nairobi: Mvule Africa, 2008.

Wamweya, Joram. *Freedom Fighter*. Nairobi: East African Publishing, 1971.

Wanjau, Gakaara wa. *Mau Mau Author in Detention*. Nairobi: Heinemann, 1988.

Wasserman, Gary. *Politics of Decolonization: Kenya Europeans and the Land Issue, 1960–1965*. Cambridge: Cambridge University Press, 1976.

Wawire, Salome N. "Negotiating Identity: Identity Dynamics in the Context of Male Circumcision and HIV/AIDS among Luo Youth in Kisumu, Kenya." PhD diss., Brown University, 2010.

Webb, Sidney, and Beatrice Webb. *English Local Government from the Revolution to the Municipal Corporations Act: The Parish and the County.* London: Longmans, 1906.

Weiss, Brad. *Street Dreams and Hip Hop Barbershops: Global Fantasy in Urban Tanzania.* Bloomington: Indiana University Press, 2009.

Werlin, Herbert H. *Governing an African City: A Study of Nairobi.* New York: Africana Publishing, 1974.

Westcott, Nicholas J. "The East African Sisal Industry, 1929–1949: The Marketing of a Colonial Commodity during Depression and War." *Journal of African History* 25, no. 4 (1984): 445–61.

Westercamp, Nelli, and Robert C. Bailey. "Acceptability of Male Circumcision for Prevention of HIV/AIDS in Sub-Saharan Africa: A Review." *AIDS and Behavior* 11, no. 3 (2007): 341–55.

White, Luise. *The Comforts of Home: Prostitution in Colonial Nairobi.* Chicago: University of Chicago Press, 1990.

———. "Separating the Men from the Boys: Constructions of Gender, Sexuality, and Terrorism in Central Kenya, 1939–1959." *International Journal of African Historical Studies* 23, no. 1 (1990): 1–25.

Widner, Jennifer A. *The Rise of a Party-State in Kenya: From "Harambee!" to "Nyayo!"* Berkeley: University of California Press, 1992.

WikiLeaks. 07NAIROBI2215. "Mungiki: Kenya's Largest Criminal Organization." 24 May 2007. Accessed 21 January 2016. https://wikileaks.org/plusd/cables /07NAIROBI2215_a.html.

———. 09NAIROBI1296. "Uhuru Kenyatta: President Ambitions and the . . ." 26 June 2009. Accessed 21 January 2016. https://wikileaks.org/plusd/cables /09NAIROBI1296_a.html.

———. 10NAIROBI11. "Kenya: Inadequate Witness protection Poses Painful Dilemma." 5 January 2010. Accessed 21 January 2016. https://wikileaks.org/plusd /cables/10NAIROBI11_a.html.

Willis, Justin. *Potent Brews: A Social History of Alcohol in East Africa, 1850–1999.* Athens: Ohio University Press, 2002.

———. "Thieves, Drunkards and Vagrants: Defining Crime in Colonial Mombasa, 1902–32." In Anderson and Killingray, *Policing the Empire*, 219–35.

Willis, Justin, and George Gona. "Tradition, Tribe, and State in Kenya: The Mijikenda Union, 1945–1980." *Comparative Studies in Society and History* 55, no. 2 (2013): 448–73.

Wilson, Monica. *For Men and Elders: Change in the Relations of Generations and of Men and Women among the Nyakyusa-Ngonde People, 1875–1971.* New York: Africana Publishing, 1977.

Wipper, Audrey. "The Maendeleo ya Wanawake Organization: The Co-Optation of Leadership." *African Studies Review* 18, no. 3 (1975): 99–120.

Wohl, Robert. *The Generation of 1914.* Cambridge, MA: Harvard University Press, 1979.

Wolf, Jan Jacob de. "Circumcision and Initiation in Western Kenya and Eastern Uganda: Historical Reconstructions and Ethnographic Evidence." *Anthropos* 78, nos. 3–4 (1983): 369–410.

World Health Organization. *Male Circumcision: Global Trends and Determinants in Prevalence, Safety, and Acceptability.* Geneva: WHO Press, 2007.

———. *WHO Progress Brief: Voluntary Medical Male Circumcision for HIV Prevention in 14 Priority Counties in East and Southern Africa*. Geneva: WHO Press, 2015.

Young, Crawford. *The African Colonial State in Comparative Perspective*. New Haven, CT: Yale University Press, 1994.

Zimmerman, Andrew. *Alabama in Africa: Booker T. Washington, the German Empire, and the Globalization of the New South*. Princeton, NJ: Princeton University Press, 2012.

Zolberg, Aristide R. "Youth as a Political Phenomenon in Tropical Africa." *Youth and Society* 1, no. 2 (1969): 199–218.

Index